EXILES AND ISLANDERS

MCGILL-QUEEN'S STUDIES IN ETHNIC HISTORY
SERIES ONE: DONALD HARMAN AKENSON, EDITOR

MCGILL-QUEEN'S STUDIES IN ETHNIC HISTORY
SERIES TWO: JOHN ZUCCHI, EDITOR

Exiles and Islanders

The Irish Settlers
of Prince Edward Island

BRENDAN O'GRADY

McGill-Queen's University Press
Montreal & Kingston • London • Chicago

© McGill-Queen's University Press 2004
ISBN 978-0-7735-2723-2 (cloth)
ISBN 978-0-7735-2768-3 (paper)
ISBN 978-0-7735-7200-3 (ePDF)

Legal deposit third quarter 2004
Bibliothèque nationale du Québec
First paperback edition 2004
Reprinted 2016

This book was first published with the help of grants from the
Humanities and Social Sciences Federation of Canada, using funds
provided by the Social Sciences and Humanities Research Council of
Canada.

McGill-Queen's University Press acknowledges the support of the
Canada Council for the Arts for our publishing program. We also
acknowledge the financial support of the Government of Canada
through the Book Publishing Industry Development Program (BPIDP)
for our publishing activities.

National Library of Canada Cataloguing in Publication

O'Grady, Brendan, 1925–
    Exiles and Islanders : the Irish settlers of Prince Edward Island
/ Brendan O'Grady.

Includes bibliographical references and index.
ISBN 978-0-7735-2723-2 (bnd)
ISBN 978-0-7735-2768-3 (pbk)
ISBN 978-0-7735-7200-3 (ePDF)

    1. Irish – Prince Edward Island – History.   I. Title.

FC2650.I6O37 2004   971.7'0049612   C2004-902825-1

Typeset in 10/12 Sabon by True to Type

For
Leah Patricia
companion for life

Contents

Illustrations and Maps

Foreword

I had the good fortune nearly forty-five years ago to have had Brendan O'Grady as one of my professors at Saint Dunstan's University. Little did I think that our paths would intertwine so often in the future, when the seed of interest in Irish literature that he had planted in my mind would germinate, grow, and blossom into a mutual love of Irish literature and culture. When we met years later our friendship flourished, and over pints and drams our talk would eventually get round to what seemed to possess us both: Ireland's cultural impact on our part of the world. We are still amazed at how the present-day culture of Atlantic Canada embodies so many aspects of the Irish culture of the time when the Irish arrived. Although my Irish antecedents came here over two hundred years ago, the milieu I grew up in was reflective of the culture my forebears had brought with them from Ireland. Similarly Brendan, whose immediate family had left Ireland for the United States after the Great War, was able to find a veritable transatlantic Ireland when he came to teach at Saint Dunstan's in 1948; and his fascination with what he discovered on Prince Edward Island has now borne fruit in the work for which I have the honour to write this foreword.

Beautifully and lucidly written, this historical account of the Irish on Prince Edward Island is a work of *pietas*, a labour of love, assiduously worked at for over twenty years. Indeed, this work may well have been gently planted in Brendan's mind when he came to the Island as a young man and began to feel the fierce Irishness of the place and to drink in what the Irish mean by the word *dinnseanchas* – the lore of places and the stories associated with them. The work is impressive for its broad research and careful array of notes, as well as for its judicious handling of events such as the famous Belfast Riot, the story of which is reworked here with the utmost sensitivity, leading to a strongly convincing presentation of what actually happened. An unusual feature of this book is its blending of folkloric and literary accounts with factual documentation, the intent being to capture the spirit of time and place in the words of the people themselves.

The author's patient attention is obvious in the way he has been able to weave back into the tapestry of the Island's Irish history bits and pieces that had faded or been lost. Part of what Brendan has done is to recreate from the detritus of forgotten or half-remembered tatters some of the rough splendour of Prince Edward Island's Irish past, both where it began in Ireland (or indeed in Scotland) and where it eventually came ashore on the red earth of the new country.

Brendan's book details Irish settlement on the Island in a way that engages and informs us as we read on; and it is free of any of the blights of bigotry or sectarianism that afflicted the children of the Gael in both the old world and the new. The sweet virtue of forgiveness wafts from its pages as catharsis does its work in the drama of Irish migration. Its large cast of characters is tracked across the stage of history from County Monaghan to the sties of early-nineteenth-century Glasgow; and from the Anglo-Irish Big House or the crowded but often fun-filled cabins of Waterford, Tipperary, Wexford, Kilkenny, or Cork to the Island in the Gulf of St Lawrence. We see the inevitable psychic wounds, some the result of migratory uprooting, some self-inflicted within a crowded, materially impoverished culture, and still others as the result of bigotry and sectarianism. But we also see the triumphs, great and small, achieved after intense struggle and against great odds, of men and women who, arriving from all parts of Ireland by fate or by design, became part of the Island and thence part of Canada, and soon after that, part of the vast continent of North America.

Nothing essential concerning the Irish on Prince Edward Island has been neglected. It is all here, from Governor Patterson and others of the Anglo-Irish Ascendancy class who ruled and ran the machinery of early colonial government, through the varied ranks of clerics and men of "the greasy till," to the poorest of the rustic Irish – who, ironically, faced the evil of landlordism here as they had in Ireland, but defeated it. They are all, in Yeats's phrase, numbered in the song. And song there is – folksong – which Brendan has woven into his narrative as the authentic voice of the culture built up by the Irish people on the Island. Their words – happy, sad, comic, and mischievous – reflect both the events and the flavour of daily life: the marriages, rows, and personality clashes, and the conflicts with the elements of nature.

This is a book deeply and thoroughly about the Irish settlers of Prince Edward Island. However, it is more than that. It fills in a neglected piece of the picture of Irish migration to North America, and as such it earns a modest place in the history of the worldwide Irish diaspora. This book is not merely of local interest but will be welcome on the bookshelves of anyone who is curious about Irish migratory culture.

I feel proud to have had some little share in gently encouraging my early mentor and friend to persevere in his work, and I am happy that he has now brought his labours to such a successful, happy, and fruitful result.

Dr Cyril J. Byrne, CM
Director of the Chair of Irish Studies
Saint Mary's University
Halifax, Nova Scotia

Acknowledgments

The author is very grateful to the Senate Research Committee of the University of Prince Edward Island for financial support of this study, to the Benevolent Irish Society for providing a forum for discussing Irish matters in its annual lecture series, to the editors of the *Abegweit Review* for publishing articles relevant to this book, and to the following persons who contributed their knowledge and skills to this project: Beryl Barrett, Boyde Beck, F.W.P. Bolger, Brenda Brady, Cyril Byrne, Robert L. Campbell, J.W. Carter, Leo Cheverie, Katie Conboy, Frances A. Dindial, Rosemary Driscoll, Joseph Fitzgerald, Vance Griffin, Benny Hackett, Betty Hall, Joan Harcourt, Mary Beth Harris, Matthew Hatvany, Harry Holman, Orlo Jones, Frank Ledwell, Carlotta Lemieux, Desmond Leslie, Sean P. Little, Seamus McCluskey, Edward MacDonald, Peter McGuigan, Nancy MacIntosh, Willie McKenna, Allan MacLeod, Theo McMahon, Frances MacMillan, George Mullally, George O'Connor, Cathleen O'Grady, Eileen O'Grady, Joseph O'Grady, Michael O'Grady, Patrick O'Grady, Thomas O'Grady, William O'Grady, Colman O'Hare, Fr. Art O'Shea, Pádraig Ó Siadhail, Frank Pigot, Victor Shea, Norman Sinclair, Frances Smits Handrahan, Frances Ann Squire, Bonnie Suen, and David Weale.

Hook Light, County Wexford, Ireland

Prologue

Travellers in jetliners traversing the skies over Atlantic Canada today are pleased when even from afar they glimpse Prince Edward Island, a slender crescent of verdant land resting in the southern basin of the Gulf of St Lawrence. To the south, the Northumberland Strait separates the Island by at least nine miles from the mainland provinces of New Brunswick and Nova Scotia. Lobster and groundfish have abounded in these waters, and dairy farming and potato growing have prospered in the relatively mild climate and arable soil. Whereas maple, birch, pine, and spruce thickly forested much of the land in the early nineteenth century, today the gently rolling landscape shelters golden grainfields and green croplands, which contrast with the rust-red soil, the many sparkling bays and estuaries, the red sandstone cliffs, and the pink sandy shores. The Island is only a hundred and forty miles long and from four to forty miles wide. Each summer nearly one million visitors augment the 135,000 year-round residents who have spread over the three counties – Kings in the east, Queens in the centre, and Prince in the west. In both area and population, Prince Edward Island is Canada's smallest province. Nevertheless, studious excavators still find treasures galore in its cultural endowment.

The aboriginal Mi'kmaq people (also spelled *Micmac*), who for centuries were the seasonal occupants, called the island Abegweit (pronounced *Abahquit* but may be spelled *Epekwitk*, meaning "lying parallel with the land," though often popularly translated as "cradled on the waves"). French colonists in the early eighteenth century named it Île Saint-Jean. After their takeover in 1758, the British called it St John's Island until it was officially renamed in 1798 in honour of Edward, Duke of Kent, commander of British forces in North America (and the future father of Queen Victoria). In 1873 the colony became a province in the Canadian Confederation. Today's residents of Prince

Edward Island are predominantly descendants of the Scottish, English, Acadian French, and Irish immigrants of the eighteenth and nineteenth centuries, augmented by recent settlers from Lebanon, Holland, Germany, and many other nations.

The first fact about Irish immigration to Prince Edward Island is that it occurred almost entirely before the Great Famine of 1845–48. While multitudes of famine sufferers bypassed the Island and took refuge in havens along the St Lawrence River, only one so-called coffin ship, in 1847, sought shelter in Charlottetown.

The second fact about Irish immigration to Prince Edward Island is that it was largely fortuitous. At times, it is true, Irish people were recruited by landowners or their agents – the most notable instance being the 1830s influx of County Monaghan families to the MacDonald lands at Fort Augustus – but the majority of the Irish settlers were not part of any large-scale well-organized effort; rather, the tides of chain migration drew many extended families into the emigration stream.

A third fact about the Irish colonists is that they became wholehearted Islanders who vigorously contributed to the growth of their adoptive land; at the same time, they were homesick exiles who remained culturally bonded to the Old Country which they would never see again. Their double fealty was a vital part of the legacy they bestowed on their descendants.

Loosely assembled as their odyssey was, the Irish arrivals may now be classified into three groups: the colonial pioneers (1767–1810), the southeastern immigrants (1810–35), and the Monaghan settlers (1830–50). The colonial pioneers were strong in influence but small in number. A much heavier influx occurred in the two overlapping waves between 1810 and 1850. The 1810–35 wave brought immigrants principally from the southeastern counties of Wexford, Waterford, Kilkenny, and Tipperary; and the post-1830 wave brought settlers mainly from such northern counties as Armagh, Tyrone, and especially Monaghan. In the final count, all thirty-two counties were represented.

Irish immigration to the Island is also unique in another way. Even the valid generalization that Irish immigration to North America in the eighteenth century was almost entirely Protestant is subject to modification when applied to Prince Edward Island. The colonial pioneers of 1767–1810 were, in fact, an amalgam of established church (Anglicans), Huguenots (descendants of French Protestant refugees), Presbyterians, and Roman Catholics, whereas the two large waves of Irish immigrants between 1810 and 1850 were overwhelmingly Roman Catholic. The proportion of Roman Catholics among its Irish immigrants was significantly higher in Prince

Edward Island than in the neighbouring provinces of Nova Scotia and New Brunswick.

Actually, each of the Irish colonies in Atlantic Canada differs from the others both historically and culturally. The setting for the following selection of essays in social history is limited to Prince Edward Island during the colonial period. The dominant concern at that time – and indeed a perennial preoccupation from the 1767 lottery to the 1997 Commission on Land Use – was land, its acquisition, ownership, and stewardship. Against this background, the focus is on the Irish settlers – some ten thousand people who constituted about one-quarter of the founding immigrants of the province.

The essays in this book trace the Irish immigration and settlement patterns, identify the successive waves of newcomers (their places of origin and settlement), record many family names, explain the immigrants' reasons for coming, and indicate their occupations, activities, and cultural impact upon the Island as it evolved from a small British colony into a province of Canada.

Map 1. Ireland: Thirty-two counties and four historic provinces: Leinster, Munster, Connaught, and Ulster (and its six-county subdivision, Northern Ireland)

CHAPTER ONE

The Legacy of New Ireland

Shortly after the British government adopted a colonization plan for Prince Edward Island in 1767, people from Ireland began to arrive. The more privileged among them represented the so-called Protestant Ascendancy, the Anglo-Irish group that controlled most of Ireland's economy and politics. In the new colony, too, despite their small numbers, they acquired much property, achieved prosperity, and assumed high office.

In that first wave, rank-and-file Irish tradesmen, craftsmen, peasants, and labourers also came – tentatively at first, partly because the original colonization plan discountenanced settlement by Roman Catholics. Later on, as such restrictions were ignored or rescinded, the Catholic Irish presence became much more pronounced in both number and influence. Meanwhile, the eighteenth century witnessed an America-bound exodus of Irish Presbyterians from Ulster, who also were victims of penal restrictions, and some few of them came to the Island. By the end of that century, however, the total Irish immigration made up only about 10 percent of the Island's population.

LORD EGMONT'S FOLLY

In the small colony that would later become the province of Prince Edward Island, the most prominent person from 1769 through 1787 was Irish-born Captain Walter Patterson.[1] But before recounting the events of Patterson's regime, it is necessary to acknowledge a peculiar prelude to the actual formation of the colony. If a distinguished member of the Irish peerage named John Perceval, second Earl of Egmont, had achieved his ambition, Prince Edward Island might have become his personal fiefdom.[2] This ambition was never fulfilled, but his proposal for colonization did have an important historical bearing on the unique socio-economic structure imposed on the Island.

Of Norman French lineage, the Percevals had inherited their Burton Manor estate in County Cork, Ireland, from an ancestor who benefited from service under Oliver Cromwell. The second Earl of Egmont (c. 1710–70) was less concerned about his properties and titles in Ireland than about his career in Britain. Assuming the mantle of his illustrious father, he flourished in the company of eminent Georgians in London (the Duke of Ormond and philosopher George Berkeley were among his friends), won a seat in Parliament, and rose to be First Lord of the Admiralty.

At a time when both aristocratic and democratic factions were assertive in Britain, Egmont personified the former. In 1763 he earnestly petitioned King George III for two million acres, consisting of newly acquired St John's Island – along with a portion of Dominica in the West Indies – wherein his governance would exemplify imperialist principles and assure fealty to the British crown while creating an economically sustainable colony in the Gulf of St Lawrence. According to Egmont's proposal, the "Earl of the County" would preside over a large number of lesser landed lords and freeholders, establish towns and villages and a series of courts to administer justice, and import black slaves from Dominica to labour on the extensive plantation. The self-supporting colony would also provide its own trained personnel to meet military obligations.[3]

Although some later critics dismissed the Egmont plan as a fantastic pipe dream, at the time of its proposal a dozen or so senior British officers and reputable gentlemen endorsed it – including the man later named to be the Island's first governor, Walter Patterson. Evidently, Egmont's supporters saw practical merit in blending military imperialism with economic feudalism. In this matter Egmont may even have consulted his friend Sir James Edward Oglethorpe (1696–1785), founder of the colony that became the American state of Georgia. Regardless, London's more pragmatic Commissioners of Trade and Commerce (or Lords of Trade and Plantation, as they were also called) withheld approval of Egmont's plan because, they said, it would not advance the primary objectives of commerce and agriculture.

While Egmont's textbook aristocracy came to naught, reaction to it seems to have engendered the commissioners' own semi-feudal plan; this called not for a single supreme earl but for more than sixty individual proprietorships, which would be determined by lottery. The two plans had a common economic objective: to make the colony self-supporting. The commissioners' semi-feudal plan, however, was more compatible with the mercantilist philosophy that powered the British

Empire's expansion at that time; furthermore, its practicability was bolstered by Surveyor General Samuel Holland's extensive survey of the lands and natural resources of British North America. When it was implemented in 1767, the disappointed Earl refused a consolation grant of a whole parish, 100,000 acres; but Surveyor General Holland saw fit to commemorate him in no fewer than eight place names in Prince Edward Island.[4]

THE GRAND LOTTERY

With the adoption of the commissioners' plan, the British settlement of Prince Edward Island began. First, Captain Samuel Holland completed a survey of the Island, dividing it into sixty-seven townships averaging 20,000 acres each (see map 2).[5] Then the crown granted sixty-four of these townships by lottery to persons who had earned rewards for their political or military service. In return, each of the new proprietors was required to settle at least one person per 200 acres within ten years and to pay annual freeholders' quitrents (land taxes) of between two and six shillings per acre, depending upon evaluation, to cover the cost of operating the government. Flaws in the commissioners' socioeconomic blueprint soon surfaced. Few of the gentlemen whose names were thus drawn ever had any personal interest in the Island, nor did many succeed either in colonizing their lands or in paying their quitrents in strict accordance with the terms of the grants. For many of them, owning property in the colony was merely a business investment, one subject to speculation. From the outset, therefore, absentee landlordism (non-resident ownership) hindered the growth of the colony; and soon, as in Ireland, truant ownership led to legal disputes and tenant insecurity, and later to violent conflicts. At first, land speculators (and, later, social reformers too) argued that underpopulated, neglected, or misused land should be subject to escheat – to revocation of entitlement. Unwisely, Governor Patterson became embroiled in this controversy, ordering the confiscation of escheated townships, ostensibly to pay the salaries of his officials but effectively to increase land holdings for himself and his friends. (He came to possess three lots and four additional half-lots.) Based on the belief that the governor's use of power exceeded his authority, the proprietors' opposition to his actions – notably by Captain John MacDonald, Laird of Glenaladale – eventually led to his recall in 1787 and dismissal from office.

During the administration of Patterson's successor, Colonel Edmund Fanning (1787–1805), progress was slow. By 1797 only twenty-six of the sixty-seven townships had been colonized in accordance with the terms of the original grants. Dr Edward Walsh, a visiting British army

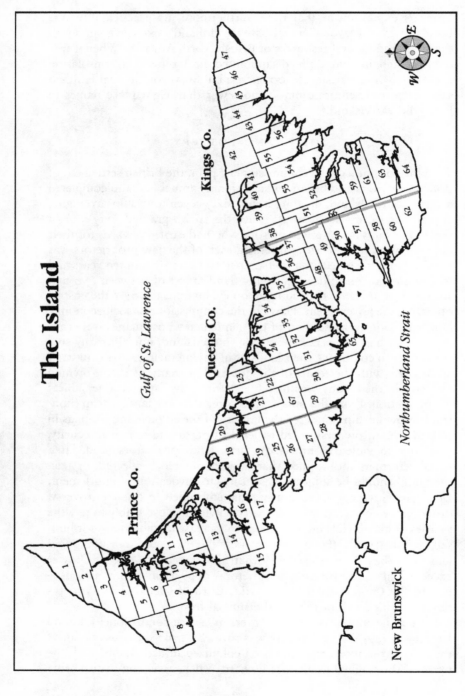

The Island

Prince Co.

Queens Co.

Kings Co.

Gulf of St. Lawrence

Northumberland Strait

New Brunswick

Map 2. In 1767 Prince Edward Island was divided into sixty-seven townships (or lots) and awarded by lottery to favourites of the crown.

medical officer, needed only a two-week sojourn on the Island in 1803 to discern that the "Principal Cause of the backwardness of the Colony" was "the original impolitic grants of large tracts of land of ten and twenty thousand acres each to proprietors who felt no inclination to improve the country, or to encourage settlers." Dr Walsh called this policy "absurd."[6]

Dr Walsh's judgment proved to be prophetic. Sixty years later, sharper criticism of the Island's landlord system emanated from the colony's own executive council. For instance, when the British colonial secretary charged the Island for the services rendered by troops who were sent to quell Tenant League disturbances in 1865, the indignant Island legislators retorted: "The feeling of discontent on the part of the tenantry owes its origin to the old Imperial error originally committed in granting the whole soil of the Colony in large tracts to individuals, an error which necessarily gave rise to an extensive leasehold system, and engendered the strife and ill-feeling between the landlord and the tenant, which from the earliest settlement of the Colony, have continued without interruption to the present."[7]

Elsewhere in British North America, residents normally could purchase the land they had tilled and on which they had built their homes; but in the Island colony, they were usually limited to leasing their farmland from an absentee or resident owner with little hope of ever acquiring the property themselves. Often in this conflict of interests, tenants were pitted against landlords. Particularly galling was the imposition placed upon the struggling tenants to pay the arrears in quitrents incurred by negligent proprietors. Furthermore, the receiver-general was empowered to seize proprietors' lands – and, by extension, he could also seize the holdings of tenants who did not pay the defaulted quitrents on top of their own lease obligations. For these and other reasons, the Island's proprietary land tenure and leasehold system (a system rarely found elsewhere in North America but familiar in the United Kingdom) gave rise to the most prolonged political issue of the nineteenth century, the many-faceted Land Question.

SECTARIAN DISCRIMINATION

Landlordism was one lamentable legacy of the Island's system of colonization. Sectarian discrimination was another. Possibly as a small instance of the larger intention of offsetting Quebec's Roman Catholic influence in North America, official British settlement policy for the Island explicitly discriminated in favour of Protestants from among

the American colonial Loyalists and continental Europeans. Simultaneously, the policy in the British Isles discriminated against emigrants
from Ireland. A double impediment therefore obstructed the majority of
the Irish – the very people, some theorists believed, who, in the absence
of a more humane economic and political system in their homeland,
should have benefited most from an enlightened emigration policy.

Despite the official restrictions, a vanguard of Irish Protestants
(both established church and Presbyterians) did come to the Island;
and substantial numbers of Catholics – mostly Highland Scots and
some refugee Acadians but a good sprinkling of Irish too – also settled
here before 1800. In this British colony, though, the Irish Catholics
who managed to gain entrance remained subject to the same discriminatory legal penalties that had oppressed them in Ireland. Fully sixty
years elapsed before the Penal Laws were formally rescinded and
Catholic men were permitted full exercise of civil rights, including the
right to vote and to hold public office, to participate in the legal profession, to attain higher education, to possess arms, and to own a
horse valued at more than five pounds. Even though the restrictions
were not always and everywhere enforced, they represented a disgraceful instance of the legalized religious discrimination practised in
the United Kingdom and British colonies. The Irish-born British parliamentarian and famed orator Edmund Burke described the Penal
Code as "a machine of as wise and elaborate contrivance for the
impoverishment and degradation of the people, and the debasement in
them of human nature itself, as ever proceeded from the perverted
ingenuity of man."[8]

The Penal Laws remained on the books in Prince Edward Island
until 1830, and even after their repeal, sectarian discrimination did not
cease. During the nineteenth century, despite several manifestations of
good will, there was little meaningful reconciliation between Catholics
and Protestants. On the contrary, while the increasing Catholic population sought recognition and equity in all aspects of society, the
Protestant majority expended much energy in maintaining its political
and economic ascendancy. The ensuing tensions between the two
major camps were not always relieved in the spirit of the golden rule.
Indeed, sectarianism in nineteenth-century Prince Edward Island was
marked more by blatant bigotry and partisan apologetics than by dis-
interested concern for truth or spiritual values or social justice.

THE COLONIAL PIONEERS

The most readily identifiable segment of the early colonial Irish were
the Ascendancy transplants – the Anglo-Irish Protestants who domi-

nated business and politics and whose function was to establish British law and British institutions and to ensure that the Island would be a loyal Protestant colony. While not the most numerous, they were the most influential settlers during the 1767–1820 period. Among this élite were governors, attorneys general, judges, administrative officials, business agents, entrepreneurs, land speculators, military personnel, and Anglican clergymen. The total Irish community also included homemakers, farmers, fishermen, shipwrights, tradesmen, and labourers, together with their families. Many of the Irish pioneers assembled in Charlottetown; others were scattered around most of the townships inhabited at that time.

A nominal census in 1798 recorded the family names and lot locations of most Island residents.[9] From this list it is reasonable to infer Irish national origin from such surnames as Delaney, Haley, Kiley, Rieley, Duffee, Cochran, Dunn, Keoughan, Flannigan, Counahan, Murphy, Ryan, Callehan, Nowlan, Quinlan, and McMahon – a veritable "McNamara's Band," including even McNamara himself. The census, though incomplete, accounts for 4,362 persons. If we consider only the surnames of heads of families, from 50 to 80 of the 748 appear to have been of distinctly Irish origin. The 1798 census data indicate that the Irish people then constituted about 10 percent of the population.

In 1803 the visiting army doctor Edward Walsh estimated that the population consisted of 150 Mi'kmaq, 650 Acadian French, and "5,000 emigrants from Scotland (by far the greatest proportion), England, Ireland, the United States, and a few Germans." He also observed: "There are several Roman Catholic Chapels in different parts of the Island, but only one Church and one clergyman of the Established Church. The Irish, Scotch-Highlanders and French Settlers, comprising three-fourths of the population are Roman Catholics."[10] Historical evidence supports Walsh's observations. The largest single contingent of immigrants in the eighteenth century arrived from Scotland in 1772 on the *Alexander* under the auspices of Captain John MacDonald, Laird of Glenaladale and Glenfinnan. These 225 Highland-Scots Catholics settled some fifteen miles northeast of Charlottetown, mainly at Scotch Fort (Scotchfort) and Tracadie in the two townships (Lots 35 and 36) purchased by Captain MacDonald, who later served as a Loyalist officer in the American Revolutionary War.

Other Scottish settlements included those of Sir James Montgomery – sixty people from Perthshire who settled chiefly at Covehead and Stanhope in 1770 – and about sixty families from Argyllshire who also arrived in 1770, on the *Annabella*, which went aground at Robert

Stewart's land in Malpeque (Lot 18). A notable English settlement was that of Robert Clark at New London (Lot 21): Clark led a group of a hundred settlers to his township in 1773, but in 1774 a second group met with great hardship when their vessel, *Elizabeth*, capsized in a storm off the Island's north shore. About eight hundred Loyalists also settled on the Island after the American Revolution.[11] Among them were the soldiers whom Surveyor General Holland brought to the Tryon area of Lot 28. The greatest colonizer of all was Lord Selkirk, who in 1803 accompanied the eight hundred Scots who settled on his vast holdings along the south shore, from Orwell to the southeastern end of the Island.

As colonizers, the Irish proprietors were not as successful as the Scottish and English landowners. Among the original proprietors of 1767, four were Irishmen: General Hunt Walsh (Lot 11), Quebec's Lieutenant-Governor Guy Carleton (Lot 15), and Captain Walter Patterson and his brother John (Lot 19).[12] By 1783, persons of Irish birth or extraction had acquired twenty-one of the Island's sixty-seven townships: in Prince County, Lots 9, 11, 14, 15, 16, 17, 19, and 25; in Queens County, Lots 22, 24, 31, 32, 33, 35, 48, 49, 50, 57, and 65; and in Kings County, Lots 54 and 61. Despite their extensive landholdings, the Irish owners had surprisingly little direct influence on the immigration of their countrymen, though there were a few exceptions.[13]

GOVERNOR WALTER PATTERSON

Among the landowner colonists from Ireland, Captain Walter Patterson stands out. The first son of William Patterson and Elizabeth Todd, he was born about 1735 at Foxhall near Rathmelton, County Donegal. As a young officer, he served in America during the Seven Years' War, after which he became involved in land deals in New York. Next, he was chosen one of the original proprietors on St John's Island. Although he and his brother John were co-owners of Lot 19, he greatly increased his own landholdings after 1769, the year he was appointed governor. As the Island's first governor, he became, so to speak, the first "public administrator of a privately-owned colony"[14] – a colony which then consisted of isolated Mi'kmaq camps, the remnants of a few once-thriving Acadian fishing settlements, and about a hundred and fifty British families. But large numbers of Scots, smaller numbers of English, and the Loyalists soon arrived, and so did nine families from Ireland, of whom Patterson noted that they would "make a good beginning."[15]

Although Patterson was a competent administrator, his controversial land transactions, political imprudence, and the indiscretions in his personal life caused him to lose the support of both the colonists and his fellow proprietors. As noted above, he was recalled to England, and in 1798 he died in poverty in London. But for one act Governor Patterson is still fondly remembered by the Island's Irish people: in 1780 he had the colonial Legislative Assembly rename the colony New Ireland.

Since then, Islanders have asked, Did Governor Patterson's love for his native land inspire the proposed name change? Ostensibly, he wanted to change the name in order to avoid confusion with other places commemorating St John and to prevent both the mails and intending settlers from going astray. Although Patterson's legislative Assembly had approved the name New Ireland, the Privy Council in London disallowed it because, the council stated, the name had already been appropriated.[16] Furthermore, the colonial governor's action, taken without prior approval from the imperial government, was considered impertinent. Thus, the name change called for by an act of the colony's Assembly, rather than by normal petition to the king, was officially nullified.[17]

Notwithstanding the official statement of rejection, it seems credible that Patterson's political adversaries may have secretly undermined his plan. Perhaps they had discovered that nine years earlier, in a letter to his lieutenant-governor (Thomas DesBrisay, who was abroad illegally recruiting Irish tenants), Patterson had referred to "the thriving state of the Island's potatoes, the proposed change of name of the Island to New Ireland, and the expected substantial immigration from Ireland in 1772."[18] Patterson's letter, a transparent propaganda piece, was meant to lure Irish settlers to the vacant lands which both he and his lieutenant-governor held in the colony. Perhaps Patterson's contemporaries thought that his motives for calling the place New Ireland smacked of something more than wholesome sentimentality. Whatever the truth, St John's Island was not renamed until 1798, when without controversy it was dutifully called Prince Edward Island.

LIEUTENANT-GOVERNOR THOMAS DESBRISAY

The Island's first lieutenant-governor, Thomas DesBrisay, was another man of Irish birth. He was a descendant of an officer of the Huguenot regiment that had landed in Ireland with Prince William of Orange. After the fall of Limerick (1691) the DesBrisays were granted property in Thurles, County Tipperary. As some people were inclined to disparage these inherited credentials, DesBrisay sometimes cited his own service as captain in the Royal Irish Regiment of Artillery as evidence of both his Irishness and his loyalty to the crown.[19]

Although he was not rewarded in the famous one-day lottery of St John's Island, DesBrisay became a major land speculator by purchasing large tracts near Charlottetown. He came to own townships 14, 31, and 33. For six years after his appointment in 1769 as colonial secretary and lieutenant-governor, he worked hard at recruiting settlers for his lands. Evidently, he hoped to emulate the Londonderry settlement that Alexander McNutt had successfully undertaken in Nova Scotia. The greatest obstacle DesBrisay had to overcome was people's reluctance to emigrate to property which tenants had little hope of ever owning outright. Neither this obstacle nor the fact that recruitment of settlers in Great Britain and Ireland was forbidden deterred DesBrisay from advertising publicly in Wexford town, Enniscorthy, Dublin, Belfast, and Londonderry. He employed agents in several towns, particularly in the north of Ireland, and even sought recruits in Scotland. By 1773 he had run afoul of British landlords, who did not want to lose their tenants through emigration, and he was ordered to desist from advertising and recruiting lest he incur "the strongest marks of His Majesty's displeasure."[20] But DesBrisay stated that "he had never taken a tenant from the north of Ireland without the consent of the proprietor or agents of the lands." Apparently his misleading publicity had no success in the south of Ireland, but in 1771 he sent nine families, mostly Protestants, to settle on his sparsely populated land in Lot 33 near Charlottetown; and in 1772 the same vessel, the *John and James*, sailed out of northern ports with 188 persons – the same year that the *Yaward*, sponsored mainly by another agent but bearing some of DesBrisay's recruits, sailed from Belfast and Newry with fifty families.

It is worth noting that DesBrisay conducted his overseas recruiting activities during a period (1769–74) when more than 40,000 Ulster Scots emigrated to North America. This heavy emigration is attributed by W.A. Carrothers to the "political disabilities under which they lived in Ireland because of their Presbyterianism." Carrothers adds that economic disabilities "gave a still greater impetus to emigration." Concerning the southern Irish who decades earlier had gone to settle in Newfoundland, he correctly notes that some later "migrated to Nova Scotia and Prince Edward Island, and were the first of the Celtic Irish to settle on the American continent."[21]

How many of the DesBrisay immigrants settled permanently on the Island is uncertain, but historian G. Edward MacDonald recently published two lists of DesBrisay's recruits, based on information found among the Selkirk papers.[22] The first list shows that the thirty people (including a few partnerships) who received leases of 50 to 300 acres in 1771 were natives of Ulster. From County Antrim were John Druitt, Edward Hodskiss, Charles Hyndman, Samuel Kennedy, William McCracken, Thomas McCrow, Barnaby McGuire, William Read, Edward Rogers and Robert Lowery, George Thompson, and possibly James Cregg; from County Armagh, John Beaty, William and Joseph Corry, John Fullerton, John Hamilton, William McKeen, James Mollone, Alexander Patterson, and James Patterson; from County Down, John Brown and William Crosby and Nelthorp Carson, Elias Harrison, Robert McConnell, and Patrick MacDonell; from County Monaghan, James Irwin and William Kidd; and from County Tyrone, Joseph Johnson. Many of these family names have survived in Island society into the twenty-first century, some having attained prominence in agriculture, commerce, and public affairs.

The second list shows that in 1772 ten people in Ireland each purchased a 100–acre farm on the Island. From County Down there was Charles McNely; and from County Antrim, Thomas Belshaw, John Bunteen, Thomas Hyde, Daniel Maguire, John Morrow, Richard Rogers, Philip Thornton, William Walker, and George Wattson. All the farms were in Lot 31. However, when some of the purchasers came to the Island in 1774, they learned that because the lieutenant-governor had already mortgaged his holdings, he could not convey legal title to them. In the same year Governor Patterson declared his absentee associate "very unfit to hold any offices under His Majesty" for having "attempted to interfere in the proper allocation of colonial funds."[23]

DesBrisay, imprudently seeking immediate profits from his ventures, actually bungled an opportunity to populate his lands with self-sufficient farmers, weavers, carpenters, and other craftsmen. Over half his Northern Ireland emigrants, after having paid their own transatlantic passage, rejected DesBrisay's extortionate terms and insecure leases, and settled elsewhere, on or off the Island.

Until 1779, to cite the words of historian Francis W.P. Bolger, the entrepreneur "did not grace the Island with his macabre and tiresome presence."[24] After DesBrisay did eventually arrive, he served as temporary administrator of the government for a year or so while Governor Patterson was in England on business. Even during his brief term of office, some of DesBrisay's land deals were questionable, and his personal reputation was impugned. "Thomas DesBrisay was a man of distasteful character," Robert Allan Rankin states. "Soon after taking up his post as Lieutenant-Governor of the

Island, he began to use the 'uncertainty of the times' to his personal advantage. DesBrisay acquired by fraudulent means fifty-eight town and pasture lots in the Royalty of Charlottetown, then granted the entirety to members of his family. He was severely reprimanded by Patterson for his loose behaviour, on the latter's return, and 'pleaded to be removed from his duties' and away from Patterson, whom he obviously hated."[25]

REVEREND THEOPHILUS DESBRISAY

Thomas DesBrisay, in his own way, served the state. His aptly named son Theophilus graced the church.[26] By royal warrant in 1774, this newly ordained twenty-year-old Trinity College, Dublin, alumnus from Thurles, Tipperary, was appointed governor's chaplain for St John's Island, and later he was appointed minister of the parish of Charlotte. There he faithfully served the established United Church of England and Ireland for more than forty-five years. He was, it seems, the only resident Protestant clergyman on the Island before 1820. He also served as justice of the peace and held some minor public offices.

En route to the Island in 1775, DesBrisay's ship was intercepted by American privateers, who had just captured the Island's attorney general and surveyor general in Charlottetown. The young clergyman was released unharmed, but when he arrived in the capital, there was neither a church nor a residence waiting for him. He therefore went to sea as a naval chaplain for about two years, during which time he was exposed to hostile fire at least once. He finally settled near Covehead, about a dozen muddy miles from Charlottetown. Married to the daughter of the chief justice and living "in the manner of an English squire-parson," he dutifully commuted on weekends between his rural home and his town congregation. Although St Paul's parish, Charlottetown, was created in 1781, the first parish church was not built until 1800. DesBrisay then moved to Charlottetown, where he resided as a widely respected clergyman until his death in 1823.

There is more to this Irish success story. Records of the Island colony reveal that originally, in 1769, the Reverend John Caulfield had been appointed minister of Charlotte parish, but he did not take up his duties.[27] Governor Patterson several times requested a replacement, and finally, in 1774, he petitioned Secretary of State Lord Dartmouth to appoint his young relative, the Reverend Edward Patterson. But as fate (or opportunism) would have it, before Patterson's letter arrived, Lord Dartmouth had been approached by

Lieutenant-Governor DesBrisay, and His Lordship "yielded to [Des-Brisay's] solicitations in behalf of his own son, who had lately taken orders."[28] After this timely interposition, Governor Patterson and Lieutenant-Governor DesBrisay had a proper falling-out, and other unfriendly encounters followed.

A postscript on the DesBrisays: it may be noted that when the Benevolent Irish Society (BIS) was founded in Charlottetown in 1825, the first elected secretary was Charles DesBrisay, grandson of the former lieutenant-governor. Later in the century, a W.C. DesBrisay was chosen president of the fledgling BIS. The DesBrisay family thus retained its identification with Ireland, as did other eminent citizens who were associated with the BIS in its early years. Colonel John Ready, lieutenant-governor at that time, was the original patron;[29] Francis Longworth was the first president; and Fade Goff and the reverend Alexander Fitzgerald were members of the original executive committee.

OTHER IRISH COLONIALISTS

Other men with Irish connections were prominent in the early public affairs of the Island. For instance, James MacNutt of Londonderry was Governor Patterson's secretary, and Phillips Callbeck, a Dublin lawyer, was attorney general.[30] While serving as temporary administrator of the colony (1775–79), Callbeck was taken captive during the above-mentioned privateer raid in Charlottetown, but he was later released with apologies by General George Washington himself. David Higgins, a naval officer who had assisted in Samuel Holland's survey, was captured by the same raiders at Canso, Nova Scotia. He and his brother Cornelius, from County Wexford, both served in the first Island legislature. Then there was Caesar Colclough, member of a landowning family in Wexford, who in 1807 became chief justice of Prince Edward Island, succeeding another member of the Irish bar, Robert Thorpe.[31] Finally, it seems appropriate to include here Patterson's successor, New York-born Edmund Fanning, who had been lieutenant-governor of Nova Scotia and was a descendant of Irish immigrants.[32]

Accounts of individual public figures give but a partial impression of a society. The common people, though depicted en masse, reflect other facets of the cultural commonwealth. In addition to Thomas DesBrisay's recruited families from Ireland, the Irish individuals and families, now mostly anonymous, who came to the Island prior to 1800 – by choice or accident or curiosity – included numerous people from Newfoundland and some from New Brunswick and Nova

Scotia. Not all of these early Irish were sympathetic to Britain; several refugees from the Rebellion of 1798 also turned up here.[33] Other Irish newcomers, as well as transients who had no particular loyalty or destination, may have been merely Island hopping on their way to Upper Canada or to the Republic of the United States of America. Those who came by chance and stayed on were known among the Irish as "blow-ins."

The Military Connection

As there is ample evidence that large numbers of Irishmen enlisted in the British forces for service before and during the American Revolution, it is not surprising that the Charlottetown garrison had its share of Irish soldiers. Even if "the first Irish to settle here" did not come with Lord Rollo's occupation in 1758 during the Acadian expulsion (as Charlottetown Mayor John McKenna speculated in 1928),[34] there were certainly Irishmen in the regiments later stationed on the Island; and some of these later troops, upon retirement (or desertion) from military service, became permanent residents.

The presence of the troops, it was said, sometimes disconcerted the local citizenry. In 1778 an Irishman named Colonel Timothy Hierlihy stationed a detachment of his Independent Rangers in Charlottetown. At the same time, Captain Edmund Dodd's frigate HMS *Cabot* was in port. That military build-up later led journalist Peter McCourt to ponder "what the presence of six hundred soldiers and a hundred or more sailors would mean in a town which did not contain half that number of civilians."[35] One part of the answer is that churchmen, in particular, found conditions in the colonial capital extremely challenging, not to say discouraging. At least one person inferred that the rowdiness of the town was one reason why the Reverend Theophilus DesBrisay preferred to live in the country.[36] Even the Reverend James MacGregor, the redoubtable Presbyterian minister who purged Pictou's riotous military garrison, was appalled at what he encountered in 1791: "In a few minutes I found Charlottetown to have wickedness enough for a larger town." Swearing and drunkenness abounded.[37]

In fairness, it must be noted that the consumption of alcoholic beverages was not a foible of the military alone. Taverns were an early priority in the colony, and importation of rum and other spirits had become a major enterprise before the end of the eighteenth century. Furthermore, since public buildings were at a premium, inns and taverns, besides being entertainment and refreshment centres, often catered to more abstemious assemblies. For some thirty years, the town's Anglican congregation held its services in a tavern building, and the first meeting of the Legislative Assembly was held at the Crossed Keys Tavern on Queen Street. On that occasion the Irish Sergeant-at-arms, Edward Ryan, wryly observed that the gathering was "a damned queer parliament" – for which perceptive observation he was dismissed from his doorkeeper's job.[38]

Full accounts of the Island's soldier settlers are not available, but it is known that in 1783 twenty-three of Colonel Hierlihy's disbanded troops settled with their families on land granted to them. Other military veterans did the same. It is noteworthy that Irish names were common among disbanded soldiers and deserters – a circumstance which suggests that some recruits may have joined the army mainly as a means of obtaining a passage to America. In this way, no doubt, a small number of men later became regular civilian settlers in Prince Edward Island.

Even before the British took possession of the Island in 1758, a few Irish people may have lived there. Sir Andrew MacPhail noted that in 1752 curé Patrick McGhee (alias R.P. Patrice Lagrée?) was garrison chaplain at Port LaJoye and that the Sieur de la Roque's census had listed a man from Picardy whose wife was Irish.[39] More credible evidence indicates that the family of Samuel Leard and Margaret Rogers of Carrickfergus in County Antrim, who settled in Tryon (Lot 28) in 1768, may have been the first Irish civilian settlers of Prince Edward Island.[40]

Irish Loyalists

Another small group of Irishmen landed on these shores among the aforementioned five hundred Loyalists who had fled from the American Revolution. Although the Irish were not as numerous in the Loyalist ranks as they were in General George Washington's army, they made up a small portion of Revolutionary War veterans who settled here and elsewhere in the region. This influx is reflected, for example, in the 1841 Claimants List. This list contains the names of Loyalists and disbanded soldiers (or their descendants) whose claims to grants of land had not been recognized or formalized, because of land disputes or other irregularities during the Patterson administration. The Claimants List is of particular interest in the present context because it includes more than thirty Irish family names that are familiar in Prince Edward Island. Even so, those among them who settled permanently on the Island have not been identified with certainty.[41]

THE COLONIAL CATHOLIC CHURCH

When embarking on his ministry in 1790, the colony's second Scottish Catholic priest,[42] the Reverend Angus Bernard MacEachern (later to become the first bishop of the Catholic diocese of Charlottetown), is described by historian Bolger as "shouldering his missionary pack and setting out to visit widely dispersed Scottish, *Irish*, and Acadian settlers throughout the Island."[43] Other chroniclers, without elucidating the matter, also acknowledge that at the time of Father MacEachern's coming, Irish immigrants from both Ireland and Newfoundland were already settling in the Charlottetown area. Nowhere at that time did the Irish constitute a dominant gathering, but by 1800 they did form an identifiable group among the Catholic people in Charlottetown. As the century began, Charlottetown "was the only truly nucleated village on the Island. It had perhaps 70 houses scattered about on lots 80 by 160 feet."[44] It also had an excellent harbour and sturdy wharves to accommodate the extensive shipping that was getting underway. This was the setting when, to assist Father MacEachern, a new Catholic missionary from France took up his duties in 1799. That missionary was abbé Jacques Stanislaus DeCalonne, a brother of the finance minister of King Louis XVI.[45]

On 28 May 1800 Father DeCalonne wrote to Bishop Denaut of Quebec, telling him of his frustrations. After stating that the Catholic Church on the Island embraced the French or Acadians (who had the least need of his services), the Scots (who spoke only Gaelic, which he did not understand), and the Irish (who were to be his painful burden), he explained that the town was made up "principally of Irish and a few Scotch, the greater number soldiers and all drunkards to an incredible excess, as well as supremely ignorant. All the religion they practise is to go to Mass on Sunday, and even on that point they are not scrupulous." Evidently the Celtic congregation, young and old, were unresponsive to their aristocratic French pastor's preaching and teaching. The relative success of later pastors suggests that the original parishioners may have preferred clergymen of their own nation, culture, and status. Father DeCalonne, however, identified another glaring cause for the town's religious indifference: "the abominable vice of drunkenness which brutalizes the people and makes them indifferent to everything." Then, with perceptive irony the troubled pastor assessed his congregation. "They are attached to their faith," he wrote. "They would suffer death rather than abandon it, but they don't observe even one of the commandments. It would be easier, if I may so express myself, to make of them martyrs than Christians."[46]

A century later the Reverend John C. MacMillan, a historian of the Island's Catholic Church, agreed with the French missionary's judgment of conditions in Charlottetown in 1800. In support of his own opinion that many of the town's Catholics were then of the lowest and poorest class, MacMillan cited DeCalonne's words: "The greater number of the Irish we have here bring with them nothing but vices because they are the very dregs of Ireland and Newfoundland. They came to this place not because they emigrate, but because they have been expelled from their own country." MacMillan then characterized the congregation of the early town as consisting of "persons most of whom had grown callous by long and continual association with crime, and for that reason could not be brought back to a life of virtue except by painstaking exhortation."[47]

An Anglican writer, Percy Pope, reviewing the same period (and not restricting his focus to the Irish population alone) placed a more generous and tolerant interpretation on moral conditions in the early colony. He opined: "It is difficult to conceive of the state of a community absolutely cut off from all ordinances of religion – yet such for many years was the condition of the inhabitants of the Island of St John (Prince Edward Island). The adventurous character of their lives, the absence of conventional restraints and the extent to which they indulged in the use of intoxicants, necessarily rendered them rather lax in matters of morality and religion, yet the early colonists were essentially men of sound judgement and fully realized that such a condition of affairs could not with safety be long permitted to continue."[48]

After Father DeCalonne had served four years as missionary in Charlottetown, Bishop Denaut transferred him to the Rustico mission. In August of that year, 1803, the mission to the town, numbering over 350 Catholics, was entrusted to the Reverend Henry Francis Fitzsimmons, a Franciscan friar, the first of a dozen Irish-born priests to serve the people there. Father Fitzsimmons may have come to the Island via Newfoundland, the route taken at that time by many other Charlottetown Irish. His stay was so brief that one chronicler was forced to remark that "if it were not that his name occurs in Bishop Denaut's register, we could not discover that he had ever been here, so completely has every trace of his sojourn disappeared."[49] Although Fitzsimmons's presence on this Island was fleeting, the imprints made by his Irish successors as Catholic priests in the diocese of Charlottetown are indelible.

By the time Bishop Denaut's successor, Bishop Plessis, made his official visit to the Island in 1812, the capital had become "a place of some pretension." Church historian MacMillan states that Charlottetown had been "well chosen for strength, while for beauty it could not be excelled. Its wide streets, elegant private residences and imposing public buildings gave it an air of importance that excited the admiration of the Bishop."[50] Although the capital had an Anglican church, a new courthouse, and military barracks, it lacked a Roman Catholic church, a parochial house, and "the requisites for the service of the altar." Bishop Plessis therefore ordered Father MacEachern to build a church on a site donated by Mrs Phillips Callbeck (widow of the early attorney general) and to name that church in honour of Saint Dunstan, a tenth-century archbishop of Canterbury.

IRISH PIONEERS IN RURAL AREAS

While the capital town was thus burgeoning and adapting to civilizing influences, scattered clearances around remote areas of the Island were also sprouting tiny Irish colonies. To mention but one example, before the nineteenth century there was already a sprinkling of Irish people located in Lot 20, along with some Loyalist families. There in 1778 Daniel Delaney, James Dunne, and John Crowley were among the first settlers of Park Corner; two years later John Poor, Mrs Lily Riely, and Patrick Duggan established homes at Sea View; and about 1790 the first settlers at Long River included John and Lawrence Murphy. These people were forerunners of a settlement soon to be called Irishtown.[51]

Using the methods and materials of their time and place, the pioneers of Park Corner, Irishtown, and other hamlets built rough log houses, filled the wall cracks with moss and mud, and shingled the roofs with sods. Woodburning fireplaces and stoves, used for warmth and cooking, provided some indoor comfort. Wood was also used to make tools and farming implements as well as rough carts and sleds for transport.

In their forest setting the pioneers faced numerous hazards. A century after the actual event, J.A. Ready recounted how James Sinnot, armed with only a hatchet, had to scramble up a tree to escape a hungry bear. The story continues: "But when the bear proceeded to climb the tree, Sinnot discovered that his hatchet was too short to reach Bruin. Then the bear made the discovery that Sinnot, unlike Achilles, was vulnerable, not only in one, but in both heels, and forthwith he helped himself to a mouthful from these parts of Sinnot's anatomy. Sinnot's screams soon brought assistance, and he was glad to escape, even with the loss of his heels."[52]

Despite the hazards and hardships of the primeval forest, the colonial pioneers put down roots in numerous outports around the Island. They began by erecting their cabins in coastal coves and along riverbanks, where water routes facilitated transport and communication, where the marshes yielded grass for their cattle, and where the sea ensured a good supply of cod, herring, and shellfish. Using hand implements they planted small plots in the clearings. Later they cut footpaths through the woods and gradually widened those paths to accommodate their crude wooden vehicles. By such sheer labour the eighteenth-century pioneers prepared for the next century's large harvest of immigrants and for the growth of several significant Irish settlements.

SECURING THE FOOTHOLD

By the end of the eighteenth century Ireland was demographically well represented here. The immigrant mix, numerically modest though it was, consisted of men, women, and children; of proprietors, tradesmen, and peasants; of Anglo-Irish, Scots Irish, and Gaelic Irish; of northern Irish, southern Irish, and Newfoundland Irish; of Irish Anglicans, Irish Presbyterians, and Irish Roman Catholics.

The tenacity of the Irish minority in the colony gave substance to the prophecy inherent in Governor Patterson's chosen name for the Island. Even the traces of one-upmanship and venality in high places, accompanied by a penchant for lawlessness and disorder among the so-called commoners, were painful reminders of the distressed society from which the Irish colonists had emigrated. Furthermore, of much greater importance in historian Bolger's view, the colony's semi-feudal land policy and absentee-landlord practices virtually ensured that the Island would become "a second Ireland"[53] and therefore that the proposed appelation New Ireland "would have been most appropriate."[54] As well, historian Ian Ross Robertson, after identifying the Land Question as the distinguishing characteristic of colonial Prince Edward Island, states: "It was a cycle of poverty, insecurity and oppression. Islanders frequently referred to their colony as 'the Ireland of the New World.'"[55]

Indeed, even two full centuries after the fact, the nullified name New Ireland lingers as an ambiguous but ironically appropriate symbol of the legacy left both by ambitious proprietors and by aspiring peasants. For Governor Patterson and some other proprietors, the name *New* Ireland no doubt signified *another* Ireland, for they wished to reproduce in this Island colony the comfortable way of life which the Anglo-Irish gentry had enjoyed when they controlled the Old Country's resources and ruled the Gaelic multitudes whom they had earlier dispossessed. On the other hand, for most rank-and-file Irish immigrants, *New* Ireland connoted a *different* Ireland, for they were determined to escape from the depressing poverty and insecurity of their exploited homeland and to establish their families in a new society that promised opportunities for decent, dignified living.

Coping with the opposing forces generated by this volatile twofold legacy became one of the great challenges for Prince Edward Island in the nineteenth century.

CHAPTER TWO

Less-Travelled Roads

During the first fifty years of British colonization of the Island, Irish immigration and settlement had progressed very slowly. The Scots, meanwhile, had clearly established themselves as the numerically dominant ethnic group. It was not until early in the nineteenth century, well before the Great Famine, that significant Irish immigration began. Even at its peak, though, it never exceeded one-quarter of the Island's total population. Nevertheless, this Irish minority created several distinctive settlements.

The development of Township Eleven, for example, illustrates how the Island's semi-feudal system initially enabled the Irish settlement of the area and how this system inevitably gave place to a more democratic economy, in which the sons of the tenant settlers became independent farm owners. Enlightened leadership accounts for much of the progress and harmony that marked the formation of this singular Irish community centred in Foxley River. Somewhat similar forces were also at work in a dozen other semi-secluded Irish enclaves, each one of which had its own fortuitous beginnings and its own distinctive local development.

Coming to the Island usually involved not only physical relocation and cultural dislocation but also adjustment to a foreign climate and terrain and to an unaccustomed way of life. However, such troubling experiences were lessened in Township Eleven because many of the settlers originated in the same general area of Ireland and many of the families intermarried compatibly. Before long, residents could identify virtually every person for miles around the settlement, not alone by name and location but often by parentage, marriage, occupation, and sometimes by family history.

Township Eleven therefore may be seen as exemplary rather than typical. Its central concerns and modalities, bridging the experiences

*of early colonialism and the expectations of later nineteenth-century
society, are clearly reflected in Irish communities all over the Island.*

For tens of thousands of Irish emigrants who realized that they would
never again see their homeland, crossing the wide Atlantic Ocean in the
early nineteenth century was a courageous act of faith. The small per-
centage who chose to settle in little-known Prince Edward Island
encountered hardships that would further test their faith. For security
and companionship, apprehensive newcomers gathered in a score of
enclaves or clusters of families here and there on the Island and formed
small communities noted for their Irishness – places such as Hope
River, Emerald, Indian River, St Marys Road, Green Road, Lot 7,
Byrnes Road, Covehead, Christopher Cross, and Kildare, each with its
distinctive origins and local history.

To consider one important example, not many people trod the rough
paths hacked through the woods and bogs of Township Eleven, but
those trusting adventurers who did so between 1820 and 1840 succeeded in founding at Foxley River a remarkable Irish community (see
map 3). In that community on the Island's north coast, strong-backed
and strong-willed immigrant families prevailed over the forces of
nature and the impediments of colonial land policies. Even so, it is true
to say that the story of Lot 11 actually begins with the fortunes of a
gentleman named Hunt Walsh (1710–95) both on the battlefields of
colonial America and on his peaceful estate in the midlands of Ireland.

Tracing how this resident landowner and his successors in Ireland
came to be absentee landlords and how they administered their estate
in distant Prince Edward Island clarifies several practical workings of
the small colony's semi-feudal system. As in each of the other proprietorships, the Lot 11 experience was singular in its origins, its ethnic
and sectarian makeup, and its evolution. Nevertheless, the foundations
of this community and the daily life of its people had numerous parallels with other rural places on the Island.

THE WALSH PROPRIETORSHIP

The name Walsh originally referrd to the Cambro-Normans who came
from Wales to southeastern Ireland in the twelfth century, gladly settled in there, and eventually generated the fourth most populous surname in the country.[1] One branch of that diverse clan is of special
interest here. Hunt Walsh's great-grandfather acquired the Ballykilcavan estate near Stradbally, County Laois (often spelled Leix; also formerly called Queen's County), about 1640; but Hunt himself grew up

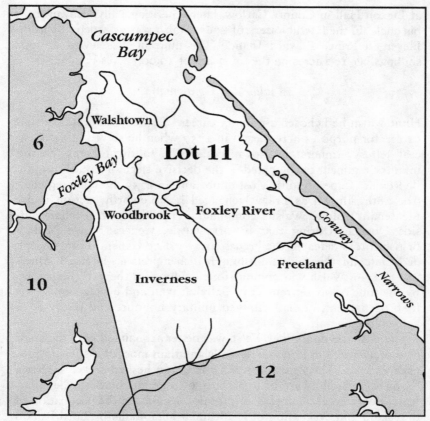

Map 3. The Walsh proprietorship encompassed Township Eleven, on the north side of Prince County.

at Burton Hall in County Carlow, later inheriting Ballykilcavan from
his uncle. In the fateful lottery of 1767, Walsh was awarded Township
Eleven in Prince Edward Island. (The quitrent was levied at four
shillings per 100 acres on the township of 20,000 acres.)

Soldier and Gentleman

Hunt Walsh had chosen a military career.[2] The leading events of that
career, for purposes here, began in 1757 when he served under General Jeffery Amherst in Nova Scotia. The following year Walsh's
infantry regiment participated in the decisive siege of Louisbourg on
Île Royale (Cape Breton). Most important, in 1759 the same regiment
(the 28th, known as Braggs) engaged in noteworthy action under
Lieutenant Colonel Walsh's command on the Plains of Abraham outside Quebec. During that historic battle, General James Wolfe's
British forces defeated the French army led by General Louis-Joseph
de Montcalm, thereby establishing British supremacy in North America. In 1766 Walsh was commissioned colonel of the 58th Regiment.
By the time of his retirement to Ballykilcavan and his election to the
Irish parliament, he had attained military honours and the rank of
lieutenant-general.

There is little doubt that Walsh was better acquainted with the lands
he was awarded in Prince Edward Island than most of his fellow proprietors were. The British forces with whom he had served in Nova
Scotia were well aware of the strategic value attributed to Île Saint-
Jean's potential as a supplier of produce. Moreover, the occupation of
the Island and evacuation of its Acadian inhabitants by Lord Rollo's
detachment in 1758 were events well known throughout the command. There is no evidence, however, that Walsh ever set foot on the
Island or took either a personal or a proprietorial interest in his estate
there. He made no known attempt to colonize it.

As Walsh, a bachelor, had no family, he bequeathed his estates to
designated heirs, who were to take the name and arms of Walsh.[3] Following his death in 1795, Township Eleven remained in the hands of
this series of heirs for the next sixty years. Even during the general's
lifetime, some Ballykilcavan transactions had been conducted by his
brother, the Reverend Raphael Walsh (1728–1808), who was the
established-church dean of Dromore from 1772 to 1802.[4] It was
Raphael Walsh who in 1802 appointed James Bardin Palmer the first
on-site land agent for Lot 11. Palmer, in turn, named a tributary of the
Foxley River after his employer, the Raphael River. Local historian J.
Clinton Morrison's description is apt: "For those with an emotional
attachment to the community's past, the warm, quiet summer evenings

along secluded Raphael River are reminiscent of the very early days of its history when nature was at its grandest and the only twilight sounds were the long, lonesome call of the distant common snipe in flight and the muffled echo of a neighbour's barking dog from deep within the shelter of the surrounding forest."[5]

THE LAND AGENTS

Thus began a series of formative influences on Lot 11 personified first by Mr Palmer and later by John Large and James Warburton. Under the patronage of the Walsh family in faraway Ballykilcavan, these three Irish-born land agents successively became responsible for the day-to-day management of the Island township. Lot 11 was indeed unique in having been owned by Irish proprietors and managed by Irish land agents.

James Bardin Palmer

The first land agent, James Bardin Palmer (1771–1833), was a wily Anglo-Irish colonist from Dublin. He was a lawyer, politician, and land agent for several absentee proprietors – including John Hill and Lord Selkirk, both of whom were soon displeased by his business dealings. During his tenure as agent for the Walsh heirs from 1802 to 1808, Palmer brought no settlers to Lot 11, but with commendable foresight he did establish some access roads for later colonization, and near the Foxley River he built a farm home and lumber mill. He named the serene, sequestered site Walshtown.[6]

In a more important public action, in 1806 Palmer founded the Loyal Electors, which is said to have been the first political society in British North America. According to Greenhill and Gifford, Palmer's party "marked the very beginning of the long fight for the political emancipation of the Islanders, first towards a government responsible to the people and then to the freeing of the people from the incubus of the landlords."[7] Palmer's political perspicacity would not be fully appreciated until later in the century, when politicians and electors acted decisively on some of his initiatives. As a land agent for the Walsh family, however, his record was not at all satisfactory.

Despite a modest beginning in the exportation of timber from Lot 11, the trusting relations between Palmer and the Walsh family did not endure. Before he left Walshtown for more promising enterprises in the centre of the Island, Palmer wrangled with his employer over the payment of bills he had accumulated. Having cited his own spartan circumstances as early as 1803 (he said he could afford himself

"neither a horse to ride nor a good coat to wear"),[8] he begged Walsh
in 1807 not to subject him to ruin and possible imprisonment.[9]
Palmer, it seems, was an opportunist who in this instance had committed a costly impropriety: he had amassed debts for unauthorized
business transactions. In the ensuing arbitration proceedings, most of
Palmer's claims for compensation were disallowed. Nevertheless, he
rebounded from this setback and resumed his controversial career as
a lawyer, militia officer, politician and entrepreneur on the Island.[10]
His family reputedly founded the South Shore haven later called
Victoria-by-the-Sea.

John Large

The agent who replaced Palmer was John Large. Circumstantial evidence points to the probability of his being related to the Thomas
Large of Derryclony, County Laois, who leased a 90–acre farm at
Drumneen (Little Hill) from the Walsh family of Ballykilcavan in
1764.[11] Ledgers kept at Ballykilcavan between 1777 and 1795 refer to
a John Large paying rents; and the names of a Richard Large and a
John Large are recorded as jurymen at an inquisition at Ballykilcavan
in 1802. Unfortunately, adequate information precisely identifying
John Large, the Island land agent, has eluded searchers. In October
1983 the provincial genealogist Orlo Jones cited estate records show-
ing that a person named John Large had died on 1 February 1849,
leaving five sons and four daughters, who had settled in several places
in Prince Edward Island and elsewhere in Canada.[12] However, another
recent genealogical search traced a John Large to a family in Dundalk,
County Louth. This veteran of the Napoleonic War is said to have emigrated with five sons to Prince Edward Island after 1815.[13] Whether
the Larges of Drumneen and those of Dundalk were related is not clear,
but the Island's public records do show the Large surname not only
within Lot 11 but also in Cascumpec (Lot 6), Springfield (Lot 67), and
York (Lot 34). (Incidentally, that family name may be an anglicization
of the French De Large, since both Dundalk and Portarlington on the
Laois-Offaly county line were centres of post-Cromwellian Huguenot
settlement.)[14]

   John Large's pedigree is of secondary importance here; what matters
primarily is that in 1818 John Allen Johnson Walsh granted him power
of attorney for Lot 11.[15] Large is believed to have sailed from Dublin
on the brig Harriet on 11 June 1817 and to have arrived at New London, Prince Edward Island, on 22 August 1817. He set up his own
farm at Walshtown and supervised the settlement of the first recruits
from Ireland. The document empowering Large to care for and man-

age Township Eleven also mentions several unnamed persons who intended to emigrate to the Island and possibly become Walsh's tenants. The terms of their tenancy included an annual charge of one peppercorn ("if demanded") for the first seven years. During that period the tenants were expected to clear the trees and prepare the land for agriculture. After that, they were to be offered leases not exceeding the term of three lives or thirty-one years (whichever period was longer) at rentals comparable to those in effect for similar land elsewhere on the Island.

Evidently Walsh's standards were reasonable enough to attract dozens of settlers. After all, even though the terms of tenancy were relatively short (some proprietors occasionally offered leases of up to 999 years), they offered more hopeful prospects than many emigrants from the British Isles had known in their homeland, and the ample acreages on this Island were invariably much larger than the pinched farms from which the settlers had come.

Even under the best of terms, however, it is clear that the leasehold principle itself became a constant irritant for immigrants who sought security and independence on the land. Although Lot 11 was not a notably volatile area, tensions between tenants and landowners elsewhere actually worsened and even became violent during the course of the nineteenth century. In dealing with the Land Question, Irish settlers especially resented the replication of social conditions and practices which had long afflicted their homeland.

Those itinerant families who simply regarded Lot 11's opportunities as temporary steps on the way to greater security elsewhere in America had to endure their situation until they were prepared to move on. On the other hand, settlers who had hoped to put down permanent roots where they landed were not long content with the feudalistic model of land settlement decreed for Prince Edward Island. They usually found short-term leases objectionable. Most newcomers probably expected to find in this colony the privileges of ownership and rights of private property extended to all who were willing to invest their labour in responsible stewardship. The prevailing social philosophy and practice virtually everywhere else in North America was that pioneers should come to possess the land which they had cleared and cultivated. In this regard, Irish immigrants were strongly motivated, since coincidental with land reform agitation on the Island, a similar movement was emerging in Ireland. To settle in Prince Edward Island during the first half of the nineteenth century was, therefore, to assert a strong faith that a more acceptable land policy would soon replace the anachronistic landlord-tenant structures devised by the original British planners of the colony. It so happened that those immigrants who were prudent enough to invest in Lot 11 leases saw their faith and foresight rewarded, for in due time they actually did acquire freehold possession of their farms.

Meanwhile, subject to the rules of the Walsh heirs, and under John Large's management, a score of families from County Laois and vicinity who came in 1823 established at Foxley River the nucleus of an Irish community, one that was mainly Roman Catholic. A smaller number of Irish Protestants also came, both before and after 1823, as did settlers from England and Scotland who had not built permanent homes elsewhere on the Island. Thus, early in the development of the Walsh township, its ethnic and sectarian character was determined. Two generations later, the census of 1881 reported that of 625 residents, 300 were of Irish origin (48%) and 334 were members of the Roman Catholic Church (52%). At the same time there were 202 Scots (32.3%) and 118 English (18.9%); the Anglicans (129) and Presbyterians (134) each constituted about 21% of the churchgoers.

James Warburton

The 1881 statistics reflect the continuing immigration during the 1834–56 administration of the third land agent, James Warburton.[16] The Warburton name and estate had taken hold in Ireland in the seventeenth century under the patronage of Oliver Cromwell. James Warburton (1810–92) was the eighth son of Richard Warburton of Garryhinch and Anne Kemmis of Shaen.[17] The Garryhinch estate was located on the northern bank of the River Barrow, where that river forms the boundary between the counties of Offaly and Laois (then known as King's and Queen's counties) near the town of Portarlington. The Garryhinch estate was only a dozen miles from Ballykilcavan, where in 1834 Sir Edward J. Walsh announced Warburton's appointment to manage his Prince Edward Island estate.[18] Immediately upon his arrival at the heavily forested, stream-laced township, young Warburton built a fine Irish-style farm residence at Woodbrook in Lot 11 and lined the lane with linden trees from Ireland. In 1837 he married Martha Compton Green.

Ten years before Warburton's arrival, John Hughes of Offaly had already settled in the vicinity. Martin Lynch and his wife Mary Quinn, both from Kilkenny, were also there in 1823. From County Tyrone, in the 1840s, came James Rafferty and his wife Mary Anne (née Bulger), who had their name conferred on a local road. Although the naming of Woodbrook district has been attributed to John Bryan, who had come to live with his uncle John Hughes in 1850, it is interesting to note that in Ireland, less than two miles southeast of Garryhinch, stands Woodbrook House, a two-storey, five-bay late-Georgian house. Furthermore, Warburton's later Island residence, named Huntingdon, probably was named after Huntingdon House, owned by the Warburtons and situated about two miles beyond Woodbrook House.[19]

James Warburton was evidently a prudent steward and a trustworthy counsellor. Certainly the tenants of Lot 11 came to respect him for his fairness and his understanding of their aspirations.[20] After he had assessed both the marginal economic benefits accruing to the absentee landowner of Lot 11 and the growing determination of the tenants to own the land they had cleared and tilled, Warburton advised the reverend Sir Hunt Johnson-Walsh to sell Township Eleven to the colonial government. In turn, in accordance with the Land Purchase Act of 1853, the government would sell the farms at reasonable prices to the current leaseholders. These recommendations were soon adopted. The deeding over of 13,865 acres to the government for £1,700 (sterling) brought to an end the Ballykilcavan Walshes' interests in Prince Edward Island.[21] As if to memorialize – and certainly to celebrate – the welcome action taken by Warburton and Johnson-Walsh, the Frederick Cove district in Lot 11 was officially named Freeland in 1856.[22]

Within the class of proprietors and their agents, whether in Ireland or the colony, Warburton's liberalism was exceptional. By contrast, his more autocratic nephew, Richard – high sheriff of Queen's County, Ireland – had served notices of eviction on several destitute tenants. The common people always regarded eviction as a most despicable action. For his callousness, Sheriff Warburton subsequently lost his left eye and "had half his face blown away" in an ambush at Maryborough in 1869. Despite the posting of a £923 reward, the would-be assassins were not apprehended.[23]

The Warburtons in Politics

The Warburtons of Prince Edward Island were not associated in any way with offences attributed to their unpopular kinsman in Ireland. Here, the Warburtons were known to be an honourable, public-spirited family, and in Lot 11, under James Warburton, the transition from a semi-feudal proprietorship to a community of privately owned family farms came about without rancour or violence.

At the time of the transfer of the unsold portion of Lot 11 to the public domain, James Warburton was active in Island politics, and for at least another dozen years he continued to exercise his political skills. Notwithstanding the critical views of a partisan Conservative editor,

who called him a self-serving "poor relation of the proprietor,"[24] Warburton was a prominent member of the Reform Party, championing the
tenants in the land debates and supporting the movement for responsible government.[25] Frequently he clashed with the wealthiest and most
powerful Conservative in Prince County, James Yeo, Jr, "the ledger
giant of Port Hill."[26] After serving in minor offices and as provincial
secretary from 1851 to 1853, Warburton won several terms as a member of the legislature. In 1868 he retired from public life, and five years
later he moved into his Huntingdon residence near Charlottetown.
Before the century was out, his son, Alexander Bannerman Warburton,
had become premier of Prince Edward Island.[27]

LAOIS-OFFALY EMIGRANTS

In considering the process of immigration that built Township Eleven,
two exceptional characteristics are at once evident: first, a larger component of Protestant Irish came to Lot 11 than to most Irish settlements on the Island; second, a larger component of Laois-Offaly immigrants congregated there than in any other Irish area of the Island.[28] By
general estimate, Protestants constituted only 10 percent of Irish immigrants to Prince Edward Island, and natives of the midland counties of
Laois and Offaly constituted almost 5 percent of Irish immigrants; yet
families from these two counties formed the nucleus of the settlers in
Township Eleven.

County Laois, a landlocked territory (about the size of Prince County, PEI) is scenically pleasant but unspectacular except for the historic
fortress of Dunamaise (*Dun-Masg*) in the east and the Slieve Bloom
Mountains in the west. The Celtic fortress of Masg – most noted as the
seat of the O'More dynasty which ruled that part of the Irish kingdom
of Ossory – was granted by the king of Leinster to the Norman leader
Strongbow in 1170, and centuries later was virtually destroyed by the
vaunted artillery of Oliver Cromwell. It is now a magnificent ruin.

At the county's western boundary the Slieve Bloom range rises some
1,600 feet above the plain. From its picturesque heights, the River Barrow winds down between Laois and Offaly, the two counties that came
under the sixteenth-century Tudor edict to supplant the native Irish
people with English colonists. At that time the county names were
anglicized to honour Queen Mary and King Philip. The plantation policy had limited success: Laois retained its Catholic majority, and Offaly
remained overwhelmingly Catholic. The Great Famine of the 1840s
was much more disruptive than the plantation policy, for the crop failure caused the death or desperate emigration of one-quarter of the
area's population.

Along the line where those two counties adjoin – between the lonely Bog of Allen to the north and the sturdy blue-green Slieve Bloom range to the southwest – arose the Huguenot town of Port-arlington, the Palatine and Quaker refuge of Mountmellick, and the Quaker village of Rosenallis.[29] All told, two hundred or so persons may have left that region to settle in such scattered places on Prince Edward Island as Mount Mellick, Springfield, Clinton, and Margate, as well as Township Eleven. A brief digression here should suffice to show how these several groups were interrelated, even though they formed clusters in separate places that were beyond the bounds of the Walsh township.

Midland Families

In 1819, ten miles east of Charlottetown (which from the outset had its own Ascendancy power base), the Lane family of County Laois became the founding settlers for the Island's Mount Mellick. In May 1819, from Ireland's largely Quaker community of Mountmellick came Samuel Lane, John Lane and his wife Joyce Lester and children Sarah and William, John Lane II, Philip Lane married to Lydia Lyster, Edward Lane married to Ann Pleadwell, James A. Moore, Samuel Hall married to Sarah Hall, Joseph Lane married to Elizabeth Pleadwell, and John Pleadwell married to Margaret Pigott (and their daughter Ellen). Mrs Edward Lane was from Mountrath.

About the same time at Springfield, twenty miles northwest of Charlottetown, the Anglican community orbited around the Haslam family – Benjamin, John, Thomas, and William – who also came from County Laois, probably from Clonaslee and Rosenallis. Stephen Weeks and his wife Elizabeth Large (daughter of John Large) arrived in Springfield in 1824. Although some of the County Laois settlers had numerous offspring on the Island, the Mount Mellick and Spring-field groups remained much smaller than the settlement in the Foxley River–Woodbrook districts.

The Lot 11 experience in particular illustrates how neighbours and relatives from the Old Country tended to form close groups in their new country. Garryhinch, for instance, sent not only James Warburton but also people who lived or worked on his family's Irish estate: the weaver Joshua Smallman (widower of Margaret Large) and his son Thomas Smallman, who had married Mary S. Murray; Huguenot descendant John Bryan, Sr, and his wife Eliza Hughes; and Eliza Hughes's brother John and his wife Margaret Bridges. John Hughes's nephews also immigrated to the Island: John Bryan arrived in 1854 and married Jane Dignan; and Arthur Bryan and his wife Amelia Evans landed in 1870. Also from County Offaly were James Edward Carroll and his wife Sarah Bridges; John Murray, Sr, and his wife Mary Bridges; George Murray, Sr, who married Letitia Heaney; George Jelley and his wife Jane Murray; and Peter Gibbs of Portarlington, who later married John Large's sister Sarah. John Large himself had married Jane Bridges.

Another remarkable genealogical network that followed from the selection of John Large as administrator of Township Eleven is recorded in the 1992 Heaney family history entitled *Some Immigrants from Offaly and Laois*.[30] John Large's brother Thomas married Jane Heaney in Ireland and they made their home on the Island until 1852; John M. Dignan, also from County Laois, married Sarah Heaney, and they settled their family in the Freeland district; George Murray of County Offaly married Letitia Heaney, and they also established their home in Lot 11; and Daniel Heaney (brother of Jane, Sarah, and Letitia) brought his wife Bellinda Abbott and their five children to Clinton, Lot 20, in 1842. (Heaney Road runs between Grahams Road and Kerrytown Road.) As these families increased and multiplied, many of their descendants were forced (or chose) to seek employment away from home. The Heaney family history and others clearly show that across North America and even in distant lands, hundreds of widely scattered families whose earlier ancestry had been rooted in Counties Laois and Offaly in Ireland now trace their later lineage via several settlements in Prince Edward Island.

POPULATION GROWTH

In 1833 the twenty-nine families in Lot 11 totalled 163 persons, and by 1841 the population reached 254. Historian J. Clinton Morrison states that 87 of the 89 immigrants had paid their own passage.[31] That being so, the Laois-Offaly settlers of the township were neither destitute refugees nor famine victims. Rather, they must be seen as earnest immigrants, some possessing skills in weaving, shoemaking, carpentry, or farming, others developing additional skills needed for successful farming or fishing in the new colony, and all seeking improved living conditions and greater opportunities than they had known in the Old Country. Generally, they had come intending to settle on the land, and when the land was made available for sale in 1856 most of the leaseholders – including several patient pioneers of 1823 – were quick to purchase their farms.

In Lot 11, supplementing the County Laois pioneers from the Dunamaise area were the families of Martin Lynch and Michael Aylesworth from Kilkenny, as well as Patrick Murphy and John

Callaghan, both Wexfordmen who came to Frederick Cove via New-foundland. Michael Bulger, Sr, came from County Laois in 1833, and during the 1830s upward of twenty other Irish immigrants who had briefly paused at other places on the Island found their way to Lot 11. About 1825, Laois-born Simon Luttrell and his wife Elizabeth Ryan, who may have crossed over from Chatham, New Brunswick, chose to raise their family in the Palmer Road district of Lot 2.

In 1861 the 78 families in Lot 11 numbered 511 souls. Some of them, however, as their families increased, removed to better farms in nearby townships. By 1870 railway stations at Portage and Conway facilitated both the outflow for those who wished to leave Lot 11 and the inflow of some railway employees and other families. Such recip-rocating mini-migrations eventually modified the ethnic and cultural composition of Township Eleven, for the later arrivals were mostly Protestants of English and Scottish backgrounds. Still, despite the lower proportion of Irish people among the newcomers after mid-cen-tury, established families of Irish origin continued to outnumber other nationals.

As the colonial period came to an end, Meacham's 1880 *Atlas* com-mented that Lot 11 had made "better progress than most of the neigh-boring Lots." By 1891 the township's population had grown to about 700 people, distributed through the fairly stable communities of Fox-ley River–Woodbrook, Conway, and Freeland. By that time, of course, adventurous islanders did not confine themselves to the Island; they could emigrate by rail to New England or even to California – and they did. Replicating the experience of their Irish parents and grandparents, young islanders became the new generation of exiles, longing from afar for their emerald isle in the Gulf of St Lawrence.

THE CHURCHES

The blend of people who settled Township Eleven proved to be quite compatible. Mostly faithful Anglicans and Catholics, they were remarkably respectful of one another's sectarian differences. For most people, civility called for generous acceptance, not grudging toleration. Having come from the same region, they had crossed the turbulent sea together; and now living as neighbours here, they assisted one another in land clearing, home building, and church building. Religious dis-tinctions certainly remained, but never, we are told, was there any sec-tarian animosity among them.

Similar good will prevailed when, a generation later, Scottish newcomers to the township erected the Presbyterian church in the Free-land district. The first church in Lot 11 was Saint Peter's (Anglican), erected on land donated by James Warburton and consecrated in 1857. Many Laois-Offaly Church of Ireland immigrants and their descendants worshipped with that congregation, and members of the Warburton family were buried in Saint Peter's churchyard. The parish church and cemetery remain historic landmarks in the community.

Saint Brigid's Parish Church

In a province noted for its finely built and tastefully adorned places of worship, the Roman Catholic parish church at Foxley River stands out as the most prominent and enduring symbol of the Irish presence in Lot 11.[32] It was erected in time for Christmas Mass in 1870 but not completed interiorly until three years later. Both the building and the parish were placed under the patronage of Saint Brigid. Traditionally venerated as "Mary of the Gaels" and "Queen of the Irish people," Brigid (452–523) founded and presided over several monasteries, most notably the large religious community in Kildare. Although she flourished in the fifth century, many people in the twentieth century came to regard her as a patroness of the Women's Liberation Movement in Ireland. Within the small but dignified wooden building at Foxley River, the decor of the altar proclaims the cultural heritage of most of the parishioners: carved sprigs of shamrock flank the tabernacle, and emblazoned above it is a stylized cross similar in design to the one on the treasured eighth-century Ardagh Chalice.

THE SCHOOLS

Besides being places of worship, church buildings enhanced the Island landscape and conveyed a sense of stability and purpose to scores of communities. Nineteenth-century rural schoolhouses added to this impression. Despite the growth and progress of the Lot 11 settlement – and notwithstanding the traditional love for learning attributed to the Irish people – formal schooling, intermittent from about 1830, was not regularized until 1859. At that time one-room schools were opened in Foxley River and Freeland.[33]

MAKING A LIVING

At first, most settlers had come to think of the fearsome forest as an abundant commodity to be exploited, and only later did they recognize it as an ecological resource to be protected and fostered. On the positive side, the depletion of large stands of virgin pine, spruce, juniper, maple, elm, and birch prepared the way for the cultivation of the newly naked fields and the production of food crops for human consumption. It took the industrious settlers several decades to cut down woodland after woodland and to bring field after field into production, until the whole Island, once an extensive forest, was transformed into the "million-acre farm."

The dense forests confronting the early settlers tested their physical and spiritual prowess.[34] When the Gain family arrived in 1801, they saw that they were intruding on the primeval habitat of some bears and wildcats, many foxes, and an abundance of rodents. Many newcomers were bewildered by the wilderness, but those who overcame their fears soon found that the gloomy forest was an important asset: wood was the preferred material for cabin building, furniture making, and household fuel. Every home required a woodpile, and soon every district had its own mills. And for some time, timber was in very high demand overseas.

Furthermore, the Island forests made possible a thriving ship-building industry.[35] Wooden sailing ships plied the water lanes and tidal rivers; inshore fishermen sailed out of every port and inlet; and scores of larger vessels conducted business with the mainland, with Newfoundland, and with the British Isles. In the fifty years beginning in 1830, more than one hundred shipyards on the Island constructed wooden sailing ships. Until the coming of the steamers in the 1870s, shipbuilding and its many attendant trades were major industries on the Island. Lot 11 enjoyed a very modest share of this economic activity.

As it turned out, only half of Lot 11 proved suitable for cultivation. There, mixed farming on holdings of 50 to 150 acres became the norm, and running the farm became a cooperative family enterprise. The early settlers burned the stumps and branches of the trees they had felled and then fertilized their garden patches with the ashes. Another common practice was to spread mussel mud on the fields, though seaweed, kelp, marsh grass, and moss also proved useful.[36] Later, they fertilized the soil by dropping smelt or capelin into the potato drills or by scattering crushed shellfish, especially lobster frames, or oyster or clam shells. Another natural soil enricher was barnyard manure mixed with a heavy coal-black sticky compost extracted from mud holes in the woods. By mid-century some progressive farmers were importing lime from Nova Scotia, burning it in homemade kilns, and applying it to the acidic soil. Although the Lot 11 boglands also contained commercial quantities of peat moss, that resource was not exploited much in the nineteenth century.

Gradually the settlers acquired new equipment and livestock. They improved their farming methods.[37] They built access paths, barns, and mills. They improved their homes. In return for unrelenting labour, the stubborn soil of Lot 11 yielded acceptable crops and provided moderate security – but certainly no promise of easy prosperity.

By 1860 veteran families could look back to their startup years when they had possessed only wooden implements and had broken the ground with one-handed ploughs; when they had used hoes to plant potatoes around the tree stumps; when they had broadcast seed by hand, cut the grain with reaping hooks, and threshed it with flails; and when they had gathered in the hay with hand rakes in much the same way as they had done in the Old Country.

Fortunately for Prince Edward Island's general economic and social development, the natural resources of the surrounding waters richly supplemented those of the land. Despite their proximity to the Gulf of St Lawrence, however, most residents of Lot 11 depended for their livelihood primarily on the bounty of the soil and woods, and only secondarily on the largesse of the sea.

Along the north shore, a twenty-mile string of sandhills buffers the mainland from the expansive gulf, except where Conway Narrows cuts through the dunes and spills into Cascumpec Bay. From that well-sheltered bay and from the tidal rivers, small boats have had access to the open sea and the gulf fishery; and long before the Island's large commercial fishery developed, the taking of cod and mackerel, clams, oysters, and lobsters for domestic consumption and for local markets had been a regular occupation. The rivers yielded trout and salmon, and the estuaries supplied mussels and other shellfish.

The Island's commercial fishery, beginning about 1870 provided some employment in Lot 11. Nearby canning factories and packing and shipping facilities created seasonal jobs, while the fishing fleet called for crewmen, as well as for workers to build and maintain boats, wharves, and equipment. But Lot 11 was never a leading contributor to, or a great beneficiary of, the Island's second most important industry, the fishery.

Incidentally, before footpaths could be widened into clay roads, the rivers served as traffic routes to the interior of the lot. For that reason, early settlers tended to build their homes near the water. In due time, the Walshtown to Cascumpec ferry (known as Large's or, later, Mac-Phee's) eliminated twenty miles of rough overland travel for commercial travellers and churchgoers.

LESS-TRAVELLED ROADS

For a full century after its settlement, Lot 11 retained traces of its early social character. Situated as it is just beyond the main highway, even twenty-first-century Lot 11 has been less threatened by tourist traffic and commercial intrusion than more prosperous parts of the Island. Apparently unenvied for its old-fashioned modesty and its varied but unspectacular terrain, Foxley River and its environs have quietly survived – like many a remote village in Ireland – because residents valued their home place, their occupations, their local institutions, and their unhurried way of life.

In the nineteenth century the way of life in Foxley River and vicinity – and also in countless other rural communities and farmlands from East Point to North Cape – was characterized primarily by unceasing labour. On the soil, in the woods, on the sea, in the home, in the shops and mills, everywhere, there was work to be done. The ultimate purpose was to transform the primeval landscape into family farms.

All over the Island, by the 1830s, woodland paths had begun to widen into clay roads, and horse-drawn carts opened up overland commerce. For the next century, on the roads and in the fields the supreme work animal was the horse; and blacksmiths, farriers, harness makers, and carriage makers were fully employed. It has often been said that the nineteenth century, on the seas, was the era of wooden sailing ships and iron men; but on the land, among the settlers of Prince Edward Island, it was the era of sturdy work animals and indefatigable men and women. The soil, like Ireland's, was promising for potatoes and grain and for grazing dairy cattle. As in Ireland, rural families tended to be large, and members were expected to work together.

Recreation

The settlers found relief from their hard work by participating in home entertainments – singing, dancing, storytelling, reminiscing, card playing, neighbourly visits – and by taking an occasional trip to a town. Those who could read shared the news from home, which they gathered from infrequent letters and newspapers or from reprints and journalistic accounts in the Island press. In this way – as well as from eagerly sought conversations with itinerant labourers, commercial travellers, and recent arrivals from the Old Country – the Irish immigrants kept abreast of Daniel O'Connell's activities, Catholic Emancipation, the Repeal Movement, the Land League, Father Mathew's temperance campaign, and the Great Famine.

In their reveries, especially on long wintry nights, the immigrants dreamed about Ireland – not necessarily as it actually was but as they idealized it. In the process, they invented versions of home that filtered out the grime and crime, the stultifying ignorance, and grinding poverty. What remained they fashioned into romantic visions of beauty, unity, and peace.

WHAT'S IN A NAME

Finally, consideration must be given to those identifying marks by which the settlers themselves knew one another. Prince Edward Island's predominantly Celtic population has always been conscious of names. In Township Eleven, no less than anywhere else on the Island, family names and place names have long been important keys to family identity and communal culture. Among most Irish, certainly, family names are still regarded as badges of identity to be worn with pride.

Historically, as early as the eleventh century the Irish had evolved their own system of hereditary surnames.[38] Linguistically, this development was signified mainly by placing the prefix O (meaning "descendant of") or *Mac* ("son of") before the name of the Gaelic sept to which the person belonged. By the eighteenth century, many emigrants – though they had not entirely severed their Gaelic roots – chose, or were coerced by practical circumstances of the English-speaking world, not only to delete these distinctive Gaelic prefixes but also to anglicize the Gaelic spellings and sometimes even to translate (or, worse still, distort) their Irish names into English versions. In the hope of succeeding in the New World, many thought they had to dispose of their Old Country cultural heirlooms. Ironically, in many ways the strategy worked, and some Irish people even became supreme masters of the alien language which at first had been forced upon them. Even more remarkable, perhaps, is the fact that despite the linguistic disguises and adaptations, much of the essential Irish culture endured.

Township Eleven illustrates the point well. There, as in a score of Irish enclaves around the Island, everyone was known by a family name and everyone had a known place of origin. Nobody was anonymous. Centuries of experience in dealing with strangers of many stripes had taught the ordinary Irish people to be, on the one hand, curious and cautious and, on the other hand, hospitable and helpful. The family name was normally the first indicator whether the newcomer was English, Irish, Scottish, or French. Often the name suggested whether the person was Protestant or Catholic. Certainly, it would reveal any likely blood relationship – or, possibly, any traditional rivalry. In the colony, family names were very important.

Remember Who You Are ...

A roll call of selected Irish surnames in Lot 11 provides a sample of what a survey of the Island's Irish population as a whole would confirm: several aspects of the history and geography of the Irish people are encoded in their family names. Among the Irish settlers of Lot 11 nearly half the surnames indicate non-Gaelic ancestry – not a surprising proportion, since most of these settlers came from Laois and Offaly, counties that had been heavily influenced by the British presence in centuries past.[39] At first glance, such names as Bridges, Jelley, Palmer, Smallman, and Warburton appear to be English, and Gibbs and Roberts appear to be Scottish. Anglo-Norman in origin are names such as Aylesworth, Barry (*deBarra*), and Bryan, though Mitchell (possibly *Misteil*) has long standing in Ireland, and Lynch (*de Lench*), though Cambro-Norman, is counted as one of the "Tribes of Galway." Descendants of King Henry II's twelfth-century Normans became, it is said, "more Irish than the Irish themselves," and most of the Elizabethans, Cromwellians, and Williamites were eventually absorbed into the Irish mainstream. Indeed, the Anglo-Irish subgroup in particular exerted a generally wholesome influence on the nation's public life and contributed significantly to the nation's literature.

Judging by surnames, the Gaelic Irish made up a slight majority of the Irish settlers in Lot 11. Two or more families, for example, are named Bulger (*Ó Bolguidhir* in Irish), from a noted medical family of Carlow, Kilkenny, and Wexford. (Ireland's Chief Herald equates Bulger and Bolger, the latter spelling being preferred in Lot 22, Hope River.) Next, consider the name Boyle. A barony in County Roscommon bears that name, which derives from the Gaelic *Ó Baioghill*, noble chieftains alongside the ruling O'Donnells of Donegal. Another early Lot 11 name, Callaghan, is strong in several counties, particularly Cork. The eponymous ancestor is Ceallachain, King of Munster, who died in 952. The Dignans of Lot 11 use a variant of the Irish spelling *Ó Duibh-grannain*, "one of the principal learned families of Gaelic Ireland" and a compiler of the Annals of the Four Masters; the name is still found in Roscommon and Offaly. The three most common names in Ireland are also represented in Lot 11: (1) Murphy (*Ó Murchada*, meaning "sea warrior"), which is particularly numerous in Cork and Wexford, where most Island Murphys originated; (2) Kelly (*Ó Ceallaigh*), which is found in large numbers in several counties, nost notably in mid-Galway, seat of the O'Kelly princes (descendants of Muiredach, great-grandson of third-century King Cormac Mac Art); and (3) Sullivan (*Ó Suileabhain*), a noble family in ancient Tipperary, which later became most numerous in Cork, Kerry, and Galway. The noble chieftain family of *Ó Maoilriain* – "by far the most numerous name in Tipperary having almost four times the population of the next in order (O'Brien and Maher)" – is known in Lot 11 and almost everywhere else by the English spelling, Ryan. Finally, the well-known Foxley River surname,

Kilbride (often MacBride or MacGilbride in Ireland), is found rather sparsely in the southeastern counties and in Cork. In Irish the name is *Mac Giolla Bhrighde*, meaning a devotee of Saint Brigid.

A knowledgeable traveller among the Island's settlers, therefore, could have discerned in the diversity of Irish family names a cultural cornucopia. So much so that Ireland's proverbial "forty shades of green" could have served as an apt metaphor for the Island's Hibernians.

... And Where You Come From

The settlers of Lot 11 were well aware that the names of their home villages – in the form they are generally found today – were, like most of Ireland's toponyms, Anglicized versions of their Gaelic designations; that is, English phonetic approximations of the original words as they were spoken in Gaelic. Deficiencies become apparent when the modernized versions fail to convey the cultural content inherent in the Gaelic terms, or when hearers or readers fail to grasp the meanings which the words embody. In such limiting circumstances, Irish place names are thought to be nothing more than quaint pleasant-sounding labels. In fact, Gaelic place names frequently allude to saints and churches or to historical events and legendary personages, resident families, local topography, architecture, occupations, or wildlife and other natural features. Such allusions become reference points for discerning the social environment and cultural ambiance of particular places, mainly in rural Ireland.

In ancient Ireland, when the sept was the principal social unit, family and land were intimately related. The sept consisted of a group of families whose immediate ancestors had lived in the same locality and who had assumed the surname of the king, lord, or chieftain who governed them. After the sept system disintegrated and uprooted families scattered to places distant from their original lands, their first criterion of identity remained the family name. The second was the place of origin. The question, "What is your name?" was soon followed by, "Where do your people come from?" To this day the same questions are considered essential for identifying Irish persons.[40]

Linking family names with particular places may become an exercise in history and political geography. Citing the four Irish provinces – formerly major royal realms or ecclesiastical jurisdictions, now known in popular parlance and song as the "Four Green Fields" but officially called Ulster, Connacht, Munster, and Leinster – is too general to satisfy curiosity about family roots. Instead, most immigrants speak of home in terms of the major political division of the province, namely, the county. The county system, modelled on the Anglo-Saxon shire, was introduced to Ireland by the twelfth-century Normans. For taxation purposes, the English occupiers later subdivided the 32 counties into 325 baronies, whose boundaries were based on the lands once held by the great Gaelic families. Next came the subdivision of the baronies into 2,500 civil or ecclesiastical parishes. Finally, the parishes were cut up into small rural segments called townlands. Originally designed by the Normans for taxation purposes, the townlands varied from less than 200 acres to more than 1,000 acres. The 1901 census counted 60,462 townlands.

The Irish settlers of Prince Edward Island, mostly rural people acquainted with the Gaelic language, never forgot their respective townlands – the smallest of social units in which their families functioned. The townland and its vicinity defined young people's earliest experience of society beyond their immediate family circle. In that miniature world they acquired the rudiments of their social formation and enculturation. There, in the small farms and villages, they first heard of a spacious continent far across the sea.

For the immigrant generation of Lot 11, it was not only the great landmarks such as the Barrow River and Slieve Bloom Mountains but also their own home places and townlands that resonated with memories and meanings. Adamstown was also called Ballyadams; and Portarlington – the Barrow harbour crossing named for Henry Bennet, first Lord Arlington – was previously known as Tanner's Nook (*Cuil an tSudaire*). Ballykilcavan (*Baile Cill Caomhan* or *Chuáin*) referred to the townland of Saint Kevin or *Cuán*'s church, and Garryhinch (*Garraí na hinnise* or *Garrdha-inis*) evidently meant a fertile spur extending into the water, or land by the river, or a garden island, while Drumneen (*Dromainn*) meant a little hill or ridge, and Stradbally (*Sráid-bhaile*) was a village of one street. For those who knew Gaelic, the place names retained both their sound and their sense. Hence, Clonaslee (*Cluain a slighe*) signified meadow of the road, and Rosenallis (*Ros na lios*) referred to a wood of the fairy fort or a wood by the clear stream; Mountmellick (*Montiagh-meelick*) was a marshy bogland, and Mountrath (*Montiagh-rath*) was a bog by the small ring fort. Dunamaise (*Dun-masg*), the ancient Celtic fortress, memorializes an ancestor of the people of Leinster, and Slieve Bloom (*Sliabh-bladhma*), a mountain range, commemorates a Celtic hero.

These were among the many places known to the immigrants of Township Eleven, people who had been nurtured by both the terrain and the traditions of the Laois-Offaly border region. Many of these Gaelic Irish settlers had also retained some knowledge of the Irish language, upon which family names and geographic names – and much else in Irish life and lore – depended.[41] No wonder, then, that for a full generation and more the gentle, lyrical brogue of the Irish midlands was heard in the environs of Foxley River and reminded the settler families about their parents' farewell exhortation: "Never forget who you are and where you come from."

CHAPTER THREE

The Meeting of the Waters

Early in the nineteenth century, in a series of developments overlapping the emergence of the Foxley River community in Township Eleven, Irish immigrants helped to populate numerous ethnically mixed townships on the Island. This second phase of Irish immigration unfolded approximately between 1810 and 1835. These immigrants were mainly from Ireland's southeast – though a smaller number were from the southwest – and they settled, almost randomly, from one end of Prince Edward Island to the other.

This phase of the immigration movement developed from two main streams, one via the fishing and trading ports of Newfoundland, the other directly from the great Irish ports of Waterford and Cork. From these principal sources and a few lesser tributaries, migrants set out, by the dozen and by the hundred, in many vessels each year when the shipping lanes were free of ice and the Island's harbours were open to receive them.

Of the several thousand Irish people who arrived in this manner, more than half probably settled on the Island permanently. How they established a firm base in Charlottetown, how they greatly augmented the parish rolls of the Catholic Church, and how they put down family roots in a score of scattered farming and fishing communities, from western Prince County to eastern Kings County, will be treated in later chapters. Here the focus is on how they arrived and where they came from.

For many thousands of Irish people who sailed into lifelong exile across the Atlantic Ocean, the last image engraved in their memories was that of County Wexford's massive white lighthouse at Hook Head. Twenty miles at sea from Ireland's southeastern shore, emigrants still

crowded the decks of their tossing brigantines and fastened their
farewell gaze on the fading tower whose beacon had long been a landmark for seafarers. When their ships finally dipped below the horizon,
the tearful passengers knew that forever after they would be exiles
from Erin.

Hook Light raises its enormous bulk 150 feet atop a craggy promon-
tory confronting the turbulent Celtic Sea. Tradition holds that, beginning about the sixth century, Irish monastics maintained their own
night-fires at Hook Head as guiding lights for mariners. In the twelfth
century, Augustinian friars became the keepers of the light when the
Norman leader Raymond Le Gros erected a tall round tower for that
purpose. Reconstructed in 1791, the present edifice continues to serve
mariners seeking the spacious harbour which the Vikings named
Vradrefjord[1] and the English translated as Waterford.

On the opposite side of the eleven-mile-long channel leading north
to Waterford basin stands a smaller beacon called Crook. This topographical entity moved Oliver Cromwell to declare that he would con-
quer the area "by Hook or by Crook."[2] The prize Cromwell sought
was the same one earlier claimed by both the Norsemen and the Normans – the strategic port of Waterford, sited at the extensive estuary
formed by the confluence of three navigable rivers, which meander
independently through the historic hinterland until, coming together,
they resolutely rush to meet the great sea.

Although these three rivers are traditionally regarded as sisters,
Edmund Spenser, "the poet's poet," personified them as "renowned
brethren," characterizing them as the "goodly" Barrow, the "stubborn" Nore, and the "gentle" Suir.[3] All three originate in the midlands'
Slieve Bloom and Devil's Bit mountain ranges, and as they wander
through the five counties of the southeast – Wexford, Waterford, Carlow, Kilkenny, and Tipperary – they enhance charming scenes of pastoral tranquility, freshen scores of trout streams, irrigate Ireland's finest
dairylands, and create a natural passage to the open sea.

The Barrow emerges from the Bog of Allen, slips between Counties
Laois and Offaly, eventually passes through Athy, Carlow town, Bage-
nalstown and Graiguenamanagh, and becomes navigable for large vessels at New Ross, where it flows southward over 25 miles toward the
sea. The Nore also springs from the Slieve Blooms in County Laois. It
enters County Kilkenny at Ballyragget, penetrates the Anglo-Norman
stronghold of Kilkenny City, glides through Thomastown and Inis-
tioge, and finally merges with the Barrow above New Ross. Meanwhile
the Suir, having started its wandering well above Cashel and the
Golden Vale of Tipperary, gains depth and momentum passing through
Clonmel, Carrick, Mooncoin, and Waterford's mile-long quays as it

hurries toward the confluence at Cheek Point. Once the Three Sisters meet at "the valley of the three waters" (*Cumar-na-dtri-nuisce*), they proceed swiftly through the broad deep channel – past Passage East and Dunmore on the west bank and Ballyhack and Hook Head on the east – into the boundless sea.

By thus twisting and turning a few hundred miles and bathing the banks of many towns and productive farmlands along the way, the Three Sisters provided convenient passage to the great seaport of Waterford for hundreds of thousands of farmers, seafarers, tradesmen, shopkeepers, and labourers, and their families. In fact, before the coming of efficient land transportation,[4] these rivers were the main thoroughfares for both inland and overseas commerce in southeastern Ireland. Geography determined that Waterford town would be the focal point, with trade lines radiating inward to New Ross, Kilkenny City, Thomastown, Clonmel, and Carrick, and then outward to overseas commercial ports. For centuries the Wexford-Waterford region had carried on trade with France, Spain, and Portugal, with English ports in Devon and Cornwall, and even with the faraway British West Indies, whereto Oliver Cromwell's cruel efficiency had banished thousands of Irishmen. Immediately important for our purposes, however, is the commercial shipping network that Waterford developed with Newfoundland.

Simply stated, the second great wave of Irish immigration in Prince Edward Island (1810–35) is closely tied in with the mercantile relationship between Southeast Ireland and Newfoundland. To clarify this Ireland-Newfoundland-Prince Edward Island chain of dependency, the following synopsis may be helpful.

Emigration out of Waterford harbour for Prince Edward Island followed two main routes (see map 4). The first route included a significant stopover in Newfoundland, while the second went directly to Charlottetown. The first produced subsidiary traffic lanes from St John's and other Newfoundland ports, leading to such Nova Scotian destinations as Halifax, Cape Breton, and Pictou; to such New Brunswick havens as Saint John and the Miramichi Valley; and to the Island's several small north-shore ports and the principal harbour at Charlottetown. Another well-travelled route between 1790 and 1830 was the passage from the Atlantic Ocean through Cape Breton's Canso Strait into the Gulf of St Lawrence and thence to Prince Edward Island or beyond. Two minor feedlines also developed, as some of the immigrants who had disembarked in Nova Scotia and New Brunswick later crossed the Northumberland Strait in small boats to settle in Prince Edward Island.

As well as the two-pronged Waterford exodus, there were similar though smaller movements originating in Cork, Limerick, Dublin,

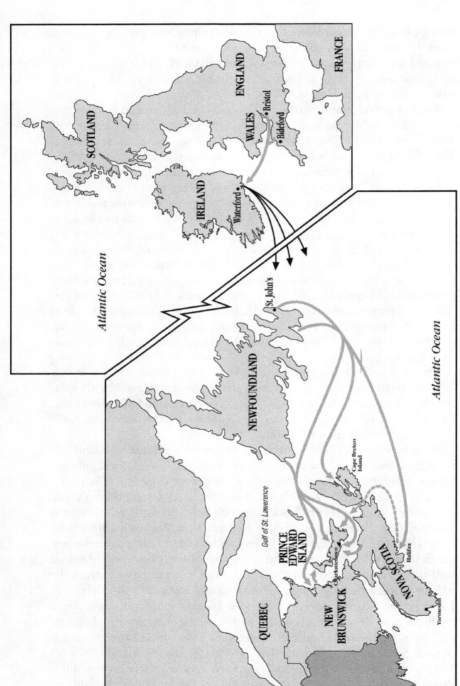

Map 4. From southern Ireland, immigrants followed several sea routes to Prince Edward Island.

and Kerry, which also brought immigrants to the Island in this period.

The pivotal point in this intricate pattern of shipping lanes was Newfoundland. To disentangle the skein of transportation strand by strand calls for an explanation of the Newfoundland connections: first with Ireland (Waterford, Cork, Dublin, and Kerry) and then with the Maritimes (especially, for present purposes, with Prince Edward Island). Finally, accounting for the ancillary movements connecting Nova Scotia and New Brunswick to the Island will complete the picture of migration routes linking Prince Edward Island with southern Ireland.

WATERFORD AND NEWFOUNDLAND

Late in the seventeenth century, mercantilists in England's West Country found economic advantages in making Waterford a base for both supplies and manpower in the conduct of their extensive fishing enterprises on the Grand Banks of Newfoundland.[5] English shipping companies therefore set up branch offices in Waterford and New Ross to supply the fishing fleet with grain, meat, and dairy products, as well as with sailors, fishermen, and general labourers. This overseas industry grew to employ tens of thousands of people annually. At first, the fishermen tended to work one season (March through October), but they later began to "winter over" in Newfoundland and fish another season before returning to Ireland. Their work schedule came to be known as "a Newfoundland season."

By the end of the eighteenth century, many of these workers, rather than commuting between the fishing grounds and their home ports, chose to settle at onshore bases in Newfoundland or to seek their fortune in the colonies to the south of Newfoundland. Among the latter were those who spilled fairly steadily into Nova Scotia, New Brunswick, and Prince Edward Island, as well as those who migrated to New England. Thus, even before the massive Irish emigration of the nineteenth century, not only did the large Irish colony in Newfoundland develop, but the "Newfoundland Irish" influx to the Maritime region also got underway.

In retrospect, it is clear that southeast Ireland's extensive involvement in the British-controlled Grand Banks fishery for over a hundred and fifty years produced both a system of transportation and a pattern of emigration that outlasted the heyday of the fishery itself. Hence, when the Napoleonic War ended and the demand for codfish declined after 1815, the Newfoundland fishery greatly receded and the unsteady economy of the place collapsed. The effect of this recession was twofold: emigration from the port of Waterford was largely diverted away from Newfoundland to other places in British North America; and emigration from Newfoundland itself to the Maritimes and New England greatly increased. In both instances, the overwhelming proportion of Irish immigrants to the Maritimes – whether they sailed directly from Waterford or came after a sojourn in Newfoundland – had originated in the counties of southeastern Ireland known historically as the Decies, a mainly Catholic territory once controlled by the powerful Butler Earls of Ormond.

In Newfoundland, the Irish immigrants were from some twenty of the thirty-two counties, but more than three-quarters of them had come from the southeastern region. They occupied that part of the western coast from the Bay of Islands and Corner Brook south to Port aux Basques. Of much greater importance, they dominated the Avalon Peninsula, including Placentia Bay, St Mary's Bay, Trepassey Bay, and the eastern coast from Cape Race up to St John's and around to Conception Bay. From these areas, especially after 1815, Newfoundland Irish came by the hundred, and established their families in Prince Edward Island.[6] The Island's nineteenth-century shipbuilding industry was a spin-off from this Cornwall-to-Waterford-to-Newfoundland fisheries operation and the subsequent trade and passenger traffic in the North Atlantic. In a dozen or more small shipyards around the Island, West Country men in particular developed a lucrative, though relatively short-lived, industry by turning out hundreds of worthy vessels for England's expanding merchant marine.[7]

NEWFOUNDLAND TO PRINCE EDWARD ISLAND

Although Newfoundland was Britain's first North American colony, its foundations could hardly be called auspicious.[8] It grew not as a normal possession but as an overseas commercial base for the huge Atlantic fishery that operated out of southwestern England. Actually, Newfoundland was a thalassocracy, whose entire economy was centred in the Grand Banks and whose civil administration functioned under the jurisdiction of a naval governor. Colonization, as such, was not encouraged; however, settlements did spring up about the middle of the eighteenth century when women joined their menfolk. At the best of times, though, Newfoundland had to contend with poverty as well as with common disorder and lawlessness.

As Prince Edward Island from the 1770s had supplied Newfoundland with cattle and produce, the shipping lanes between the two islands had become well established, and these same lanes later served for passenger traffic. The sailing distance between Port aux Basques, Newfoundland, and Charlottetown is more than 300 miles, and between St John's and Charlottetown considerably longer. Although the names and numbers of Irish immigrants from Newfoundland were not recorded, over the decades the two-way traffic across the Gulf of St Lawrence certainly involved thousands of passengers. The unregistered influx to Prince Edward Island from Newfoundland's Irish havens, therefore, along with the large reported numbers who came directly from southern Ireland up to 1835 or so, amply explain the origins of many family ties between these two Canadian provinces as well as the claim of thousands of Islanders to ancestry from Wexford, Waterford, Carlow, Kilkenny, and Tipperary. From East Point to North Cape numerous tombstone inscriptions, obituaries, family records, and parish and community histories attest to the pre-Famine immigration from those five Irish counties. Much of that evidence also alludes to Newfoundland. By the 1830s, southeastern family names abounded: Aylward, Cavanaugh, Cullen, Deacon, Doyle, Dunn, Dunphy, Hanlon, Harrington, Hennessey, Kickham, Landrigan, Mullally, Murphy, Phelan, Power, Reardon, Reid, Roche, Rossiter, Ryan, Sinnott, Walsh, and others. Later chapters will show how these southeasterners formed substantial but scattered communities in Charlottetown, Souris, St Peters, Morell, Iona, South Shore (Lot 65), Hope River, Covehead, Kensington, Kinkora, Foxley River, Burton, Tignish, and the western coastal village named Waterford.

Those "two boaters" who came to the Island mainly from southeastern Ireland via southeastern or western Newfoundland were truly Irish, regardless of the length of their sojourn in Newfoundland. They had hardly been assimilated into an alien social milieu, for in Newfoundland they had replicated their Old Country ethnic customs in scores of coastal enclaves. In the Avalon Peninsula and elsewhere, insulated as they were, they had retained much of their homeland culture: language, religion, feast days, holy wells, parades, games, mumming, traditional poetry, and even factional fights. Some early schoolbooks were brought over from Ireland, and the church services were often conducted in the Irish language. Whether these people had resided in Newfoundland for two years or two generations, they were the "Irish abroad" and were treated as such by civil and ecclesiastical authorities, as well as by employers and neighbours. Irish culture was so pervasive that Newfoundland was sometimes humorously referred to as "Ireland's fifth province."

Official reluctance to colonize Britain's first North American foothold, it is sometimes said, was based partly on the British perception of the numerous Irish there as being pro-Jacobite and pro-French, and therefore as potential rebels and pirates. Early in the nineteenth century some of the Penal Laws were still being enforced in Newfoundland, and conscientious objection to the oath of allegiance still curtailed the civil liberties of Catholics. In many social, political, and economic matters, Newfoundland progressed slowly. Furthermore, British fishing interests did little to promote normal colonization, one reason being that they usually wanted to control the industry from their home base rather than risk competition from overseas operations. Only the exodus of many Newfoundland labourers, which followed the fisheries depression after 1815, relieved some British anxiety over the obstreperous Newfoundland Irish. By then, the neglected colony had become so unruly that a visiting Gaelic poet, Donnach Ruadh MacConmara, called it "the wild plantation."

The displaced Irishmen from Newfoundland generally fled south. Referring to the summer of 1815, for instance, Paul O'Neill estimates that "no less than 11,000 Irishmen came to St John's, but in the fall many of them went to Prince Edward Island or the United States."[9] In large numbers they also descended on Nova Scotia and New Brunswick, where they mingled in the workforce along with their countrymen who were then coming in large numbers to the Maritime region directly from Ireland. Thus, the exodus from Newfoundland greatly affected ethnic patterns in the region and aggravated certain social problems, especially that of poverty.[10]

Beneficial as the influx from Newfoundland later proved to be, early on it brought to Prince Edward Island a rash of poverty. This phenomenon deserves an explanation. In Prince Edward Island as elsewhere in North America, few pre-famine settlers from southern Ireland were actual paupers. Truly destitute people or those who required public charity for support could not have afforded passage to Canada.[11] The early arrivals generally were people of very modest means, who by careful parsimony had managed to pay their own way. Even though many had lived in subsistence poverty under the odious Penal Code (whose laws were intended "to make them poor and keep them poor"),[12] they cannot be equated with the impoverished, emaciated refugees from the late 1840s who were so often depicted in the Great Famine literature. Although they were far from being prosperous or well off, the pre-famine Irish immigrants were generally better off than the refugees from Newfoundland.

A full generation before the Great Famine in Ireland, the victims of Newfoundland's post-1815 economic collapse fled into the Maritime colonies by the thousand. In that movement Prince Edward Island received hundreds of families who became permanent productive settlers, as well as hundreds of families who were transients on their trek toward New Brunswick and New England. There was, as well, an unfortunate minority – aged, disabled, indigent people, who fell exhausted on these shores and became dependent upon the Island's scanty public welfare resources. In caring for these people, the Benevolent Irish Society, the Ladies' Benevolent Society, various church groups, and relatives and friends supplemented the assistance available from the public asylum, the workhouse, and the government purse. Reports from these agencies indicate that Irish paupers outnumbered those of other national origin – an expected statistic inasmuch as the Irish made up fully half the population of Newfoundland and the bulk of the fisheries' workforce.

Indicative of its extreme distress, Newfoundland initiated at least two policies that had adverse repercussions in Prince Edward Island. First, it deported many unemployable people "to the neigbouring colony of Prince Edward Island where there is a demand for labour in the winter." Governor Sir Charles Hamilton explained this action to Colonial Secretary Lord Bathurst in these words: "I have adopted this measure to lessen the expense of keeping some hundreds of starving men, women and children who would require to have some provision made for them which would invariably fall on Governments."[13] This policy must have been helpful to families who found employment, but many poor wretches ended up on the meagre public relief rolls in Charlottetown. In this way, Newfoundland's problem was shifted, not solved.

The problem of dealing with criminals was handled in a similar manner: Newfoundland decided to banish its felons by placing them on ships destined for Prince Edward Island or mainland ports. However, the Island's legislative assembly reacted firmly by passing its own "Act to prevent the bringing persons convicted of felonies and misdemeanors to this Island from the Island of Newfoundland, or elsewhere in America."[14]

It is impossible to ascertain how many unemployable refugees or unwanted deportees came to Prince Edward Island as a result of Newfoundland's sanctions, but it seems reasonable to assume that Newfoundland's social and economic woes significantly increased the proportion of Irish names (particularly those of apparent southeastern Ireland origin) in the published lists of paupers. As this particular crisis passed, though, it became evident that the great majority of Newfoundland Irish immigrants had become normal hard-working, self-supporting settlers on the Island.

THE DIRECT ROUTE

Far more important for their effect on Irish immigration in the Maritimes were the direct sailings from several ports in southern Ireland to

Halifax, Pictou, Saint John, Miramichi, and Charlottetown, for they accounted for the thousands of permanent settlers (as distinct from the thousands of transients) who came to the Maritimes, and to Prince Edward Island in particular, between 1810 and 1835.

Aside from the North Atlantic fisheries, Waterford had long enjoyed trade links with Bristol and Barnstable, Cadiz and St Malo, Newfoundland and the West Indies. But around 1815 it began to increase its commerce with the Maritime region of British North America. As soon as the Napoleonic Wars and the War of 1812 had ended, the sea lanes were safely opened to civilian traffic. At the same time, as the military's demand for fish declined and Newfoundland's marine-based economy temporarily collapsed, America-bound passenger vessels from Ireland generally bypassed Newfoundland in favour of mainland ports.

Meanwhile, important new forces at home had begun to motivate emigration from Ireland. During this period the population in Ireland burgeoned, the Irish economy continued to decline, and the imperial land policies proved disastrous to the Irish people. After the Irish rising of 1798, civil strife, agrarian discontent, sectarian struggles, and widespread poverty beset the country. Increasingly, the Irish adopted the view that the might and majesty of the world's greatest imperialist power was presiding over the impoverishment of their country. Morale suffered another setback in 1822 when the crops failed in the province of Munster. In that first quarter of the nineteenth century, many people chose to emigrate for a better livelihood. Then, hardly a generation later, came the supreme national tragedy – the Great Famine – when over a million Irish people were forced to flee for their lives.

Long before the Great Famine, though, Irish people had often looked to North America. Early in the nineteenth century, certainly, the Maritime colonies beckoned. Lumbering, roadmaking, and shipbuilding were thriving; fertile land was waiting to be cultivated, and the waters were teeming with fish. Passage to the Maritimes cost less than to New England, and for those who chose to move on, the United States was easily accessible. Irish newspapers frankly publicized that option. For example, an advertisement for the brig *Thomas* sailing to New Brunswick in 1818 stated: "This may be found a most eligible opportunity for passengers to any of the contiguous parts of the United States or British Colonies." Similarly, in the same year the notice that the *Harp* was sailing to St Andrew's, New Brunswick, stated: "This is an excellent opportunity for Tradesmen and others who cannot go to the States, as St Andrew's is within a mile of them."[15]

The *Hibernian Chronicle* (Cork), the *Waterford Mirror*, and *Ramsey's Waterford Chronicle* were among the newspapers that regularly announced sailings from Cork and Waterford to ports in British North America. Such ships' names as *Pandora, Jane,* and *Molly Moore* became household words among emigrant families; and just as familiar to them were the names of the Waterford shippers Jacob Penrose, Anthony Jackson, and Richard Pope. High-pressure advertising was unnecessary. As a large part of Ireland was overcrowded, discontented, and depressed, people were willing to "turn their backs on rack rents, tithes and presentment jobs"; and a British commission in 1826–27 even recommended assistance to settle 10,000 Irish people in 300,000 acres of Nova Scotia, New Brunswick, and Prince Edward Island, which were to be surveyed by Colonel Cockburn.[16] Not only for the depressed populace but also for the ambitious and far-sighted, the portals of opportunity were open in British North America. Clearly, Sir Robert Peel was not alone in realistically regarding emigration to the British colonies as "one of the remedies for Irish misery."[17]

In contrast to the discouraging economic and social conditions in Ireland, prospects in the colony of Prince Edward Island seemed particularly promising. Leasehold land was available, the soil was fertile, the woodlands were extensive, and fish were plentiful. The Island was exporting produce and timber and was building many wooden trading ships. These economic conditions held the promise of employment for many of Ireland's willing workers in the rural trades, mills, and shipyards. En route to the Island, of course, very few emigrants could afford first-class cabins; most came steerage in whatever transport happened to be available and affordable. Usually, in order to serve a dual purpose, ordinary freight carriers were converted into passenger ships simply by fitting them out with a common galley, with rows of rough bunks below decks. The bunks, or berths, were in effect large storage bins, each capable of holding several people. Such sleeping quarters provided neither comfort nor privacy, and the poor ventilation and unsanitary conditions below decks often exposed the occupants to vermin, rodents, and contagious diseases. But emigrants endured such hardships in the belief that they would find security at the end of the four-week voyage.

SHIPPING DATA

The exact number (and names) of ships that entered Island harbours and the exact number (and names) of the Irish immigrants these ships disembarked can only be conjectured. As noted earlier, in 1771–72 the *John and James* made two trips with passengers from northern Ireland, and the *Yaward*'s single voyage in 1772 brought fifty families via the ports of Belfast and Newry. In the eighteenth century only two other immigrant ships are actually recorded as having called at or originated at an Irish port: the *Elizabeth* in 1775 and the *Union* in 1793, both from Cork. No records of Irish ship arrivals in the busy twenty-four years between 1793 and 1817 are known to exist. The Prince Edward Island Heritage Foundation accounts for only sixty-one vessels from Ireland between 1817 and 1848, with a tally of about 5,500 Irish passengers. There is virtually no accounting for the large volume of steady Newfoundland traffic, and no incoming ships at all are listed for 1821, 1824, 1825, 1845, or 1846. More information about the listed ships will be provided presently, but first some general explanations may be useful.

Despite information gaps amounting to twenty-nine years in the 1775–1850 Island immigration period, it is evident that, for our purposes, the leading Irish ports of embarkation in the nineteenth century were Waterford (with at least twenty-seven departures) and Belfast (with at least ten departures). The statistics concerning shipping from these ports are, unfortunately, far from complete. Passenger lists were not required prior to 1855, and even then regulations were not fully enforced. Only about 1,300 Island-bound emigrants are recorded in aggregate to have sailed from the Waterford–New Ross estuary, whereas the Belfast complement was over 3,500. Incomplete records accounting for only nine of the vessels from Cork attribute a mere 142 immigrants to that port; the six recorded sailings of the many from Dublin yield only 19 immigrants; and the port of Limerick's several recorded sailings to the Island account for only 111 people. In noting even these very incomplete statistics, it seems realistic to assume that no master would have had cause to overestimate the number of his passengers, whereas some might have been tempted to report lower-than-actual figures or to make no report at all.

The two ships named *Pandora* out of Waterford disembarked immigrants at Charlottetown eleven times; the *Hannah* from Wexford or New Ross made four visits; the *Benjamin Shaw* came from Waterford in 1823 and 1829; and the *Quebec Trader* sailed from Waterford in 1830 and from Dublin in 1831. Of particular interest was the notice of "Emigration from Ireland" in the 30 November 1839 edition of the *Colonial Herald*, which stated: "The well known regular Trader Barque Argyle, William Baldwin Commander will sail from Waterford with passengers about the beginning of April next, for this port. Those who wish to avail themselves of this eligible mode of conveyance will please apply to Thomas F. Nevins Esq., Waterford, or to Daniel Brenan, Charlottetown. Nov. 1st, 1839."

The *Lawrence* from Waterford brought 21 passengers in September 1840. The two ships named *Pandora* had an aggregate of 582 immigrants during their eleven voyages, but they were surpassed in 1841 by the single sailings of the *Consbrook* (700 passengers) and *Margaret Pollock* (685 passengers), both ships out of Belfast. A century and a half later, people still marvelled that early Charlottetown, with a population of just over 4,000, could handle so many immigrants.

Judging by the 1848 census, about 15 percent of the Irish-born Island residents lived in Charlottetown; the larger task lay in placing the majority of the immigrants around the countryside. As explained earlier in this study, a minority did have prearranged plans for settling here: there were several concerted (albeit small-scale) efforts at colonizing certain townships, and there was some recruitment of tradesmen especially for such industries as shipbuilding and lumbering. Generally, it seems, for settling in the farming areas, most newcomers relied on an informal information network, variously consisting of land agents, parish clergy, the local newspapers, resident relatives and friends, correspondence, the verbal advice of compatriots, rumours, and blind chance. Immigrants who came between 1810 and 1840 tended to settle in Queens County at first, but later they spread out further, even to the ends of the Island. Some people soon managed to settle on farmland which they purchased or leased; others moved and moved again, until they found a suitable place, their wanderings puzzling their ancestor-hunting descendants four or five generations later.[18]

Most difficult to trace were the itinerant day labourers, who earned their meals and shelter by casual work on farms or docks, in the woods, or at construction sites. Skilled tradesmen and professional persons were generally more stable, establishing themselves in the capital or in villages where their talents were needed and rewarded.

OTHER COLONIAL SOURCES

To a lesser extent than Newfoundland, the nearby mainland colonies of New Brunswick and Nova Scotia contributed significantly to Prince Edward Island's Irish population.

New Brunswick Crossovers

The emergency created during Napoleon's blockade of Scandinavia gave impetus to a huge continuing lumber-exporting industry in eastern Canada. Over the years, this industry drew tens of thousands of Irish labourers from Newfoundland and Ireland to New Brunswick and Quebec.

Natives of Wexford, Waterford, Kilkenny, Tipperary, and Cork along with smaller numbers from Kerry and a sprinkling from Clare, Offaly, and Limerick, poured into Chatham, Newcastle, and numerous lumbering towns along tributaries of the Miramichi River in the 1820s and 1830s. More than half of these lumbermen eventually made their way to the United States or to Lower or Upper Canada, but those who remained built impressive Irish settlements in northern New Brunswick.[19] A small number, however, chose to sail over to Prince Edward Island and to establish themselves permanently along the Island's western shore (see chapter 4). Reciprocating this process later in the nineteenth century, many young Islanders sought seasonal employment in lumber camps along the Miramichi.

Nova Scotia Crossovers

Add to the New Brunswick connections the regular commerce between Prince Edward Island and Nova Scotia. Pictou and Pugwash on Nova Scotia's north shore were springboards for newcomers to the Island; and both Sydney, in Cape Breton, and Halifax were also temporary shelters for dozens of Irish people who later moved to Prince Edward Island. The return routes were of course available for any Islanders who chose to transfer to Nova Scotia. Hence it is clear that the Island Irish, though remote from large population centres, were not totally isolated from their compatriots elsewhere in the Atlantic region. In fact, a fairly effective network developed. Intercolonial commerce and migration activities assisted communications among scattered groups of settlers; and merchant vessels calling at smaller Island ports such as Georgetown, Murray Harbour, St Peters, Crapaud, Port Hill, Cascumpec, and Green's Shore (later called Summerside) participated in this communications process. They also provided a means for some Irish immigrants in the region to find their way to Prince Edward Island. And virtually all of this activity was common at least twenty-five years before the Great Famine of 1845–48.

CORK AND PRINCE EDWARD ISLAND

Like Waterford, the port of Cork with its deepwater cove (Cobh) was an important base for the Grand Banks fishing enterprise – long before Cork Harbour achieved fame as the gateway to America for hundreds of thousands of famine victims in the late 1840s. Youghal, also in County Cork, served a similar function on a smaller scale. Before the Great Famine, both ports scheduled sailings for passengers to St John's, Halifax, Miramichi, Saint John, and, occasionally, Charlottetown.

Hundreds of Island-bound settlers boarded vessels in Cork's extensive basin, which receives the flood of the celebrated River Lee.

Whether or not their home places had been comfortable, in their romantic reveries many Corkonians and their descendants have fondly recalled that their lovely river flows eastward from Saint Finnbar's arcadian hermitage at Gougane Barra, then graces the environs of Ballingeary and Inchigeelagh, winds past Macroom, Coachford, and Dripsey, and pours through the center of Cork city before it spills into the complex harbour.

There, in 1775, the *Elizabeth* out of London moored briefly before sailing with fourteen passengers for Prince Edward Island – only to be shipwrecked on 5 November off the shore of Township Eleven.[20] In 1793 the *Union* brought the businessmen Hennesie and Mayhew to Charlottetown. Fragmented records verify only nine other direct sailings from Cork. The second *Elizabeth* (1812), the *Endeavour* (1820, 1821), and *Saltren's Rock* (1820) did not list any passengers, and the *Anna* (1834) named only one. The *Nelson* brought three passengers in 1818, and the *Carron* brought eleven more two years later. In 1823 the *General Elliot* landed 113 people. In 1836 fifteen more immigrants arrived on the *Thomas Hanforth*. The largest number from Cork, 131 immigrants, sailed to Charlottetown in May 1842 on the *Sir James MacDonald* (*MacDonnell*). Incomplete as these statistics may be, they clearly indicate that Cork, the primary port of embarkation for settlers of New Brunswick, was of secondary importance for settlers of Prince Edward Island.

Arrivals from County Cork included William Broydrick, William Collings, Richard Fowler, and John Hennesy from Youghal. Daniel, Ann, and William Collins came from Kanturk; Michael and Margaret Shehan, Anne Patterson, and Maurice Ronayne from Midleton; Jeremiah Coghlan from Bantry, Thomas Condon from Mitchellstown, Daniel Donahy from Doneraile, and Mike Green from Castletown. Mrs Hanora Collins was from Kilbolane, John Driscoll probably from Baltimore (via Chatham, N.B.); Jeremiah McCarthy was born in Queenstown (Cobh), Mrs Johanna McCarthy in Everary; David Noonan was of the parish of St Brigid, and Edward Barry came from Lady's Bridge. Even this small sample of emigrants clearly suggests that their assemblage was accidental, leaderless, and uncoordinated. There is no evidence that these people were recruited. They came on their own and paid their own passage.

Similarly, when the Cork immigrants arrived on the Island and dispersed to various localities, there seemed to be no concerted plan or pattern to their settlement. Hence, John O'Keefe went to Kinkora, Catherine Ryan and her husband John O'Donohue settled at Palmer Road, Michael and Margaret Shehan went to Bedeque, while William Collins and Jeremiah Coghlan ended up in East Point, John

Murphy in Lot 65, Daniel Ferris in Summerfield, and Daniel Neill and his wife Margaret Murphy in Morell. John O'Flynn and his wife Catherine went to Indian River, where Michael Saunders also settled, and William Daley and his wife Ellen O'Neill (and her mother, Fanny O'Neill) resided in Sturgeon. William Sweeney lived in DeSable, and Edward Laughlin established his family in Lot 16.

It is evident that the settlers who came from County Cork were not a cohesive group. They were not part of a specific movement. They were merely a collection of individuals or families who happened to travel together from County Cork to Prince Edward Island. Even on the Island, the Cork immigrants did not congregate as a county group; they were randomly dispersed.

LIMERICK AND PRINCE EDWARD ISLAND

The rugged Irish coastline evidently forced the ninth-century Viking invaders to locate their strongholds in sheltered estuaries of the major rivers – Dublin on the Liffey, Wexford on the Slaney, Waterford on the Suir, Cork on the Lee. Limerick is perhaps the most notable example of such a Viking haven, situated fifty miles inland at the head of the estuary of Ireland's longest river, the stately Shannon. The Shannon starts out as a mere spring in the Cuilcach foothills of County Cavan, and as the rivulet widens and deepens it forms lakes (including Lough Ree and Lough Derg) and occasional rapids on its resolute course through Ireland's heartland. After flowing nearly two hundred miles, the Shannon empties into the estuary at Limerick and gladdens that city. Finally, it slips through the embracing headlands of Clare and Kerry and loses itself in the vast Atlantic. It was the Limerick estuary the poet Spenser had in mind when he wrote of "the spacious Shenan spreading like a sea."

Limerick has long been a major west coast port serving several counties. Although "Limerick ships brought a steady stream of emigrants to the Gulf of St Lawrence and usually returned to their home ports with cargoes of timber,"[21] this heavy commerce did not greatly affect immigration to Prince Edward Island. Despite steady traffic conducted between Limerick and Miramichi, over many years, only seven ships are on record as having sailed from Limerick to Prince Edward Island. The *Sarah* brought eighteen passengers in 1817, the brig *Fawcett* called at Charlottetown in 1819 but left no passenger list, and the *Alexander* delivered 93 immigrants in 1820. After that, incoming ships did not specify the number of passengers. However, newcomers to the Seven Mile Bay area in 1826 are believed to have arrived on the brig *Martin*; and the *Spy* (1830), *Ellen Stewart* (1840), and *Mary Jane* (1843) also carried unknown numbers of immigrants from the port of Limerick.

Among the County Limerick settlers were Daniel McCarthy of Capamore, who lived in Charlottetown; Michael Ryan and Timothy Ryan, who lived in Tignish; William Ryan (senior and junior), who made their home in Georgetown; Patrick O'Brien, who died in 1885 at Palmer Road; and Mrs Ellen Ruth, who arrived about 1818 and lived on the Souris Line Road until 1886. Clearly, the County Limerick people, as well as their fellow travellers from neighbouring counties, simply went their separate ways when they arrived in Prince Edward Island. Despite all they held in common, they did not congregate as a tight-knit immigrant group.

DUBLIN TO CHARLOTTETOWN

Extant records of sailings to Charlottetown from Dublin yield limited information related to the settlement of the Island. Newspapers reported that J.B. Palmer, Daniel Brenan, Richard Goff, Dennis Reddin, W.W. Lord, and other Island businessmen made personal and commercial voyages between Charlottetown and Waterford and Dublin, but the voyages of other migrants from Dublin are scarcely reported, even in the aggregate. The *Prince Edward Island Gazette* of 7 September 1818 informs us that the brigantine *Ocean* was here in 1818. The scow *Sarah* called at Charlottetown in 1821, and the brig *Collina* disembarked some passengers in 1829. The following year, the *Favourite* and *Quebec Trader* brought only five passengers between them; but in 1831 *Venus II* delivered forty passengers and the *Quebec Trader* nineteen. In 1844 the arrival of the *Mary Jane*, along with two visits by the *Antelope*, yielded at least forty settlers. The *Douglas* brought fourteen more immigrants in 1848.

Judging by such records, Dublin's contribution to the population of Prince Edward Island was numerically slight. The immigrants from a wide area who might have followed the Dublin-to-Charlottetown route were not a unified body of settlers. They formed no discernible communities or organizations of their own, nor did they brandish bonds of loyalty to their former localities. As a regional subgroup, it seems they made no memorable mark on Island history. However, a number of individuals who had Dublin connections – such as the entrepreneurs mentioned above – devoted their lives to public service, business, and the professions in Prince Edward Island.

THE KERRY CONNECTION

Professor John Mannion's extensive research reveals that the ports of Waterford and New Ross accounted for about 85 percent of New-foundland's Irish population. Concerning the remaining 15 percent, two points must be made. First, the fishery also attracted fishermen from the ports of Cork and Youghal and even smaller numbers from Tralee; second, in keeping with the example set by the southeastern Irishmen, some members of those southwestern and western Irish contingents left Newfoundland in search of employment in the Maritime provinces. A brief account of the County Kerry connection should illustrate both points.

As it happened, the fishing activities out of the coastal Gaeltacht – the designated areas, mainly in the south and west of Ireland, where Irish is the primary language – had particular relevance to Prince Edward Island. The noteworthy presence of Kerrymen among settlers of central Queens and western Prince counties, for instance, raises the question, "How did they come to be in those places?" The general historical context outlined above certainly begins to explain the movement of many persons from western and southwestern Ireland, first, to the fishing grounds off Newfoundland and later to Prince Edward Island. But there is more to relate about the Kerry "two boaters."

Writing in Irish, Eibhlín Ní Mhurchú (Eileen Murphy) in an article entitled "An tIascach a Bhí" (The Fishing That Was) recalls County Kerry's centuries-long dependence on the sea for survival. Even in medieval times, she notes, Kerrymen, well aware of the legendary voyages of Saint Brendan,[22] sailed into the Atlantic in their wooden boats and their curraghs covered with animal skins. She continues:

It is still remembered here that fishermen, in the early nineteenth century migrated from here, but not to England or America. America had not yet started to build railroads and there was no pay for laborers. These fishermen went to *Talamh an Éisc* (Land of the Fish) which had beautiful harbors and excellent fishing. They were occupied there for only half a year because of the ice in the winter. Obviously some of them came home after the fishing season, as mentioned in the poem:

> To Talamh an Éisc he went
> On his return home to port
> He folded up his nets
> He shared with the local people
> All he fished for a month in the harbor.[23]

Especially at the outset of this transatlantic industry, Ireland's west coast fishermen were known to sail in season to the Grand Banks and to return before winter to their homes in the Dingle Peninsula and elsewhere in the Gaeltacht. In due time, however, some of the men from places such as Ventry and Fenit and Dingle Town chose to make Newfoundland a launching place to explore opportunities in the Maritime colonies or in the New England states. Thus, Kerrymen were among the pioneers who participated in the movement southward from Newfoundland. Equally at home on the sea or on land, they were also among the early voyagers who bypassed Newfoundland and headed directly for the continental mainland.

Later Kerry immigrants, other than those engaged in the fisheries, followed similar routes. They normally embarked for the Maritime colonies from Cork City, Youghal, and Limerick. Kerry immigrants arrived from Cork on the brig *Martin* in 1820, on the *General Elliot* in 1823, and on the *Alexander* out of Limerick in 1820. They also embarked for America from Blennerville on Tralee Bay, a port which figured prominently during and after the famine exodus but which earlier had received many timber-laden ships from New Brunswick and sent out passengers on the return voyage to the Maritimes.[24] Those Kerrymen, in turn, became lumbermen, road builders, fishermen, and farmers in various places in eastern Canada.

Kerry immigrants to Prince Edward Island were not systematically recruited. Some had Island-hopped from Newfoundland; others had migrated across Northumberland Strait from the Miramichi forestry encampments; still others had sailed directly to the Island from Ireland. They had come from such diverse places as Annagh, Ballyheige, Capa Clough, Castlegregory, Dingle, Kenmare, and Tralee. They proved to be sturdy settlers, and their names became honourably rooted in local Island history: Dalton, Dorgan, Fitzgerald, Hanifin, Lane, McCarthy, Nelligan, O'Halloran, O'Shea, Reardon, Reilly, Slattery, Sullivan, and others.

BON VOYAGE

In the pre-Famine decades, newspaper accounts and oral reports about opportunities in the New World spurred interest in emigration from the crowded townlands of southern Ireland. Ship owners announced their sailing schedules and provided information for travellers. Recruiting agents also spread their propaganda. Although some of the information thus engendered was unreliable – even occasionally deceptive – honest information proved helpful to intending emigrants.

In 1828, for instance, a Limerick newspaper presented practical information and guidelines for emigrants setting out for the Gulf of St Lawrence.[25] According to that article (which was apparently based on A.C. Buchanan's *Emigration Practically Considered, Etc.*), the Atlantic crossing in the 1820s cost from two to three pounds, with much lower rates for children; and it took from thirty to forty-five days from Ireland to Quebec, and between twenty-five and thirty-five days from Ireland to Halifax or Saint John. There was no luxury accommodation. Except for passengers sailing for Gaspé or Quebec City, the most convenient places for disembarkation were Miramichi and Prince Edward Island. April and May were the months recommended for the journey, but travellers were warned "on no account to go in July or August, as, from the prevalence of south-west winds, you will have a tedious passage." Another warning was: "Be sure that the ship is going to the port you contract for, as much deception has been practiced in this respect. It is important to select a well-known captain and a fast-sailing ship, even at a higher rent." A sinister aspect of the seaport subculture is revealed in the caution, "Beware of those crimps that are generally found about the docks and quays" and "designing people who often give their advice unsolicited."

Other practical suggestions included packing baggage in small wooden chests and placing oatmeal in iron-hooped barrels. A family of five would require two and a half hundredweight of oatmeal, half a hundredweight of biscuits, 48 stone of potatoes (672 pounds), a 20–pound keg of butter, a gallon of molasses, 20 pounds of bacon, a 50–pound keg of herrings, a little vinegar, and a gallon of spirits. The ship's captain was required to supply five pints of water daily for each adult. These supplies would cost six or seven pounds sterling and would last two months or more. A most thoughtful recommendation, perhaps, was this: "If the emigrant has the means, let him purchase besides one pound of tea and fourteen pounds of sugar, for his wife."

To ensure their arrival in good health, emigrants were advised to eat moderately, keep clean, "air the bedding daily, get up at five o'clock and retire at eight." They should not overlook "thread, pins, needles, and a strong pair of shoes" and a woollen cap for winter. For unmarried emigrants, there was this word: "From the great disparity of male over female population in Canada, I would advise every young farmer or labourer going out (who can pay for the passage of two) to take an active young wife with him."

Emigrants setting out for Prince Edward Island were told to expect winters to be "cold but dry and bracing," milder than in New Brunswick or Lower Canada. The summers were said to be "extremely hot, particularly in July and August" – a season requiring "only coarse

shirts and linen trousers, cheap moccasins and straw hats." The new settlers, equipped with spades and reaping hooks and such tools as augurs,
planes, hammers, and chisels, would have to "consult the seasons in all
undertakings, and leave nothing to chance or to be done another day."
The writer concluded with this urgent plea: "I beseech you, if you have
any party feeling at home, if you wish to promote your own prosperity,
or that of your family – wash your hands clean of it, ere you embark.
Such characters are looked upon with suspicion in the colonies; and you
could not possibly take with you a worse recommendation."

References to dreadful conditions aboard passenger vessels arriving
in Charlottetown are, in fact, extremely scarce. Nevertheless, a surgeon
on six different emigrant ships, Dr J. Curtis, observed that whereas
crime was punished in Hell, it "flourished without retribution" in an
emigrant ship. He added, "Take all the stews of Liverpool, concentrate
in a given space the acts and deeds done in all in one year, and they
would scarcely equal in atrocity the amount of crime committed in one
emigrant ship during a single voyage."[26] The number of Charlottetown
arrivals deserving such a classification will never be known.

"THOSE ELUSIVE IMMIGRANTS"

In a public exhibit mounted by the Prince Edward Island Heritage
Foundation in 1990, one caption stated that between 1815 and 1840,
950 immigrants arrived from Waterford, 300 from Cork, Limerick and
Dublin, and another 600 from unidentified southern Irish ports. While
thus accounting for at least 1,850 Irish settlers, the Heritage Foundation historian noted that the total figure was "undoubtedly low" and
the "true figure may be double that number." Circumstantial evidence
clearly supports this estimate.

Unfortunate gaps in the data and the scarcity of information continue to frustrate social historians and family historians alike. Consider, for instance, the two-part article "Those Elusive Immigrants"[27]
by provincial genealogists Orlo Jones and Douglas Fraser. Although
the authors are able to state that "between 1830 and 1835, an average
of 276 vessels per year called at Island Ports," available records contain the names of fewer than 150 transatlantic ships, all from the
United Kingdom. Jones and Fraser further believe that during the same
five-year period, "at least 4,600 passengers arrived in the colony." Yet
the statistics tally no more than 2,800 passengers, all from the United
Kingdom. Data on travel from Newfoundland to Prince Edward Island
do not exist. The same study lists twenty ships transporting about 600
immigrants from Ireland to Prince Edward Island between 1830 and
1835; even these figures are minimal.

Although incomplete records and imprecise data blur many desirable details, in this instance they do not obfuscate the overall picture. It is now known that from May through October each year, starting about 1770, the Irish immigrants sailed by barque and brig, barquentine and brigantine, topsail schooner and fore-and-aft rigged schooner, coastal trader and commercial carrier, fishing ship and timber ship, into the welcoming bays of Prince Edward Island. By 1835, probably more than five thousand people who had originated in southern Ireland had come to settle on the Island.

Although smaller vessels from the neighbouring provinces often sailed into any of the dozen safe havens around the Island, passengers who came directly from Ireland usually disembarked in the spacious, picturesque harbour of Charlottetown. As their sea-weary ships entered Hillsborough Bay, they cleared Point Prim, where now the Island's oldest and tallest light tower stands sentinel.[28] As soon as their ship had navigated the narrows between Rocky Point and Keppoch, the immigrants crowding the decks discovered that they were once again at the meeting of the waters – this time at Three Tides, the steadily swirling confluence of the Hillsborough, North, and West rivers. Sometimes, we are told, when their ships dropped anchor, the immigrants broke into spontaneous song and dance, the captain and crew joining the celebration of their safe arrival.

The following chapters detail how those exiles from southern Ireland adapted to their new conditions and became adopted Islanders.

CHAPTER FOUR

An Irish Principality

By 1835 families from southernmost Ireland, many via Newfound-land, had located in Charlottetown and in virtually every rural town-ship of the Island. They spread sparsely from the more fertile lands in the central area into the two large peninsulas that form the Island's extremities. This chapter explores the western peninsula of Prince County, while the following will view Irish settlements in the eastern Kings peninsula.

A rosary of Irish communities encircled the western peninsula, where newcomers from Ireland's southeastern counties blended with "crossovers" from lumbering and fishing centres in New Brunswick; an infusion of Kerry folk also contributed to the lively mix. Irish co-existence with a large Acadian French population in the Tignish area tested the good will and hardiness of both ethnic groups. Nearly two centuries later, vital signs of Irish culture and French culture – greatly modified, of course, by the Island milieu – are still evident in Prince County. Extracts from the letters, folklore, and diaries of the time provide important glimpses into the colonial way of life.

About twenty-five miles west of the present small city of Summerside, on the border of Townships Ten and Eleven, all traffic funnels through a narrow isthmus called Portage. The word *portage* denotes a land route for carrying boats and goods between two navigable waterways. At this particular Portage, Cascumpec Bay and the fingers of the Fox-ley River pinch the land from the north, almost touching the incursion of Egmont Bay where its thumb, Percival Bay, presses in from the southwest. Once past the place where these tidal indentations have squeezed the land to a 2¼-mile passage and have virtually divided Prince County, the traveller is said to be "up west," and the peninsula itself is generally called West Prince (see map 5). Around much of the coast of the peninsula, well over a century and a half ago, Irish immigrants hacked out a haphazard principality.

IRISH PLACE NAMES IN THE REGION

To this day, numerous place names scattered through western Prince County recall the Irish presence. Several miles northwest of the "bottomless lake" near Portage (in Lot 6) is the farming centre called O'Leary. Like scores of villages in Ireland, O'Leary was a *stradbally* (a one-street community) with an obviously Irish name; otherwise, there was nothing particularly Irish about it. Apparently, the name derived from the fact that an immigrant named Michael O'Leary had once lived at the western end of the road. Upon returning from a visit to Ireland in 1858, he drowned in Halifax. This is the standard version of the place name's origin.[1]

Some residents prefer to believe that the village derived its name from a kinsman of Ireland's liberator, Daniel O'Connell – namely, Dr Cornelius Richard Purcell O'Leary, who died in Tignish in 1887. Dr O'Leary of Mallow, County Cork, was the grandson of the celebrated Art O'Leary, whose slaying was mourned in a classic Irish lament, *Caoineadh Airt Ui Laoghaire* (Lament for Art O'Leary), composed by his widow, Eibhlin Dubh Ni Chonaill (Eileen O'Connell).[2] Dr O'Leary, a medical officer aboard the ill-fated Quebec-bound emigrant ship *Spartan*, came to the Island in 1852, when the storm-damaged vessel took refuge in Georgetown. He opened a medical office, the first in Souris – where he married Mary Ann Scully – and then he moved his practice to Alberton, and finally to Tignish. The place where he lived acquired the local name of O'Leary's Cape.[3]

Not far from O'Leary, on the line separating Lots 5 and 6, another place bears a name that has little reference to its heavily Acadian population. The community is called Howlan.[4] George William Howlan (1835–1901), an articulate advocate of farmers' demands for land ownership, was this district's assemblyman when the road was built in 1865. In 1873 he was appointed (and in 1891 reappointed) to the Canadian Senate, and in 1894 he became the Island's lieutenant-governor. Born in County Waterford in 1835, he was four years of age when his parents emigrated to Charlottetown. In later life, as a prosperous merchant and successful politician, Howlan was known to follow the course of expediency in such contentious 1860s issues as religious elements in public schools and the Island's debates about Confederation. He is best remembered as the first public man to propose a permanent transportation link (a tunnel) between Prince Edward Island

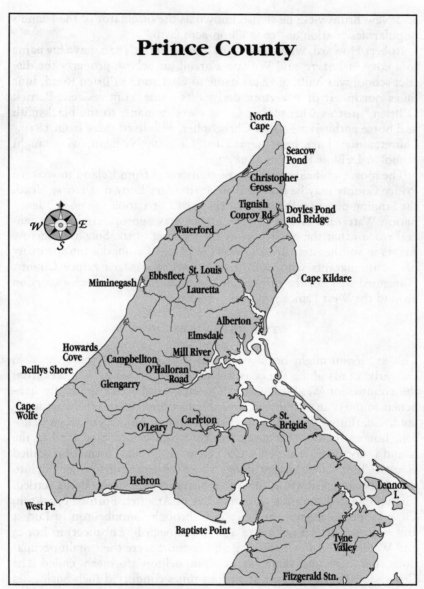

Prince County

North
Cape

Seacow
Pond

Christopher
Cross

Tignish
Conroy Rd

Doyles Pond
and Bridge

Waterford

Ebbsfleet   St. Louis

Miminegash

Lauretta

Cape Kildare

Alberton

Elmsdale

Howards
Cove

Mill River

Campbellton

O'Halloran
Road

Reillys Shore

Glengarry

Cape
Wolfe

Carleton

St.
Brigids

O'Leary

Hebron

Lennox
I.

West Pt.

Baptiste Point

Tyne
Valley

Fitzgerald Stn.

Map 5. Western Prince County attracted both Acadian and Irish settlers.

and New Brunswick; he is also known as the originator of the Island's popular designation as "the million-acre farm."[5]

Robert Howard, who came from Ireland about 1820, gave his name to a cove in Lot 7;[6] and William Carroll, on whose property the district school was built, gave his name to Carleton.[7] O'Brien Road, four miles northwest of Alberton, derives its name from resident Patrick O'Brien,[8] just as Christopher Cross owes its name to the blacksmith and horse enthusiast Patrick Christopher, who lived there from 1830.[9] Lauretta may have been named for Lauretta Nelligan, who taught school at DeBlois Road in 1898.[10]

The most significant place name transferred from Ireland to western Prince County may be that of Waterford. Once known as Horse Head, the landing place on the western shore of Lot 1 took the postal designation Waterford in 1885.[11] The choice was appropriate for the general reason that the great port at the meeting of the Suir and Barrow Rivers in southeastern Ireland was the place of embarkation for many of the immigrants who built their homes in western Prince County. Waterford was not the only point of origin, however, as an excursion around the West Prince peninsula reveals.

TOWNSHIP SEVEN

This excursion might begin where an Irish settlement was formed in the early 1820s along the coastline of Township Seven. Families from the counties of Wexford, Laois (Queen's), and Kerry gradually happened to move in. Some had first sought opportunities in Newfoundland, Charlottetown, Bedeque, Tryon, and perhaps Kerrytown (Clinton, Lot 20) before they settled in the sparsely occupied land in the Island's northwestern peninsula. Near a coastal formation called Giant's Chair – and, farther along, where three red cliffs projecting into the sea became known as the Three Sisters – Irish descendants settled. They populated the rural communities of Ankatel, Burton, Brockton, Cape Wolfe, Glengarry, and beyond: through Campbellton in Lots 4 and 7; Roseville in Lots 3 and 4; to Miminegash (Ebbsfleet) in Lot 2; and Waterford in Lot 1. Fishing and farming were their main occupations, but here and there, as at Campbellton (formerly called The Cross), local entrepreneurs at various times conducted such businesses as small-scale shipbuilding, lobster packing, cheese making, brewing, milling, and blacksmithing.

The Irish first came to this coastal strip in the 1820s, and about twenty-five years later their sons and daughters built a Catholic mission church, St Mark's, which became the focal point of the community. Nearby, the home of Thomas Doyle of Wexford and his wife

Alice Knowles of Kilkenny was the model of hospitality and geniality. There, the neighbours often met for a cup of tea and for singing, dancing, card playing, and humorous storytelling, or to share news from near and far. At intervals along the shore lived the families of Lawrence Butler, Thomas Dalton, Maurice Griffin, Robert Howard, Maurice O'Halloran, Garret O'Reilly, Patrick O'Reilly, and Michael White.

The Irish immigrant schoolmaster James Heron Fitzgerald[12] – who styled himself "a teacher of knowledge and cultivator of brains" – recalled in a public letter in 1839 that, when friends invited him to teach in Lot 7, the locale later known as Campbellton was "a thicket of forest and the haunt of wild beasts."[13] So primitive was the region, said Fitzgerald, that the school inspector "had to strap his valise on his back and trudge on foot, over torturous and muddy foot-paths, a distance of ten miles" to visit the school, and it took "nearly four months" for the teacher to receive his newspapers. "The greater part of the West was an unbroken forest, which the surveyor and the hunter alone penetrated. There were no roads ... The only way was by woodpath, zigzagged and crooked, from tree to tree kneedeep in mud and mire or ... creeping along the brow of cliffs eighty or one hundred feet above the surfy beach and attended with no small danger to life and limb." Even though Fitzgerald called the place Mount Pleasant, his observations make it clear that natural obstacles, on the land and in the waters, would probably have discouraged all but the hardiest pioneers from settling along that western shore.

Tombstone inscriptions in St Mark's churchyard and notations in family histories indicate where some of these hardy settlers originated and how their genealogies interlocked in patterns as intricate as Irish lace. For instance, in 1820 the brig *Martin* out of Cork evidently brought to the Island the O'Halloran, O'Reilly, Griffin, and Howard families, among others.[14] The first three families split, one male member from each family going east toward Souris, the other west toward Lot 7. Each western O'Halloran, Griffin, and Howard man married an O'Reilly girl, and the family compact grew. Maurice O'Halloran's son Patrick, who remained in Lot 7, had (besides his sons) five daughters. Concerning these young women tradition states, "None were courted, all were wed." Two of them married Donahue men, one married a Kelly, another a Doyle, and the last was wed to Larry Butler.[15] In colonial society double-marriages (a brother and sister of one family marrying a sister and brother from another) were fairly common.

Parish records reveal not only a remarkable interlacing of marriages among Irish families but also the rapid growth of community through the progeny of these marriages. For instance, as recently as 1978 St Mark's parish history noted that the Irish descendants Bernard and Therese Reilly, when observing their sixtieth wedding anniversary, counted thirteen living children, eighty-seven grandchildren, and thirty-seven great-grandchildren.[16]

The lore of numerous Irish families contains tales of lovers fleeing from disapproving parents, eloping to America on emigrant ships, and pledging marriage vows on the high seas. One such legend has enlivened the chronicles of Township Seven. Bridget Reilly, it seems, met and married Robert Howard at sea. After a brief stay at Bedeque, they travelled west to the uninhabited land along the gulf shore and built their home at the place since known as Howards Cove. Nine years later Bridget's brothers, Garret and Patrick, took up farms nearby and thereby conferred on their locale the name Reillys Shore.

Meanwhile, Mr and Mrs Maurice O'Halloran (*née* Reilly) of Tralee arrived in 1820 on the brig *Martin* and gave their name to the road in Lot 7. Although Maurice's brother Matthias O'Halloran went east and settled in Souris, brother Patrick O'Halloran, who may have preceded the others here, chose to live in Lot 7. The names of both Maurice and Patrick appear on the 1844 list of Lot 7 contributors to the Irish Repeal Movement, along with George Kelly of Laois, Mr Lecky of Waterford, Martin Doyle of Adamstown, County Wexford, and schoolmaster James H. Fitzgerald of the Cove of Cork.[17]

John and Patrick Dalton, also active repealers, emigrated from Ballyheigue, County Kerry, in the 1830s. Patrick married Margaret McCarthy (whose father, James, had settled near Tignish), and their son Charles later rose to wealth and fame as a fox breeder and as lieutenant-governor of Prince Edward Island (1930–33). Also in Lot 7 was Thomas Dalton, a tailor and farmer, whose son Patrick married Mary Barrett in 1854 and remained at the original homestead. By that time, the O'Halloran Road had gained additional Irish family names: Butler, Doyle, Dunn, Fitzgerald, and Reilly.

LOCAL CULTURE RETAINED: STORIES AND SATIRES

In the next generation in the Lot 7 area, Thomas Dunn was a well-known teller of tall tales, and the irrepressible Larry Gorman – an "intruder" from Bideford, PEI – achieved widespread renown as a versifier and composer of satirical songs. Dunn, a Wexfordman, loved to tell old stories about kings and queens in their castles, as though he personally knew the royal characters. He often placed himself in the hero's role in the guise of a miller's son, whose adventures among the nobility ranged from the risky to the risqué. Overstatement and wild imagination accounted for the humour in the tales, we are told, but for Dunn's contemporaries the appeal of such stories probably depended in equal measure on the plot itself and the dramatic style of the story-teller.[18] Though a small number of Dunn's stories linger in oral tradition, only a few samples have appeared in print (those fondly preserved by Island folklorist John Cousins).

In this folk activity, the achievement of Larry Gorman has received both lasting popularity and scholarly attention. An itinerant songmaker, Gorman wandered into the West Prince Irish enclave in the late 1860s. In his father's native Kilkenny he might have been called a spalpeen (*spalpín* in Irish), for he made his temporary home wherever he happened to be, and he paid his way by hiring on with any farmer, fisherman, miller, or shipbuilder who happened to need a hand. Gorman was no mere tramp, though. Indeed, with his bright blue eyes, natty clothes, fastidious manners, and fondness for comforts, he had the bearing of a self-possessed gentleman. In Prince County, where he was born and grew to maturity, and in the Miramichi district of New Brunswick, where his parents Thomas Gorman and Ann Donahue met and where he himself went lumbering after he left (or was driven from) the Island, as well as in the woods and milltowns of northern Maine, where he spent his last years, Larry Gorman was known for one talent: he was the man who made the songs.[19] In many ways, he personified the large number of popular versifiers, storytellers and tune makers who brought music and humour to a great many Celtic communities on the Island. In his satirical skills, though, he surpassed his contemporaries.

Notorious is the epithet sometimes used for Larry Gorman, because his verses often raised hackles in the tight-knit society of West Prince. Like some Irish poets (*filí*) of old, he often used his "gift of words" to ridicule, even villify, those who incurred his disfavour. Sparing no one, he was feared as much as he was admired. In "Horse's Confession,"[20] he exposed his brother James's harsh treatment of a horse; and in "Monaghan's Raffle" and "Mick's Wives," he maligned his brother-in-law, Mick Monaghan, nicknaming him "Brigham," – a name that connoted bigamy.[21] (Larry's sister Bridget was Monaghan's third wife.) Gorman ridiculed another widower who had remarried with unseemly haste, in this opening stanza:

If she's gone, let her go,
I will soon get another;
There are lots of pretty girls
At the head of Grand River.

Later in the song, he described the girl the widower had found:

> She can dance to a pipe
> She can dance to a fiddle,
> She's neat around the waist
> As a cow around the middle;
> She has two rows of teeth
> And a tongue in the middle.[22]

In another satirical piece, entitled "Michael O'Brien," Gorman poked fun at a neighbour who supposedly had publicly advertised for a wife.[23] Usually, one cutting poem was sufficient for Gorman to expose the folly of a neighbour, but he lavished his most extended abuse – over thirty songs – on Michael McElroy, the humourless operator of a fish factory in Miminegash.

One of Gorman's most incisive and best-known satires is "The Gull Decoy."[24] It is believed that when a certain Lot 7 fisherman offended him, perhaps by underpaying him for his work, Gorman gained revenge in this song. The title refers to the fisherman's ability to whistle in a way that mimicked the cry of the seagull. One verse describes this phenomenon:

> When I stand up and begin to whistle
> You'll see all the gulls around me fly,
> And in the sand they seem to nestle,
> From whence they call me the Gull Decoy.

This song begins with apparent gentleness, but soon the Gull Decoy reveals himself to be rough and illiterate – a tight-fisted freebooter who has a neighbour read the weekly newspaper to him. Finally, he confesses to outrageous forms of negligence and wickedness that any respectable Irish community would condemn:

> To my own church I have been neglectful,
> My mind being on everything that passed;
> To my Christian duties I've been neglectful,
> It's been forty years since I went to Mass.
> My oldest brother I did him torture,
> I tortured him 'till he had to fly,
> All on account of the girl he married,
> And still in anger I did rage.
> To the place where his child was buried
> I went by night and dug up the grave.

Of all my actions and my bad doings,
I set a dog on an orphan boy,
And many other cruel and dirty action
Which adds more grief to the Gull Decoy.

Folklorist Edward D. Ives, collector of the songs of Larry Gorman, clarifies the last two stanzas by citing a story he had heard: "The Gull Decoy had hounded his brother for marrying a Protestant; and when the brother's child died and was buried in the family plot, the Gull Decoy dug up the body and left it on his brother's doorstep. The brother reburied the child on a hillside facing the Gull Decoy's house, marking the grave very plainly so that it would be the first thing the Gull Decoy would see on stepping out of his front door in the morning. And as for the Gull Decoy's having 'set a dog on an orphan boy,' we can be sure, at the very least, that Larry has worked his material to a fine edge. Veracity was all very well in its way, but for Gorman's purposes it was not a necessary consideration."[25] Another song with a sectarian bias, "The Baptists," employs a parody of a Protestant hymn to ridicule a newly formed Baptist colony on the Nauvoo Road.[26]

Regardless of the purely personal motivation or provocation behind many of his songs, Gorman's humour – ranging from subtle to earthy – and his penchant for piercing satire link his art with folklore and with writing practices in the Irish language in the seventeenth and eighteenth centuries. Ostensibly, Gorman often took pleasure in revealing sordid, sensational, and scandalous incidents concerning his neighbours; implicitly, he ridiculed social indiscretions and moral frailties against a backdrop of standards and ideals that were professed by his people, including the offenders themselves. Of immediate and continuing importance to the cultural historian is the fact that even the fragmentary remains of Larry Gorman's prolific repertoire candidly depict many actualities of Irish-settlement society.

Just as myth and reality often shed light on one another, so fiction and folklore may illumine facts and events. To this day, a folk festival held annually in Prince County commemorates the name of Larry Gorman. Furthermore, residents and visitors alike testify that familiarity with the local-colour artistry of folk composers such as Thomas Dunn, and Larry Gorman – and, a generation later, Alec Shea – adds vitality to their rambling around West Prince peninsula.

THE WESTERN END OF THE ISLAND

On the western coast of the peninsula, the village of Campbellton spans the line between Lots 7 and 4. There, along the shore, the Irish community stretches westward into Roseville (Lot 3) and Miminegash and parts of Palmer Road (Lot 2).[27] Relatively few Irish settled inland. They were noticeably scarce in Lots 5 and 6.[28] However, with the mainly Acadian village of Tignish as a hub, Irish farmers and fishermen populated an outer circle of districts in Lots 1 and 2. Francophone communities, mainly inland, buffer Tignish itself: Harpers Road, Peters Road, Palmer Road, Pig Brook, DuBlois, Union Road, St Peter and St Paul, St Josephs, and St Felix. The Irish, on the other hand, had majorities around the perimeter or coastal land, in Horse Head (Waterford), Skinners Pond, Nail Pond, Christopher Cross, Norway, North Cape, Seacow Pond, and – continuing eastward along the gulf shore – in Kildare Capes, and especially Central Kildare, with a scattering through Greenmount (in Lot 2), and in Cascumpec and Alberton-Northport (Hills River) in Lots 4 and 5. By the 1840s the Irish made up more than half of the people in the Island's seven westernmost townships.

Before pausing to observe certain features of selected Irish communities in western Prince County, visitors might safely assume, first (as place names such as Cascumpec, Miminegash, and Tignish intimate), that the Mi'kmaq bands were the earliest occupants of the area; second, that the British takeover of the Island assured English and Scottish control of most of the land and other economic resources; and, third, that substantial Acadian settlements in Tignish and vicinity and in nearby lots set the stage for interaction with the Irish newcomers. The third factor, especially, deserves elucidation here.

The Irish and the Acadians Meet

Tignish village was founded in 1799 when eight Acadian families from the Malpeque district paddled fifty miles up the gulf shore to the marshy inlet now called Tignish Run. Their family names were Arsenault, Bernard, Chaisson, DesRoches, Doucette, Gaudette, Poirier, and Richard. These pioneers were joined by several more Acadian families the following spring and later by many others when the cutting of clay roads through the woodlands opened up overland travel. Meanwhile, in 1811, the first Irish families had sailed across the fifteen-mile strait from New Brunswick, where they had been working at lumbering and fishing encampments on Chaleur Bay. They moved to the Norway and Nail Pond sites on the Island's western shore. The fusion of Acadian and Irish settlers which soon took place was marked by a mixture of friction and friendship.[29]

Acadian-Irish relations got off to an unpromising start when the first Irishman on the scene, Edward Reilly, split a wooden shovel on the head of Acadian resident Joseph Bernard.[30] In that encounter the Irish-man lost both the shovel and the fight. That incident came to be known as *fendeur de pelle*. There were other fisticuffs, no doubt, but no pitched battles; nor were there (as in New Brunswick)[31] public clashes over ecclesiastical appointments. Despite the Acadians' justifiable pref-erence for francophone clergy, a fairly harmonious community evolved.[32] The mingling of Acadian and Irish people was facilitated at every level by the fact that both groups worshipped in the one church, and therefore no sectarian impediment discouraged intermarriage.[33] Over the next hundred and fifty years, normal assimilation produced families surnamed Arsenault, Buote, Gaudet, Poirier, and others whose dialect contained traces of Irish rhythms, expressions, and pronuncia-tions, as well as families with Irish names like Casey (Caissie) and Maddix whose genealogies and dialects were strongly Acadian.

The Language Question

Adapting to an English-dominated colony presented fewer linguistic difficulties to the Irish than to the Acadians. The Irish in exile dealt with the language issue as pragmatically as most of their kinfolk did in their homeland; in exchange for possible economic, social, and political recognition or advancement, and with mixed feelings, they simply surrendered (often with some reluctance) their ancestral Gaelic and embraced English.[34] After all, they realized that English was the dominant language of the worldwide British Empire, and within that orbit (or that of the United States of America) they would have to sur-vive. By making this investment, the Irish people incurred a deliberate deficit in at least the linguistic component of the cultural balance sheet. The Acadians, on the other hand, resolutely chose to preserve their native French, the language they correctly deemed essential to their culture.[35] On the centennial of the founding of Tignish, the local historian and editor Gilbert Buote summed up the Acadian heritage in these words: "N'oublions jamais d'observer fidèlement les préceptes qu'ils nous ont enseignés: l'amour de la patrie, la préservation de notre belle langue française, l'obéissance aux lois et une fidélité invio-lable à notre religion."[36]

There is much evidence to support the belief that the social philoso-phy of the Irish people, like that of the Acadians, also normally embraced patriotism, native language, civil law, and religion. Although the elements were similar, the priorities or emphases were different. The ethnic mix and social pressures, which varied from place to place in the new colony, certainly had a bearing on the retention or loss of the original languages. Inevitably, the gradual merger of Acadian and

Irish people that took place in remote western Prince County produced both cultural loss and cultural gain for both groups.

The Rev. A.E. Burke's late-nineteenth-century purview of Tignish and vicinity was notably, perhaps naively, magnanimous. He saw the descendants of Irish and French immigrants "side by side," labouring for a living, worshipping together in their church, and building a peaceful society: "Two branches of the great Celtic family in exile – as their fathers loved and trusted each other in that old land whence they came, they live in mutual regard here."[37]

Origins of the Tignish Irish

In his sunshine sketch of Tignish parish, Father Burke evidently was aware that the Irish people who assembled around the northwestern tip of the Island originated in such diverse places in Ireland as Waterford, Wexford, Kilkenny, Tipperary, Louth, and Monaghan, and, notably, Kerry.[38]

From County Louth came Edward O'Brien and his wife Martha Doherty, as well as James Phee, who married Catherine Woods from County Monaghan. Catherine's sister Mary married Patrick McCue from her home county, and when McCue drowned in 1818 she married William Handrahan. Handrahan had come from County Waterford before 1820 and resided briefly at Malpeque. Also from Waterford were James McGrath, Thomas Noonan, Richard Aylward, Patrick Hogan, and John Gavin. Prior to 1817, Mr and Mrs Gavin and eight Irish-born children had lived in New London, PEI.

County Tipperary was represented in the Tignish area in 1826 by John Carroll and his wife Ann Horan, as well as by 1835 arrivals William Dillon and Patrick Carrigan. In 1838 County Kilkenny sent to Seacow Pond (via Miramichi) Thomas Hackett and his wife Ellen Condon; to Nail Pond, Catherine Clohossey and her brother Patrick, who later wed Johanna Foley of Central Kildare; and to Kildare Capes, James Fitzgerald.

From 1835 the politically prominent family of Thomas Conroy (son Nicholas was especially active in provincial affairs) lived in Tignish and named their mansion the Grange after their former Wexford residence. A Christopher family, also from Wexford, gave their name to a crossroad near Tignish. Around 1839 Martin Doyle and his wife Catherine Sullivan settled on the western shore at Miminegash, and their three sons became successful farmers at Nail Pond; and in 1820 three Ahearn brothers (Joseph, Peter, and James) left Charlottetown to reside on the north side at Kildare.

Michael Brennan (in 1818) and John Broderick (in 1839) came to the Tignish area from Newfoundland; Timothy Casey, who had married a Miss Flynn in Miramichi, came west in 1844 from Cape Traverse and raised six children in Tignish. The counties of birth are not recorded for these three Irish families, but they are assumed to have emigrated from the southeast of Ireland.

The Kerry Influence

Generally on the Island, pre-Famine emigration from Kerry and Clare (where Irish was still the dominant spoken language) was not so prominent as from the southeast or Ulster or the midlands. Kerry folk were not numerous anywhere else on the Island, but they were generously sprinkled around western Prince County. We have already noted several Kerry families in Lot 7. Another mini-colony developed at Nail Pond, near Tignish. There, John Ready and Elizabeth Reilly were a pioneering couple who landed in 1811 in the company of brothers Edward and Michael Reilly. Mrs Elizabeth Ready was Michael Reilly's daughter. Edward's daughter (also named Elizabeth) was married to John Mansfield. Apparently all of these people travelled together from County Kerry via New Brunswick to the Tignish area. They were joined there in 1818 by Michael Brennan, and in 1819 by James McGrath and his wife Mary Kennedy.

In 1822 James McCarthy settled in the area; his daughter Margaret (as noted earlier) married Patrick Dalton. Also in 1822 John McCarthy, a weaver and farmer, first tried Lot 7 and then moved with his wife and family to Nail Pond. There, in the next generation, the McCarthy family tree sheltered Johanna Morrissey (married to Cornelius McCarthy), Bridget O'Halloran (married to Eugene McCarthy), and Bridget Doyle (married to Charles McCarthy). John McCarthy's daughter Margaret and her husband – she had married Patrick Dalton in County Kerry – arrived together in 1829 and established a large family in the Nail Pond–Tignish district.[39]

In 1830 John Dorgan and Margaret Lane, a couple from Capaclough in Kerry, settled in Seacow Pond near Tignish, where they too raised a large family. The family of schoolteacher Thomas Mansel (Mansfield) also lived there. In the same year John Kennedy, married to Mary Phee, came to Nail Pond. Two years later Patrick Nelligan and his second wife, Hanora Kennedy, arrived with his three sons. In 1839 Maurice Nelligan immigrated; in 1842 he married Margaret Phee, and their ten children grew up in the Tignish parish. Later arrivals in Tignish were Michael Ready and his wife Ellen Sullivan. Coming from Kerry via the Miramichi area of New Brunswick, they settled on the Island in 1844.

Also near Tignish, descendants of a post-famine immigrant family take pride in their genealogical connection with a famous American family. Edward Fitzgerald, apparently a Kerryman who had come to the Island from New York in the 1850s, urged his two brothers to follow him. One did, namely, Garrett Fitzgerald, who, in 1858 with his wife Mary (née Fitzgerald) settled on a farm in Waterford with their seven Ireland-born children. Mary's brother James, after a brief stay in Newfoundland, also settled in nearby Norway and married Christy Ann O'Brien. But Edward Fitzgerald's second brother, Thomas, who had wed Rosanne Cox in Ireland, chose not to come to the Island but to live in Acton, Massachusetts, near Boston. Thomas and Rosanne had a great-grandson named John Fitzgerald Kennedy. He became the thirty-fifth president of the United States of America.[40]

Other County Kerry immigrants included the Hanifins from Annagh, the McCarthy and O'Shea families from Kenmare, and schoolteacher Robert Slattery and Anglican Church minister David Fitzgerald, whose professional careers took them from Tralee to Charlottetown. In addition, as early as 1816, Irishtown (in Lot 20) was settled by a group of Kerry families (thus the place names Kerrytown Road and Kerrytown, later named Clinton); and before 1830 small numbers of Kerry folk arrived in Charlottetown via Newfoundland and continued their trek toward the western precincts of the Island. North of the capital, Michael and Charles Reardon built their homes in Covehead (Lot 34), as did Anne Reardon (Mrs William Carroll), who raised her twelve children there. In Hope River (Lot 22), schoolmaster William Sullivan and his wife Mary McArthy saw one of their nine children – son William Wilfred – become the first Roman Catholic premier of Prince Edward Island.

In summary, over half of the Island's known Country Kerry immigrants bunched together in the western peninsula, while the others dispersed to several other places on the Island.

LOCAL LEGENDS

Extensive marine traffic around the western region of the Island provided much employment in shipbuilding, sailing, fishing, and commerce. It also led to numerous mishaps and tragedies at sea. These accidents and hardships in turn engendered stories and legends – some factual, some far-fetched – which became embedded in the Island's lore and informed the consciousness of its nineteenth-century inhabitants just as profoundly as similar experiences affected their cousins in the distant Aran Islands or Dingle Peninsula.

A story well known locally relates how, one night in late October 1866, a fierce storm ripped the masts from the deck of the timber ship *Fanny Fern* (out of Miramichi, bound for Cork) and drove the hapless barque onto the reefs at North Cape. By mid-morning, first mate Smith and six crewmen reached shore, where they enlisted the help of Michael Shea and Mr McCarrey. Smith and the two landsmen then set out into the billows to rescue the crewmen on the stricken ship. A witness described their heroic attempt:

The Captain and the remainder of the crew got into the boat, and when about half the distance to the shore, a large sea struck the boat, upset her, and all the poor fellows were struggling in the water. Two boats were on the beach, which were immediately pushed off. They were not prepared, but out they went. Several of the persons on shore rushed to their necks in the water to try and save the poor fellows. It was a sad sight. The Captain was the first to reach wading ground, but he could not stand; the sea was breaking over him, and [he] would soon have perished had not a friendly hand come to his assistance. Four others of the boat's crew were saved in a fainting state. But sad to relate, Michael Shea, and McCarrey were drowned, besides Mr. Smith, the mate, and two other seamen. Mr. Shea was an honest, upright man, he leaves a widow and four small children; he is greatly regretted in the neighborhood. McCarrey was a stranger; he leaves a widow and three small children here – totally destitute. Mr. Smith, the mate, was a gentleman in appearance and conduct – a very superior man. He was an Irishman from Wexford, and was buried today at Tignish, together with those others of the poor fellows who lost their lives at the same time.[41]

The frequency of mishaps in Island waters called forth much heroism and caused much sorrow. Questions and rumours about the causes of these shipwrecks, as well as about profiteering from salvage operations, have enriched the Island's folklore. Accounts abound of treasure troves (including Captain Kidd's), of mysterious lights on the North Cape reefs and disembodied voices in the Hoar Bush woods.

Perhaps more engaging than speculation about mischief or stories of fortune-hunting along the beaches are the traditional tales of phantom ships. People in several locations on the Island have reported such mysterious sightings. Particularly in West Prince, residents have claimed that they have occasionally seen a burning schooner, the image being clear enough to discern passengers running about on the deck. This phantom ship is said to appear between late August and early October. Rather than dismissing these sightings as nonsense, some local sages who normally tend to be sceptical about reports of pirate treasure or forest apparitions have supposed an inexplicable connection between phantom ships and actual seacoast tragedies of long ago.

Amateur folklorist F.H. MacArthur, for example, tells about a similar mystery in "Phantom Ship of Sea Cow Head."[42] This strange occurrence was first reported in 1786 and has recurred on numerous occasions since then. MacArthur's version of the story begins:

It was midnight and a fine scotch mist blew in from the sea and spread itself over land and forest. The mournful cry of herring gulls mingled with the voice of the sea as it beat savagely against the rocky coast – it was a bad night for man or beast or ship to be out.

Into the teeth of the mighty storm rode a sturdy little schooner under full sail. A red light shone from her port side, a green light from the opposite side; and she was headed directly toward the high rocky cliffs.

Persons who were abroad that dreadful night caught momentary glimpses of the unknown, unnamed vessel, and vowed that she had neither captain, helmsmen, nor crew. In other words, she steered a reckless drunken course, toward what appeared to be her final doom.

Unlike the unfortunate vessels that actually crashed upon the rocky shore, the phantom ship in this story escaped such a tragedy. Since then, according to report, she has been seen many times in the Northumberland Strait, always managing to elude pursuers. Not so strange to say, perhaps, many Islanders seem to know more about phantom ships and similar mysteries than they do about factual history and the actual maritime tragedies that may have given rise to the local legends. In this matter, the Irish settlers were not alone in preferring a good story artfully embellished to the plain factual account of events.

KILDARE CAPES

In numerous havens all along the Island's coasts, from North Cape to East Point, people have divided their time, work, and interests – truly, their entire lives – between the land and the sea. Although these havens have much in common, each has singular features. On the gulf side of the peninsula, southeast of Tignish, for instance, extend the deep red cliffs and blue inlets of Kildare Capes. From there, in a line stretching over twenty miles to Richmond Bay, the golden sandhills gleam one mile offshore and yield their annual lavish tribute of wild blueberries. At one inlet, a particular craggy formation close to the shore became popularly known as Nature's Pulpit. Not far from there, when Jacques Cartier came ashore briefly in 1534, he remarked that the locality was "the fairest land that may possibly be seen."[43]

For the Irish people, the name Kildare resonates with legends of Saint Brigid (c. 453–524), who founded a great double monastery at Cill dara ("the cell of the oak grove") in the fifth century. A thousand years later, Kildare was also a title of the British nobility. It was no doubt the latter that Surveyor General Samuel Holland had in mind when in 1765 he conferred the name Kildare on a cape, a river, and an island (or point) in the unpopulated north shore of Townships Three and Four.[44] In naming nearly two hundred geographic features of the Island, Holland commemorated eminent military and political figures – in this instance, James, the twentieth Earl of Kildare (1722–73), heir of the distinguished Hiberno-Norman family of Fitzgerald and member of both the English House of Lords and the Irish parliament.[45]

More Irish Arrivals

In the first half of the nineteenth century, a motley collection of Irish families, along with other nationals, came by chance to the Kildare district of western Prince County. A small group of Acadians had been there since 1812. The Irish arrived a dozen years later. They had no recognized leader, no colonizer, entrepreneur, or clergyman to guide them. Though one was from County Louth, all the other settlers seem to have initially sailed from Ireland's southeastern region. None is known to have come directly from Ireland to Kildare Capes and vicinity, nor is there a dominant pattern to their arrival except in the sense that they were all wanderers. Some had tested the shores of Newfoundland, Nova Scotia, or New Brunswick before coming to Prince Edward Island. Even after they had found this Island, they tended to search about before putting down roots in Kildare. In any event, by the twentieth century the roots of virtually all the Irish family trees in that district had intertwined.

Patrick Cahill, married to Catherine Coady, came to the Island from Bannow, County Wexford, shortly after the 1798 rebellion in Ireland. He was one of several known PEI veterans or refugees from that struggle. The belief is that he was "actually engaged in the Rebellion of '98 in Ireland and was perhaps the last survivor of those of them who emigrated to America."[46] When Patrick reached Kildare about 1816, Walter Cahill, married to Anastasia Coady, was already there. John Cahill arrived in 1824. Moses Foley from Cowensworth was another 1816 arrival. Edward Foley landed in Halifax in 1798, and after coming to PEI and losing his original farm in Crapaud in a poker game, he ended up in Kildare, where he married Margaret Lane from Newfoundland. The Ahearn brothers – Joseph, Peter, and

James – arrived in Charlottetown in 1813 and moved to Kildare in
1820. Patrick Cluney and his wife Mary Cummings were late arrivals
(around 1850), having lived in Charlottetown and Brae before settling in Lot 3. Clearly, County Wexford was well represented in the
Kildare area of the Island.

William Ryan, Maurice O'Connor, and William Dillon represented
Tipperary. John Fitzgerald and his wife Christina MacDonald came to
this area in 1834, from Kilkenny. Timothy Gavin from Waterford
landed at New London in 1817, then moved to the western end of the
Island. County Carlow's only representatives were James O'Rourke
and his wife Mary Brennan, who came in 1841 via Chatham, New
Brunswick. The road they settled on in Lot 3 was named for them.

Other Irish family names on Meacham's 1880 map include Fitzpatrick, Connors, Lynch, Hammill, and McArthy in Lot 2; Fitzsimmons, O'Brien, Whelan, Power, and Mackay in Lot 3; and spilling over
into South Kildare in Lot 4 were families named Foley, Cahill, Quigley,
Moran, McAlduff, Larkin, and Cunningham. It is believed that the
McAlduff family had lived briefly in Quebec before coming to the
Island.

A charming connection between Central Kildare and Nail Pond is
related by Roy Clohossey, grandson of an 1848 immigrant from
County Kilkenny. When the elder Clohossey, named Patrick, arrived on
the Island, he was "dressed well, in a swallow-tail frockcoat, wool
knickers, and a top hat." Soon he purchased 65 acres and built a
sturdy house. Next, the family history records:

Patrick decided to take a wife. He heard that Edward Foley, formerly of Crapaud, Queens County, and now of Central Kildare, where the beautiful red-soil
capes are, had many beautiful daughters. Patrick walked to Kildare [some ten
miles], and he arrived late in the day. He rapped on the door of the Foley home.
Edward Foley came to the door. Patrick told him he was looking for a wife.
Mr. Foley sang out, "Johannah!" Johannah came down the stairs. Edward
Foley introduced daughter Johannah to Patrick. He told her that Patrick was
from Ireland, and that he lived in Nail Pond, and that he was looking for a
wife. She acknowledged, "I've always done your bidden, Da!" She packed her
things and went with Patrick to the farm at Nail Pond.[47]

For Patrick and Johannah the ritual of courtship was startlingly
brief, but their marriage was enduring, prosperous and prolific. Most
of their ten children chose to live in the Nail Pond–Tignish district.
Hasty courtships such as theirs are part of the lore in other colonial
families as well. Marriages were often facilitated by relatives, parish

priests, Old Country friends, neighbours, or even matchmakers – and marriages arranged between persons residing as much as a hundred miles apart were not unheard of. The wedding festivities sometimes lasted a fortnight, with week-long dancing and merrymaking at the family home of each of the newlyweds.

THE O'CONNOR DIARIES

Fortunately, many concerns of everyday life in Kildare around 1880 and earlier are captured in the matter-of-fact diaries of a local shop-keeper named Maurice O'Connor.[48] Although most of the entries are devoted to business transacted in his store (which dealt mainly in food-stuffs, hardware and some clothing), he was also preoccupied with the weather and fishing. These latter interests, of course, were characteristic of the whole district, and indeed the whole Island. The livelihood of many people depended on the fishery, and success in the fishery was obviously influenced by the weather. Often, therefore, notations that might seem dull to the urban dweller reflected serious concerns to the coastal dweller.

In this context O'Connor's notations were far from inane: "Big snow storm commenced" ... "Snow about 4 feet deep, the weather very stormy" ... "Feb. 13th Snowstorm about 8 feet of snow on the level" ... "Storm began and ice went" ... "Wind began to blow from north." Underlying such observations was O'Connor's practical concern about transportation and communication, and the business of the community. In 1884 he entered these notes: "May 11th snowstorm. 12 and 13th snowing still. Wednesday 14th fine day. Thursday 15th snowing heavily and wind North. Heavy body of ice along shore and very little farming done yet."

That year, the first schooner did not enter the harbour until 27 May, perhaps two or three weeks later than usual. Ice still clung along the shore, and northerly winds brought cold rain. Nevertheless, O'Connor sowed his wheat and early potatoes, and the next day he put in oats. On 29 May he began to mend his salmon nets. Then, suddenly, the west wind brought a fine morning, which drove out much of the harbour ice and enabled him to set one net. Judging the signs of the weather and prudent timing were keys to success in both planting and fishing. O'Connor's frequent observations on the severity of the climate are occasionally offset by pleasant notes such as this very Irish expression about the 1885 New Year's thaw: "January 1st, fine soft day. The fields are bare and covered with water."

June was normally a good month for netting salmon. In 1879

O'Connor set the nets late in May, and by 17 June he was able to record: "Have 33 salmon ... blowing from the north." Eleven days later he seemed pleased to note: "Got 17 salmon during the week, making 50 in all up to date." His catch was also good on 3 July: "Got one salmon this morning. afternoon 3." The diary alludes to herring, mackerel, and lobster, but salmon was the fish of first choice in O'Connor's business. His clientele included such Irish families as Ahearn, Cahill, Conroy, Fitzgerald, Foley, Heron, Mackay, O'Brien, O'Connor, and Whelan. Even while focusing upon the livelihood of only one shopkeeper, Maurice O'Connor's personal diaries reveal much about the community of which he was an important member.

ALBERTON AND CASCUMPEC

Less than ten miles down the coast from Kildare Capes, the town of Alberton developed. The Irish component of this town and the vicinity produced a remarkable share of the area's commercial and professional persons. A local history compiled by the Alberton Historical Group refers to many Irish-born citizens who operated stores or offices in early Alberton and nearby Cascumpec.[49]

Alexander Larkin (who had emigrated at age nine in 1829) ran a family store for forty years, until 1885. James Reid came to Cascumpec via Newfoundland in early 1850 and ran his store until he died in 1866. His two sons continued the business until 1874. From 1860 to 1882, George W. Howlan, who had a distinguished career in politics, conducted his store in Alberton. Dr Joseph P. Sherlock and Dr Cornelius O'Leary were early medical practitioners in Alberton. John C. Keefe was a carriage builder and hotelier (1866); Patrick Cunningham built carts, and John R. Larkin and Joseph Leonard were blacksmiths. Michael Foley dealt in dry goods and clothing, as did the Gavin brothers. In the 1870s Daniel O'Brien was a harness maker, Edmund Burke a tanner and shoemaker, William Kelly a tanner, Thomas Gamble a carpenter, B.D. Reddin a baker, and William Walsh a printer.

In some instances, succeeding generations continued the businesses which their pioneer forebears had begun. Well before the twentieth century, increasing mobility enabled entrepreneurs to change businesses, allowing both professionals and tradespersons to come and go. In these turnovers the names of many pioneers disappeared, but often they were replaced by other Irish names belonging to Island-born persons, such as Ahearn, Callaghan, Dunn, Foley, Keefe, McAlduff, McCue, MacKinley, Moran, Murphy, Noonan, O'Brien, O'Meara, Rooney, and Weeks.

St Anthony's Parish

St Anthony's parish in nearby Cascumpec, founded in 1803, was pre-dominantly Acadian.[50] It served the Catholics of Lots 4, 5, 6, 10, and 11 in the early years, but the church was rebuilt at Bloomfield in the 1860s, and separate parishes were later created at Foxley River and Alberton. Irish Catholics were numerous in Foxley River (as chapter 2 explained), and in Hills Point in Alberton. The Bloomfield parish and district remained heavily Acadian, though some Scots and English families also lived there. A small number of Irish were there too: Gavin's Inn was at Bloomfield Corner (also known as Gavin's Cross); George Howlan, who ran a business in Alberton, was a parishioner for seventeen years; and Patrick Lynch and Catherine Bulger established their family there in 1849. From early in the nineteenth century, in fact, Irish immigrants dispersed around Cascumpec Bay. In the Cascumpec area, as in the dozen communities surveyed in this tour of West Prince, many of the Irish family names carved on tombstones well over a century ago are still being inscribed on their descendants' roadside mailboxes and on storefronts, parish lists, sports pages, and school registers.

A Letter from Home

In 1968, when Roy Clohossey of Nail Pond was renovating his family farmhouse, he discovered concealed in the kitchen wall a letter written to his grandfather Patrick Clohossey and Patrick's sister Catherine, shortly after they emigrated to the Island. The letter was from their parents in Freshford, County Kilkenny. It reads:

Ballydoole December 28th, 1848

Dear Patrick and Catherine,

We received your long expected letter on the 23rd day of December, in which gave us the most consoling satisfaction in hearing of your safe arrival and good health at the destined port. Thanks be to providence for goodness to us. Dear Patrick, I am likewise happy to hear of my sister's good health and prosperity and hope she will prove a father and mother to you both which I have so much confidence she will do. And also that you both my dear children will be a consolation and prove satisfactory to her in her old days. Dear Patrick, I am sorry to have to inform you of the death of your sister Anty which took place on the 17th day of September 1848, and also of the death of your cousin James who died a fortnight before the death of Anty, and also the death of Patt Nary of Leiugh son to James. Dear Patrick, your brother Edmond is doing well and very much esteemed by his master. Dear Patrick, the crops in general proved very unsuccessful, not the least productive, wheat, not producing more than 5 barrels to the acre. And in the whole town land of Ballydoole, beyond the river, with the exception of John Martin, were noticed to give up their land and quit which some of them have done presently. Dear Patrick, I am very sorry you have not requested of us to be remembered to your worthy clergy, the Rev. Father Hart and Rev. Father Ryan, who had a great anxiety to see your letter. But from that mistake of yours, we were delicate in letting them see the letter which I hope you will not forget in your next. Dear Patrick, I am sorry your Uncle Thomas Roberts had been dead before your arrival, which I am well aware of would be as willing and as welcome to embrace you both as your Aunt. Dear Patrick, I have sent a newspaper with this letter, whenever it arrives. And, also, I will send you a paper weekly in the future. Dear Patrick, I am much surprised you did not mention in your letter anything about the climate of the country, or any information regarding that place, which I hope you will not forget in your next. Mr. and Mrs. Maxwell are in good health and happy to hear of your safe arrival and Mike Kale wishes to be remembered to you also.

Dear Patrick, we are much surprised that Catherine has not sent or spoke one word about herself to father or mother or to her nearest and dearest friend, as to whether she was sorry to leave home or anything else. James Hickey of Sart and family are gone to America and in fact, all families, if they can afford it will go in the spring. All friends and well wishers are in good health and very happy to hear ye were safely landed and in good health. And thank God the bears have not devoured ye. Dear Patrick, let us know whether your Aunt received the letter you sent in the past yourself not last July. So no more at present from your ever doting and affectionate parents.

Mr. and Mrs. Edmond Clohosy Ballydool

Dear Patrick, Mike Bisk sends his best, too, and respects to you both, and intends very probably next spring to sail for P.E.Island, if he thought that place good for his business, or any other situation he would be able to fill. Send an account in your next letter.

Although the letter is very personal and appeals most directly to family members and friends in the Nail Pond community, it also reaches a wider audience because it touches upon many aspects of Irish life: family closeness and responsibilities, crop failures and evictions in Ballydoole, deaths, respect for the clergy, neighbourly notes, desire for personal news and information about the colony, continuing emigration to America, and parental love for family members. The writer's homely style is pleasing too. This letter, one of the few still extant from the Island's Irish settlement period, is now cherished as an authentic relic of Irish culture of 150 years ago.[51]

TRADITION AND TRANSITION

By retaining many of its ethnic characteristics well into the twentieth century, the Irish principality in the western peninsula of the Island has demonstrated a remarkable hardiness. Despite local assimilation and cultural adaptation, the underlying spirit of an Irish Catholic rural community (however modified) has persisted for nearly two hundred years. Such stability might be expected of a planned and planted colony, but the West Prince settlements surveyed in these pages derived largely from the overflow of immigrants to the central part of the Island and the human flotsam carried there mainly from Newfoundland and New Brunswick.

After 1850 there was no further appreciable immigration to the Island from Ireland. Therefore this Irish concourse in western Prince County survived on its own human resources, with occasional replenishment from other parts of the Island. The relative remoteness of the area, the centrality of the church in the communal life, and the social stability of the family farm and other rural institutions all contributed to the retention of traditional values and customs well into the twentieth century. As these benign influences began to lose their active power, however, the old order made way for some new forces in culture. These new forces – largely products of advances in transportation and electronic communication in several forms – continue to gain ground. Still, in the 1990s the New Ireland Society in the West Prince district was conducting its own annual cultural gathering and festival of traditional Irish music, dancing, and entertainment – its members taking a nostalgic backward glance while stepping inexorably forward into the twenty-first century.

CHAPTER FIVE

Kings County's Irish Domain

Come all ye hardy sons of toil
Pray lend an ear to me
Whilst I relate the dismal state
Of this our country
I will not pause to name the cause
But keep it close in view;
For comrades grieve when they must leave
And bid this Isle adieu.

Lawrence Doyle[1]

In several respects the peninsula at the eastern extremity of the Island matches the West Prince peninsula. However, it is slightly smaller in area and population, and the Irish descendants and the French are less numerous. All over Kings County the Scots are much more prominent than any other nationality. An English nobleman was only briefly successful in his attempt to settle a group of Irish refugees near Bay Fortune in 1811; otherwise, Irish settlements in eastern Kings County appear to be creations of happenstance rather than design. In fact, several unrelated incidents account for families who augmented the general influx from Ireland's Waterford hinterland.

Historical documents contain important passages for establishing the factual framework of eastern Kings' story, but folk sources and less formal writings – such as memoirs, legends, fiction, verse, and song – may reveal the spirit of the place better. The following account therefore relies on a blend of factual history and less evidential tradition and popular culture to approximate the way residents have seen themselves.

For nearly three centuries, eastern Kings peninsula (Lots 42–7 and 56), with its sparkling bays, sandy inlets, and natural harbours has been a picturesque setting for inshore fisheries. The land itself has some productive farming tracts as well, but generally settlers found much of the area swampy, rocky, or thickly wooded.[2] This was one reason why the area was thinly populated; another was that the commercial concerns of such landowners as Sir Samuel Cunard and Robert Bruce Stewart, whose interests were in shipbuilding and lumbering, did little to encourage the settlement of their extensive holdings. Cunard alone controlled 212,000 acres, one-sixth of the Island's land mass (see map 6).

Moreover, in the early nineteenth century the area was remote and primitive. Before the Scots built roads, they tied tags on the trees or axe-chipped blazes into the bark to mark footpaths through woodlands where bears and other wild animals still prowled; and for transportation of goods between coastal settlements, they relied mainly on rough-hewn canoes, other small boats, or rafts. Illustrative of the hardships newcomers faced in that time and place is the story of a woman from Little Harbour whose fire happened to go out. This was before matches were available. "She had to walk a distance of nine miles and wade through two harbours, one of which was quite dangerous even in low tide, for there was a strong current and quicksand which were very difficult to pass through. On arriving at the French Marsh, South Lake, she filled a little pot which she was carrying with live coals buried in ashes and returned to rekindle her fire."[3]

Gradually the pioneers tamed the Eastern Kings wilderness and acquired the amenities of civilization. Lumbering and shipbuilding became important activities, complementing fishing and farming, and the port at Souris began its slow development into a busy town. By the early 1900s, the provincial railway had been cut through the core of the peninsula to its terminus at Elmira, and the perimeter trail and inland paths had been widened into roads linking the fishing stations that punctuated the coastline, so that at last eastern Kings could keep pace with the rest of the colony.

Today the traveller who enters eastern Kings at the upriver farming community of Dundas may follow the coastal road some sixty miles around East Point – where a stately lighthouse marks the northeastern tip, named *Kespemenagek* ("the end of the island")[4] by the Mi'kmaq – then westward along the north shore to the village of St Peters at the head of a long sheltered bay. On this coastal route, with detours into several inland hamlets, the attentive traveller may discern several Irish imprints on the cultural landscape of eastern Kings County.

SOME IRISH IMPRINTS

A dozen place names such as Rock Barra, Annandale, Glencorradale, and Selkirk signify that in eastern Kings the Scots (who had moved into

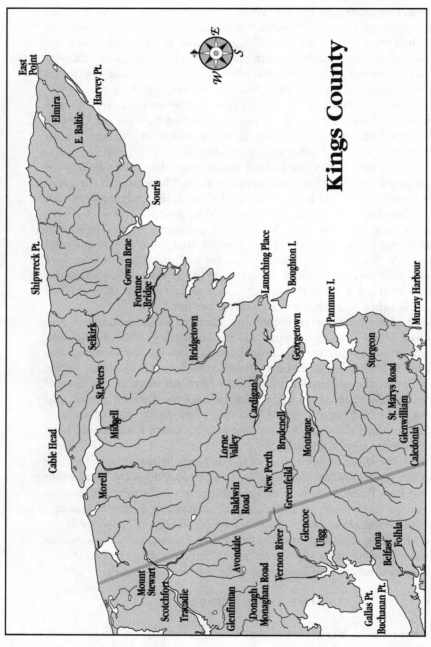

Map 6. In eastern Kings County the Irish were interspersed among the more numerous Scottish settlers.

that area late in the eighteenth century)[5] far outnumbered all others settlers. Nevertheless, from the 1720s the French were present at East Point
and St Peters Bay (St Pierre);[6] and other French signposts include Fortune, Souris, and Groshaut. English and Loyalist settlers, though present
in the peninsula since the 1780s, seemed content with Samuel Holland's
assignment of geographic names and left few place names of their own.

Relative latecomers, the Irish were equally neglectful. A notable
exception was Gowan Brae, the name that Attorney General Peter
McGowan (d. 1810) had conferred on his farm and residence three
miles from Souris. It became the name of the district in the 1860s.
Other Irish geographic designations seem more arbitrary, though
Greenvale (in Lot 46) was named by the Irish immigrant Daniel
Mooney in 1842; Creed Point (in Lot 59) took its name from an Irish
family there as early as 1789; and the district generally known as Baltic
was once called Irish Baltic because families bearing names such as
Dunphy, Griffin, Holland, Mooney, Moran, and Ryan settled there.
But the Irish have only partial claim to the place called Harmony, for
that name commemorates the long-standing amicable relations among
all four national groups in the area;[7] and even St Columba's parish at
Fairfield, though named for an Irish saint of royal lineage, really honoured him as the sixth-century founder of the historic monastery of
Iona, a tiny island in Scotland's Inner Hebrides. The Irish, it seems,
were scattered by mere chance through eastern Kings, and they left few
public reminders of their presence – other than their family names.

Yet even in memorializing their family names and origins, they
seemed neglectful. After all, they obviously believed that their neighbours knew who they were and where they came from, and they did
not realize that later generations might not be so well informed. Tombstones of fewer than 10 percent of the Irish settlers in Eastern Kings
County record their county of origin, and only a handful note the
native town or parish. Nevertheless, such evidence as there is on tombstones in Rollo Bay, Souris, Fairfield, Little Pond, and St Peters Bay
supports the general impression that the Irish immigrants in eastern
Kings County came mainly from southeastern Ireland. This conclusion
is adduced from the historical background of the names themselves,
from family records and traditions, and from the time and place of settlement. This being so, Daniel Mooney from County Antrim and
Thomas O'Donnell from Donegal, as well as Michael McWade,
Thomas McGaugh, Patrick McCluskey, and Thomas Manning (born
Monaghan), and a few other people from County Monaghan must be
regarded as independent travellers rather than forerunners of a potential movement of northern Irish settlers into this area. It was not until

1863 that James O'Brien and Mary McCullagh from County Monaghan established their home in Windon, by which time the James McGuire family from County Fermanagh had settled in Morell. Still, Ulster names remained a distinct minority.

Much more typical in eastern Kings up to 1850 are certain Tipperary names: James and Anastasia Mullally (from Mullinahone and Balicudon), Patrick Scully (a woodranger and landlord's assistant), and John Sullivan in Souris; Edward Kickham in Rollo Bay; John Pierce in Fairfield; and Daniel Mullin, James Whelan, Thomas Flynn, Richard Flynn and his wife Mary Hughes, Patrick Larkin, David Larkin and his wife Margaret O'Brien, Kearon Larkin and his wife Mary Ryan, Edward Power and his wife Margaret McCarthy, John and Johannah Bulger, and William and Ellen Decoursey – all buried at St Peters Bay.

Kilkenny names also are found at Rollo Bay (Richard Hayes); in Souris (Edward Grinsell and his wife Alice); at Little Pond (Patrick Power); and at St Peters Bay (Anastasia Fox married to James Whelan; Mary Mahar married to James Aylward; and Thomas Dwan, Michael Walsh, and Nicholas Power). The Morell district attracted the family of John Phelan and Honorrah Carey, who came via Nova Scotia from Freshford, County Kilkenny. County Wexford is represented at St Peters Bay by Jermiah O'Brien, in Souris by James Burris, and in Morell by the Rossiter family. Members of the Carey family, buried at St Margarets, came from County Mayo and settled in Monticello.

In *ABC of Kings County*, Joan Easton notes that prior to 1800 the Irish name Broh was found in Lot 47, and Creed and Keoughan in Lot 59; before 1832 Patrick Stephens owned property in Montague, where the O'Holleran, Rourke, and MacDiarmid families settled; by 1834 William Sanderson's diary counted more than thirty-five persons in Georgetown, including the families of Dr McKeown and John Kearney, and the tavern keepers Patrick O'Keefe and Jane Hadley. In the nine lots or townships constituting the eastern Kings peninsula (Lots 41 through 47, plus Lots 55 and 56), the number of Irish-born persons still resident there in 1848 was only 353 in a total peninsula population of 7,347.[8] In addition to the native Irish, of course, there were numerous Island-born Irish descendants – and numerous Newfoundland Irish as well.

NAMES IN THE NEWS

By reporting the rallies of various Island chapters of the Repeal Association, Edward Whelan's *Palladium* rendered a valuable public service to genealogists and historians. Genealogists are grateful for the lists of scores of Irish immigrants who contributed to Daniel O'Connell's Repeal Fund. Historians appreciate the records of an important political activity avidly engaged in by "the Irish in exile."

The Repeal Fund of 1843–44 supported the Irish movement led by Daniel O'Connell to repeal Britain's Act of Union (1800), which had bound Britain and Ireland in a unitary parliament. The movement, though unsuccessful in its primary objective, won adherents around the world; in Prince Edward Island, twenty-six districts formed chapters. In several places subscribers' names, and sometimes their places of origin, were recorded in Whelan's newspaper – and these lists proved to be a boon to family historians decades later, notably in Kings County.

For instance, the 7 March 1844 issue of the *Palladium* recorded the subscribers at East Point. From County Cork came Jeremiah Coghlin (Bantry) and Daniel, William, and Ann Collins (Kanturk); from County Kilkenny, Edmond Shea (Callan), Thomas Stone (Kilmurry), and Thomas O'Brien (Ardpatrick); from County Tipperary, James Morrissey (Cashel), and Thomas Morris (Grange); from County Wexford, Patrick Cavanagh (New Ross), Michael O'Brien (Tintern), and Felix Finn; from County Clare, Thomas MacMahon (Kildysart); and from County Sligo, Thomas Irwin.

In the issue of 28 December 1843, the *Palladium* listed the repeal subscribers at the St Peters Bay rally. From County Kilkenny came John Phelan (Freshford), John Ryan (Shannakill), Edmund Shea (Callan), Patrick Hickey (Gowran), Richard Cody and Thomas Mallowney (Mullinavet), John Walsh (Kilmacow), Patrick Tobin (Windgap), James Roach (Thomastown), and Thomas Murphy (Ballydole); from County Tipperary, Michael Mullally (Mullinahone), Thomas Gleeson and Michael Wyse (Thurles), Patrick and John Sweeny (Anacarthy), Daniel Hogan (Borrisokane), Patrick Keefe (Caher), and Michael Scully, Sr (Kilderin); from County Waterford, Thomas Hennessy (Ballybricken), John Kennedy (Cappoquin), and Thomas Donovan (Kilmacthomas); from County Wexford, Patrick Redmond (Taghmon), James McKay (Knockbyrne), Simon Kehoe (Pollparty), and Michael Thomas (Saltunnels); from County Cork, Patrick Hillgrose (Youghal); from County Limerick, Thomas Condon (Wilbarry); and from County Monaghan, Peter Kairns (Kilmore). In addition to the Irish subscribers, there were four from Inverness Shire in Scotland (Dougald MacIsaac, Angus MacAulay, Donald MacDonald, and Mrs E. Cooke); one from Newfoundland (John Butler), and one native of Prince Edward Island (Archibald MacAulay).[9]

Taken at face value, the newspaper reports of local rallies simply listed the names and homeland addresses of Island contributors to the Repeal Fund. But more importantly, by printing these lists, the newspaper was documenting a communal event in which Irish exiles publicly declared their moral and monetary support for a patriotic cause. The act itself was an expression of pride; it consisted of each individual declaring his convictions and identifying himself by his name, his family, and his hereditary home. This ritualistic act exemplified an old Irish custom carried over to the new settlement: the people stood up and were counted. Among the Irish people – in Kings County, Prince Edward Island, no less than in, say, County Offaly, Ireland – the mystique of ancestral names and the memories of ancient home places continue to possess force and significance. They loved the land they had left behind them. Depending on the circumstances of their arrival and settlement, most Irish immigrants were also happy to acclaim Prince Edward Island their new home.

ORDEAL AT SEA

Aside from the data already cited, scattered fragments of information pertaining to Irish immigration and settlement in Kings County sometimes lend themselves more to imaginative narratives than to historical accounts, for what little is recorded tends to reflect popular legend and tradition rather than authoritative documentary evidence. A case in point is the ordeal endured by passengers aboard a vessel called the *Aeolus* – the ship on which Patrick Pearce, Valentine Needham, and other Irish immigrants were once believed to have sailed to Prince Edward Island.

Local history maintains that in 1811 HMS *Aeolus* anchored in Fortune Bay (Lot 43) to disembark several families from Belfast, who were to settle on Lord Townshend's lands in Lot 56. It now seems clear that the *Aeolus* was the British naval ship that brought the settlers from Halifax to the Island, certainly not the commercial vessel that transported them from Ireland to Halifax. Furthermore, it is possible that the emigrants sailed from Dublin rather than (or in addition to) the port of Belfast. While these matters require further research, immediately germane is the November 1982 newsletter of the Prince Edward Island Genealogical Society, containing a passenger list of Irish emigrants, submitted by Annabelle Powell.[10] As the information in Ms Powell's article appears to be valid, and as it complements an oft-cited narrative written by the popular novelist Captain Frederick Marryat, it is reasonable to construe that the high seas adventures of those 1811 Irish immigrants consisted of two episodes: the first off Newfoundland, the second near Halifax.

In the Powell correspondence, the emigrant ship is identified as the *Belisarius* commanded by Captain Morgan, sailing for forty-two days from Dublin and arriving in New York on 5 July 1811. West of Georges Bank, Newfoundland, the British sloop HMS *Atlanta* intercepted the *Belisarius* and "forced on board" sixty-two Irish passengers who, it was alleged, had failed to "clear out or pass the custom-house."

This action took place on 24 June 1811. A witness described "the shrieks of the unfortunate parties on being dragged into the boats, the lamentations of the aged parents who were left behind, the wife clinging to her husband, – the child grasping the knee of its more than distracted father, on giving up his last hope to provide for his little ones, and doomed to serve his tyrants."[11] Precisely what this distressing scene describes is not explicitly stated; but it appears that in keeping with policies of that time, the British warship forcefully removed the able-bodied male civilians from their passenger ship and conscripted them into the Royal Navy. Judging from a later statement, it seems that of the sixty-two men who had been seized, only seventeen were ultimately detained on the warship. The others were taken to an undeveloped colony in eastern Prince Edward Island. Sad to relate, even the safe landing in Bay Fortune of these refugees after their trauma on the high seas does not conclude their story.

First of all, it must be noted that Captain Frederick Marryat's fictionalized version of these transactions, in *Frank Mildmay, or The Naval Officer*, differs from the Powell document in several particulars. In Marryat's novel, the meeting of his naval vessel with the emigrant ship is not described as a distressful incident at all. He says nothing about the seizure of the Irishmen, nor does he allude to the *Atlanta* or identify by name the Irish merchant vessel his sloop encountered soon after sailing out of Halifax. Instead, he writes:

We had not been long at sea before we spoke an Irish Guineaman from Belfast, loaded with emigrants for the United States – I think about seventeen families. These were contraband. Our captain had some twenty thousand acres on the island of St John's, or Prince Edward's, as it is now called, a grant to some of his ancestors which had been bequeathed to him, and from which he had never received one shilling of rent, for the very best reason in the world – because there were no tenants to cultivate the soil. It occurred to our noble captain that this was the very sort of cargo he wanted, and that these Irish people would make good clearers of his land, and improve his estate. He made the proposal to them, and as they saw no chance of getting to the United States, and, provided they could procure nourishment for their families, it was a matter of indifference to them where they colonised, the proposal was accepted, and the captain obtained permission of the admiral to accompany them to the island to see them housed and settled. Indeed, nothing could have been more advantageous for all parties; they increased the scanty population of our own colony, instead of adding to the number of our enemies. We sailed again from Halifax a few hours after we had obtained the sanction of the admiral, and passing through the beautiful passage between Nova Scotia and the island of Cape Breton, known by the name of the Gut of Canso, we soon reached Prince Edward's Island.[12]

The Powell document relates that at Halifax, a *Belisarius* refugee named William Phelan witnessed the transfer of forty-three of the sixty-two Irish captives from HMS *Atlanta* to an unnamed sloop (presumably the *Aeolus*), which took them to Prince Edward Island. William and Patrick Phelan were the only *Belisarius* captives who were permitted to leave the *Atlanta* and remain in Halifax. The other seventeen men (whom William Phelan recalled by name) had been impressed – drafted into enforced service aboard the British naval vessel, presumably the *Atlanta* – and, presumably, separated forever from their families and friends.[13]

After subtracting the names of the two Phelans and the seventeen impressed men, the list that remains provides a putative roster of the Irish immigrants who were set ashore at the estate of Lord James Townshend in eastern Prince Edward Island. William Phelan referred to forty-three individuals who were sent to the Island, but he singled out only the following twenty persons and their families: Richard King, Jane King, James King, Mary King, Jane King, John Gilbert, John Birk, Eliza Birk, Thomas Walsh, Thomas Newman, Lawrence Current, Thomas Bird, Mary Bird, Valient Needham, Catherine Needham, Eliza Needham, Joseph Gilbert, Ann Gilbert, Ally Burton, and Michael Murphy.[14] Among those not individually named by Phelan (though they were included among the original sixty-two Irish passengers and therefore may be presumed to have been among the forty-three persons who were directed to the Townshend settlement) are the following: "Benjamin Tuckerbury and family, Mary Ann Gilbert, Denis Menteur (Menieur?), Rev. Mr Ryan, Robert Hughs and family, William Nailor and family, Jane Connor and family, Patrick Pierce, William MacDonald, Stephen Mathews and wife, Henry Stanhope and wife, William Harding and wife."[15]

Tracing these names forward from the early nineteenth century remains a challenge for individual family historians; but it is evident from cadastral maps, censuses, and other sources that few of these families attempted to put down roots in eastern Kings County. For the many who obviously chose to settle elsewhere, landing at Abells Cape served at best as a temporary toehold, a mere springboard. It may be more precise to describe their situation as having been precarious, or bordering on disaster. Certainly, the minutes of a meeting called by Governor Joseph F.W. DesBarres on 18 July 1811 acknowledge the refugees' distress: "His excellency informed the Board that he had called a meeting in consequence of a messenger having arrived from Fortune Bay who represented that forty persons in extreme want of provisions had lately arrived from Ireland at Fortune Bay and had prayed for some relief from Government."[16] After viewing an abstract of the public accounts, the board decided "that relief cannot with propriety be afforded to the above mentioned persons."

The evident lack (not to say, refusal) of emergency relief for the refugees who were deposited on a strange shore, when added to the stressful circumstances of their enforced recruitment and the traumatic separation at sea from their families and friends, justly portended the ultimate failure of Lord Townshend's Irish colony. Ms Powell's intriguing communication to the genealogical society therefore adds interest to the longstanding speculation about the fate of one group of Irish emigrants who were cast ashore in Kings County.

Unfortunately, Captain Marryat's novel provides only a generally romantic depiction of the event. Nevertheless, although he was writing fiction, not history, the popular author seems at times to have drawn upon eye-witness experience in the persona of Midshipman Mildmay, aide-de-camp to the captain, Lord Townshend. When, for instance, Marryat tells about the arrival of the emigrants at "a small harbour near the estate" in Prince Edward Island, his fairly precise description is entirely credible:

A large party of the ship's company came on shore with the carpenter, bringing with them every implement useful in cutting down trees and building log-houses. Such was to be our occupation, in order to house these poor emigrants. Our men began to clear a patch of land by cutting down a number of pine-trees, the almost exclusive natives of the wood; and having selected a spot for the foundation, we placed four stems of trees in a parallelogram, having a deep notch in each end, mutually to fit and embrace each other. When the walls by this repeated operation were high enough, we laid on the rafters, and covered the roof with boughs of the fir and the bark of the birch-tree, filling the interstices with moss and mud. By practice I became a very expert engineer, and with the assistance of thirty or forty men, I could build a very good house in a day.

We next cleared, by burning and rooting up, as much land as would serve to sustain the little colony for the ensuing season; and having planted a crop of corn and potatoes, and given the settlers many articles useful in their new abode, we left them, agreeable to our orders, and to my great joy returned to dear Halifax.[17]

Setting aside both fiction and hearsay, the question remains, How successful was the actual colonization effort in Lot 56? By the 1848 census (thirty-seven years after the *Aeolus* adventure), 6,821 acres were under lease, 520 acres occupied under verbal agreements, and only 342 acres listed as privately owned. Therefore, occupied acreage was less than half the township. The population had reached 783, of whom 352 were under sixteen years of age. Of the 140 foreign-born persons living there in 1848, 30 had come from England, 39 from Scotland, 38 from British colonies, and 33 late arrivals from Ireland. As some (many?) of the British colonials were presumably Newfoundland Irish, perhaps about one-third of the immigrant population referred to was Irish.[18] Ironically, well before the end of the nineteenth century virtually none of the Townshend-planted Irish families were still represented in or near Lot 56. Writing in 1910, Bay Fortune historian J.C. Underhay observed: "None of the farms settled by Lord Townshend at the time of his visit here are now occupied by any descendant of the emigrants, their only known descendant now being Edward Needham, a well-known citizen of Charlottetown, who was about a year old at the time of [Land Agent Edward] Abel's death" in 1819.[19] Thus the Townshend enterprise held no lasting appeal for Irish settlers. As a plantation it lacked healthy roots.

INCIDENT AT ABELLS CAPE

Although it was once hopefully believed that the infamous seventeenth-century Scottish privateer Captain William Kidd had cached pirate treasure in the vicinity of Bay Fortune, a more verifiable legend about the area concerns a tragedy at Abells Cape, about eight miles from Souris. There, in 1819, a mortal conflict occurred between an Irish immigrant named Patrick Pearce (also spelled *Pierce*) and the resident land agent named Edward Abell (also spelled Abel). At the outset we should recall that Viscount George Townshend, an English officer who had served with General Wolfe at Quebec and who later was appointed Lord Lieutenant of Ireland, was awarded Township Fifty-six in the grand lottery of 1767. His son James, the naval officer discussed above, inherited the township. Though young Lord Townshend did indeed visit his property for a few weeks in 1811, occupying Edward Abell's house and barn, and erecting log cabins for his newly arrived tenants, he was thereafter an absentee landlord.

He entrusted the administration of his estate to Edward Abell, a farmer and merchant as well as a land agent. Officious and obnoxious in his dealings with tenants, Abell, it is said, "applied for so many summonses and foreclosures against the tenants in distress that he sometimes found it difficult to get a Justice of the Peace to act for him."[20] Meanwhile, he lived in comparative prosperity on 500 acres known as Red House. A contemporary fictional account describes the steward of the Townshend lands in Prince Edward Island as "rascal enough for the stewardship of any nobleman's estate in England."[21] The local historian J.C. Underhay asserts that Susannah Abell was a good match for her husband, being "a selfish and unscrupulous woman who goaded him on to acts of harshness and injustice."[22]

Patrick Pearce, born in 1789 in Ireland, may have immigrated to the

Island in 1811 as a hostage in the *Aeolus* incident; or as some people believe, he may have come out in 1815 after having served at Waterloo. He began farming, paying a rent of what was said to have been one English shilling per acre per year.[23] On his 100–acre leasehold beside Fortune Harbour, Pearce built a small cabin not far from Red House, acquired a trusty black horse, and settled down to unrelenting labour. Needless to say, in colonial Prince Edward Island, a sturdy horse was both a practical asset and a symbol of social status. Neighbours at the time wondered, as their descendants do now, whether Edward Abell coveted Patrick Pearce's sleek black horse. Or did Mrs Abell, perhaps, covet that animal even more than her husband did?[24]

Folk tradition and a newspaper report have preserved the salient beliefs about what happened on 24 August 1819.[25] It seems that as Pearce did not possess in British currency the combined lease and quitrent payments that Abell demanded, he went from neighbour to neighbour until he had collected the required amount. Included in the total, however, was some non-British coinage, which Abell rejected because, he said, it was unacceptable currency in England. Abell, we are told, then threatened to seize the hard-working tenant's black horse in lieu of the required currency. Even when Pearce's second collection among his neighbours produced the required coins, Abell would not accept the money. He had already determined to take the horse. Thus provoked to anger, Pearce resorted to violence – not in cold-blooded premeditation but in the heat of righteous indignation. A former soldier, he ran to his cabin, fetched his Queen Anne musket with its long bayonet attached, and stabbed Abell first in the arm and then in the groin or "through the back part of the thigh into the intestines."[26] Four days later, Edward Abell died. In his will he left his entire estate to his wife. It is not known whether she ever got the coveted black horse.

Meanwhile, Patrick Pearce became a fugitive, taking shelter among his fellow tenants, who sympathized with him. Perhaps some people saw in the violent incident near Red House a parallel with the lamentable experiences endured during the penal times in Ireland, when possession of a fine horse was considered to be the exclusive prerogative of "fine Ascendancy gentlemen," and Catholic "bogtrotters" could therefore be dispossessed of any horse valued at over five pounds. Pearce's friends, regardless of their national or sectarian background, probably realized that in sheltering him in their woods and cellars, they were re-enacting a long-standing Irish practice of harbouring fugitives from abusive authority. They certainly knew that helping Pearce escape was a violation of Governor Charles Douglas Smith's orders. While they left the finer points of legality and morality to future generations to ponder, the ordinary people of that time did what they thought necessary to assist their neighbour in distress.

Not only did they ignore the fact that a reward of twenty pounds had been offered for Pearce's capture;[27] but they materially helped him escape.

One hundred and eighty-five years after the event it is not possible to establish all the details, but a composite version of traditional accounts indicates that Pearce managed to hide in the woods or with sympathetic friends during the winter of 1819. First, a family named Burke sheltered him in their cellar, then Joseph Brown and John Black took turns concealing him at Cape Spry. In the spring of 1820, writes Adele Townshend, Pearce "swam across Blackett's Creek and stayed the night in the attic of George Banks' home in Annandale. The next day the young Banks girls, Mary and Elizabeth, dressed the fugitive in their mother's clothes and rowed him out to a vessel anchored in Grand River."[28] From there, an American sea captain, Nicholas Falla, transported him to safety.

What later became of Patrick Pearce or his family is not recorded. His cottage, soon abandoned, eventually disappeared. Edward Abell's place, long believed to be haunted by his ghost, was still in use early in the twentieth century. There is no trace of that house now, but the official names Red House and Abells Cape still evoke images of one of the most sensational incidents in colonial times. And, for the Irish, one of the most symbolic.

SHIPWRECK SURVIVORS

As the account of Lord Townshend's attempt to colonize Lot 56 has shown, at least one small group of Irish refugees who were set ashore in eastern Kings County were mere pawns of the international power struggle on the high seas; but a few other small groups, who also deserve recognition, landed on eastern Kings shores as victims of shipwrecks. Although no armadas were destroyed in the Gulf of St Lawrence, sailing mishaps were quite frequent in the vicinity of Prince Edward Island – and these shipwrecks occasionally accounted for unexpected arrivals of refugee settlers.

The notorious Yankee Gale, lasting three days in 1851, caused eighty-three wrecks and a hundred and sixty drownings along the Island's north coast and drove fifteen ships ashore in the forty miles between East Point and Savage Harbour. The following year, as local historian George A. Leard relates, twenty-one ships piled up against the cliffs of Souris East, and "two hundred shipless fishermen were billeted that night in the hospitable homes of Souris."[29] Back in 1824, *True Friend*, a brigantine caught in a gale, had gone aground on the

East Point reef. In October 1829 five lives were lost when the *Marchioness of Donegal* from Belfast was wrecked at Little Pond. Four years later another brigantine, the *Planter*, was wrecked near the same place, and in 1856 three lives were lost when the *Henrietta* capsized near Kingsboro. Perhaps the best documented incident involved the *Sovinto*, a Russian brigantine bound for Australia with a cargo of lumber from New Brunswick. The ship's master misjudged the coastal lighthouses and crashed his ship upon the rocks near Priest Pond, twelve miles short of East Point.[30]

Another seafaring mishap, in 1822, accounts for a small group of Irish families becoming established in eastern Kings County. The *San Domingo* (Lewis, master) arrived in Charlottetown on 20 June 1822 with eighty-seven passengers from Ireland.[31] This seems to be the same schooner that met with misfortune three days later. While taking Irish immigrants to Newfoundland after their stopover in Charlottetown, it is believed that the vessel was blown off course and tossed upon the rocks at Beaton Point near the northeastern tip of Prince Edward Island. There, a threatening reef that extends two and a half miles out to sea is still known locally as the San Domingo Rocks.

An Island writer, George Keefe, recently published a poem about a visit to East Point, in which he discovered personal significance in an historic event:

It was the same reef
that so many nights before
(a hundred years or more)
cut into the innards
of a freighter
laden with Irish folk
fleeing from you-know-what
to God-knows-what
on the shores of Quebec.

For here at East Point,
blown far off course
the freighter fell
upon the reef
one dark night
and a man
whose spirit
stirs in my blood
clawed his way to shore.[32]

Local accounts of the *San Domingo* shipwreck are confusing. For instance, the vessel is variously called *San Domingo*, *Santo Domingo*, and *St Domingo*, and the Irish port of origin has been given as both Ross and Wickford (a supposed place name, which seems to be a jumble of Wicklow and either Wexford or Waterford); but in another context one of the passengers is said to have sailed from Queenstown (i.e., Cork). There is even disagreement about whether the wreck occurred in 1822 or 1823.[33] Despite such discrepancies and some gaps in the records, general information about the passengers seems reliable. Some of them certainly settled in eastern Kings County, notably in the community then known as Portage (signifying the land route between North Lake and South Lake) but after 1872 called Elmira (or, as in the 1880 *Atlas*, Almira).

Local speculation persists that some of the *San Domingo* passengers may have been Scottish rather than Irish, but Adele Townshend, a well-informed local historian, states: "All but one of the young families, English soldiers stationed in Ireland married to Irish girls, decided to settle in Elmira."[34] The family names generally associated with the shipwreck include Campion, Drummond, Harris, Hughes, Pierce, Price, and Tierney. (Moses Harris and his wife both lived more than a hundred years.)

OTHER EXPERIENCES

The adventures of the *Aeolus* and the *San Domingo* were certainly not typical of the immigrant arrivals. Most Irish families came to eastern Kings County unassisted by a coercive proprietor or a frightening "act of God." Most newcomers, having endured a tedious, sickening voyage, then undertook a back-breaking trek through woodland paths in search of hospitable places to settle.

In their quest for suitable farmsteads in Kings County, the Irish usually extended the beaten forest paths. The French had been present as early as the 1720s in St Peters Harbour, Bay Fortune, and elsewhere. Farther east, in St Peters Bay and beyond, the English had come late in the eighteenth century, and the Scots followed in much greater numbers. Slowly moving in early in the nineteenth century, the Irish (from Newfoundland as well as from Ireland) managed to populate several coastal areas. At that time clay roads in gridlike fashion linked inland settlements with the coastal villages. On the first of these roads, in Elmira, there were families named Bailey (Bayley), Campion, Druhan, Hackett, Harris, Holland, McMahon, Murphy, Pierce, Price, and Sweeney. Even before these Irish people came – possibly as early as 1798 – Scottish families were already established there. As the place name Harmony implies, the Irish lived harmoniously with the more numerous Scots. In 1848 there were still forty Irish-born residents in Lot 47, but by 1880, as the Meacham *Atlas* indicates, the Elmira Irish community had dwindled. This decline may be attributed to both out-migration and assimilation.

Along the East Baltic Road, starting at Red Point with the Hackett family and running through to Priest Pond, there were once Irish settlers with such surnames as Dunphy, Ellsworth, Fay, Griffin, Holland, Mooney, Moran, Murphy, O'Grady, and Ryan. Also inland, at Greenvale, were the Irish families of Mooney and Cavanaugh. In 1848 there were still forty-four Irish-born residents in Lot 46. This East Baltic Irish community survived into the twentieth century. At St Catherines (Lots 45 and 46) there were settlers named Morris and Hennessey, and at New Zealand (Lot 44) resided the Conways, while in Chepstow (Lot 45) and Little Harbour (Lot 46) were found such family names as Foley, Johnston, Kennedy, McMahon, Nolan, O'Hanley, and Power.

In none of these communities were the Irish dominant. Nor were they dominant in Souris, Rollo Bay, or St Peters, even though they were numerous there. In Elmira and the Townshend territory their colonies were small at the outset and negligible by the end of the nineteenth century. It is therefore fair to conclude that in eastern Kings County generally the Irish remained a significant minority.

New Acadia

Nevertheless, those small groups of Irish settlers adapted well to the multicultured mix in the area. The parish of St Charles Borromeo was founded in 1882 to serve about thirty Acadian families from Rustico who had moved into the Bear River area of the northern sector of St Alexis parish in Rollo Bay. (This is where Lots 42 and 56 meet.) They called their settlement New Acadia. Just west of it was the settlement they called Groshaut, where about twenty Irish and Scottish families had lived for a generation or two before the Acadians arrived. On the Groshaut Road were found such Irish surnames as Bolan and Bowlin, Gorman, Cooney, McCarthy, Sullivan, Shea, and Cahill. In the Bear River area Meacham's 1880 *Atlas* shows such Irish names as Costello, Kickham, Kelly, McCluskey, Moriarty, and O'Keefe, but not all who owned land in the area actually lived there.

The small rural parish of St Charles became notable, indeed notorious, for an annual social event – called a tea party, or picnic – which parishioner Lawrence Doyle commemorated in a ballad. In many places on the Island, church teas were popular warm-weather entertainments, both as social gatherings and as fundraisers. Often held on church lawns, they normally featured a light lunch and beverage, the auctioning of cakes and pies, and musicmaking and dancing. As well, inevitably, there was some surreptitious sipping of whisky or rum, and sometimes brawls erupted. At Groshaut in 1897 or 1898 the offending agent was a supply of hard cider delivered ("mistakenly," some said) to the parish picnic. The parish priest, a strict teetotaller, took umbrage at the whole affair and thereafter banned the picnic. Good-natured Lawrence Doyle, a normal hard-working farmer who lived nearby, taking a more traditional Irish view, captured forever the jovial spirit of the event in popular rhythm and rhyme.

Doyle's ballad, entitled "The Picnic at Groshaut," tells how the sedate parish tea party turned into a lively frolic – with fisticuffs as well as dancing – after some picnickers broke open a few barrels of strong cider. The ballad ends with these verses:

Perhaps it was a shame but there's no-one for to blame,
'Twas nothing but an accident you know;
'Twas continued the next day but the spirit died away
And the cider changed to water at Groshaut.

So now the tea is over and the boys again are sober
And they'll always taste the cider for to know;
If it's hard, they'll take it light, if it's soft they'll leave it quite,
But they'll not forget the tea was at Groshaut.[35]

Over a century later this amusing ballad still brings to mind the event that inspired it and the composer whose skill kept it alive. In his time and place Lawrence Doyle (1847–1907) was the leading balladeer among a host of storytellers and minstrels who created their own unpretentious entertainments. Collectively, they were bearers and custodians of secular tradition.

In some country places immigrants played flutes or fiddles, a few had concertinas, and here and there could be found a set of uillean pipes. Commonly, in Island cabins people danced to "mouth music" or "jigging," as well as to humming on a paper-covered comb or to the music of a harmonica. The luxury of pianos and parlour organs was unknown until late in the nineteenth century. Local songmakers often fitted their lyrics to popular Irish airs, and the singing of such ballads as Doyle's "When Johnny Went Plowing for Kearon" or "The Picnic at Groshaut" was usually unaccompanied by musical instruments. Those early folk compositions are still valued for the insights they provide into the cultural adaptation of Irish immigrant families.

The mention of music among the Irish in eastern Kings recalls another occurrence early in the past century. It seems that venerable Dr Gus, returning home at daybreak after an all-night emergency house call in St Charles, heard music coming from the deep dark woods along the lonely Sheehan Road. He halted his horse and listened. Again he heard the unmistakable strains of a fiddle. Presently, through a dim opening in the trees he spied in the distance, silhouetted against the golden dawn, the figure of a man joyfully stroking his fiddle – playing his heart out at the rising sun. A minute later, the doctor quietly returned to the road, patted his curious horse assuringly, and resumed his long journey home. Years afterward, neighbours in Souris still speculated that the doctor had seen an apparition, a spectre who haunted the mystic woods. Some even guessed it was a spirit from the Celtic past paying homage to the rising sun. Less poetic souls, however, knowingly insisted that the happening was not emblematic at all but was merely a local fiddler, Jack Lawlor, up to one of his unpredictable pranks. The good doctor never did pass judgment on the incident; he simply made light of it.[36]

St Peter's

Before the building of St Charles's Church, the Irish from the Mansfield district (as it was then called) generally worshipped at St Peter's Church. The village of St Peters (formerly written St Peter's) is situated at the head of a seven-mile-long bay on the peninsula's north side. The substantial Irish component of this largely Scottish parish originated in Ireland's southeastern counties, and they evidently came to the St Peters district as a byproduct of the long-standing commerce between Prince Edward Island and Newfoundland. As north-shore ports that could accommodate smaller trading vessels became involved in this trade, they also received a portion of the immigrants from Newfoundland. Other immigrants may have come via Halifax or via Cape Breton by sailing through the Strait of Canso to St Peters and other Kings County anchorages. In the Catholic cemetery at St Peter's Church, ninety tombstones refer explicitly to birthplaces in Tipperary (41), Kilkenny (32), Wexford (11) and Waterford (6). As noted earlier, Professor John Mannion's studies have established that the same counties supplied about 80 percent of Newfoundland's Irish population. Even while acknowledging the importance of the Newfoundland connection in accounting for the southeastern Irish influx to Kings County, we must be mindful that after 1815 a number of passenger vessels skirted Newfoundland and brought immigrants from those same Irish counties directly to Charlottetown and other Island ports.[37]

Fortune Road

By whatever route they took, settlers from Ireland's southeast certainly established some semblance of community along the Fortune Road, from Five Houses through the Farmington district, in the direction of Bay Fortune. Both the 1861 census and the 1880 *Atlas* include family names commonly found in southeastern Ireland: Curran, Larkin, Butler, Ryan, Flynn, Walsh, Bulger, Cahill, McTeague, and Power (from Five Houses); Russell, Ryan, Walsh, Cleary, Hogan, and Sullivan (in Farmington district); Flynn, Tobin, Doyle, Larkin, Whitty, Walsh, Murphy, and Conahan (toward Bay Fortune). Clearly, the Fortune Road settlement was predominantly Irish and Catholic. Among the settlers in 1841 were James Doyle and his wife Sarah O'Hanley, jokingly said to have been "kicked out of Newfoundland." It was their son, Lawrence Doyle, who later became renowned as "the farmer poet."[38]

Remarkable as lyricist Doyle was, he did not stand alone. Like Larry Gorman, his contemporary in Prince County, Doyle was a product of a society that enjoyed music and singing, and in which songmaking was a common home entertainment. It is said that the woods were once full of fiddlers, stepdancers, singers, rhymers, and storytellers. Most of their compositions, having been inspired by local events in their own lifetime, passed away with them, but the songs that have survived (or have been revived) give later generations glimpses of a way of life that was greatly enriched by the shared folkways of the founding peoples of the Island.

IRISH PEOPLE IN THE SOURIS AREA

The coastal road that rims the eastern Kings peninsula passes through Souris and thereby serves as the main street of the area's largest community. It was the building of John Knight's breakwater in the 1830s and the coming of the railway in 1875 that truly enabled Souris to flourish as a fishing and trading centre and led to its incorporation as a town in 1910. Incidentally, the town acquired its name when the early French inhabitants, having suffered a plague of mice in 1724, called the place *Havre à la Souris* (Mouse Harbour).[39]

Local historians tell of Mi'kmaq bands spending summers fishing on the tidal flats of Souris River long before the first group of Acadians arrived at Bay Fortune in the 1720s. Early in the nineteenth century, a later generation of Acadians arrived at Souris, including Michael Cheverie (1805), Jean and Toussaint Longaphie (1810), Fidele and Cyprian Paquet (1813), and François Cheverie and Paul Boucher (1820).[40] Soon mingling with them were Scots named MacDonald, MacPhee, MacAulay, MacLellan, MacKinnon, and Campbell.

Next came the Irish. The west bank of the river then became a very busy place with stores, wharves, and an extensive shipbuilding industry (eighty-five wooden ships were launched there in the 1870s). By 1864, we are told, thirty-eight families in the Souris area (including the Scullys, MacCormacks, Lyons, Mullallys, and O'Donnells) worked as "the shipwrights, carriage makers, block makers, pump makers and caulkers."[41] Among the area's shipbuilders were English people named Rice, Gregory, and Mallard. At the same time in Souris East, in the mixed society of Acadians, English, Scots, and Irish, "there were thirteen farmers, seven sea captains, seven general dealers, four shoemakers, two teachers, two ship owners, two mill owners, and a tailor, cooper, blacksmith, carpenter, harness maker, physician, clergyman and road commissioner."[42] Once entrepreneurs like John MacLean and Uriah Matthew, as well as Loyalist John Knight, established their businesses, the east side of the river became the locus of commerce.[43]

Meacham's 1880 *Atlas* shows in Lots 44 and 45 a fair number of Irish settlers, or property owners, on both sides of the Souris River. From New Zealand and Gowan Brae to Souris West are found such Irish surnames as Mullally, Kickham, McQuaid (and McWade), O'Donnell, Doyle, Keefe, Whitty, Scully, McCabe, Conroy, and Sweeney; while on the other side of the river, from Souris East up to the Scottish neighbourhood of Souris Line Road, there are such familiar Irish names as Mullally, O'Donnell, Whelan, Lyons, Haley, O'Hanly, Mooney, Walsh, McQuaid, and McCartey. The influx of Ulster immigrants by the 1840s is reflected in the mixture of some County Monaghan and County Donegal names with the more prevalent family names from the southeastern counties.

In his account of the 1839 Mission of St Mary, in Souris, after fully acknowledging the founding role played by Scottish and Acadian clergy and laity, the Reverend A.E. Burke lists among the early Irish parishioners Martin Whelan, Thomas O'Donnell, Martin Lyons, James Mullally, and Patrick Birmingham. He notes that he "gained much information regarding the early days of the mission and its first church from a fine old Irish gentleman from Tipperary, who with his beautiful old wife reside in affluence upon the fertile and picturesque farm which fifty years ago their energy and industry won from the uncleared forest."[44] After three or more generations, intermarriage assured that many of St Mary's parishioners would have at least one Irish branch in their family tree.

The Irish presence in Souris, while not paramount, remained notable through the nineteenth century. The illustrious Edward Whelan, for example, represented the second district of Kings in the Island legislature; the Benevolent Irish Society hall was a landmark in Souris in the early decades of the twentieth century; and the annual St Patrick's

Day parade along Main Street brought out residents of sundry backgrounds.

THE BENEVOLENT IRISH SOCIETY

Perhaps the clearest assertion of Irish loyalties in the area was the incorporation of the Benevolent Irish Society (BIS) of Souris in 1890. Among the charter members were James J. Hughes, James Brennan, James Dunphy, Matthew Fahie, John Kickham, James Landrigan, James McQuaid, and Michael Mooney. Even before the Act of Incorporation and continuing thereafter, the BIS held an annual picnic to raise funds for the building of its hall and for other charitable purposes. The picnics were well attended, and on those occasions excursion trains ran between Souris and Georgetown, and Souris and Charlottetown. At the old tea grounds, there were games and contests, races and speeches, and a plentiful supply of food and liquid refreshments to suit all tastes. For many years, at their St Patrick's Hall, the Souris BIS staged plays, lectures, concerts, and other family entertainments. This newspaper account of St Patrick's Day about 1910 captures part of the spirit of the time and place:

The day at Souris was observed with more than the usual enthusiasm. At an early hour the flag on St. Patrick's Hall and the Stars and Stripes of the American Consul were seen floating in the breeze. Promptly at 10 o'clock, the members of the B.I. Society headed by the band, formed in line and marched to St. Mary's Church where high mass was celebrated and an eloquent and appropriate sermon preached by the Rev. Father McIntyre.

The closing event of the occasion was the grand entertainment given in the evening at St. Patrick's Hall which was literally crowded to the very door by an appreciative audience of villagers and people from the surrounding country ...

The first on the programme was an Irish melody by the band. Then came the orator of the evening, the Rev. Dr. Doyle of Vernon River. His address was carefully prepared and showed masterly familiarity with the history of the Irish race. Towards the close he touched upon the appropriateness of the celebration of the day, and concluded with an eloquent allusion to the laws and institutions established and the liberties enjoyed in this fair Canada of ours, telling his fellow countrymen present that, while they loved the new country, they should never forget the old.[45]

There followed a series of solo songs, duets, choir renditions, readings and recitations, a Scottish song or two, a few humorous sketches, a skit satirizing local characters and events, and the finale – a one-act comedy. All the entertainment was provided by local performers, good neighbours from Scottish, English, Acadian, and Irish families. For a few decades before the turn of the twentieth century and continuing thereafter, the town of Souris was a centre of much commercial and recreational activity for eastern Kings County.

ELSEWHERE IN THE COUNTY

The eastern peninsula was not the only area in Kings County that displayed Irish cultural tenacity. Several hardy Irish gardens also sprouted in the central and eastern districts. Inland farming communities developed around Morell, St Patrick Road, Byrnes Road, Baldwin Road, Peakes Road, and St Marys Road, while the coastal communities of Cardigan, Montague and Georgetown grew into busy fishing, shipping, and shipbuilding ports.

No high-seas coercion, shipwrecks, or misadventures spurred immigration in the inland places. Instead, in typical fashion, the Irish sought out spots in areas the Scots had not occupied. In the 1820s settlers from southeastern Ireland formed small scattered clusters, often in places which then seemed to have only marginal social and economic prospects. A generation later immigrants from County Monaghan and contiguous Ulster counties greatly augmented the Irish Catholic population in that mainly Protestant region of the Island.

That was the social situation in the 1840s in Lot 61, for example, where a vigorous Irish community took root in the grudging soil of St Marys Road. The Irish people actually spread well beyond that one road. As Peter McGuigan nicely described the area, the "major settlement was in the form of a 'T,' the body being St Mary's (sic) Road, the cross being Mink River Road from Mink River in Lot 65 to Sturgeon Bay. Additionally there were related groups in Albion, Gaspereau and Murray Harbour North as well as a few Protestant Irish on Peter's Road and other areas away from St Mary's."[46] The origins of most Irish settlers could be discerned from their family names. Those named Brophy, Dunn, French, Kearney, Lanigan, Tobin, and Walsh, for instance, were 1820s settlers from Wexford, Kilkenny, and Tipperary; whereas anyone named Gormley, Hughes, McCarron, McGuigan, McKenna, or Ronaghan signalled the later wave of immigrants, those from Counties Monaghan, Tyrone, and Armagh. Whether they originated in the south or north of Ireland, the settlers were ardent supporters of their parish churches. This fact was notably demonstrated in the St Marys Road area where the growing numbers of Irish persons necessitated the building of the Harris-designed church of St Paul.

In some areas the homes of the Irish were strung out along a road or two; in other places they were knotted at intersections or in villages. Regardless, the settlers of the eastern end of the Island never felt so remote that they lost touch with their compatriots in the more populous settlements in Queens County. In fact, they too joined in the Irish national Repeal campaign; they too engaged in local Orange versus Green squabbles; and they too played a strong role in the Islandwide Tenant League struggles. In Kings County the settlers and their descendants held fast to their Irish ways.

A LETTER HOME

John McNally [Nallen], a furniture maker residing in East Point in 1832, wrote a letter to his brother in County Mayo describing the Island "as wholesome as Ireland, but not so large."[47] Besides squirrels, foxes, hares, rabbits, and mice (but no rats), McNally observed bears and wild cats, "which are ... injurious to cows, sheep and pigs and to the inhabitants." Putting aside such natural nuisances, however, in a burst of optimism he assured his brother, "Dear Ulick, if you were here you would make a fortune." He himself was "getting five dollars for a spinning wheel and six pounds for a turned chair." Tradesmen were much in demand. According to McNally, "There is no trade in any part of America better than a wheel-wright, blacksmith, carpenter and taylor."

The only reason McNally gave for not encouraging his brother to emigrate to the Island at that time was that "the land to be got here is taken up by old settlers." On the other hand, he claimed, "If a man got two or three hundred pounds he could purchase from four to five hundred acres, while the grass grows. Dear brother, this is the truth – you can get 100 acres of woodland for five pounds but there could be no gain by it for five years."[48]

Most of all, John McNally seemed to relish his freedom. "Every man does anything he wants – they tan their own leather," he wrote. Then, apparently alluding to the much-resented tithe imposed to support the established church in Ireland, he assured his brother: "Likewise there is no pound or taxes – every religion pays their own clergy here." In this letter to his home in County Mayo, McNally was not so much boastful as hopeful. In this respect, his voice was probably representative of most Irish immigrants in eastern Kings County, Prince Edward Island.

CHAPTER SIX

County Monaghan before the Emigration to Prince Edward Island

> Monaghan hills
> You have made me the sort of man I am
> A fellow who can never care a damn
> For Everestic thrills.
>
> Patrick Kavanagh

The third and most concentrated wave of Irish immigrants brought more than four thousand settlers to the Island. This influx extended from 1830 to about 1850, and the effects on Island society can be seen to this day. By the mid-1830s the Island's Irish population consisted mainly of natives of the southern, particularly southeastern, counties. Generally these Leinster and Munster immigrants adapted well to the Island. Now the Ulster newcomers, though they were equally sociable, were not quite so pliable. They were overwhelmingly from northern County Monaghan and contiguous parishes in the neighbouring counties of Armagh, Tyrone, and Fermanagh. They had been solidly shaped by the customs and characteristics of Ulster, and their arrival made an appreciable difference in the Island's social, political, and religious life. But before tracing, in chapter 7, the Island adventures of the flood of immigrants who came to be known as the Monaghan settlers, the present chapter will review several main lines of their pre-emigration regional history and will acknowledge some distinctive cultural features indigenous to County Monaghan and environs.

The three thousand or more Irish emigrants from the parishes of Donagh, Errigal Truagh, Clontibret, Tydavnet, Tyholland, and Monaghan town who sailed to Prince Edward Island between 1830 and about 1850 measured everything in multiples of the little hills of County

Monaghan. Even in their new Island homes, their old milieu still mattered greatly. Their native geography and history made them distinctive, and their cultural heritage continued to nurture them in the overseas communities they formed. Standing upon foreign soil and beneath an alien sky, they remained Monaghan people, and the unfortunate history of their county was at the heart of the legacy they bestowed upon Prince Edward Island.

Most of these people came from villages and townlands in the northern baronies of the county, tucked up against the borders of Armagh, Tyrone, and Fermanagh, in that portion of the ancient kingdom of Oriel popularly called McKenna Country. Centred in the Barony of Truagh, these people were related by blood, by community ties, by secular history, and by sectarian affiliation. As Ulster Catholics, their Irishness was transfused, indeed permeated, by social and sectarian experiences more intensely felt than by the southern Irish immigrants who had preceded them to Prince Edward Island. Toward the end of this wave of immigration some of them had also been tempered in the crucible of the Great Famine, a catastrophe that hardened and sharpened their attitudes in various socio-economic and political matters.

THE NEWCOMERS

Although every county of Ireland was represented on Prince Edward Island by 1850, the County Monaghan contingent far outnumbered any other county group. By the time they arrived, most of the Island's coastal lands had been claimed, so they tended to congregate in several rural areas in the central, inland parts of the Island. This served to concentrate and strengthen their forces and to ensure their cohesion. Their compatriots from the southeast, on the other hand, generally lived in mixed communities or in smaller enclaves scattered mainly along coastal areas, a situation that tended to dilute or disperse their influence.

In their tightly knit settlements at Fort Augustus, Kellys Cross, Emyvale, and Kinkora, the Monaghans perpetuated many of the religious, social, and political customs of their homeland. They tended to stand together, to assist one another, and to marry within their own county group. Notwithstanding their gradual adaptation to the local practices and beliefs in their new setting, the comparative stability of the nineteenth-century rural way of life assured the survival of their Old County traits and values for at least a few generations.

To some outsiders, therefore, the Monaghan people – mindful as they were of family names, family ties, and their places of origin – appeared to be strongly clannish or chauvinistic. In fact, the cohesiveness that gave them a sense of identity and security also engendered factional fights, agrarian activism, political and social sensitiveness, and sectarian clashes. In periodic factional fights, for instance, they taunted their rivals from other counties with such names as Southies and Yellow Bellies, while they themselves were sometimes accorded the epithet Monaghan Bastards. Their early reputation for pugnacity earned them the grudging respect implied in the common parental admonition, "Never say *Boo* to a Monaghan!"[1]

In a more constructive vein, wherever Monaghan people settled they became forceful exponents of tenants' grievances and aspirations. In nineteenth-century Prince Edward Island, when the tenant-landlord struggle was the dominant political issue, Irish immigrants (along with tenants of other ethnic origins) stood four-square for reform of the Island's outmoded system of land proprietorship. Electoral practices, corrupt and corrupting as they were, had hampered efforts at land reform; and social conditions being what they were, the aggressive conduct of the Irish sometimes contributed to altercations – most notoriously in the Island's Belfast Riots of 1846–47.[2]

The militant sectarianism of the time also motivated some temperamental Monaghan men – and others – to demonstrate their prowess by mounting vocal and sometimes physical resistance to Orange parades. A more edifying expression of strongly held convictions among the Monaghan settlers was the steady flow of aspirants to the priesthood and religious life which emanated from their families.[3]

CONDITIONS IN COUNTY MONAGHAN

The odyssey that took these hundreds of families from the hamlets and farmsteads of northern County Monaghan (see map 7) had a long prologue. Their homeland, as they knew it, had come into being in the sixteenth century when English forces overran the area, divided it into five baronies, and attempted to anglicize and anglicanize the natives. Largely that attempt failed, for the Gaelic and Catholic roots of Monaghan culture survived even after three centuries of oppression. Unvanquished but severely wounded, the people who became the emigrants of the 1830s and 1840s were just emerging from a long dark night of deprivation, persecution, violence, and sectarian animosity. Once they had lifted their heads, they were not likely to be docile and submissive again.

It so happened that one year after Ireland won emancipation for the Catholic people, in 1829, a small group of emigrants known as "the Glasgow Irish," forerunners – indeed, catalysts – of the extended Monaghan emigration, took up farms in Fort Augustus, Prince Edward

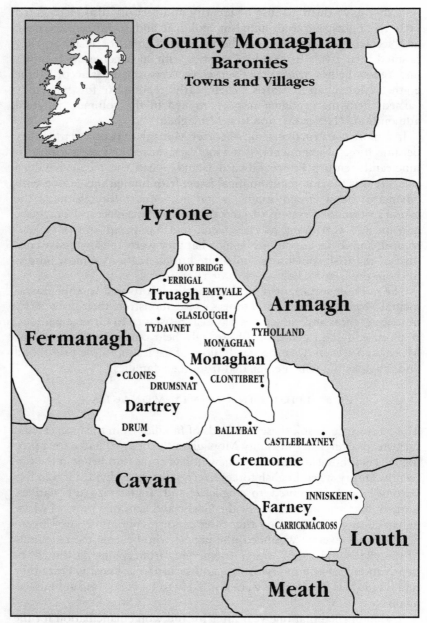

Map 7. County Monaghan sent out the largest contingent of settlers.

Island. Although there was no causal connection between Daniel O'Connell's long campaign for the political liberation of his fellow Catholics and the setting forth of the first contingent of Monaghan settlers to PEI, O'Connell's success had certainly heightened political awareness among the new emigrants. In fact, the Monaghan election of 1826 – a riotous encounter which Henry Westenra, supported by O'Connell, had won – has been cited as the first instance of direct intervention by O'Connellite forces in an Irish election.[4] Even though emancipation had little immediate effect on the day-to-day life of ordinary citizens, the restored right of Catholics to represent their people in Parliament grew in significance both in Ireland and in the British North American colonies. This new political awareness mattered profoundly both to suppressed Catholics, who now gained an important measure of self-esteem, and to the members of the Protestant Ascendancy, who now feared any lessening of their long standing control of the country. It caused some members of the "landocracy" to quit Ireland altogether. In others, it aroused dormant bigotry. Moreover, it led to the eviction of tenants who, under the new standards, were too poor to qualify for a vote and were therefore no longer a political asset to landlords who sought popular support (for themselves or their lackeys) during elections. In these ways the Emancipation Act of 1829, which restored civil rights to Catholics, created new problems even while it corrected old grievances.

Most important, though, through the far reaches of the British Empire, the Emancipation Act elevated the sense of Irish pride and rejuvenated the aspirations of a downtrodden people. The future statesman Charles Gavan Duffy recalled that even at nine years of age he had felt that "Catholic Emancipation meant the deliverance of our race from the subjection to Orange ascendancy in which we habitually lived." Indicative of their new morale, many of the Irish in Prince Edward Island displayed in their homes portraits of the liberator, Daniel O'Connell, and they contributed generously to the Repeal fund in the early 1840s.

POLITICS IN COUNTY MONAGHAN

The Monaghan settlers were, in truth, heirs to two distinct political traditions. One was the tradition of constitutional reform: social improvement through reasoned pleading and, when necessary, through civil resistance that espoused only non-violent actions. Essentially, this was the philosophy of Daniel O'Connell, a philosophy that had clearly succeeded in restoring some civil rights in Ireland. Admirable as this philosophy was, it failed to achieve the repeal of the 1800 Act of

Union, which had dissolved the Irish parliament and placed Ireland under the direct jurisdiction of the British government in Westminster. Contention over the Act of Union underscored Irish-British relations for more than a century. During this time the efficacy of O'Connell's pacifist approach to the glaring injustices was put to numerous tests both in Ireland generally and in County Monaghan itself, and even in the distant colony of Prince Edward Island. Notably during the 1840s, in a dozen places in the Island colony, chapters of the Repeal Association sprang up to contribute both funds and moral support for the Repeal Movement in Ireland.

The second political tradition found in Monaghan was exemplified in scores of encounters in which physical force took precedence over reasoned argumentation. Quite apart from the frequent internal struggles among the ancient chieftains of Ulster, and of Oriel itself, County Monaghan was well schooled in violence: the hellish pursuits by Danish marauders, Lord Furnival's 1417 devastation of Oriel, Queen Elizabeth's confiscations, Prince William's occupation of Monaghan town, Oliver Cromwell's atrocities, and three centuries of assorted cruelties inflicted by occupation forces, militia, yeomanry, and secret societies. These protracted visitations of violence had taught the people of Monaghan to defend themselves. Although they generally preferred to find peaceful solutions to problems and although they sometimes employed tactics of passive resistance or civil disobedience, they were willing – when required or challenged – to stand and fight. In fact, to outsiders they sometimes appeared to be unduly pugnacious; their fairs were often riotous, their market days were commonly rowdy, and their elections were frequently coercive and violent.[5]

Combative practices in Monaghan had an unhappy history. Some went back at least three centuries; others were precipitated by events within the living memory of the older Island settlers. The secret societies, for instance, originated in the latter half of the eighteenth century. At first they were mainly concerned with such agrarian issues as rents, tenure, and tithes, but by 1800 their activities had become both political and sectarian. By that time several forces seemed to converge. The formation of militia units known as the Volunteers, for instance, was intended mainly to defend Ireland against the threatened French invasion, though its purpose was also to maintain domestic order. When Volunteers who held republican or United Ireland sympathies became too numerous, the more carefully screened Militia was formed. Still later, an even more selective group, the Yeomanry, took over domestic police duties.

Matters came to a head with the disastrous rebellion of the United Irishmen in 1798 and its impolitic aftermath – Britain's controversial and perhaps excessively reactionary Act of Union (drawn up in 1800 and enforced the following year), to which the Irish parliament sub-serviently acquiesced. Once the Irish parliament was dissolved, the country came under the direct rule of Westminster. Meanwhile, in 1795, in County Armagh (which abuts County Monaghan's eastern border) a militantly Protestant and pro-British organization had come into being. It was known as the Loyal Orange Institution, or Orange Order. Before long, the militantly Catholic people formed their own counterorganizations. Thereafter, it became difficult to distinguish political, economic, and sectarian motives behind the frequent factional clashes that upset the stability of Ulster for more than two centuries.

Land Problems

Among the Island's older immigrants from Monaghan in the 1830s were veterans not only of the sectarian battles but also of the military and civil strife of those earlier years. Many remembered how the Volunteers (whose Catholic members were forbidden to bear arms) were employed as a police force to suppress farmers' protests. While it is true that the possibility of foreign invasion linked with agrarian grievances terrified some landed gentry, the real causes of the mass discontent had much deeper roots.

First of all, there had been a great deal of land trouble in Monaghan between 1758 and 1767, including arrests, injuries, and deaths in 1763, when armed troops put down the Oakboys, an agrarian society, at Glaslough and (in nearby County Fermanagh) at Wattlesbridge. As well, unrest was evident among the relatively prosperous Presbyterian planters (and some Catholics too) along the Glaslough-Clones line. Oakboys in Armagh and Tyrone joined those in Monaghan in resisting the practice of compulsory labour for road building and maintenance. The whole area, in fact, was restless.

In County Monaghan's heavily populated, underdeveloped pre–Famine society, land was all-important. A neighbour once counselled young Charles Gavan Duffy: "Mind this, my boy, 'tis not so much the question of kings or governments which concerns us here in Ireland as the question of land from which the people get their daily bread." Land determined one's social and economic status and even one's personal identity. Landless cottiers were a step above paupers; peasants holding leases were slightly more secure; frugal owners might subsist on small acreages; farmers with forty or more acres were counted among a fortunate small minority; and the few great landlords who held many thousands of acres constituted the social and economic élite. Many of the landlords lived in England and hired agents to manage their Irish estates. At times this feudalistic system functioned efficiently, but combined with laissez-faire mercantile practices it proved woefully inadequate to meet the natural needs and aspirations of the poorer classes. Indeed, during the tragic 1840s, the exploitive system of land distribution and management proved a major factor in turning a natural affliction, potato blight, into a national catastrophe, the Great Famine. Most of the Irish emigrants to Prince Edward Island had experienced very difficult times even before the famine years, but those who fled after 1845 personally witnessed the terrible distress that irreparably scarred the face and character of south Ulster.

The Ulster Custom

One of the most practical Oakboy grievances focused on the landed gentry's challenge to the Ulster Custom. The custom centered on the traditional right of a tenant to occupy a defined portion of land and to sell this right of occupancy to another person, subject to the landlord's approval. It was a custom that recognized the tenant's claim to compensation when he gave up his lease on a farm he had occupied and improved. The Ulster Custom therefore not only recognized simple equity but also provided rural families with some means of buying their passage to opportunities overseas – a consideration of great importance to would-be emigrants. It was not until 1848 that a bill was introduced to legalize the Ulster Custom, and the bill was defeated. Even so, Ascendancy gentry usually came to terms with their small tenant farmers – if not out of a sense of justice, then for reasons of self-interest. Cautious landlords tried not to arouse the retribution of aggrieved tenants who were beginning to organize societies to assert their rights.

The Penal Laws

By the end of the eighteenth century the discriminatory Penal Laws, inconsistently enforced as they had been, were being systematically but slowly dismantled. Most civil rights – such as the right to vote, to sit in Parliament, to hold public office, to enter certain professions, to carry arms – were denied to Catholics until 1793 or even 1829; but some concessions had been made to bishops and members of religious orders, and Catholics were permitted to open schools. As well, a small number of Catholic businessmen kept pace with the ruling minority in enterprises of trade and commerce. Nevertheless, regardless of the later, uneven leniency in the enforcement of the Penal Laws, the very existence of such statutes was, and was intended to be, degrading and demeaning to the vast majority of the people. No wonder, then, that sectarian resentments were often part of the emigrants' cultural baggage.

In Irish agrarian matters, by 1771 Catholics were permitted to lease 50 acres of bogland for 60 years; by 1778 they were allowed to lease land for 999 years; by 1782 they were even allowed to purchase land in their native country. Then a chain of economic factors further complicated the land question. One was the rapid increase in population. Along with the growing demands of the provisions trade during the years of Grattan's Parliament (1782–98), the pressure of the expanding population increased the demand for land. Increased demand in turn raised the value of land. Higher land values led to rent increases. And rent increases forced many small farmers to divide and subdivide their holdings to the point of economic inefficiency. In default of meeting the increased rents, tenants faced foreclosure or eviction.

Caught in such a network of frustrations, many peasants became cynical and bitter. More and more, they tended to fight back. Sometimes, land agents who were unscrupulous in their methods and uncaring for their neighbours were subject to acts of vengeance such as house burning and shooting.

RESISTANCE TO TITHES

More galling for many people than the feudalistic landlord system or the greedy land agents, whom that system spawned, was the statutory collection of church tithes. Both Presbyterians and Catholics, already disabled by the Penal Code, objected to paying taxes to support an established church which their conscience rejected. Clearly, the Tithe Law was a major cause of hostility between Catholics and Protestants. Exacerbating the sectarian imbalance, the tithe collectors were prone (in the words of William Carleton) "to forget too frequently that the garb of justice may be often thrown over the form of rapacity, and that the authority of law is also in too many instances, only another name for oppression."[6]

The Tithe War coincided with the political movement for the emancipation of Catholics, but the former was of much greater urgency to the poor tenant farmers because the tithe proctors were empowered to seize tax defaulters' personal property or their crops and cattle. Understandably, the tithe proctors came to be regarded as a "despicable lot," and the enforcement of what was perceived to be an unjust law created among some of the peasantry disrespect for all laws.

In County Monaghan as elsewhere, opposition to the tithes often took the form of passive resistance; discontented taxpayers tried every imaginable tactic of evasion and lawful obstruction, for instance, refusing to buy goods or cattle seized from defaulters, treating proctors and landlords' agents with contempt, and punishing informers with ostracism. On occasion, however, protesting tenants took up whatever weapons they could find and threatened, coerced, or attacked the tithe proctors. Especially in the 1830s, the direct levy and forcible collection of tithes led to violent encounters not only in Carlow, Wexford, Kilkenny, and Tipperary, but also in such County Monaghan communities as Tyholland, Magheracloone, and Ballybay, where police and military forces were called out to break popular resistance.[7]

Monaghan historian D.C. Rushe describes what happened in 1831 when the proctors of Tyholland attempted to collect tithes that were owed to the rector, Mr Crookshank:

Large crowds assembled to resist the collection. The proctors were assailed by a crowd of people and fled for their lives through the country. The rector heard of it and sent for the police. There were only four men and a sergeant in a barrack which was then in Tyholland, and the sergeant wisely declined the invitation of Mr Crookshank to aid in collecting the tithe in the face of such an angry assemblage. A troop of dragoons and some police came out from Monaghan. The people assembled in great crowds, most of them armed, on the hills, and there was general expectation of a real battle being fought. But the proctors could not be induced to continue their work even under such protection. This was the first resistance in this county, which was rapidly followed by similar scenes in several districts.[8]

The following year more violence occurred at Aughnaseda when the rector of Monaghan sought to collect the tithe from John Hughes, a man whose family had been active in the insurrection of 1798. On that occasion, historian Rushe relates, Mr Hughes "declined to pay, and produced a printed document which he said was an order from the Grand Club [evidently a secret society] to pay no more tithe":

John Hughes' brother then came forward and shouted to a young man at some distance to sound the horn on Goudy's Hill, which was forthwith done, and had the effect of gathering a crowd who abused and hunted [the two proctors,] Watson and Longmore. As soon as the news of this reached the town, the police and military were sent out to arrest the Hugheses, and Michael Hughes gave the authorities a race for his capture. Having run about a mile, hotly pursued by the police, he changed clothes with a young man named Barkey in Carn, who, being fresh and mistaken for Hughes, gave the police twice as severe a run through Tyholland for several hours, until at last he was surrounded and captured about Leitrim townland. The whole body of police and military brought Barkey a prisoner into Monaghan in great triumph. But, alas! on his being confronted with the proctors, the authorities were informed that they had caught the wrong man.[9]

More Violence

In financial straits by 1832, some clergymen hired the notorious Ballybay land agent, Sam Gray, to collect their dues. Gray's henchmen did their dirty work, and in the process Gray allegedly shot to death a protesting farmer, a crime for which he was later acquitted. Elsewhere, particularly in the heavily Catholic barony of Farney, police and soldiers actually accompanied the tithe collectors. Rushe describes one incident:

On 9th November 1832 a body of dragoons under command of three magistrates (one a Catholic) protected the tithe proctors of the Rev. Patrick Cummings in collecting the tithes of Magheracloone. The people assembled, armed, some with guns, pitchforks, scythes, etc., to resist the collection, and a regular fight took place. The soldiers charged and cleared the roadway of people, who got behind the ditches and fired shots and stones at the troops and proctors. The dragoons charged into several of the fields, driving the people over the fences, who, as soon as they were driven out of one field, formed behind the fences of another. Ultimately the people crowded on the top of a high hill, whence they were driven and scattered by a desperate charge of the whole force. In this fight, which lasted several hours, many people and soldiers were wounded, as was also one of the magistrates, a Mr James M. Reid, who was hit with a ball. The proctors returned empty-handed that evening.[10]

Attempts to collect tithes at Donaghmoyne also failed. Despite a planned pincer attack by police and dragoons, the protestors – forewarned by allies who sounded alarm horns – successfully resisted with "guns, pitchforks, scythes, sticks, stones, etc."[11] In this encounter a constable was killed. Many others on both sides were wounded before the official forces retreated.

These and similar setbacks incensed the members of the Ascendancy, who had believed that at least in Ulster they could enforce their will as they pleased. Consequently, they had recourse to the fearsome power of the courts – which they controlled – to imprison, transport, and hang those who dared to resist even an unjust law. D.C. Rushe was not exceptional in holding the opinion that as "the Courts were generally hostile to the poor, and always hostile to the Catholics, it is not to be wondered at that the people took the law into their own hands."[12]

Evidently, the admonition attributed to James Doyle, the celebrated "JKL" (bishop of Kildare and Leighlin), had more than one application: "Let your hatred of tithes be as lasting as your sense of justice."[13]

By 1838 Ireland's heinous Tithe Law had ostensibly been rescinded. In fact, though, the tax remained. It was levied not on the tenants directly, as before, but on the holdings of the landlords. The landlords, as expected, simply passed the new tax on to their tenants in the form of increased rents. Another thirty-one years elapsed before the Anglican Church was disestablished (1869) and the tithes were transferred from the coffers of the established church to the general revenues of the state. Still another twelve years passed before William Gladstone's legislation lowered the jacked-up rents to (or below) their 1838 levels. There were no rebates. In the interim, the rural people of Monaghan (and of Ireland generally) had endured poverty, bloodshed, injustice, exile, and famine. They had resented, resisted, and rebelled. And whether they remained at home or went abroad, they remembered.

These events were unfolding in County Monaghan at the very time that people by the hundred were emigrating to a more hospitable place they had heard about, a place where good large acreages were being leased on reasonable terms – Prince Edward Island.

THE REPEAL MOVEMENT

Around the time that the violence associated with the Tithe Law began to subside, the movement to repeal the Act of Union came to the fore. The arguments over the enforced union of Britain and Ireland in a unitary parliament split the smaller country into several camps. Although Britain's initial reason for dissolving the Irish parliament had been a matter of retribution for the Irish Rebellion of 1798, during the next half-century or so the controversial Act of Union was variously rationalized as a means of restoring and maintaining order in Ireland or as a means of strengthening Ireland's defences against a possible French invasion.

Within Ireland itself, it was difficult to divorce this issue from others of burning importance; the Act of Union was favoured, or opposed, for its impact on political autonomy, economic power, the exercise of religious freedom, access to education and local government, and a host of other issues. One thorny issue took the form of this question: Would the British parliament be more likely than a restored Irish Ascendancy to honour the pledges of religious liberty upon which the Act drawn up in 1800 had been based? Catholic Archbishop John Troy and other prelates believed that Catholic interests would be better served from London than from Dublin. Daniel O'Connell and his followers disagreed and led the agitation for repeal of the Act. The underlying question, however, was not narrowly sectarian; rather, it was rooted in recognition of Ireland's right to govern itself in its own parliament (but still under the British crown), even if this meant granting Catholics equal status with the Protestant minority in such matters as voting and holding public office, and by exempting them from oaths that perforce made them deny tenets of their religion.[14]

Novelist William Carleton was one contemporary writer who strongly took issue with the advocates of repeal, claiming that their divisive views "debauched and contaminated" such virtues of the people as "love of truth ... simple devotion and patriarchal piety ... [and] sincerity in all social intercourse."[15] In the heat of his tirade, Carleton declared: "The Irishman of the present day – the creation of agitation – is neither honest, nor candid, nor manly, nor generous, but a poor, skulking dupe, at once slavish and insolent, offensive and cowardly – who carries as a necessary consequence, the principles of political dishonesty into the practices of private life, and is consequently disingenuous and fraudulent."[16]

Carleton's harangue is indicative of the strong feelings the repeal campaign aroused. In Britain the campaign was sometimes perceived as a sign of growing Irish alienation from the United Kingdom. In Ireland, too, many saw the Repeal Movement as an expression of Irish nationalism, and some linked it with the idealistic appeal of Thomas Davis and the Young Irelanders for an independent Irish nation. Among the leaders of the Young Ireland movement were three well-known Monaghan men: Terence Bellew MacManus, Thomas Devin Reilly, and Charles Gavan Duffy. Duffy, Monaghan's leading citizen, shared many of O'Connell's views, but when his belief in peaceful constitutional reform was protractedly mocked by British intransigence, he became more revolutionary. Thomas D'Arcy McGee, who later became a founding father of Canada, called Duffy "morally and intellectually the greatest Irish production of the century."[17]

A parenthetical observation seems necessary here. In 1798 many in the Protestant establishment had favoured and even fought for Irish independence from Britain. Earlier still, Anglo-Irish landowners had successfully agitated for the repeal of Poyning's Law, which had given legal sanction to Britain's claim to legislate for Ireland. By the late eighteenth century, of course, the Anglo-Irish Ascendancy had come to respect and love the land their ancestors had usurped. They owned or controlled 90 per cent of the country; their cultural attainments were admirable, and they were active in London's social and intellectual circles. Furthermore, they had demonstrated an aptitude for governing in a civil and responsible manner; it may be said that the Irish parliament, when guided by Henry Grattan, crowned a mini-Golden Age. In 1780 the grand jurors and freeholders of Monaghan were so self-confident that they formally resolved: "We do affirm that no parliament had, has, or of right ought to have any power or authority whatsoever in the kingdom, except the parliament of Ireland: and that no statute has the force of law in this kingdom, unless enacted by the King with the consent of the Lords and Commons of the land."[18]

By 1840, however, the Anglo-Irish Protestant establishment – perhaps fearful of the implications of Catholic Emancipation and no doubt reluctant to share power equitably with the Gaelic Catholic majority – generally aligned themselves with the forces favouring retention of the Union. Coincidentally, the Orange Order performed a similar about-face. In 1800 Orangemen had dutifully opposed the Act of Union because they believed it would deprive the ruling Protestants in Ireland of their complete control over the country. A generation or so later, however, without compromising their sectarian intents and purposes at all, Orangemen readily reversed their political position. The absentee landlords, as expected, were unanimous in their support of the Union. The rank-and-file of County Monaghan, also as expected, once again stood firmly with O'Connell in support of repeal. The repeal campaign failed. O'Connell died in 1847.

SECRET SOCIETIES

The problems related to land tenure and secret societies were other sources of vexation and violence. Early in the eighteenth century the outlaw Rapparees were militant defenders of the peasantry. In County Monaghan the countryside was terrorized by "the formidable and dangerous Parra Glass" (i.e., Green Paddy),[19] whose grandfather's estate, it seems, had been confiscated by the Cromwellians. Next, the Hearts-of-Steel society – somewhat similar to the Munster Whiteboys in their agrarian objectives – was composed in Monaghan of both Catholics and Protestants, though mainly of Protestants in the rest of Ulster. Later, to protect their own spheres of influence, Ulster Protestants formed the Peep-o-Day Boys, and Ulster Catholics retaliated with the Defenders, also known as the Ribbonmen. Secret societies mushroomed in Monaghan in the early nineteenth century.

As acknowledged above, the most prominent secret society was the Orange Order. It was founded in Loughgall, County Armagh, in 1795 and, in the words of the original oath, it pledged to support "the King and his heirs as long as they support the Protestant Ascendancy." Monaghan historian D.C. Rushe was not alone in his belief that British officialdom encouraged "the Orange wedge" in order to alienate Irish

Protestants from the United Irishmen movement.[20] Be that as it may, after the failed insurrection of 1798 and the consequent Act of Union of 1800, numerous demoralized patriots left the country. Of the many militants who remained, those who were Protestant tended to join the Orange Order, while the Catholics tended to join the Ribbonmen or a similar anti-Orange society.

Not all secret societies, however, were pro-Orange or anti-Orange. Patriotism or agrarianism as much as sectarianism motivated some groups who still hoped to liberate their country from Britain or to stamp out the worst evils of landlordism. In particular, rack-renting proprietors, selfish land agents, and officious tithe proctors became targets of the pent-up vengeance of oppressed tenants.

Within several secret societies there were often differences of opinion, and when the various undisciplined factions could not be reconciled, internal rivalry sometimes erupted into violence. Both for their oath taking and for their recourse to violence, secret societies were unequivocally condemned by the Roman Catholic Church. Still, membership in them increased and their baneful activities continued. The Orange Order was strong in the Monaghan-Cootehill-Clones triangle, particularly in the Ballybay district, while the Ribbonmen were well organized in the Clones area, in Errigal Truagh, and in Donagh where they formed a chapter in response to "wholesale evictions at Glaslough."[21]

The Westenra election victory in Monaghan in 1826 and Daniel O'Connell's personal victory in 1828 in County Clare (even though Catholics were not then permitted to sit in Parliament) brought out rival marchers in the tens of thousands, but they did not clash. However, at a huge Orange assembly on 12 July 1848 in Monaghan town, thousands of men armed with guns and bayonets – including pathetic evictees and malnourished refugees – did come into conflict. On this occasion no one was punished for the fray. The direction that Orange activities were now taking had been foreshadowed as early as the order's first parade in County Monaghan – at Black Kesh near Newbliss on 12 July 1796. Even then there had been signs that energies once directed toward a united Ireland might become diverted and dissipate in tedious sectarian squabbles and violent clashes. When those premonitions did come to pass, as William Carleton said, "There was no law against an Orangeman and no law for a Papist."[22]

Historian J.E. McKenna, putting the blame on both landlord terrorism and mock-justice in the courts, offers this account of the inception of secret societies in northern Monaghan:

In the days of open voting, the tenant farmers were wont to be driven to the polling booth, to record their votes for the landlord or his nominee, as sheep are driven to the slaughter. Woe betide the man who dared to raise his voice against his landlord's command. Very soon there would be another occupying his farm and reaping the fruits of his industry ... Some little attempt had been made to organize and direct the Catholic vote prior to the Parliamentary election of 1826. The aggressive policy of the Orange party, in different districts, had compelled Catholic young men to band themselves together, sometimes in secret societies, for defensive purposes. Prior to 1813, this parish [Donagh] was free from secret societies. At the Emyvale fair, in that year, Captain Singleton's yeomen shot down a number of inoffensive Catholic Truagh men. The local magistrates refused to return the murderers for trial until compelled to do so by the Court of King's Bench. The Assize Court, in Monaghan, duly acquitted them. Some years later, on the 30th October, 1818, a body of Truagh people returning from Aughnacloy races, were pursued to the Blackwater bridge by a body of Orangemen, and a free fight took place. Roger Anketell succeeded in separating the combatants, and the Truagh people were proceeding homewards when a detachment of Moore's Aughnacloy yeomen arrived on the scene and poured a deadly volley into the densely packed body of Catholics on the Truagh side of the river. A few of them were killed and many wounded, but a Monaghan jury, in the following year acquitted the murderers.

These and many other murders committed in the neighbourhood and condoned by the executive, fostered the growth of the secret societies. The same thing was occurring in every part of the county, secret societies sprang up in every parish. Rival societies soon developed into aggressive factions; and every succeeding fair and race meeting left its tale of blood and a grievance to be washed away in the blood of the victorious faction, on the first available opportunity.[23]

The sad truth is that County Monaghan in the early nineteenth century was a land infested with disorder and injustice, with encounters between rival factions, and with corruption in the secret societies. William Carleton, the region's leading novelist of that time, who as a young man had been recruited into the Ribbonmen, bitterly recalled: "The members of that accursed Ribbon Society, instead of confining themselves to these objects for which it seems to have been originally designed – a union of Irishmen against their Protestant enemies, and the penal enactments which oppressed them at the time – departed from their original object, and employed its murderous machinery not against its open and common enemy, but in the following up of private and personal feuds, and enmities among themselves."[24]

It is not surprising that Benedict Kiely, Carleton's explicator, should describe Carleton's country – a territory lying mainly in County Tyrone but also embracing northern County Monaghan, where the older novelist had received part of his schooling – as a place "where men were bitterly discontented about rent and tithes, where men really knew slavery and oppression and the black neighbourhood of perpetually threatening hunger, where men hated each other because of differing creeds. That wicked rivalry of creeds, the sufferings of the majority at the hands of a rabid, government-supported minority had already touched his home and his people vividly enough to be remembered."[25]

By faithfully depicting the actualities of Ulster life in the eighteenth and nineteenth centuries, Carleton's stories – most notably in the collection entitled *Traits and Stories of the Irish Peasantry* – reveal much about the people of the Tyrone-Monaghan border country, the people who would soon emigrate to Prince Edward Island. Carleton denounced violence and secret societies in *Valentine M'Clutchy* and in "Wildgoose Lodge," and he exposed the notorious rowdiness associated with Scarnageera in "The Fair of Emyvale." As Thomas Brendan O'Grady has observed, the latter short story has special value for Prince Edward Island because it portrays the contemporaries of the Island's County Monaghan settlers. The story includes a donnybrook, which "was probably the most violent and terrific one of the kind which ever occurred in Ireland."[26]

THE GREAT FAMINE

Then, in 1845, the potato blight struck Ireland. The following year the potato crop was a total failure. Worse still, "Black '47" brought the full fury of the national disaster known as the Great Hunger. The whole national economy collapsed. The social order, with all its disorder, was uprooted. A million people perished from famine-related causes: hunger, fever, scurvy, and cholera. Upwards of a million people emigrated to North America. The devastation caused by the Great Famine (1845–48) and the social upheaval accompanying the disaster pushed all other issues into the background.

Before isolating for closer scrutiny some effects of the Great Famine as witnessed by County Monaghan people who later emigrated to Prince Edward Island, it must be acknowledged that the famine devastation was much greater in the west of Ireland than in the east or north. Cecil Woodham-Smith's *The Great Hunger*, to mention only one account, describes the nationwide tragedy. Here, however, we focus on a limited area and a leading Monaghan historian's judgment that "of all the Ulster counties, Monaghan suffered most."[27] There had been crop failures in 1817, 1821, and 1822, but none that caused nationwide misery, illness, and death. As well as these periodic agricultural setbacks, Monaghan suffered from extensive unemployment, and as early as 1839 food had to be distributed to the poor in Monaghan.

These poor and unemployed people who depended heavily on potatoes for daily sustenance were among the earliest victims of the blight.

It is now recognized that the socio-economic structure of the countryside itself made up a large part of the problem. The townlands encompassed the farms, and the farmlands were in turn divided and subdivided into individual or family units. For a century prior to the emigration period, most farmers had worked holdings of ten acres, more or less, while cottiers lived on smaller acreages, and subtenants scraped by on the least land of all. Subsistence farming was the norm. For nourishment, families relied occasionally on fowl, beef, or mutton, but regularly on porridge, bread, milk, and eggs, and extensively on potatoes. This small-farm society sufficed until late in the eighteenth century, when the population greatly expanded and the size of individual holdings was sharply contracted. Thus, the disaster was caused not by the potato infestation alone but also by several social conditions along with the political policies of the era.

Not all the news out of Monaghan was bad. In the early 1840s there were some accounts of rural progress. The farming societies formed in several places spurred interest in improved farming methods. For instance, on the Rose estate near Tydavnet, the tillage and grazing was poor. The native breed of small black cattle, which took three years to fatten and in winter were fed on coarse natural grasses and rushes, provided a tolerable stock of manure. Here the landlord introduced a loan scheme to improve pig and cattle stocks. In 1840 James Smith published *Remarks on Thorough Draining and Deep Ploughing*, and in 1841 the Scotch or iron plough came to Tydavnet. These were among the signs of improvement in agriculture on the eve of the Great Famine, but unfortunately they were not sufficient to avert the disaster.[28]

County Monaghan's Protestants suffered as much as Catholics during the Great Famine, with dwellers in the western and southwestern parishes suffering more than those in other sections. According to historian Peadar Livingstone, Monaghan's population between 1841 and 1851 dropped from over 200,000 to less than 142,000 (a net loss of more than 58,000 people, or nearly 30 percent of the population). The Tyholland district lost more than 37 percent of its people, Donagh 32 percent, Tydavnet close to 28 percent, Clontibret over 27 percent, Clones over 27 percent, Truagh 26 percent and Monaghan nearly 21 percent. The towns fared better than the countryside, but the villages were hard hit. Emyvale, for instance, decreased from 694 residents to 518, and Glaslough from 562 to 463. Bellatrain village was wiped out, and the entire townland of Drum, outside the village itself, became deserted.

However, not all of this population loss should be attributed to the famine, for some emigration had preceded the disaster. In 1843 a Church of Ireland history pamphlet recorded: "A number of men and women emigrated from the Leslie estate and founded St Joseph's Mission, DeSable," in Prince Edward Island.[29] Recent studies indicate that more than 2,000 persons had fled from northern Monaghan to Prince Edward Island before 1847, and another 700 or more followed in 1847–48. How many scattered to other British North American colonies is not known.

The severity of the crop failure and attendant evils may partly be explained by the fact that Monaghan had a very high proportion of vulnerable people, including unemployed persons, part-time labourers, cottiers, and farmers with very small holdings (less than ten acres). These were the classes most unprotected against this type of disaster. The collapse of the linen industry early in the century had left many men unemployed, living in hovels and mud huts, and squeezing out a mere subsistence from small patches of potatoes. By the 1840s the number of cottiers, too, had increased. The prevalence of subtenants on many subdivided small acreages further aggravated the problem. In all, about 30 percent of the people relied totally on a diet of potatoes, and another 40 percent (including small farmers, employed cottiers and casual labourers) were greatly dependent upon that crop. Farmers who had more than ten acres, along with shopkeepers and their employees, were not so badly affected, though they did have to cope with food shortages, higher costs, loss of rental income from destitute cottiers and labourers, and pressure to meet their own rental obligations to their landlords. The dreadful spectre of imminent eviction and a dreary workhouse constantly loomed before landless tenants.

Landlords were affected too, for their incomes were reduced and they lost many of their tenants to hunger or disease (typhus, dysentery and relapsing fever were rampant); they lost others to northward migration and emigration to North America. In Magheracloone, where the discontented tenants had bravely rebelled in 1843, the famine gave rise to evictions, migration, and hundreds of deaths from starvation and disease. On the Shirley estate in southern Monaghan there were many evictions, and it was said that a hundred hovels were crushed into the ground; on the other hand, the Leslie family in northern Monaghan earned a good reputation for caring for the poor on the Glaslough estate. The area hardest hit by the famine was the heavily colonized Monaghan-Clones-Cootehill triangle, where the linen industry had prospered before British trade policies and unenlightened industrial practices had snuffed out its life.

Workhouses established under the 1838 Poor Law Act to provide institutionalized relief for the destitute, as well as temporary centres for the distribution of soup and porridge, certainly helped to lessen the tragedy in Monaghan. Still, scenes of destitution and death – of poor people dropping dead on the roads and in the fields – were common. The survivors lived in dread of hunger and disease. In his comprehensive *Monaghan Story*, Peadar Livingstone graphically illustrates how the fever "changed the whole attitude of people to their neighbours"; their consciences became so deranged by grief and fear that they numbly deserted the sick and dying.[30]

The trauma of the Great Famine scarred the national psyche and etched itself indelibly in the national memory. It changed the collective personality of Ireland. By 1848 the famine itself had passed, but the old work habits, diets, agricultural practices, land distribution and farm sizes, family life, emigration patterns, and trusting attitudes toward the British government would never be fully restored.

MONAGHAN SOCIETY AND ECONOMY

Most of the County Monaghan settlers had departed for Prince Edward Island before their home suffered the full brunt of the Great Famine and before the social structures they had known either collapsed or were subsumed in new or revitalized institutions. For them, the "home place" remained permanently identified with a townland (a defined area, ranging from a few hundred acres to over a thousand acres). They had originated in the numerous townlands of the county's northern sector: in, around, and above Monaghan town, in the districts of Clones and Clontibret, but principally in the three Roman Catholic parishes of Donagh, Errigal Truagh, and Tydavnet.[31]

Besides enfolding the townlands, the rolling hills sheltered hamlets and villages. For instance, there was Scotstown (*Baille an Scotaigh*), a market village that in 1834 consisted of one three-storey house, six two-storey houses and eighteen one-storey houses, most of them thatched; in 1841 its population reached 210. At that time Glaslough ("the green lake") was no more than a small collection of houses and stores bordering on the Leslie estate; and Emyvale, originally named *Scairbh na gCaorach*, ("the ford of the sheep"), was a one-street town, with 148 houses with a population of 694, which was noted for its clamorous markets and seasonal fairs.

The Monaghan Story[32] relates that residents of these rural communities produced and dealt in potatoes and turnips, corn, flax, butter and eggs, fowl, pigs, sheep and goats, black cattle, horses, donkeys and mules, plants, glassware, earthenware and hardware, socks, and coarse linens. Versatile by necessity, these country people were carpenters and builders, linen manufacturers, operators of forges and mills, processors of salted and pickled pork, and (even in a small place like Glaslough) delft makers and wood turners. In Donagh there were potters, and in Glennan stonecutters along with dozens of furniture makers, and in Emyvale mill workers who turned out spades, shovels, and other implements. Emigrants skilled in such trades and occupations stood a good chance of becoming productive settlers in other lands, as they did indeed become in Prince Edward Island.

Among the small industries found in eighteenth-century County Monaghan, historian D.C. Rushe includes linen manufacturing, tobacco manufacturing, tanning, brewing, and distilling; and among the tradesmen and craftsmen he lists shoemakers, hatters, tailors, dressmakers, dyers, and even specialists in the making of wigs, bonnets, gloves, coats, breeches, waistcoats, shirts, collars, frills, and underclothes. Rushe also acknowledges such diverse rural and town occupations as watch and clock makers, coach builders, harness makers, farriers, wheelwrights, whitesmiths and blacksmiths, mechanics, artisans, printers, musicians (harpers, fiddlers, flutists), publicans, and shopkeepers.[33] All of these secular skills were in demand both in Ireland and in the New World.

What County Monaghan's emigrants-in-waiting lacked most was formal education. This deficiency Rushe attributes to the 1712 enactments which statesman Edmund Burke had labelled "the two ferocious Acts of Anne" – royal statutes which effectively prevented Catholics from being educated and which made outlaws of itinerant schoolmasters.[34] Despite such laws, some teachers in the so-called hedge schools strove to perpetuate "the old racial love for learning."[35] In 1731 a committee reported that there was a "Popish" school in Donagh, another in Monaghan town, three in Clones, and three in Errigal Truagh.[36] Even when church-sponsored schools were permitted a century later, they were not state supported; therefore, in many towns, each denomination was forced to support its own school. In these local schools, country students could prepare for university or seminary studies; but because few professions were open to Catholics and very few families could afford the cost of higher education, enrolments remained small. Moreover, university education was not available to women, who, if they were fortunate, sometimes attended convent schools or private finishing schools.

The "national schools," which provided free primary education in the English language, were introduced in 1831. Earlier than that, though, some pastors in Monaghan had made some provision for the education of young people. The Reverend Charles MacDermott, administrator of Errigal Truagh from 1818 and parish priest there from 1834 until 1844, established primary schools before the National

Board existed, and "he maintained at least two very good classical schools."[37] (As a youth, John Hughes, the highly influential archbishop of New York, had attended the school at Mullyoden.)[38] Father Mac-Dermott's successor as parish priest in Errigal Truagh, Father John Mullan, was a noted Latinist and teacher of the classics. The Reverend Patrick Moynagh, longtime parish priest of Donagh, "built six primary schools in his parish, mostly at his own expense, and contributed generously to the salaries of the teachers," besides devoting much of his own time to instructing the children.[39] These were pastors whom immigrants to Prince Edward Island, to their lasting benefit, knew and admired.

It has been estimated that at the start of the nineteenth century, only one-third of the Irish men and perhaps one-sixth of the Irish women were literate. In an earlier, predominantly oral culture, literacy had not been as important as it would become in the nineteenth century. As traditional culture declined, formal schooling became more and more necessary. In the 1830s and 1840s Monaghan wrestled with this problem. Errigal Truagh had a lending library as early as 1842. In their homes and public houses literate people read aloud to the others – not only newspapers and the popular fiction of the day but even, occasionally, works of history and classical literature. At that time many people were articulate in conversational Gaelic, however imperfectly, as well as in English (that is, in an Irish dialect of the English language). Noting the 1835 reprinting of *The Spiritual Rose*, a popular prayer book, D.C. Rushe concluded that there must have been "a considerable number of people who read Irish in Monaghan."[40] Perhaps one-half the Monaghan people who came to North America spoke Irish, and it seems that virtually all spoke English. Many of them, upon arrival, were materially deprived, but not so many of them were culturally or linguistically destitute.

Renewed Hope

The period under review here (mainly the pre-famine decades of the nineteenth century) constitutes a transitional period in Irish social history, for the people generally were emerging from the vestiges of the penal age and preparing themselves for normal citizenship. The preserved bohogs (*bothóga*, "hidden chapels"), mass rocks, and penal crosses served as reminders of the old sectarian persecutions; myths and folk memories of those dark ages persisted; and the psychological scars of a deeply wounded people continued to sting. As the Roman Catholic Church regained its public prestige and undertook a massive rebuilding program, some outstanding priests came to the fore of social progress and guided their people to improvements in their moral and intellectual education. Adjudged by a later generation, on the other hand, some clergy seemed to have been too severe, too authoritarian, perhaps too prone to seek security for themselves or for the institutional church; if so, an offsetting characteristic of that time and place was steadfast religious belief. In 1811 at Corracrin, Father Daniel MacMullin confidently erected a new church on the site of the old Mass House used in penal days, a place (tradition relates) where Saint Oliver Plunkett administered confirmation in the mid-seventeenth century.[41] An even more dramatic assertion of Monaghan's liberation was the laying of the foundation, in 1861, for the magnificent Cathedral of St Macartan.[42] Such events enriched the memories of the County Monaghan people who chose to emigrate.

On Their Way

Improvements in Monaghan's infrastructure proved opportune for people on the move. Between 1780 and 1830 many roads had been built or improved. More importantly, in 1832 the Ulster Canal had been completed to Charlemont, giving Monaghan residents water access across Armagh to Lough Neagh and thence to the eastern seaports of Belfast and Newry. By 1842 the same canal crossed Monaghan westward to Lough Erne in County Fermanagh. And by 1848 the railway linked the town of Armagh with the seaport of Newry. These advances in transportation clearly facilitated the mobility of those who chose to join the exodus from Ulster – to Scotland and England as well as to North America.

For these emigrants, as for their cousins who did not venture forth, the family home – small, sparse, humble – remained the immediate school for character and the conservatory of culture. Talking, listening, reading, singing, entertaining neighbours, observing, musing by the turf fire, attending to the routine chores, family members daily transmitted their values to one another. In this cultural setting, the mother ordinarily was the first and principal teacher, the care provider and guardian of morals. Perhaps this explains the view that the Irish home was a kind of matriarchy, possibly at times overprotective, too possessive, puritanical; but there can be no doubt that in the traditional Irish kitchen the mother was the sovereign. In most instances, no doubt, the kitchen was the family's private oratory, where prayers were recited daily. In less fortunate instances, the kitchen became the setting for callous conduct and bitter argument. There, in any event, habits were engendered, attitudes formed, lessons learned, judgments passed, relationships cemented, decisions made, and family bonds cultivated. For better or for worse, all over Ireland, the home was the foremost place for the education of the heart and the formation of character.

When they came to Prince Edward Island, typical emigrants from the little hills of Monaghan carried few material possessions and little money, but assuredly they took with them the burden of their county's history, the mores of their villages and townlands, the precepts of their parishes, and the guidance of their homes.

CHAPTER SEVEN

The Monaghan Settlers:
A People Set Apart

My thousand farewells, my dear country, dear Truagh,
I am now far away, we are now far apart;
But in trials I know that your gates won't be bolted –
You'll open your doors and you'll open your heart.
                                    "The Green Woods of Truagh"

More than one hundred and fifty years after the exodus of a few
thousand people from the northern baronies of County Monaghan,
their descendants have been restoring familial and cultural links with
their places of origin, tracing their ancestral roots, and visiting their
ancient townlands and homesteads in the "County of the Little
Hills." In return, each summer since 1990, delegations from Mon-
aghan have been flying across the Atlantic Ocean to become person-
ally acquainted with their distant cousins in Canada's smallest
province. This chapter identifies the settings and backgrounds of
many of the Monaghan immigrants, and indicates their native
parishes and some of the 1,853 townlands as well as their places of
settlement in Prince Edward Island. Although official passenger
rosters are practically non-existent, all of the ships known to have
brought the Monaghan settlers are listed here, along with the date of
their arrival.

The piecing together of a plausible history of these people and the
restoration of social ties with the homeland should continue to bene-
fit descendants on both sides of the Atlantic. The findings are pre-
sented in their historical, geographical, and cultural contexts only,
and although many surnames are mentioned, no conscious effort is
made here to provide specialized genealogical information or individ-
ual family histories. Furthermore, the study is limited to Prince
Edward Island and does not account for County Monaghan immi-
grants in Nova Scotia or in such interesting settlements as Miramichi,

*New Brunswick; Peterborough, Ontario; and Providence, Rhode
Island.*

Of the ten thousand immigrants who came directly from every county
in Ireland to settle in Prince Edward Island in the first half of the nineteenth century, the largest single group unquestionably originated in
County Monaghan. From the rural parishes of Donagh, Tydavnet,
Errigal Truagh, Tyholland, and Clontibret they came, from the villages
of Emyvale, Glaslough, and Clones, and from Monaghan town. They
came mainly from the baronies of Truagh and Monaghan, in the north
and northeast of the county. In rapid waves between 1830 and 1848,
over three thousand strong, they came. Then they ceased coming.

PROLOGUE TO THE MIGRATION

To account for the phenomenon known as the Monaghan Settlements,
it is first necessary to trace the activities of an Island-born Scottish
priest, John MacDonald (also spelled McDonald), in the city of Glasgow in 1830. Father MacDonald, then about thirty years of age, was
the third son of the estimable Captain John MacDonald, Laird of Glenaladale and a Loyalist officer in the War of American Independence.
Of particular relevance to our story is the fact that Captain MacDonald, a resident proprietor, had purchased Townships Thirty-five and
Thirty-six, and founded in 1772 the first Scottish Catholic settlement
in Prince Edward Island. Both John MacDonalds, father and son, were
destined to influence the course of Island history: the father, by design,
in the planned Scottish settlement of Scotchfort and Tracadie; the son,
by inheritance, in the opportune Irish settlement of Fort Augustus, his
portion of the family estate.[1]

From the outset, it seems, the destinies of the Scots Catholics and
Irish Catholics who later came to Prince Edward Island were providentially intertwined, for an Irish Dominican priest named Father
Wynne had been a catalyst of Captain MacDonald's Scots migration of
1772,[2] just as the Island's Scottish priest, Father John MacDonald, precipitated the Monaghan migration nearly sixty years later. More
remarkable, perhaps, is the fact that the two movements were causally
linked.

As recorded by Lorne C. Callbeck and others, the story is as follows.
Father Wynne, assistant to the aging Rev. Alexander Forrester, in the
course of his ministry on the Isle of South Uist in the Outer Hebrides,
saw fit in 1768 to reprimand Colin MacDonald, son of Alastair Mor

MacDonald, Laird of Boisdale. The headstrong elder gentleman of the Western Highlands reacted not with repentance but with defiance. He renounced his Catholic faith and thereafter tried by various means, but without success, to convert his tenants to Presbyterianism. A popular version of the event relates that Boisdale "was wont to station himself at the fork in the road on a Sunday morning where, brandishing his long yellow staff, he would attempt to herd the Roman Catholics up the branch that led to the Presbyterian kirk. His peculiar type of evangelism became known as *credimh a bhata bhui*, the religion of the yellow staff."[3]

In response to Boisdale's intimidations, at least two bishops advised the Catholic tenants to emigrate. Bishop George Hay in Edinburgh and Bishop Richard Challoner in London greatly assisted John MacDonald, a Clanranald tacksman, in his venture to resettle these Highlanders on his recently purchased estate in St John's Island – later named Prince Edward Island. Thus in 1772 the Scottish Catholics (100 from South Uist and 110 from the Arisaig and Moidart districts of the mainland) sailed on the *Alexander* for the New World and landed at a place later to be named Scotchfort. There, they became tenants on Lot 36, the principal locus of which was called Tracadie. Glenaladale, as the proprietor was titled, later also purchased the adjoining Lot 35, so that his holdings totalled 40,000 acres.

In time Captain John MacDonald and his second wife, Margaret MacDonald of Guernish (who came to be called "The Queen of Tracadie"), had four sons and a daughter. The third son, John, studied theology in Rome and Paris.[4] Upon ordination as a Roman Catholic priest in 1825, he was appointed assistant pastor at St Andrew's Church (at that time it was called a "chapel")[5] in Glasgow, an extensive parish which embraced the towns of Airdrie and Hamilton and numerous villages as well as the entire city itself,[6] including slum districts where many poor Irish immigrants lived. St Andrew's, opened in 1816, was an impressive Gothic structure that could accommodate more than two thousand worshippers. For Glasgow in the nineteenth century, the building of St Andrew's exemplified the revival of Catholicism, which had been in a shambles since the Reformation and in the doldrums under the Penal Laws. Swelling the membership of the Catholic Church in the city were many thousands of northern Irish, refugees from the periodic crop failures, the decline in the linen industry, the general poverty, and the limited opportunities in their homeland. The Scots nicknamed these Irish immigrants Barneys, but to outsiders they came to be known as the Glasgow Irish.

THE GLASGOW CONNECTION

From pre-Christian times, sailing vessels had shuttled twelve miles across the North Channel that geographically separates but commercially unites Ireland and Scotland. The two Celtic states had social and political ties as well. For centuries, in fact, across the wider expanses of the Irish Sea, Ireland had conducted sporadic exchanges of goods and people with Scotland, England, and Wales – and the ancient Gaelic kingdom of Dal Riata actually encompassed large parts of both Antrim and Argyll. Over all these centuries, mutual attitudes and actions had wavered between hostility and hospitality as one state or the other conducted or endured raids, invasions, plantations, and migrations.[7]

By the early nineteenth century, several thousand seasonal migrants from Ulster were annually commuting to Scotland on crowded sailing ships and (by the 1820s) on steam packets. These Irish labourers were usually tolerated, for they brought in the harvest, built canals and railroads, and toiled in shipyards and sweatshops. They were willing to undertake almost any type of physical labour that would enable them to buy their daily food and perhaps some clothing, and still save a few pounds to take back to Ireland to pay the rent and get through the winter. On such precarious pickings thousands of Irish migrants and their families subsisted.

In time, many of these labourers chose not to return to Ireland, and in Scotland they sought jobs that offered steadier income and security. Some of the more resourceful workers aimed ultimately at emigrating to America – a dream that eluded the vast majority, who remained too poor ever to afford such a voyage. In 1834 Bishop Andrew Scott of Glasgow estimated that only a few Irish had "raised themselves to the rank of respectable shopkeepers," whereas the great bulk of the men were "hand-loom cotton weavers, or labourers employed on day's wages on roads, canals, coal-pits, draining, ditching, serving masons, coal porters, etc.," and the women were "generally employed at the steam looms or in the cotton manufactories."[8] Wages were low and employment irregular, and most of the Glasgow Irish lived in appalling poverty in overcrowded tenements, where they were exposed to frequent epidemics, violence, and moral degradation.

By 1830 the forty thousand Irish denizens of Glasgow constituted fully one-fifth of the city's population. Some Scots, understandably, viewed the Irish workers as intruders who took jobs away from them. Other Scots, sternly Calvinistic, feared that the large influx of Irish Catholics would threaten the dominance of Protestantism in Scotland. Sometimes these fears gave rise to bigotry and intimidation.[9] The Irish sojourners in Glasgow – like their countrymen struggling for survival in the slums of Dumbarton, Stranraer, Greenock, Kilmarnock, Edinburgh, and a dozen other places – must have wondered if they would ever be able to improve their lot in life.

James Edmund Handley, in his study of the Irish in Scotland, states that central Glasgow in the first half of the nineteenth century exhibited "the most revolting conditions of life to be met with in the whole of Great Britain."[10] He describes one small sector of the extremely overcrowded city in these terms: "No proper system of drainage or removal of refuse, an imperfect supply of water from the more or less polluted river that flowed through the city, no privies, or a few that women and children could not use, no baths or means of bathing even in the houses of fairly well-to-do – one can imagine the effect of such a state of affairs on the health and morals of the people. It was into this congested city that thousands of Irish poured and added to the already terrible congestion. In the decade 1831–41 the population of the city increased by 78,000 while the number of new houses built was only 3,551."[11]

In his account of crime in Glasgow, Handley cites the official report of Police Superintendent H. Miller:

"In the very centre of the city there is an accumulated mass of squalid wretchedness, which is probably unequalled in any other town in the British dominions." In the dwellings in this area "there is concentrated everything that is wretched, dissolute, loathsome and pestilential. These places are filled by a population of many thousands of miserable creatures. The houses in which they live are unfit even for sties, and every apartment is filled with a promiscuous crowd of men, women and children, all in the most revolting state of filth and squalor. In many of the houses there is scarcely any ventilation; dunghills lie in the vicinity of the dwellings; and from the extremely defective sewerage, filth of every kind constantly accumulates. In these horrid dens the most abandoned characters of the city are collected, and from thence they nightly issue to disseminate disease, and to pour upon the town every species of crime and abomination."[12]

After describing in great detail the miserable habitat of the desperate and destitute Irish in Glasgow and the antisocial behaviour often engendered by the deplorable conditions there, Handley makes these wry observations:

A peculiar feature of quarrelsome Irish immigrants was the inter-province and inter-county rivalry that existed among them, though in a strange land a sense of prudence should have dictated otherwise. Connacht men disapproved of the men of Ulster, Tyrone men frowned on natives of Antrim, and Monaghan men scowled at immigrants from Donegal. Reports of fights among them are not uncommon. The greatest rivalry seems to have existed between Monaghan and Donegal immigrants, occasioned principally by jealousy on the part of the Monaghan men, who were mainly labourers, against the more pushful and successful Donegal men. Once on a Sunday evening a fierce fight involving some three hundred broke out between them in the Saltmarket of Glasgow. The battle rolled backwards and forwards for hours. Irishmen coming home from evening service in the Catholic chapel of St Andrew's in the neighbourhood rushed into their houses to change from their Sunday clothes into fighting gear. At the height of the disturbance some of the leaders gave vent to their exuberance by executing step-dances on the edge of the battlefield before joining the combatants. A crowd of 10,000 spectators assembled in the Bridgegate and Saltmarket. The police arrived but were kept on the outside of the throng feebly waving their batons to no purpose.[13]

Eventually the combatants exhausted themselves and, sore and weary, they stumbled back to their miserable slum dwellings, often to cause further anxiety and disorder there. Unfortunately for the families involved, such factional fights were quite common. On the larger scene, the propensity for excessive drinking and rowdiness deeply damaged the general reputation of the Irish people abroad.

A WAY OUT

Poor wages and poor working conditions, poor housing and poor health, poor education and poor social assistance, poor prospects and poor morale – for many Irish these were pervasive realities in Glasgow and vicinity early in the nineteenth century. Is it any wonder that such a social, economic, and moral miasma as Handley and others describe bred large measures of drunkenness and violence, pestilence and injury, bigotry, injustice, and crime? Is it any wonder that even the minority of Irish residents of Glasgow and vicinity who managed to earn a modicum of security and build up small savings would choose to emigrate when given the opportunity? And is it any wonder that decent people in Ireland would gladly embrace any reasonable alternative to the cycle of sporadic employment and endemic poverty in Scotland?

It was in this general setting, and particularly to the parishioners of St Andrew's – a mixed congregation of regular Glasgow residents (including some of Irish descent), Glengarry and some other Highlanders,[14] and a large number of seasonal and temporary Irish immigrants, mainly from Ulster – that Father John MacDonald addressed his invitation to emigrate with him to Prince Edward Island and to take up farms on the large estate he had inherited. Those who could afford the one-way journey listened attentively.

It is not known whether it was political, humanitarian, or sectarian motives that inspired MacDonald to propose to transplant Glasgow dwellers to Prince Edward Island, though it seems that it was mainly a straightforward business enterprise, intended to populate his own idle farmlands. Evidently, MacDonald did not subsidize the transportation costs of would-be settlers, though he did offer start-up loans for livestock and equipment.

The Corsair

The response to MacDonald's invitation may be judged from this report in the *Glasgow Chronicle* of 2 April 1830:

About thirty-two families, almost all of Roman Catholic faith, were to sail on Thursday from Greenock for Prince Edward Island under the superintendence of Mr MacDonald, assistant Clergyman of the Catholic Chapel in this city. The greater part of them are residents of this city and the Western Isles. We understand that they have been promised to receive grants of land from Mr MacDonald, who is a native of the Island, and is said to possess large tracts of ground there which he has taken the resolution of letting out to emigrants at the mere trifle of 1 shilling per acre. Each family averaging three or four children is to receive 100 acres and is to be furnished with farmsteads, a cow, a horse, and other stock, which, however, are to be paid for as soon as the emigrants have it in their power. Under these impressions they have set out with great spirit and many of them have left very comfortable situations in the country, allured by the high prospects held out by their spiritual guide. They are by no means the poorest of our Catholic population, as all of them have taken away a considerable amount of money.[15]

When the *Corsair* sailed out of Greenock, neither the poorest of the Irish poor nor the truly well-to-do of Glasgow were aboard. The passengers were mainly members of Irish families who had lived in Glasgow and vicinity for varying lengths of time. Some had lived in Glasgow long enough for their children to be born there or their elders buried there. Tombstone inscriptions in Dumbarton, for instance, clearly confirm historical evidence that northern Irish families had been settling in Glasgow for a generation or longer; but genealogical research has been slow to identify among the Island's "Glasgow Irish" people of Irish parentage who were born in Scotland. Regardless, they generally thought of themselves and were thought of by others as "the Irish abroad" or even as "the Irish in exile." Although they had been living in Scotland, they had not ceased to think of Ireland as their home.

After several weeks at sea, Father MacDonald and his recruits arrived in Charlottetown. The date was 19 May 1830. The Prince Edward Island *Register* reported the historic event: "Two hundred and six settlers arrived in the *Corsair* from Greenock on Wednesday last. The bulk of them proceeded up the Hillsborough River about 10 miles to be located above Johnston's River, on the property of the Rev. John MacDonald. They are chiefly natives of the north of Ireland and apparently seemed pleased with the change. Two births occurred on the passage and one since their arrival."[16]

Records and tradition indicate that these settlers included the families of James Brogan, Peter Duffy, James Gillan, John Haggarty, Bernard Heron, Edward Kelly, John Kelly, William Kelly, Thomas Logan, Peter McGill, Peter Murphy, Peter O'Hare, and Bernard Sweeney.[17] It seems quite possible that some of the following persons also arrived on the *Corsair*: Ann Brady, relict of John Flynn; William Crozier; James Heron; Arthur McGill (married to Sarah Curran) and his mother; James McLaughlin and his wife Mary Phillips; Elizabeth McQuaid and James and Mary Moynagh (née McQuaid), sisters of settler Francis McQuaid; John Mooney, Henry Mooney and (less likely) Robert Mooney; James O'Hare; and Samuel Wilson. Also believed to have been aboard the *Corsair* were the Jennings brothers: Bernard (born in Ireland and married to Catherine O'Rourke), who settled in Lot 34; and Peter (born in Scotland and married to Catherine, family name unknown), who settled in Lot 36. Also settling in Lot 36 at Tracadie Sandhills were Peter and Daniel Powell, the latter married to Jane Curren of County Down. Others who might have sailed on the *Corsair* include James Waddell and his wife Elizabeth Craig of Monaghan; Daniel Hughes of Tyholland, County Monaghan; Patrick and Jane O'Donnell of County Mayo; and Thomas Frizzell of County Antrim. Also worth noting is the belief that the *Corsair* may have disembarked a small number of people while passing through Nova Scotia's Strait of Canso.

Along with their still unidentified compatriots who settled at Fort Augustus in 1830, the *Corsair* passengers came to be labelled the Glasgow Irish. Initially they sheltered close to the Hillsborough River in "the settlement of the five houses," an area once occupied by Acadians, near where a number of Scots and southern Irish (including Patrick and Mary Hennessey of County Wexford) were already living when the newcomers from Glasgow landed (see map 8). "For the first few years," relates the Reverend A.E. Burke, "they suffered greatly

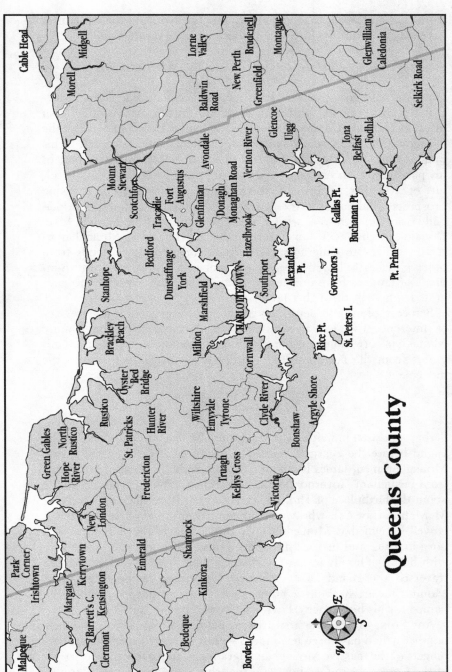

Map 8. The Monaghan settlers founded several notable communities in Queens County and spread into both adjoining counties.

Queens County

from cold and want, then experience taught them, and the wilderness gave way to farms," which in time became quite productive.[18]

EMIGRATION FROM COUNTY MONAGHAN

Once the Glasgow pioneers had become acclimatized, Father Mac-Donald corresponded with the Reverend Patrick Moynagh, parish priest of Donagh, County Monaghan, the native parish of some of the Glasgow Irish. Apparently satisfied with MacDonald's account of his budding colony, Moynagh encouraged and materially assisted some of his parishioners to emigrate to Fort Augustus. Choosing the difficult life of colonists in British North America over the unpromising prospects of labourers in the British Isles, a number of families principally from Donagh soon set out for Prince Edward Island. Later, Mac-Donald sent his agent, James Trainor, back to his native Monaghan to recruit still more emigrants. As a result, relatives and friends from other parishes followed the Donagh pioneers, and in that way hundreds of families from northern County Monaghan continued to emigrate from 1835 through 1848.

Before exploring in detail this Monaghan migration, it is necessary to interpose two explanatory notes concerning, first, the County Monaghan forerunners of the sustained migration and, second, immigrants from the neighbouring counties who also participated in the movement.

Forerunners

Perhaps a dozen individuals from County Monaghan had come to the Island before the Glasgow Irish. For instance, as early as 1771, two Monaghan men, James Irwin and William Kidd, had leased farmlands from Lieutenant-Governor Thomas DesBrisay.[19] We can only speculate about the birthplace of Tho. Duffee (Lot 5) or Rob McConnel or Peter McMahon (Lot 65), who were enumerated in the 1798 census; but it is well known that Monaghan's Colonel Thomas Dawson, who was born in 1762 and married Elizabeth Frances Tait in 1784, came here with his large family in 1801. Before he died three years later he had traversed the Island as a dedicated Methodist lay preacher. Near Mount Stewart he built a home on a 600–acre property, which he named for his birthplace, Dawson's Grove.[20]

Any Monaghan immigrants arriving before 19 May 1830 – and their number would have been few indeed – must be regarded as chance harbingers of the massive Monaghan migration that began with the arrival of the *Corsair* from Greenock. Of that ship's 206 passengers who set-

tled on Father John MacDonald's lands at Fort Augustus, ten miles up
the Hillsborough River east of Charlottetown, the Glasgow Irish were
certainly the great majority.

Neighbouring Counties

It would be a serious mistake to assume that Ireland's county lines con-
fined or defined the chain of migration which ensued from the Glasgow Irish colonizing venture that was initiated by the Reverend John
MacDonald of Fort Augustus, Prince Edward Island, and abetted by
the Reverend Patrick Moynagh of Donagh, County Monaghan. Their
brief collaboration, along with other factors, gradually embraced family after family along tributaries in adjoining areas until the Monaghan
movement touched, however lightly, every county in Ulster.

The County Armagh parish of Tynan, for instance (including the
Middleton district and extending along Monaghan's northeastern
border down to Keady and inland to Armagh town), sent at least a
score of families. Philip Hughes immigrated to Tracadie in 1834 at
age forty-seven and settled his family in Hunter River. Patrick and
Mary Hughes also settled there in the same year. James Murtagh of
Lot 26 came from Armagh in 1840. The Corley family, whose daughter Mary later married a man named Dunn, had been weavers in
Middleton. Edward Hughes, from the same place, came to Kinkora
in 1841. That year also brought James McAdam to Lot 48 from Der-
rynoose. Margaret McDade immigrated with her mother and sister;
and Michael MacGuigan and his wife Catherine Murphy settled in
Hope River.

The 1841 immigrants may have sailed together on the *Thomas Gelston*. Those who had arrived two years earlier, including Philip Duffy,
who settled in Fort Augustus in 1840, probably sailed on the *Margaret
Pollock*. Among the other County Armagh newcomers were Thomas
Crehan, James Garland from Armagh town, Ann McGee and husband
Francis Hughes, and James Hughes and his wife Jane Irving, who settled on St Marys Road and raised a son who became a prosperous merchant and a member of parliament. At the outset of the movement,
Armagh's Samuel Wilson (1785–1867) may have sailed on the *Corsair*
in 1830; toward the end of the movement, Armagh's Owen O'Neill
arrived on the *Lady Constable* in 1847.

Still retold at family reunions is the story of Hugh Campbell's 1841
emigration. Campbell, his wife Margaret Smart, and their five children set out in early April from their home in Cavan townland
near the Blackwater River in Clogher district of County Tyrone. Son
Hugh John, age fourteen, and his three sisters (Mary, Margaret, and

Catherine) accompanied their parents, who boarded the 917–ton barque *Margaret Pollock* in Belfast; but the elder son, Thomas, embarked from the next pier in a smaller ship, the *Thomas Gelston*. Both ships were bound for Prince Edward Island. Soon the friendly race was on – first one vessel and then the other taking the lead, all the way across the wide Atlantic. A month later the *Pollock* entered Charlottetown harbour with her 685 passengers, many up on deck, straining to locate the rival *Gelston* carrying their 139 countrymen. Two hours later, to the waving, shouting, and cheering of the happy immigrants, the two vessels moored alongside one another. The singing and dancing continued on the wharf until the newcomers gradually dispersed. Guided by Charlottetown's pastor, the Reverend Malachy Reynolds, they headed across country to the settlements he recommended. The Campbells first put down roots in Westmoreland, but later generations scattered to Charlottetown and to other Island communities, then to many localities across Canada and the United States. Three County Tyrone neighbours of the Campbell family became their neighbours in the Westmoreland–Kellys Cross area on the Island; within the radius of half a mile lived Thomas Hagan married to Bridget Brennan, John Hughes married to Mary Mullins, and John Cusack married to Johanna Heuron.

Francis and Mary Hagan (Hagen) also spoke of the Clogher district of County Tyrone as their homeland. Preceding them were Cookstown natives James McLaughlin and his wife Mary Phillips, who came in 1830, evidently on the *Corsair*; Michael Mullin and his wife Ann McCarrron (1835); John Dreehan (1839); James Donnelly from Mullybrannon, and the Bedeque settler Patrick Kelly (both before 1840). Other Tyrone immigrants included Edward Laverty, Mary Laverty, and Michael Laverty, all of whom settled in Fort Augustus and vicinity, and Mrs James McAvinn. Thomas McDonald, who settled on the Georgetown Road, was also born in Tyrone. Other families surnamed Cusack (Cuisick) and Owens may also have Tyrone antecedents.

Although Letitia Mayne (married to James Murphy) came from Enniskillen, and Thomas McAnalty (who settled near Georgetown) came from Ederney Bridge, most other County Fermanagh immigrants to the Island seem to have resided much closer to the Monaghan county line. Evidently, Patrick McKenna and William McIntyre resided in that area, as did Philip and Ann McMahon. The Maguire family, later well known in Morell, originated near Maguiresbridge. Roslea, not far from Clones, sent James Flinn to Charlottetown and Aeneas McCabe to Iona, PEI. The Patrick Prunty family may also have come from that district. In May 1847 Owen McCarvill arrived on the ill-fated *Lady Constable* and settled in Kinkora. Also aboard that plague ship were two couples who had set out from Roslea intending to raise their families in Iona: Patrick McCluskey and his wife Ellen Dougherty, and Philip Rooney and his wife Mary Dougherty. Of the four Rooney sons born in Ireland, three died en route. Another son, named Philip (born in PEI) later married Ellen McKenna, daughter of Owen McKenna and Ellen McInnis. Into that family were born five priests and two nuns.

James Heron, born in Donegal, lived in Dumbarton, Scotland, before he sailed with the Glasgow Irish to Fort Augustus. Robert Dean, and Mrs Mary Ann Heggs were among other settlers from Donegal. From County Antrim came the Art McGill family, also part of the *Corsair* complement. He was born in 1794 and lived in Scotland from 1800. Other Island settlers with roots in County Antrim include Ephraim Craig, Neil Lafferty, James Strain, George Russell of Ballymena, and four Belfast natives: Mrs Eleanor McKiernan, Mrs Elizabeth Thomas, James Finley, and Thomas Sullivan. Sea Captain James Hemphill of Ballyshane settled at Burnt Point near Georgetown.

Descendants of Patrick Beagan, Peter Cosgrove, Samuel W. Mitchell, and Mrs Francis Stagman regard Cavan as their ancestral county, while descendants of Robert Laurie, John Shankster, and Mrs Ann Brady Flynn think of County Down as their ancient homeland. County Derry was the birthplace of Mrs Mary Clouston, Mrs Jane Robertson Beer, John Dean, Robert Gibson, and James McNutt (Londonderry). Also from Derry were James Gillan and John Kelly, Fort Augustus settlers who arrived on the *Corsair*.

How all these families, and many more, emigrating from Ulster's nine counties and possibly numbering more than four thousand people all told, reached the shores of the Island is partly answered by the following account of the shipping that entered the port of Charlottetown during the 1830s and 1840s.

IMMIGRANT TRANSPORTATION

In 1835 the *Grace* of Newcastle (196 passengers) and the *Margo* (80 passengers) arrived from Belfast, but no names or birthplaces of the passengers are available. Not until 4 July 1837 does the *Royal Gazette* offer the following type of information: "The Brig *Lady Anne*, of Newcastle, James Sims, Master, having on board 48 passengers from the County of Monaghan (Ireland), sailed from Belfast on the 19th May, bound for Wallace, Nova Scotia, where she arrived on the 28th June. The destination of the greater part of the passengers being Prince

Edward Island, a sloop was hired by Capt. Sims, for the purpose of conveying them to Charlottetown, where 35 of them landed in good health."

Next, the *Royal Gazette* of 28 May 1839 announced: "*The Consbrook* arrived on Saturday May 25, in 34 days from Belfast, with 308 passengers, chiefly from the County of Monaghan, and came here with the intention of settling on lands of Rev. John MacDonald." The *Agitator* left Belfast at the same time and evidently arrived on 4 June with 314 passengers, having as their guide James Trainor, official agent for Father John MacDonald. Seventeen months later Francis Kelly of Fort Augustus, agent for Donald MacDonald (older brother of Father John), announced that "the Monaghan Emigrants who came to this Island in the month of May, 1839, in the ships *Agitator* and *Consbrook*" could claim a refund on the Board of Health deposits they had made before they sailed from Belfast.[21]

In 1840 the *Rosebank* arrived from Belfast on 2 June with 208 passengers. Less than a year later, as reported in the *Royal Gazette* (18 May 1841), that number was quadrupled in a single record-setting day when the *Margaret Pollock* from Belfast brought 685 passengers and the *Thomas Gelston*, also from Belfast, brought 139 passengers. Except for the sad fact that an epidemic of measles had taken the lives of twenty-eight children aboard the *Margaret Pollock* and a quarantine had to be imposed, the crossing had apparently been pleasant. Up to that time, we are told, "this vessel had the largest passenger list of any ship either steam or sail that ever entered Charlottetown harbour ... [During the quarantine] the captain, officers and crew did all that was possible to make the passengers happy and contented. Games and amusements were started and the young men and women danced and sang on the deck of the vessel. This must have been a gala day in Charlottetown ... These newcomers had no arrangements for settlement, preferring to see the land themselves before settling. This they did without delay, some of them leaving the same day to view the prospective localities, and were to report back to the others on the conditions as they found them."[22]

The Reverend Malachy Reynolds, parish priest of Charlottetown, assisted many of the newcomers, and it is believed that under his guidance fifty families from Monaghan and Armagh chose to settle in Kinkora while others became established in the Kellys Cross and Emyvale parishes. According to the erstwhile Charlottetown mayor, John McKenna, these people, unlike most Irish immigrants "were all fairly well supplied with money and whatever household effects they could bring with them. Before disembarking, an address was presented to the captain, thanking him for his kindness during the voyage. The address took the form of a ballad of twenty-four verses, which praised the captain, praised the crew and ships, and in fact everything that helped make the voyage so pleasant. The captain and mate both replied, bidding them a sorrowful good-bye and hoped that their days on the Island would be as pleasant as those spent on board the *Margaret Pollock*. They also praised them for their splendid behaviour during the voyage."[23]

In 1841 the *Consbrook* also made a satisfactory crossing, with as many as 700 immigrants from Counties Monaghan and Armagh. At least fifty persons from these two counties settled in Middleton that year. The *Morgiana* and the *Thomas Gelston* arrived on 28 and 30 May 1842, respectively, with a total of 425 passengers, "principally labourers, all from the County of Monaghan. Two old persons and one child died, and two children were born on the passage."[24] The *Morgiana* returned in September, again from Belfast, with sixty-six passengers.[25] In 1843, the year of the settlement of Kellys Cross, two other vessels out of Belfast transported immigrants to the Island: the *Chieftain*, which arrived in Charlottetown on 15 May with 208 passengers, and the *Rosebank*, which followed a week later with 150 passengers.[26] No doubt, most of these newcomers were from County Monaghan, but precise names and numbers were not recorded.

In his article on the early Irish settlers, Mayor McKenna refers to two vessels not recorded in the *Royal Gazette* or in the *Island Magazine* (Fall/Winter 1989): "The *Margoretta* arrived in 1844. This vessel went aground after entering the harbour and the passengers were taken off in lighters. I was unable to find the number. The *Fanny*, that afterwards went to California, also made a trip with emigrants."[27] One oversight in McKenna's account is found in the following shipping item reported in the 30 July 1844 issue of the *Royal Gazette*: "The ship *Independence*, John McCappin, Master, 34 days from Belfast, arrived here on Friday, with about 360 passengers, 156 of whom will be landed here, the remainder will proceed, in the vessel, to Quebec."

McKenna concluded his survey of the Irish arrivals up to June 1847 by stating with assurance: "On these ships from Belfast, every county in Ulster was represented, but a very large proportion was from the County Monaghan. They settled principally on the Monaghan Road, St Marys Road, Fort Augustus, Kellys Cross, Emerald, Millcove, Scotchfort, and Bear River, where hundreds of their descendants now live on land that was cleared and cultivated by the hard labour and toil of these pioneers."[28]

In passing, McKenna alluded to an ill-fated vessel, later identified as the *Miracle*, which set out from Ireland in 1847, the darkest famine

year. Its destination is not known, but its destiny was determined in the
Gulf of St Lawrence. During the voyage many passengers and crew
became ill, and those who died were buried at sea. Next, when the ship
was forced off course by extremely stormy weather and capsized near
the Magdalen Islands, many people died in the wreckage. Finally,
though the survivors were taken by a rescue ship to Pictou, Nova Scotia, several of them died there from the ordeal they had suffered. No
memorial records the names of the *Miracle*'s victims or survivors. All
alike are now recalled, if at all, as anonymous souls among the countless refugees from Ireland's Great Famine.[29]

While there is no evidence to indicate that the *Miracle* intended to
come to Prince Edward Island, another vessel carrying famine refugees
did arrive, as planned, from Liverpool with 419 northern Ireland settlers. This was the *Lady Constable*, which dropped anchor in Charlottetown on 24 May 1847. Over thirty fatalities during both the crossing and the period of quarantine were attributed to a highly malignant
type of ship fever.[30] The survivors of this tragic voyage made up virtually all of the Irish immigrants to the Island in 1847. In the post-famine
years Irish immigration to the Island declined to a mere trickle.

The mistaken belief persists that the Irish settlers of Prince Edward
Island were mainly famine victims who fled Ireland on the abominable
fever ships of the late 1840s. But as the documentary evidence
reviewed in this study confirms, the vast majority of Irish settlers had
come to the Island before the Great Famine. Moreover, the Island
rarely faced the pestilence more properly associated with the Grosse Île
quarantine station and burial sites along the shores of the St Lawrence
River. In the Maritime region, Saint John and Chatham were the most
significant sites for famine refugees. This is not to deny that before the
Great Famine of 1845–48 many Irish immigrants had already fled
from poverty and localized crop failures. Indeed, some of them certainly landed on the Island "poor, pinched with hunger, scantily clad."
Having said that, the fact remains that the *Lady Constable* was the
only "fever ship" to berth in Prince Edward Island during the Great
Famine years. (Chapter 8 discusses the *Lady Constable* incident in
greater detail.)

BLIGHT IN PRINCE EDWARD ISLAND

The Irish who had already settled on the Island were, of course, well
aware of the national catastrophe caused by the Great Famine in Ireland. Moreover, they themselves had experienced, first-hand but on a
much smaller scale, a potato blight similar to that which practically
wiped out the crop in their homeland. The blight period in Prince

Edward Island (1845–48) coincided with that in Ireland, and the same scourge might have had disastrous effects here too if the colonial legislative assembly had been manacled by the unbreakable *laissez-faire* policies and inhumane mercantile interests that proved so devastating to Ireland. Instead, to ward off the most harmful effects of the Island's potato crop failure of 1845, the assembly passed a series of short-term Acts prohibiting the export of potatoes. This legislation was enacted in 1846, renewed in 1847, and in 1848 it was extended to include grain and meal exports as well as potatoes.[31] Another Act, in 1846, also in response to the potato blight, provided seed and food for the many settlers who would otherwise have been unable to obtain those necessities for the ensuing seasons.[32] Because of such humane, sensible measures, the Islanders – unlike their unfortunate relatives in Ireland – were enabled to combat a widespread natural affliction and avert a social disaster. For this reason among others, to this day many Islanders hold the belief that famines are caused less often by crop failures or food shortages than by shortsighted economic and political policies that are not primarily designed to serve the common good.

Meanwhile, immediate relief for the Irish people at home was not neglected. For instance, 14 May 1847 was designated by royal proclamation as a day of general fast for all Christian denominations on the Island. Appropriate sermons were preached and large sums of money were collected, on that occasion and others, to help the famine victims in Ireland.

MONAGHAN SETTLEMENTS IN PEI

Upon their arrival, most of the pre-famine newcomers from County Monaghan quickly established themselves on land which they leased. At once they began the long process of turning the wilderness into productive farms.

D.J. Lake's map of Prince Edward Island,[33] the first to show the location of rural residents by name, lists many persons who were living in the Fort Augustus area in 1863. The map includes, of course, names of Irish and Scottish occupants who predated even the Glasgow Irish in Lot 36. Along the Hillsborough or East River were N. Lafferty, O'Brien, O'Hare, Hagarty, B. Webster, J. Brogan; nearby were H. Duffy, Fisher, J. McCanna, P. Hennessey, and P. Hughes. Along the principal road in the vicinity of the church and the school lived John Mitchell, James Mitchell, J. Poor, M. Hughes, the Hon. F. Kelly, H. Corley, D. McCannel, J. Kelly, T. Kelly, J. Duffy, P. Duffy, J. Gillan, E. Holland, J. Keenan, P. Callaghan.[34] On the same map, the Monaghan Road running from Fort Augustus through Lake Verde toward Vernon

River includes the homes of the following: Mrs Queen (Quinn?), P. Clarkin, F. McAree, B. McAree, J. Callaghan, Jas. McEntee, P. McEntee, J. McKoen, F. Carroll, J. McAlear, H. McEntee, L. Simpson, T. Carroll, O. Simpson, P. McKoen, J. McKenna, J. Lynn, J. Mullen, J. Trainor, and E. Cody.[35] These lists are not complete, nor is the print on the map always clear or the spelling always standard or consistent; but the 130 to 150 names on Lake's map identify most of the Irish (and many Scottish) families in the extended settlement that stretched from Fort Augustus to Millview. Many of their relatives and compatriots spread into Vernon River and branched out through Kings County; thus the colony which Father John MacDonald had founded soon extended well beyond the bounds of his own estate.

It is neither possible nor necessary to ascertain the specific place of origin of each of the families named on Lake's map (even in the cluster at the conjunction of Lots 35, 36, and 48, which was nostalgically named Donagh). The generality is clear enough: County Monaghan names are very common among the residents of Fort Augustus (St Patrick's parish), and their numbers decline as colonization proceeds eastward through Vernon River (St Joachim's parish), branches out in Kings County to Peakes and Baldwin Road (St Cuthbert's parish) as well as to Montague and St Marys Road, and to the Georgetown and Cardigan districts. In this thirty-mile-long irregular swath, there are many non-Monaghan Irish as well as many Scots and English settlers. In Iona (Montague West), for instance, Waterford, Wexford, and Kilkenny people preceded those from Monaghan, Armagh, and Tyrone by up to twenty years, and surnames from Ireland's southern regions were scattered around Kings County prior to 1835. Still, no pattern of immigration or concentration of settlers is more evident than that formed by the County Monaghan immigrants.

COUNTY MONAGHAN FAMILY NAMES

One way of identifying settlers who probably originated in County Monaghan is by their family names. However, designating certain surnames as "Monaghan names" remains risky indeed, even when matching Island names with the hundred most common names recorded in County Monaghan.[36] Fortunately, the circumstantial evidence of family names identical to those commonly found in County Monaghan and its immediate vicinity is supported by a modest number of tombstone inscriptions,[37] family and local histories, and by tradition. Further confirmation is often found in the known dates of settlement and the dates on land leases and deeds, especially when they correspond to the time of arrival of passenger ships from northern Ireland. Such sources when taken singly are often tenuous, but considered cumulatively they indicate the main lines of Irish settlement, and especially of County Monaghan presence, in several parts of rural Prince Edward Island. Nor is that all. Published biographical sketches[38] and newspaper stories and obituaries often provide useful information on place of origin. Finally, clues may be found even in the transferral of such place names as Donagh, Dromore, Truagh, Emyvale, Tyrone, and Monaghan Road. Unfortunately, allusions to the emigrants to Prince Edward Island in accounts originating from County Monaghan itself are very scarce.[39]

Four rural districts where County Monaghan family names abound are Fort Augustus, Kellys Cross, Township Sixty-five and Emyvale, and Kinkora. Lesser concentrations are found in Sturgeon, Hope River and Emerald.

Fort Augustus

The mission parish of St Patrick's at Fort Augustus, ten miles east of Charlottetown on the south side of the Hillsborough River, was once divided into quarters: Monaghan, Fort Augustus, Glenfinnan, and Johnston's (Johnstons) River. Each quarter had twenty-three or twenty-four families, and each quarter was at least unofficially represented on the chapel committee in 1836. The Monaghan quarter was represented by Francis Kelly (co-president), John McAree, Owen McAree, and Patt McKeown; Fort Augustus by James Brogan, James Gillian (Gillan), John Mitchell, and John Hegarty; Glenfinnan by James MacDonald (co-president) and Peter Duffy; and Johnston's River by Hugh Campbell and Angus Campbell. On 1 November 1838, when a new committee was chosen, Allan MacDonald (Johnston's River), Angus MacDonald (Glenfinnan), and Henry Mooney (Monaghan) replaced John Mitchell (Fort Augustus), John Hegarty (Fort Augustus), and Owen McAree (Monaghan). The register lists the 1838 committee in four groups, apparently according to the four quarters of the parish, the only seeming discrepancy being that the fourth Monaghan man (Francis Kelly) is listed now with the two Fort Augustus men (Brogan and Gillan).

It also appears that from the start an attempt was made to recognize the two national backgrounds of the parishioners by naming James MacDonald and Francis Kelly co-presidents. The 1838 committee, as listed, suggests a further attempt at ethnic balance, for now there were three MacDonalds and two Campbells along with a Duffy, followed by the six Irishmen mentioned above. Whether or not the balance was intentional in this instance is a matter of conjecture; but in countless other decisions and appointments in Prince Edward Island's history, equitable representation helped to maintain harmony between Celtic cousins from Scotland and Ireland. Even so, analysts should be wary of assumptions on surnames alone, for some Duffys and McIvers may have been born in Scotland just as some McAdams, Campbells, and McDonalds rightly claim Irish ancestry.

Allowing for some assertively proud exceptions,[40] the gradual assimilation of descendants of both Scottish and Irish settlers, and their common involvement in their new homeland, generally outweighed tendencies to ethnic rivalry. In Fort Augustus particularly, the Glasgow Irish and Monaghan Scots lived in harmony, both groups being well aware that they were byproducts of historical events that had occurred long before anyone in either Old Country had ever heard of Prince Edward Island. Whatever cultural differences there were, in mid-nineteenth century Fort Augustus the Scots and Irish came together in religious belief. Here, in a place named by a Scottish laird after an historic landmark in Inverness, the mainly Irish settlers along with their Scottish neighbours erected an impressive parish church bearing the patronal name of St Patrick.[41]

Practically from the outset, it should be noted, the Monaghan settlers were interested in improving their farming methods. In 1840, for instance, the Monaghan Farming Society was formed "to advance the general interest of Agriculture, by the introduction of new seeds, improved implements of husbandry, the improvement of stock," and similar measures. Besides the landlord, Donald MacDonald – who may have initiated and certainly encouraged the idea and who was named president – the officeholders of this society encompassing the Fort Augustus area included Patrick Hughes and Edward Kelly, vice-presidents; Francis Kelly, secretary-treasurer; and John King, John Quinn, James McCarron, James Kelly, Patrick McKowan, Peter Duffy, and Owen Simpson, committee members.

Beyond Fort Augustus

A brief detour to the northerly portion of Captain John MacDonald's Lot 36 lands lying across the Hillsborough River from Fort Augustus leads to the Scottish communities of Tracadie Cross, Scotchfort, and Blooming Point. Except for an occasional McKenna or McGuire, Carroll or Hughes, few Irish people settled there.

Captain MacDonald's Lot 35 embraced Grand Tracadie (where virtually all the original residents were Scottish), Mill Cove, and Tenmile House. A score of Irish families settled in Mill Cove: Bearney, Bradley, Byrne, Court, Coyle, Dougan, Hughes, Lawler, McGrath, McQuaid,

Meagher, Morris, Murphy, Reid, Rielly, Trainor, Walsh, and others. At Tenmile House, Irish family names such as Dwyer, Fitzpatrick, McCarron, McNally, McQuaid, Mitchell, Mooney, Moynagh, Mullin, Power, and Smith indicate a mixture of early southeastern and later northern Irish families.

Before the Glasgow Irish and their successors arrived in the two MacDonald townships, neighbouring Lot 34 had a substantial Irish settlement composed of people mainly from the southeastern counties.[42] By mid-century, prominent among the farming families along the Covehead Road were these Irish surnames: Carroll, Connors, Curran, Delaney, Doyle, Higgins, Hughes, Kelley, Landrigan, McGrath, Mullin, Power, Reardon, Ready, Reid, Riley, Tracy, Whalen, and Whelan. Later, Monaghan natives John McCabe and Anne Duffy settled on the Stanhope Road.

Patrick Berney immigrated to Lot 33 in 1840 from Straduff townland, Myshal parish, County Carlow. He was accompanied by his half-sister, Ellen Berney, and his stepmother, Catherine Berney. Later he married Maria Troy of Greenfield and took up farming in Lot 35.

Eastward Expansion

Starting from Fort Augustus again, a longer excursion reveals the eastward expansion of the Monaghan immigrants. Meacham's 1881 *Atlas* clearly shows that the original Monaghan Settlement spread well beyond Fort Augustus into such rural communities as Lake Verde, Keefe's Lake, Avondale, Vernon River, and Elliottvale, thus overlapping southern Irish settlements along the way through Peakes and Baldwin Road into Iona. This stream of immigrants also branched out to the Cherry Valley, Orwell, and Newtown areas along Hillsborough Bay.

The Monaghan Road was an important strand of this network, for it linked Fort Augustus with Vernon River. It passed through Lake Verde, where the Callaghan, Corley, Corrigan, Kelly, and Wood families settled; and through Avondale (named in honour of the Irish political leader, "the Chief," Charles Stewart Parnell), where Arthur Delaney from Emyvale in County Monaghan had neighbours named Kelly, Callaghan, Hughes, Keoughan, Keefe, Larkin, O'Donnell, Sullivan, Ryan, Power, and others.

The Vernon River parish of St Joachim embraced Elliottvale and Lot 66 (at 6,000 acres, the smallest of the Island's townships), where a strong Irish enclave extended to the Sparrows Road district (first named Shamrock and later Greenfield); it also spread along the main road community of Summerville and ran along the Brothers Road (named for a Wexford family residing there), which forms part of the

Queens-Kings county line. From there the Monaghan settlers infiltrated the Three Rivers district of Kings County (Georgetown-Bru-
denell, Montague and Cardigan) as well as St Marys Road. Along the
way a vibrant community developed where the Baldwin Road meets
the Peakes Road. There, for instance, Francis Curran married to Mary
Mooney settled in 1840 and raised twelve children. A family reunion
160 years later brought together over one thousand descendants to celebrate their spiritual and cultural heritage. The Kenny family was also
prominent in that area.

ANOTHER MONAGHAN COLONY

On the Island maps that record nineteenth-century land ownership and
residency,the Monaghan settlements resembles a huge ink blot running
eastward from Fort Augustus and intruding deep into Kings County.
This impression, however, represents only half the achievement. West
of Charlottetown, the Monaghan settlers created a second very large
imprint on the map.

Kellys Cross

Distinct from the more extensive Fort Augustus settlement but not
unrelated to it,[43] the Monaghan colony in Kellys Cross and vicinity lies
about twenty miles to the west of Charlottetown. This colony begins
at South Melville Road (near DeSable) and envelops the community of
Kellys Cross (St Joseph's parish) before it branches through the northern part of Lot 30 into Tyrone and Emyvale (St Anne's parish), and
reaches into North Wiltshire (Lot 31) to the east and down the handle
of Lot 65. In addition, a spinoff to the west of Kellys Cross took some
Monaghan settlers to Maple Plains, in the direction of Kinkora.

   The development that began on the South Melville Road and progressed inland in Township Twenty-nine (the estate of Robert Dundas, second Viscount Melville) has been called Kellys Cross (or
Kelly's Cross) since the beginning of the twentieth century. Originally it was known as Truagh. This Irish name provides a key to the
origins of the settlement, for *Truagh* (or *Trough*), the northernmost
barony of County Monaghan, was evidently the birthplace of early
immigrants of this area. But in local lore there is more than one
account of how and why the Truagh people came to Kellys Cross.
Apparently the pioneer Irish family in the area was that of John
Creamer, a native of County Longford, who after his military service
– possibly under Wellington at Waterloo – stopped briefly at Saint
John, New Brunswick, before taking possession of some land here in

1835 or earlier.[44] Creamer's wife, Mary McGuire, was probably born in County Cork – though a local guess is that she was born in County Monaghan. This latter assumption concerning her birthplace gave rise to a local theory that Mrs Creamer played a key role in bringing Monaghan people to Kellys Cross. Supporting this theory was the belief that some of the new immigrants resided in the large Creamer home while they were erecting their own dwellings. It is also believed that John Creamer helped mark off and assign farms for the new tenants. In any event, after the South Melville Road was occupied, people moved into the heavily timbered northern area of Lot 29, congregated at "the cross," and from there spread east and west.

Without rejecting the role that tradition assigns to the Creamer family, a very credible and perhaps even more compatible scenario suggests that another local entrepreneur may have had an important hand in the early settlement. William W. Lord (1798–1890) of Tryon was such a businessman: an innkeeper and tavern owner, merchant, property owner, banker, shipbuilder, and exporter. It is well known that Lord, owner of more than forty vessels, had established a lucrative trade with the British Isles, where wooden sailing ships and timber were in demand. It is reasonable to assume that, following a fairly common practice among shippers of timber in those years, he provided passage for emigrant labourers on his vessels returning to Canada.[45] As Lord required woodsmen to work in the forest and carpenters to work in his shipyards, such speculation has much merit. However, as his shipping business was known to have been conducted in southern Ireland, it is likely that his early Irish recruits would have come from southern counties such as Wexford and Waterford, and that the later emigrants from County Monaghan would have taken a different route. A local opinion explains Lord's role this way: "In order to cut wood to build ships for sale in England, William Lord required men that could handle axes and saws. This employment problem was solved when he brought out a few families from Ireland and settled them on a valuable tract of forest he owned."[46]

Echoing the recollections of Kellys Cross resident George Fall at the turn of the century, Mary C. Brehaut states: "Wm. W. Lord brought out pioneers from Ireland in his vessel; they settled on the land now called Kelly's Cross. These young Irish people took up their farms at one shilling per acre, and went into business cutting timber for Mr Lord who sold it in the Old Country. The timber was cut in the winter, hauled out to Sturdy's mill with spring tides. Small rafts of the timber were pulled below the Bridge and then made into one big raft which was then rolled out into the basin."

These Irish people, according to Brehaut, were excellent neighbours. When they were not cutting lumber for export, they cleared their own land and hoed in potatoes and grain in the burnt-over places. Despite hardships and mishaps, they managed to build a wooden church which lasted over fifty years. The building was never properly finished; in fact, "there were no pews; men stood on the north side of the church, women in the south."[47]

In the long view, the creditable contributions attributed to Creamer and Lord concerning the peopling of Kellys Cross are of secondary importance. The real impetus for the entire Monaghan emigration – and therefore for the eventual colonization of Kellys Cross, Emyvale, Hope River, St Marys Road, and other Monaghan settlements on the Island – was primarily generated by Father John MacDonald's initiative in Glasgow in 1830 and Father Patrick Moynagh's assistance in Donagh a few years later. In the ensuing chain of events that bound County Monaghan families with the Island, the settling of Kellys Cross and vicinity was a related link, not an independent development.

In Kellys Cross, farms of 100 acres were rented at a rate of three-pence per acre for three years, sixpence per acre for the next three years, ninepence per acre for another three years, and one shilling per acre for the next 999 years. The first dozen settler families under this arrangement were those of Robert Craig, John Haughey, Mrs Mary Kelly, Felix McGuigan, Patrick McMurrough, Peter McNally, John Monaghan, and Henry Woods, all from Donagh; Owen McDonald from Tyholland; William McKenna from Errigal Truagh; Francis Malone from an unspecified place in County Monaghan; and Thomas Hagan from Tyrone. According to strong tradition here, the views on emigration held by Father Moynagh, parish priest of Donagh, prevailed over the opposition of his curate, Father McKenna, and Donagh area residents continued to emigrate to the Island in the early 1840s. Patrick McMurrough, mentioned above, is said to have been Moynagh's parish clerk, and numerous couples were pleased to relate that the revered pastor of Donagh had presided at their wedding. He also provided financial assistance for needy emigrants. There should be no doubt about the essential role that Father Moynagh played in the Monaghan emigration movement.

It is believed here that "those who came to Township Twenty-Nine were chiefly from the estate of Colonel Leslie who, although having a reputation of a good landlord, had agents and sub-agents who were hard and cruel."[48] In fact, the adjoining Island parishes of St Joseph's and St Anne's became populated with families many of whose surnames correspond to those in documentary records of the Leslie estates: Bradley, McKenna, Monaghan, Malone, Trainor, McNally,

McQuaid, Hughes, McDonald, Connolly, and McGonnell.[49] Other County Monaghan names include Clarkin, McGuigan, McGaughey, McMahon, Flood, Smith, Carragher, and Duffy.

The duplication of surnames in the Kellys Cross district is illustrated by data drawn from the 1841 census, but is more colourfully expressed in the local parlance. Big Pat Monaghan was married to Margaret Johnston, and Pat Monaghan was married to Catherine Johnston; and two other Monaghans, both named Johnny, were their neighbours. White Johnny Monaghan had one brother known as Little Pat and another brother known as Peter the Great. Peter the Great's children were called Tom the Great, Jim the Great, and Mag the Great. This situation gave rise to this verse:

There was White Johnny,
Black Johnny, Peter and Pat,
And twice as many more –
Now, how many's that?[50]

Father Duffy, Parish Priest

Among the priests who served St Joseph's mission at Kellys Cross was the Reverend James Duffy of Aughnamullen, County Monaghan. He did not accompany the Monaghan settlers to the Island; he had arrived in North America many years earlier. Before coming to the Island, he had ministered in Newfoundland for twenty years and in Nova Scotia for eight. He spent only two years among the people in Kellys Cross and in the neighbouring missions of St Anne's in Lot 65 (where he drove the first wagon ever seen there) and in Kinkora. He died in 1860 and was buried, as he had wished, near the pathway to St Joseph's Church. In 1900, after a new church building had been constructed, Father Duffy's coffin was exhumed to be placed near the new building. During the removal process the astonished villagers discovered that the corpse had not decomposed at all. A pontifical requiem mass was held and Father Duffy's body was buried again, near the walkway to the new church. A prominent Celtic cross marks the grave.[51] To this day, the pious pray for Father Duffy, and some ask his intercession in their needs.

The present church stands a few hundred yards from the place where three roads cross: Maplewood Road (Maplewood was originally called *Seskinore*), where Tom Kelly lived; Lot 30 Road where John Kelly lived; and Melville Road, where Ned Kelly lived. It is no wonder that the community that developed at this intersection came to be called Kellys Cross.

Township Sixty-Five and Emyvale

Not entirely cut off from Kellys Cross but spreading five or six miles across country to the east, other Irish family groups formed in Township Thirty (in Brookvale and Green Road, for instance) and notably in the area where Township Thirty abuts the northern strip of Township Sixty-Five. The latter settlement is often referred to merely as Lot 65, probably because the parish church is located there, but in fact the parish is much more extensive than the place name implies. It includes, for instance, Tyrone and Emyvale, and it reaches into the North Wiltshire district of Lot 31. In 1839, when the *Consbrook* and the *Agitator* arrived in Charlottetown from Belfast with hundreds of settlers aboard, Township Sixty-Five was owned by shipping magnate Samuel Cunard and was largely occupied by early Scots settlers. Local history records that the new settlers were from County Monaghan's parishes and townlands of Carrickroe, Ballyoshen, Clare, Tydavnet, Donagh, Clontibret, and Tyholland, and a few from County Tyrone. Before the building of St Anne's Church in Lot 65, priests from Charlottetown held religious services called "stations" at the homes of Michael McCardill, Patrick Clarkin, and "Little" Patrick Murray, and also at the home of Martin Devereaux (from Wexford). These men and Francis Trainor, under the leadership of a successful farmer named Patrick Dougherty, are credited with erecting the church in 1851. A burial ground was consecrated in 1855, and a parochial house was built by carpenter Patrick Beagan in 1859.

The first settlers of St Anne's Mission, Lot 65, have been identified as Thomas Murray, John Callaghan, and Patrick Clarkin (all from Tydavnet); Frank Trainor and Patrick Trainor (both from Donagh); Peter McGonnell and Hugh McGonnell (both from Monaghan); Andrew Hagan (from Tyholland); Patrick Murphy (from Clontibret); and Patrick "Little" Murray, Patrick "Melior" Murray, and Patrick "Thresher" Murray (all from Truagh). The 1881 *Atlas* shows mainly Monaghan families (and a few southeasterners) on the strip between Hartsville and Howells Brook: Clarkin, Murray, Callahan, Cody, Cullen, Trainor, McCourt, McCluskey, Berrigan, Wynne, Docherty, McKenna, Malone, Murphy, McQuade, and Eagan. Other County Monaghan family names in the Emyvale district included McArdle, McCarron, McCloskey, McGinn, and Moan.

It is said that the Lot 65 settlers often reminisced about the Truagh district in Monaghan, recalled its legends, and recounted stories of the football grounds, "where the tenants of Colonel Ancatell and of the Murtraghs and Captain Singleton were rivals on practice days, only to form a grand coalition team when a match was played and they were called to confront their hereditary foes, the clubs of Tydavnet and Tyrone."[52] They were also reminded of the Old Country observances of festivals honouring the Assumption and St Patrick, as this narrative relates:

All persons who can possibly attend from every parish in the country meet in Monaghan Town, where a grand procession called in these parts a "walk" is formed. The boys turn out in green sashes and caps, the colleens in green ribbons. After attending high mass, they march through the town, to the stirring notes of many brass bands, and then separate to their respective villages of Ballyoshen, Carrickroe, Clare, Tyholland, Tydavnet, Dundalk, Calcachen, Rosslea, and Sunnyvale. Each village has its brass band, drawn by four horses, and its gorgeous banner. "But," said my informant, "sure there is ni-one among them all that can compare to the one wid the motto, 'Truagh for ever, and the sky above it.' Och, that was the rale beauty, and it's the truth I'm telling ye, and no descindant of a lie about it."

This account concludes: "Very loyal to the old sod is the population of St Anne's mission, very true to the good teachings of their dear Father Moynagh, who trained most of them in the paths of religion and morality."[53] How loyal they were to the old sod is indicated by the name which either Michael McArdle or Patrick Dougherty gave to the postal district: Emyvale.[54]

Quite apart from the Emyvale settlement but also within the bounds of Lot 65 (along the south shore and not connected with the later inland community just described) a small Irish colony had been formed by 1820s immigrants from southeastern Ireland. Gravestones at St Martin's Church there record many of the names belonging to farm families living between Nine Mile Creek and Rocky Point: Murphy, Dowling, Hogan, Foley, Griffin, Hennessey, Lannon, Scott, Smith, Quilty, Doyle, Feehan, Leonard, McMahon, and others – virtually all of whom came from Wexford, Waterford, Kilkenny, or Tipperary.

Kinkora

The settlement of Kinkora[55] (formerly spelled *Kincora*) was named for the royal domain of Brian Boru, the putative first High King of Ireland. His castle was near present-day Killaloe, County Clare, on the west bank of the Shannon River. The resourcefulness and achievements of the people in new Kinkora, PEI, engendered a pride of place and sense of community matched by few other localities in Prince Edward Island. The level fields in this area proved highly suitable for growing potatoes – the bane and blessing of the Irish and the crop that became the mainstay of the Island's primary industry: agriculture.[56]

The Kinkora district straddles the Queens-Prince county line and encompasses several distinct communities in Lots 26, 27, and 67 – Emerald, South Freetown, Shamrock, Newton, Middleton, Maple Plains, and the village of Kinkora – all of which have been consolidated into one school district in recent times, but none of which has surrendered its local identity. Scottish, English, and Loyalist settlements surround Kinkora district, and Acadian descendants are now found within it. Although the parish gradually became ethnically mixed, the Irish remained most prominent. The Catholic church at Kinkora, dedicated in 1851, was placed under the patronage of St Malachy, in honour of a saint much venerated in northern Ireland and in recognition of the devoted service of the area's first missionary, the Reverend Malachy Reynolds.

Kinkora was first known as Sou'West (although that name may more properly designate Middleton) and later Reverend Patrick Doyle called the community Somerset in recognition of an outstanding parishioner named Maurice Sommers. After the railroad station was opened in 1872, the place was given the name Kinkora. Although one source states that several Irish families were in Lot 27 as early as 1798, it is generally believed that the first permanent settlers from the south of Ireland arrived in that area in 1835. The township was owned in part by Colonel James Searle, whose daughter and heiress married Horatio Mann. In 1849 Mrs Mann in turn bequeathed the land to her daughter, Mrs Giliean, who had married a lawyer in Philadelphia. The agent for the Manns and the Gilieans, Joseph Pope, came to admire the hard-working Irish settlers. Since Pope was an influential politician in that era, his friendship was considered as important to the Irish as their voting support was to him.

A parish history records the names of the first settlers: John Brenan, Michael Cahill, Andrew Clear, John Keefe, Maurice Sommers, Edward Ryan, and James Walsh. Evidently their descendants, along with the others whose native counties were not in Ulster came to be known as Southies. The influx from the north of Ireland started no later than 1839 when Philip Began, Patrick Murphy, Owen Shreenan, and John Smith arrived. Valentine Shreenan and Felix Mulligan joined them two years later; Patrick Duffy arrived in 1844; and James Farmer, Matthew Kelly, Leslie Kelly, John McCarville, and Patrick Young probably came in 1847.

It is impossible to track all the movements of many of the unaffiliated and unrecruited immigrants who – coming on their own and by chance, singly and in family units, but numbering in the hundreds – arrived in the 1840s aboard vessels shuttling between Charlottetown and Belfast. Most of these northerners dispersed to settlements in or near Queens County, including the Kinkora district. It is reasonable to surmise that many had been tenants of Lord Rossmore (Henry Westenra) in northern Monaghan, where they had subsisted on poor holdings of from two to seven acres. Some others had lived in the neighbouring Armagh parish of Tynan where the Bishop Estate, administered by twelve clergymen, is reputed to have offered many worldly inducements to those who would join the Protestant Church. For those who lived in such difficult conditions, Prince Edward Island offered better prospects. The farms usually consisted of one hundred acres, a normal rental being two years free, followed by twenty years at sixpence per acre, and then 999 years at one shilling per acre. In 1875 the Land Purchase Act enabled tenants to purchase outright the acreages they had occupied.

Before the Gilieans (who were Catholics) sold their share of Lot 27 to the Pope family in 1865, they had endeared themselves to the Irish settlers because of their many generous contributions to the parish. The mutual respect and affection between landlord and tenant in this particular instance evoked a celebratory gesture well known in Monaghan. It is captured in the following anecdote: "After mass there was a christening at Mr Brenan's and Mrs Gilian stood godmother to the little Isobel. She also spoke to all her tenants with a kindly word and a promise of some comfortable, useful presents to the poorer among them, after which she and her husband started to drive back to Bedeque. Then the enthusiasm of the grateful hearts broke out, with a cheer which is seldom heard in America. The people unharnessed the horses and dragged their honoured visitors' cart along the dusty road, uttering characteristic good wishes for their welfare and calling down blessings upon their heads." [57]

Thistle and Shamrock

Where the old Anderson Road from Springton intersects the county line is the school district known as Thistle and Shamrock. This place name bespeaks a social situation predating its 1867 commemoration by the landowners, who named the little schoolhouse after the floral emblems of Scotland and Ireland. The eastern part of the road was settled by Scottish families named MacDonald, Matheson, Gillis, MacKenzie, and MacKinnon, while the western section was occupied by people with County Monaghan names such as MacGuigan, Trainor, Moan, Duffy, McCarville, Hughes, and Greehan, as well as Kelly, Murphy, and Rooney. The road that passes the school leads into the village of Kinkora.

Newton

In a once heavily wooded area where Lots 26 and 27 meet, lies Newton (formerly Newtown). Settlers found that tributaries of the Elmo and Dunk rivers provided water for their cattle, and the soil proved highly suitable for potatoes and grain. Local tradition relates that Peter Corr, Thomas Hammill, Patrick Smith, and Mr McGyral left Ireland on Easter Sunday 1841 aboard the *Margaret Pollock* and, upon arrival, bought 200 acres in Newton, which they divided into four farms. Other land seekers rapidly followed, and twenty years later the first school enrolled thirty-five students under master John Foley. The list of teachers from 1869 until the school's recent closure (for the sake of administrative consolidation), reads like a register from County Monaghan: Francis Greehan, Thomas McCabe, Michael McKenna, Kate A. Hammill, Francis McIver, Anastasia Duffy, Frank McCarville, Regina P. Smith, A.C. Deighan, William J. McGinn, Peter F. Hughes, Susan Murtagh, Mary Hagen, John H. Moan, Adelaide Mulligan, Bernice Corr, Borden Greenan, Georgie Johnston, and others.[58]

Emerald

Tucked away inland between Newton and Summerfield, and spanning the borderline of Prince and Queens counties, rests a picturesque settlement of tidy white homesteads amidst rich green fields. When the railway lines were laid through this area, the postal designation was changed from County Line to Emerald Junction – or simply Emerald.

Although this community appears to have been an outgrowth of the larger Kinkora development, its local history and geography made it distinctive. Its situation within the parish of St James in Summerfield certainly contributed to its sense of identity. Another factor may have been the early clay road which the Haslam family constructed between their sawmill on the Dunk River and their home in Springfield, which gave Emerald residents access to the town road without passing through Kinkora.

Drawing mainly upon the general influx of County Monaghan immigrants, Emerald's population flourished in the 1840s. A later generation took special pride in the large hall that once housed an active chapter of the Benevolent Irish Society (c. 1885–1910). In addition to performing charitable works, the BIS held picnics, dances, concerts, card games, lectures, plays, and banquets. Prominent members in the early years included P.L. Cash, William Clarke, Michael Croken, William Deighan, Patrick Duffy, Peter Duffy, Terrance Goodwin, Peter

Hughes, James McEntee, George McMahon, James Power, and Patrick Whelan.[59]

Additional family names in Emerald also point to many ancestral roots in or near the "county of the little hills": Corr, Clow, Mayne, McAtee, McKenna, Greenan, Lamb, Kelly, McGuigan, Moynagh, Mulligan, Shreenan, Murtagh, and Murphy. To this day, an annual festival at the community centre is a sign of the residents' continuing interest in their Irish heritage. Visitors are informed that the name of the community derives from Ireland's sobriquet, the Emerald Isle. They do not have to be told that Emerald is a jewel.

On the Main Road

Lake's map of 1863 records the following selected Irish family names on the main road through Kinkora village: G. Hughes, J. McCrehan, J. Doyle, R. McArvill, W. Thomas, J. Kelly, M. Kelly, P. Duffy, J. Trainor, P. McGarvill, H. Farmer, M. Rooney, O. Rooney, J. Thomas, D. Gallagher, T. Trainer, J. Welsh, P. Welsh, J. McCarvill, O. McCarvill, N. Murphy, P. Murphy, F. Murphy, E. Hughes, T. Hammill, W. Daughrey, M. Cunningham, T. Greenan, F. Mulligan, S. Nowlan, F. Murphy, J. Hacket, J. Young, A. Clear, J. Farmer, Mrs Ryan, Mrs Crehan, J. Crehan (tavern), J. McGuigin (tavern), M. Sommers, and Mrs Goodwin; and, near the Middleton post office, J. Rennaghan, M. Brennan, T. McBride, P. Beagan, O. Shreenan, and T. Murray. Other names in the cluster designated as South West include: J. Keiff, L. Gamble, P. Garrigan, J. MacManus, O. McIver, R. McCourt, P. McKenna, P. Prunty, and Croaken. These lists, of course, do not include all the names or even all the communities in the vicinity of Kinkora, but they do confirm the numerical dominance of County Monaghan settlers in the area.

The land itself and the public buildings in Kinkora proclaim a continuing concern for agriculture, religion, and education. Some of the most productive farms and the most prosperous and progressive farmers have been found in this area of the Island. The present church of St Malachy, designed by William Critchlow Harris in 1901, is not only a worthy successor to the earlier building but is one of the finest examples of church architecture in the province. From the opening of the first school in Kinkora in 1849 (a one-room building accommodating seventy-six pupils under teacher John Gallagher), through the development of the first rural grammar school and the first rural senior high school in the province (conducted by the Religious Congregation of Saint Martha), to the recent consolidation of district schools, Kinkora has exemplified the Irish immigrants' reliance on education as the principal route to economic and social advancement.

Irish settlement of Kinkora and adjoining communities was well established by 1850 and remained strongly intact for another century. In fact, additional Irish pieces in the farmlands mosaic were found here and there among the thriving Loyalist and Scots properties in the Albany and Bedeque districts to the Green Shore area, where the Irish played a modest role in the post-Confederation development of Summerside.

THE FATE OF THE REVEREND JOHN MACDONALD

To complete this account of the Monaghan settlers of Prince Edward Island it is necessary to recall the story of the Reverend John Mac-Donald – priest, linguist, scholar, scion of New Glenaladale, and original promoter of the Monaghan migration. Although his colonizing activities ultimately produced rewards for both his church and civil society, these activities had very unhappy consequences for the clergyman-landlord himself. Paradoxically, from the time he assumed the proprietorship of the Fort Augustus portion of his late father's 40,000–acre estate, the priest's fortunes inexorably declined. As had happened forty years earlier under his autocratic father at Tracadie, Father MacDonald's original settlers became disillusioned and discontented with the terms and conditions of their tenancy, and the influx of later Scots and the Monaghan Irish did nothing to improve landlord-tenant relations. As a landlord, the priest generally dealt at arm's length with his tenants,[60] employing agents – James Trainor, Francis Kelly, William Forgan, and John Ogle Nantes, at various times – to attend to his business affairs, while he himself concentrated on his priestly duties.

At first Father MacDonald lived at Tracadie, where his oldest brother, Donald, presided. Even then the veteran Bishop Angus MacEachern, not long before he died, expressed concern that the priest was not sufficiently disengaged from his family's business. In fact, he wrote to the archbishop of Quebec saying that Father MacDonald "is so entangled with their land affairs, lawsuits in recovering rents, etc., that our adversaries take an opportunity of making him odious and disrespected."[61] After 1835 Father MacDonald accepted an appointment to the missions at the eastern end of the Island, and there, for about nine years, he ministered to the Catholic people – many of them Gaelic-speaking Scots – in St Margarets, East Point, Souris, and St Peters Bay.[62]

Predictably, the public perception grew that the pastoral duties of the priest and the business interests of the landlord were in conflict. In St Margarets a crisis developed when a member of the Legislative Assembly, John MacIntosh, who was a spokesman for the mainly Scottish tenants of Kings County, disrupted a church meeting to argue with the priest-landlord, ostensibly over the selection of parish trustees. In response, and against the stated advice of his bishop, the pastor brought legal charges against the aggrieved parishioner.[63] Bishop Bernard MacDonald, like his illustrious predecessor, knew well how deep-rooted was the animosity of the tenants toward the proprietors, particularly in eastern Kings County, where Hay River was a hotbed of anti-landlord agitation. He also knew how suspicious those tenants were that Father MacDonald had at least acquiesced in the sending of troops to quell an uprising at the Cunard estate in East Point in March 1843 – a charge which the priest always denied. In October 1843 the bishop removed Father MacDonald from the eastern missions and offered him pastoral charge of the Tracadie townships. A year later, however, as Father MacDonald was still adamantly claiming rights to the parish house and church at St Margarets, the bishop felt constrained to relieve him of all his priestly faculties within the diocese of Charlottetown.

Father John MacDonald retired briefly to New Glenaladale, his family's residence at Tracadie, and there, in his own defence, he published an account of the affairs that had alienated him from the people whom he had wished, on his own terms, to serve.[64] He then chose to exile himself to England, where in the vicinity of London he dutifully served as a priest of the Catholic Church for the remaining twenty-nine years of his life. He died in Brighton, England, in 1874. By that time the power of the landlords had been broken, and the descendants of the Acadians, the West Country people, the Loyalists, the Scottish Highlanders, and the immigrants from Ireland had taken freehold possession of the land and together were forming the Island colony into a responsible province of Canada.

Although Father John MacDonald's priestly career in Prince Edward Island was fraught with deep disappointment, he may have been consoled late in life by the expectation that both his church and his native island would greatly benefit from the Monaghan Settlements he had launched. This consummation, indeed, has stood as his lasting memorial.

CHAPTER EIGHT

The Crown and the Harp

In Prince Edward Island the influence of the Irish settlers, comprising about one-quarter of the immigrant population, has been both undeniable and immeasurable. The great majority of the people who sailed to the Island from Ireland disembarked in the capital city, Charlottetown. Most of them then dispersed and spread throughout rural areas of the Island. Those who remained in the capital constituted the colony's largest Irish community.

This chapter describes, to some extent, the cultural impact of the Irish men and women who settled in Charlottetown. How many Irish people resided in the capital? When did they arrive? Where did they originate? What occupations did they pursue? What did they contribute to the cultural institutions and activities of the capital? These questions, and others, prompt the following review of the Irish presence in nineteenth-century Charlottetown. The answers may explain why Charlottetown was once known as "an Irish town."

At the confluence of the North, West, and Hillsborough rivers in the harbour formerly called Port La Joie, Surveyor General Samuel Holland designated a point of land to be the capital of St John's Island, and in honour of the queen he named the site Charlottetown. Here in 1770 the first colonial governor, Walter Patterson, established his administrative offices and military headquarters. By 1800 the combination of historical circumstances, natural resources, and enterprising people had made Charlottetown the Island's leading port of entry and its principal market and export centre (see map 9).

The early townspeople, mainly from the British Isles, were augmented in 1784 by Loyalist refugees from the American Revolution, who were a mixture of English, Dutch, German, and Irish.[1] Before the

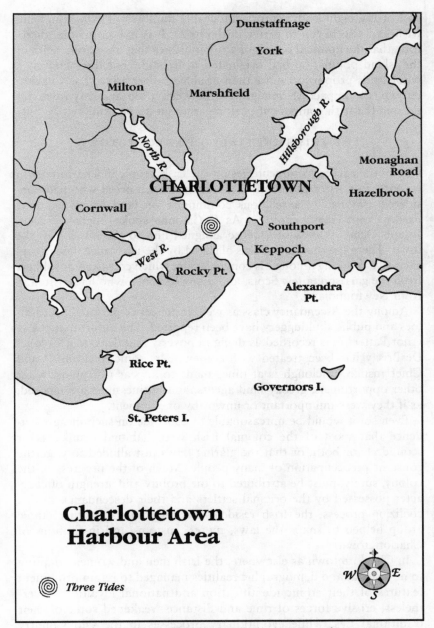

Dunstaffnage

York

Milton

Marshfield

North R.

Hillsborough R.

CHARLOTTETOWN

Monaghan
Road

Hazelbrook

Cornwall

Southport

West R.

Keppoch

Rocky Pt.

Alexandra
Pt.

Rice Pt.

Governors I.

St. Peters I.

Charlottetown
Harbour Area

Three Tides

W O E
S

Map 9. For most immigrants, Charlottetown harbour was the gateway to
the Island.

end of the eighteenth century noticeable numbers of Newfoundland Irish had also begun to arrive in the town. It is not surprising, therefore, that the nominal census of 1798 indicates that about one-tenth of the Island population had originated in Ireland.[2] For the Island as a whole, this proportion more than doubled before 1850. For Charlottetown, the impact of immigration between 1800 and 1850 was far greater, the Irish component peaking at about 40 percent.

THE IRISH IN EARLY CHARLOTTETOWN

One of the earliest commentaries on the Irish people in Charlottetown is found in a letter of abbé DeCalonne, a French priest who had considered establishing a religious community on land he owned near Rocky Point (see chapter 1). As DeCalonne spoke English, Bishop Joseph Octave Plessis of Quebec assigned him to the mission in the town. There the missionary was alarmed by the ignorance, laxity, and excessive drinking among his congregation, which consisted of soldiers from the garrison, a few Scots, and many Irishmen who had drifted in from Newfoundland.[3]

Among the Ascendancy class as well, instances of personal peccadilloes and public skulduggery have been reported. The unfortunate Governor Patterson is recorded as dying in poverty and dejection; Colonel DesBrisay has been treated with contempt by some historians;[4] and Chief Justice Colclough is at times made to appear ridiculous. Most other opportunists, greedy land agents, and businessmen are ignored, as if they were unimportant or unworthy of comment.

Even so, it would be unreasonable to conclude on such meagre evidence that most of the colonial Irish were habitual drunkards or scoundrels or both, or that the glaring flaws just alluded to were the constant preoccupation of many people. Much of the progress of the colony, surely, must be attributed to the probity and strength of character possessed by the original settlers and their descendants. In this civilizing process, the Irish residents no less than any other ethnic group helped to shape the laws, mores, customs and institutions of Charlottetown.

In Charlottetown as elsewhere, the Irish men and women adapting to new social and demographic realities managed to retain prominent features of their ethnic identification and national loyalties. Nevertheless, erosive forces of time and distance weakened some of their traditional ties, while evolutionary processes in the Old Country modified old ways to suit the changing conditions there. Thus, with the passage of time, the Irish culture in exile necessarily diverged from the culture of the homeland, each society retaining or acquiring some values and customs not relevant to the other, but neither severed its bond with the other, and both preserved a great deal of their common heritage.

Among the majority of the Irish immigrants the ideals aspired to, which were harmonized in their families, churches, schools, and social organizations, delayed the depleting of their cultural legacy and assured the continuity of certain values. They gave up the Gaelic language and neglected the written word to the point that a great deal of their lore and literature faded, but they clung to many patriotic myths and to religious values, most notably to Christian concepts of the family. Even when they were unfaithful to their heritage, they tended to believe in it, to defend it against opponents, and to judge themselves by its standards.

THE BENEVOLENT IRISH SOCIETY

Among the social institutions the Irish established in Charlottetown, one was exclusively theirs. On 18 April 1825 at the Wellington Hotel, a nonsectarian charitable society was founded and called the Benevolent Irish Society (BIS) of Prince Edward Island.[5] The first meeting for the purpose of paying in quarterly dues was held in the Roman Catholic chapel on Sunday, 8 May. Membership was open to "natives of Ireland and their children." Dues were two shillings and sixpence on entrance and quarterly thereafter, to be applied to the charitable fund to "relieve the indigent of every nation." Other purposes of the society were the performance of works of benevolence, and the perpetuation of Irish national sentiment.

The *Prince Edward Island Register* states that the seal of the BIS consisted of a shamrock with a harp and crown, and on all public occasions the officers were expected to wear "a green sash with harp and crown thereon." On the annual festival of 17 March, each member was to "wear his hat, and on his breast a sprig or emblem of shamrock, tradition informing us our patron Saint made use of it, as a type, to explain to our ancestors the existence of three distinct persons in one God." These words were warmly approved by the society's first patron, Lieutenant-Governor John Ready. The first president was Fade Goff, the secretary was Charles DesBrisay, and among the active founding members was Father Alexander Thomas Fitzgerald.

In striking contrast to abbé DeCalonne's 1800 depiction of Charlottetown's "dregs of Ireland and Newfoundland," the BIS historian Peter McCourt presents a favourable portrayal, mainly of the Anglo-Irish residents of Charlottetown and vicinity a generation or so later. These founders of the BIS, McCourt states, were as a rule "a well

educated class of people, with cultured manners, intense love of
country, unswerving loyalty to the British crown, and a spirit of phil-
anthropy which may have been equalled but has not been surpassed
by that of succeeding generations, or by that of any other race."[6] He
adds: "It is also worthy of note that they did not permit religious differences to dwarf their charity or lessen their patriotism; on the contrary, they found in those virtues a common standing ground on
which they met as brothers in the new world to perform works of
charity and benevolence."[7]

On St Patrick's Day 1826, the society inaugurated its annual festival
at an elegant dinner at the Wellington Hotel. The *P.E.I. Register* reported
that the following toasts were given: the king, St Patrick, the lieutenant-
governor, the president; the land of Erin and her sons; the shamrock,
rose, and thistle; religious and civil liberty; Prince Edward Island, its
agriculture and commerce; the bishop of Rosen; the Rev. Mr Fitzgerald;
the memory of Rev. Mr DesBrisay; the governor general of British North
America; and the Benevolent Irish Society of Prince Edward Island. The
banquet started at 4 o'clock, and "the company separated at 12 o'clock
precisely."[8] Incidentally, not uncharacteristic of Irish practice, a rival
Irish group simultaneously held its own dinner at the Commercial Inn,
in competition with the BIS festivities, and celebrated with its own "loyal
and constitutional toasts and several excellent songs."[9]

Both the St Patrick's Day parade and the patron saint's banquet
became annual traditions for BIS members and were notable social
events in the Island capital. In testimony of how faithfully the gregarious, voluble Irish of Charlottetown upheld the tradition of feasting,
fanfare, and exuberant fellowship, this typical report appeared in the
Examiner of 20 March 1876:

The day sacred to the memory of Ireland's Patron Saint was duly observed in
Charlottetown. At ten o'clock the members of the Benevolent Irish Society
formed in procession at their rooms, and headed by Galbraith's Band marched
to St Dunstan's Cathedral. The Society presented a very fine appearance. During the service which followed, Rev. Allan MacDonald preached an eloquent
sermon. In the afternoon, the members of the St Patrick's Total Abstinence
Society – in tasteful and appropriate regalia – with banners flying and music
playing – marched in procession through our streets and attended Vespers at
the Cathedral. The entertainment at St Patrick Hall, in the evening, was the
crowning act of the time-honoured celebration. Mrs Maurice Blake, the Misses
Rankin and McEwen, Professor Caven, Doctor Creamer, and Charles Her-
mans, were among the vocalists, and we need not say, the music was excellent.
Miss Newbery, Miss McEwen, and Mr Blanchard, of St Dunstan's College,
played the accompaniment on the piano. Mrs Robinson read "Shamus

O'Brien" with good effect. The dramatic part of the evening was contributed by the boys of St Joseph's Society. They seemed to bear in mind the old couplet, "Honour and fame from no condition rise, / Act well your part, there all honor lies."

The report concluded with this trenchant understatement: "There was some drinking in the evening; and the Stipendiary Magistrate's 'entertainment' on Saturday morning was unusually long and interesting."

In the formative years of the Benevolent Irish Society, Anglo-Irish leaders such as Fade Goff, J.B. Palmer, Francis Longworth, and Charles DesBrisay shared executive positions with prominent Catholic immigrants like Daniel Brennan, John Doyle, Dennis Reddin, and Cornelius Little. Within twenty years southeastern Ireland was represented by such newcomers as William Fitzpatrick, Thomas Broderick, John Walsh, and Thomas Tobin. By the twenty-fifth anniversary, the second generation began to assume some offices. William Longworth was president; Edward Whelan, vice-president; Dennis Reddin, treasurer; and Edward Kickham, secretary. The Charity Committee consisted of Pierce Gaul (Dennis Reddin's son-in-law), Richard Walsh, Patrick McKenna, Garret Toole, James Carroll, and John Egan. New family names also appeared on the rolls: Blake, Broydrick, Cawden, Dougan, Hickey, Hogan, Pippy, Quinn, Ryan, and Warburton. In the early 1850s several northern names presaged the County Monaghan build-up during the next decade, when the BIS ranks were augmented by such surnames as Connolly, Hughes, Kelly, McGrory, MacIntyre, McQuaid, Mitchell, Sweeney, and Trainor. During the same period several new members from the south of Ireland joined the Society: Byrne, Carroll, Hennessey, Holleran, Mullin, Phelan, and Sullivan.

The evolution of the membership was such that by the end of the century the BIS had come to be regarded as a completely Catholic Irish organization, though constitutionally it remained nonsectarian. (The perception of sectarianism persisted until the 1990s, when a number of non-Catholic Irishmen enlisted. A more radical development, requiring an amendment to the society's constitution, occurred in 1993 when full membership status was granted to women. Five years later, Anne Marie Dowling became president.) In several ways the changing profile of the Benevolent Irish Society has been a barometer of Irish culture in Charlottetown.

THE SAD STORY OF THE *LADY CONSTABLE*

History clearly shows that Irish Charlottetown had emerged before the Great Famine decimated Ireland and glutted the major cities of eastern America with more than a million displaced persons. Numerous accounts of the famine tell of the coffin ships that came to Canadian shores during the tragic years 1845–48. Dozens of vessels disgorged their dead and dying on Middle Island near Chatham and at the Partridge Island quarantine station near Saint John, New Brunswick, and especially at Grosse Île in the St Lawrence River near Quebec City. Charlottetown was all but spared such grisly visitations. Although several earlier Island-bound vessels had reported some loss of life, there was a considerable decline in Irish immigration to the Island during the Great Famine. As noted in the preceding chapter, only one so-called "coffin ship" bearing contagion and death entered the port of Charlottetown. That ship was the *Lady Constable*, a barque from Liverpool transporting 419 Ulster emigrants.

Twenty-five persons had died during the Atlantic crossing, and at least eight more – perhaps upwards of thirty more – died of malignant ship fever after the vessel reached port.[10] This sorrowful event occurred 21 May 1847, within days of a similar disaster at Saint John.[11] For immigrants to the Island, Charlottetown had always been the leading port of entry. Into this serene deepwater harbour came passenger ships and freighters by the hundred, from the British Isles and Newfoundland, from Nova Scotia and New Brunswick, from New England and the West Indies. People in the tens of thousands, and supplies in the hundreds of thousands of tons, passed through this port. As the volume of traffic mounted, the 1842 legislative assembly decided to impose a head tax on newcomers from the United Kingdom. This tax was to meet the cost of medical and other aid for the sick, aged and poor.[12]

Charlottetown was more or less prepared to accommodate increasing immigration and commerce, and to deal with the common hardships of newcomers. But pestilence was another matter. Evidently the *Lady Constable* arrived unexpectedly. The medical officer did not object when the harbour pilot broke the rules and permitted the ship to moor at the wharf. Although the Board of Health believed that the ship should be sent back to quarantine ground, about fifty sick and dying passengers were landed and placed in a temporary quarantine hospital (which had accommodation for twenty people), while other destitute wretches wandered about the town seeking food, shelter, and employment. Charged with incompetence, the members of the Board of Health resigned, and the pilot was severely reprimanded. By mid-June the suffering refugees were transferred to the hastily vacated Lunatic Asylum. Twelve patients had died in the temporary hospital, and eleven more died in the asylum. The killer was typhus fever, complicated by malignant dysentery. Despite the fears of the citizenry, the contagion did not spread beyond the refugees themselves.

The fact that the capital town lacked the resources, personnel, and facilities to deal effectively with such a major crisis led the *Islander*, on 4 June to charge that it was England's responsibility to use the resources of the British Empire to assist the colonies in such emergencies. The editorial declared, "Under existing circumstances unchecked emigration is an evil."

In Charlottetown, the townspeople watched and waited in fear as the dreaded procession of coffins passed on its way to the cemetery on St Peter's Road. A witness recalled: "Counting eight coffins at one time, probably those held the people who died whilst the ship was in Quarantine. We have also counted three and four each day, and sometimes one and two twice a day as long as the fever lasted."[13] The victims were buried in rough board coffins in anonymous graves. No tangible monument commemorates the tragic event.

A story survives, however, of a young Irish widow who lost her husband and child to the fever. For a long time she busied herself at whatever tasks she could find in an effort to overcome her grief. Tears streaming down her face, she would sing the old folk songs of her beloved homeland. When she was asked why she cried while she was singing, she replied: "I am saddest when I sing, and when I laugh the loudest my heart is sorriest. Sometimes when I think that those I loved best and left home and country for are now living in the cold churchyard, I feel my heart will break."[14] The young widow spoke for many similarly bereaved people who wept over the unmarked graves of Irish immigrants in the old Catholic cemetery on St Peter's Road.

During those terrible famine years, Charlottetown residents read many accounts of fever ships entering distant ports. The *Examiner* of 13 November 1847, for instance, reported: "A vessel lately arrived at the Quarantine Station of Quebec, with a large number of emigrants. 100 persons died on the voyage, and many others are in a sick and destitute condition. Two vessels have also arrived at the Quarantine Station of St John, N.B., with 470 poor emigrants, banished from the Estate of Lord Palmerston, in Ireland. These people are represented to be in the most miserable condition." Appended to the report is this salient editorial question: "What better proof can be found as to the fitness of an English Government for Ireland, than is thus given by an English [Cabinet] Minister?"

Attitudes toward Britain

A subtext of the *Examiner*'s question is the view that the Great Famine was caused and exacerbated less by natural forces (the blight) than by Britain's political and economic policies, in which laissez-faire principles and market interests obviously took precedence over human needs. This blunt interpretation of the national catastrophe certainly strengthened the resolve of the Fenians and others by fuelling the fires of rebellion against British rule in Ireland.

Perhaps because the great majority of the Island's Irish settlers had not personally suffered the deepest on-the-scene devastation of the Great Famine, they were not so overtly anti-British as their fellow immigrants were in those areas of America where tens of thousands of famine refugees disembarked. In Charlottetown, for example, supportive as the *Examiner* was for the Repeal Movement for self-government, and indignant as that newspaper was over the suffering and injustice endured by the Irish people under British rule, publisher Edward Whelan's editorial policy followed the O'Connell tradition of calling for constitutional reform, not violent revolution. Whelan's policy evidently reflected the dominant temper of the Irish people who had settled in PEI, for they never openly expressed support for the Fenian movement or any other violent revolutionary cause.

The notorious "Fenian alarm" of 1866, for example, was a false alarm.[15] In fact, when the Catholic Young Men's Literary Institute sponsored a discussion on the Fenians, the Reverend Angus MacDonald, rector of St Dunstan's College, condemned the movement in very strong terms. George Coles spoke in the same vein. Even when Fenianism was called "a villainous swindle," no one present expressed a contrary view.[16] In the House of Assembly, too, the speaker and Messrs Haviland, Coles, and Longworth rejected and ridiculed Fenianism, and Edward Whelan called it "a mischievous organization" – even though he stoutly upheld the validity of several of Ireland's grievances.[17]

Frightened by the remote threat of violence, however, some legislators, some journalists, and a portion of the general citizenry called for military preparations.[18] By coincidence, troops were called in from Halifax, but their purpose was to put down the Tenant League – not, as some people may have thought, to protect the province against a possible Fenian uprising. To house these troops, the Victoria Barracks were built in 1865.[19] To what extent local members of the Ancient Order of Hibernians (which had chapters in Charlottetown and Tignish) were in agreement with Fenian tactics was never stated. What is clear, in retrospect, is that the so-called Fenian menace in Charlottetown was largely a figment of fearful imaginations. Some people who may have had personal reasons to be fearful were, in this instance, traumatized by the myth rather than by any immediate threat of Fenianism.[20] In union with compassionate people everywhere, Irish Charlottetown strongly resented the fever ships, the famine, the evictions, and the catalogue of injustices, but Irish Charlottetown was not disposed to put a match to the fuse.[21]

Overt anti-British sentiment, in short, was not characteristic of mid-nineteenth-century Irish Charlottetown. After all, the Irish immigrants were legal British subjects. The sense of Ireland being a state within the United Kingdom – though this status was being severely questioned – was at that time more or less accepted, and loyalty to the British monarchy was at least perfunctorily proclaimed. When the nineteen-year-old Prince of Wales (who forty-one years later would be crowned Edward VII) visited the Island in 1860, among the invited organizations that turned out to greet him was the Benevolent Irish Society. Members, we are told, wore sashes of "green silk, adorned with the golden harp of Ireland, and wreath of Shamrocks."[22] Along with the BIS were the St Andrew's Society, the Fraternity of Masons, and the Sons of Temperance. At Government House the Irish volunteers, under Captain Murphy, formed the guard of honour. The escort marshall was Colonel Francis Longworth. The Irish participated in the official reception and presentation of addresses, the garden party, the fireworks, and the formal ball. There were no untoward incidents. Everyone seemed jubilant. The question of Irish sovereignty was not raised.

SOCIAL LIFE IN CHARLOTTETOWN

The visit of the Prince of Wales was, of course, an exceptional occasion. But as Charlottetown was the site of the garrison, the capital was frequently a festive place. In addition to the regular army detachments which performed civil police duties locally (mainly protecting property and quelling Tenant League disturbances), militia units mustered each June in Market Square to march and do other training. The company of cavalry often paraded through the streets, and several companies of volunteers were organized. Among them was the Irish Rifles Company, which was distinguished by its black uniform with green facings. Traditionally, the volunteer companies paraded on holidays and organized dances and other social gatherings. In 1863, for instance, they sponsored a grand tea party, to which the well-to-do people of the town brought their silverware and fine china. They decorated the tables in bright colours and bedecked the hall with flags and banners. Soldiering in Charlottetown had its social rewards.

Tea parties and picnics were popular entertainments of civilians too. Often they were a means of raising funds for building projects or other worthy causes. The Sons of Temperance held teas at Colonel John Hamilton Gray's property at Spring Park, and Sunday schools often had teas on the riverbank at Kensington (later known as the Exhibition Grounds), where a tent was erected for serving food. At such gatherings there were various games and other amusements, as well as music and speeches. Often the people marched to the picnic grounds in groups, carrying flags and singing. Another site for picnics and boating was near the blockhouse at the mouth of the harbour. Boat racing in the spacious harbour was also popular, culminating in Regatta Day each August. Residents also enjoyed horse racing, especially in September and October at Croker's, three miles from town on the St Peter's Road. In early October there was a fall fair in the Market Square, and during the winter townspeople attended concerts, lectures, teas, and bazaars, and went for sleigh rides through the streets of Charlottetown. The highlight of any season, surely, was an invitation to attend a dance or garden party at Government House.[23]

The Hospitable Town

For centuries, the gregarious Irish have regarded their pubs as social centres – places to meet friends, drink, laugh, tell stories, sing, and especially talk. In nineteenth-century Charlottetown, too, the tavern was a well-established institution, and despite various temperance campaigns both in the town and in the country, over the years old Charlottetown supported numerous taverns and inns. No scandal was attached to the fact that a tavern known as the Cross Keys served as a meeting house for the first session of the colonial legislative assembly in 1773.

Connolly's Irish Tavern, one of fifteen taverns and nine stores licensed in 1820, was operated by James and Catherine Connolly at 218–20 Euston Street in a house that was still at that site in 1990.[24] Dennis Reddin, John Howell (Wellington Hotel), and Joseph Pippy (New Inn) were other tavern owners at that time, and James Reilly, Joseph Higgins, and Thomas Murphy ran licensed stores.[25] In 1843 Arthur O'Neal (O'Neill), a baker and tavern keeper, leased a building on Sydney Street near Union Street.[26] By 1846 at least four more Irishmen were in the business: Martin Griffin, Edward Kickham, James Maloney, and James Toole. Two years later Mrs McNeill was also operating a tavern.

The 1861 census lists Martin Hogan and William Croak as publicans, and ten years later John Murphy ran a tavern at the corner of Queen and Water streets. John McKenna was a grocer at the corner of Pownal and Richmond Streets in 1864, but by 1877 he was also running a tavern. In 1875 when John Kelly, formerly of Summerville, opened his business on Dorchester Street, he called himself a "saloon keeper" and later an "inn keeper." Kelly was a dealer in groceries and general merchandise as well as liquor, and he ran a second store on the north side of Queen Square. His son, Francis Clement Kelly (Kelley), became an influential American churchman, bishop of Oklahoma.[27]

By 1873 or later, John Carroll was proprietor of L'Etoile du Nord, an oyster parlour (and tavern, presumably) at 64 Great George Street, across from the cathedral.[28] But it was the adjoining premises, at the corner, that housed the best-known place of entertainment in early Charlottetown: the Wellington Hotel, operated by John Howell. Irene Rogers, in her indispensable guide to the old city, *Charlottetown: The Life in Its Buildings*, calls the Wellington "the centre of social life in Charlottetown in the 1820–50 period." She continues:

It was a popular meeting place for the Members when the Legislature was in session; a time, it was said, of increased festivity rather than one of arduous parliamentary labour. A newspaper article described it thus: "Then it was that the Wellington, or rather Howel's as it was more frequently called, was in its glory. Rum, gin and brandy punch were the usual accompaniment of the evening session of the Howel Parliament lasting till far in the night ... It was quite a common occurrence in those days for men high in rank to spend the evening at Howel's solacing themselves with the creature comforts above mentioned."

The event that best illustrates the importance of this hotel in the growing town was a dinner given by the local gentlemen for Lieutenant-Governor Ready when he arrived from England in 1824. The guests ate "turtle and other delicacies" while crowds surrounded the hotel and a bagpiper and band played music in front of the house. A salute was fired from three 12–pounders drawn up in front of the hotel. On another occasion a company of equestrian performers from the United States, seated on their Arabian horses, executed feats of horsemanship before a large crowd in a handsome marquee in the yard of the Wellington. This took place in 1829 and was the first performance of its kind to be held on the Island.

But the Wellington Hotel was not just a place of entertainment. Several societies basic to the well-being of the community were formed from initial meetings held here. In 1824 the Saint Andrew's Society formed, and most important of all, on 24 March 1827 the Agriculture Society was established at the instigation of Governor Ready.[29]

The drinking of alcoholic beverages was a regular practice in colonial society. West Indian rum was said to be "the cheapest commodity not essential to life," yet a large proportion of the townspeople's money was expended on it – to the profit of the importers, dealers, and tavern keepers. The abuse of this cheap rum was not uncommon, and the city magistrate's dockets testify to many instances of drunkenness and fighting. During 1877, for instance, Judge Rowan R. Fitzgerald announced 729 summary convictions for drunkenness and sentenced 66 persons for assault. That same year, incidentally, operating licences were issued to twenty-three taverns, eleven saloons, and eight stores.[30]

Abuses aside, Charlottetown's inns hosted many gracious and sumptuous parties. The 1857 testimonial banquet at the Victoria Hotel honouring the politician and newspaper owner Edward Whelan was one such splendid affair. More than thirty of his personal and political friends attended, including George Coles and Mayor Robert Hutchison. "Never at a public dinner was there more joyous good feeling," Whelan's newspaper boasted. "The solids were such as might tempt any palate, and the liquids were unexceptionable." When the party broke up at 1:30 AM, the euphoric guests agreed that "no public entertainment had ever afforded them so much gratification."[31]

An ebullient Kerryman, writer Bryan MacMahon might well have had Charlottetown's Irish community in mind when he described his compatriots as "gregarious, loquacious and addicted to celebration." Indeed, ample evidence affirms that the entire colonial town had cultivated the virtue of exuberant hospitality. Fortunately for Canada, this virtue was abundantly revealed at the Charlottetown Conference of 1864, when the Fathers of Confederation met in a friendly setting and got to know one another sociably, preparatory to their founding of the Canadian nation.[32]

RELIGION IN CHARLOTTETOWN

Although the Irish were active in all walks of life, their presence was perhaps nowhere more evident than in the conduct of the church. The first colonial churchman was Theophilus DesBrisay, a graduate of Trinity College, Dublin, and an ordained minister of the established Church of England (see chapter 1). Of Huguenot descent, he was a native of Tipperary. Worshippers in DesBrisay's St Paul's Anglican parish in Charlottetown included several prominent families of Irish origin. One of DesBrisay's notable successors was David Fitzgerald, a Kerryman. He was followed by Charles O'Meara.

A few blocks from St Paul's, J.P. Hetherington of the Irish Wesleyan Conference erected a Methodist chapel, the 1835 forerunner of the large Trinity United Church. When the new building was completed in 1864, the estimable Irish-educated Dr Matthew Richey occupied the pulpit. Earlier (in 1847–48), across town, Samuel Browne, a licentiate of the General Assembly of the Presbyterian Church in Ireland, was interim minister at the Kirk of St James. Several other churchmen who had Irish origins or connections presided in Protestant assemblies beyond the capital, but nowhere on the Island was there a Protestant congregation that was mainly Irish.

Besides the dozen Irish Protestant ministers who served from time to time on the Island, another dozen Irish-born clergymen were Roman Catholic priests.[33] Despite their numbers, in not a single instance did an Irish minister or priest accompany any group of emigrants on their arduous journey from Ireland. Nevertheless, to say that the Catholic Church in colonial Charlottetown was numerically a strongly Irish institution is a tenable generalization, for the Irish influence was evident everywhere – from the town's motley congregation so unflatteringly described by abbé DeCalonne to the hard-working citizens involved in building and staffing the cathedral parish in the nineteenth century.

Bishop Plessis of Quebec offered the first public mass in Charlottetown on 16 July 1812. The courtesy of Wexford-born Chief Justice Caesar Colclough enabled the bishop to conduct the service in the courthouse. Generally, mass had been offered in private homes or at a Sydney Street inn run by Mrs MacPhee, a devout convert. Later, for about twenty-five years, a small wooden building served as the town chapel. In 1815 Father Fitzsimmons arrived, the first in a long succession of Irish missionary priests; but, as he had prior commitments elsewhere, his stay in Charlottetown was very brief and uneventful. In July 1822, with the arrival from the Newfoundland mission of an Irish Dominican friar named Alexander Thomas Fitzgerald, Irish leadership in the Catholic parish of Charlottetown began in earnest.

The Cathedral Parish

At the core of Irish Charlottetown was St Dunstan's parish. The name of the patron saint was conferred by Bishop Plessis when the Island was still under the ecclesiastical jurisdiction of Quebec. The bishop, not averse to complimenting those who wielded power but careful not to favour one segment of his own people over the others, chose not a French saint to be patron, nor a Scottish one, nor an Irish one, but a great Englishman, St Dunstan. While the Irish have no special claim to St Dunstan, who was the tenth-century abbot of Glastonbury and archbishop of Canterbury, it may be recalled that Dunstan had a particular spiritual kinship with the Irish, for in his youth he had often prayed at the shrine of St Patrick near his home in Glastonbury.[34] Be that as it may, an immediate and enduring bonding occurred between the parish of St Dunstan and the Irish Catholic people of Charlottetown.

Shortly after his arrival, Father Fitzgerald enlarged the original wooden chapel and announced a campaign to raise building funds. Among the first subscribers were Donald MacDonald (West River), John Doyle, John McCarthy, John Gainsford, and Thomas Fitzgibbon. Contributions also came from Governor John Ready, J.B. Palmer, and several other members of Protestant denominations. Father Fitzgerald ceremoniously opened the first parish church of St Dunstan on 17 March 1825. Since 1829, when the diocese was created, the successive churches of St Dunstan have been cathedrals.

In 1830 Fitzgerald left the Island, and for the next six years the parish was administered by an Island-born priest of Scottish descent, Bernard D. MacDonald. His trustees were an English convert named John Gainsford and five Irishmen: Dennis Reddin, James Kelly, John Doyle, John Breen, and Garrett Toole. In 1836 Father MacDonald was appointed the Island's second bishop, and an Irish priest named James T. Morris became pastor (1836–38). Father Morris was succeeded by Charles MacDonnell from Mohill, County Leitrim, who died suddenly on 1 January 1840.[35]

Father MacDonnell's cousin, Malachy Reynolds of Drumlish, County Leitrim, immediately took over the duties of pastor and accepted the responsibility for building the first cathedral. His building committee consisted of John Gainsford and five Irishmen: Daniel Brenan, James Kelly, Edward Kickham, Patrick Gaffney, and Dennis Reddin. The master carpenter was Daniel Carroll. Besides attending to the construction of the new building and performing his pastoral duties, Father Reynolds personally welcomed the immigrant vessels that arrived at Charlottetown in the 1840s, and he helped the newcomers settle on farmlands, particularly in Lot 65 and Kellys Cross, and in Kinkora where he later served as pastor.

In 1851, before the completion of the cathedral, Bishop MacDonald assigned Father Reynolds to smaller rural parishes. A few years later, possibly after some friction with the bishop, Reynolds returned to Ireland, where he died. Thomas Phelan, a native of County Kilkenny, succeeded him as rector in Charlottetown, and in 1855 he completed the interior of the cathedral.

In the years between 1832 and 1872, St Dunstan's rectors witnessed 616 marriages of Irish parishioners. Only 10 percent of these involved mixed nationalities. Three brides and one groom were converts to the

Catholic faith. Only one interfaith marriage is recorded, between a Catholic man and a Protestant woman.

SUPPORT FOR THE IRISH REPEAL MOVEMENT

Just as Irish loyalty to their church is legendary, so too is their love for the land of their birth. In no political cause did Irish immigrants display their patriotism more publicly than in their support of the Repeal Movement. It galvanized Irish national sentiment from one end of the Island to the other and, indeed, throughout the Maritime region. The object of the movement was to persuade the British parliament to repeal the Act of Union, enforced since 1801. As noted in chapter 7, this legislation, enacted in excessive reaction to the republican rising of 1798, had dissolved the Irish parliament and absorbed it into the unitary government of Great Britain. Daniel O'Connell, who in 1829 had succeeded in winning for the Irish Catholic people emancipation from the Penal Laws that had long deprived them of basic civil rights, had now turned his charismatic powers toward the repeal of the Act of Union and the restoration of the Irish parliament.

The Repeal Movement did not advocate complete separation from Britain, nor did it reject the concept of a United Kingdom. It did not threaten the British monarchy or lessen British sovereignty, nor did it sanction violence to achieve its ends. It was a popular movement of peaceful persuasion bent on self-government for Ireland under the British crown.

In Prince Edward Island during the early 1840s, repeal associations sprang up in a dozen places. As Terrance M. Punch, a Nova Scotian historian, notes: "Prominent repealers from Newfoundland and Halifax converged on Charlottetown that summer [1843] to help organize the movement there and succeeded in holding Repeal meetings northeast of Charlottetown at Fort Augustus and Monaghan Road, and to the west at Barret's Cross Roads and Bedeque, as well as a meeting of over three hundred in Charlottetown itself."[36]

The 6 July 1843 meeting at Patrick Coughlan's hotel on Pownal Street, presided over by John Slattery of St Andrew's College, appointed the following repeal wardens: Dennis Reddin, Walter Phelan, Richard Walsh, Thomas Broydrick, James McKenna, P.R. Doyle, and William Fitzpatrick. In the words of one resolution, those present deemed it "an imperative duty, in the present crisis of the affairs of Ireland, to express our sympathy with our Countrymen, in our native land, who are seeking, by peaceable and constitutional agitation, for the repeal of that obnoxious statute, the Act of Legislative Union between Great Britain and Ireland."[37] Other resolutions expressed admiration for Archbishop McHale and "other clergy who supported the cause," and gratitude to Daniel O'Connell, "the Father of His Country." The meeting also gave three cheers for "Rev. James Lowrie and the Presbyterians of North Ireland, the descendants of the glorious volunteers of 1782, who have joined in the Repeal movement"; three cheers for "the independent clergymen of Old Scotia who separated from the Established Church rather than allow their religious rights to be trampled upon"; and three cheers for "our gracious and beloved Sovereign, Queen Victoria." Under the chairmanship of Charlottetown lawyer John Little, the meeting concluded with a collection of £33 for the Repeal Movement.

A public meeting of the Charlottetown Repeal Association called for simultaneous gatherings throughout the Island on 22 January 1844 to petition "Queen and Parliament for a redress of Irish wrongs" and to "demonstrate their sympathies for oppressed Ireland by a vigorous and determined action."[38] Similar meetings were held at numerous places on the Island, and frequently the names of the subscribers (and sometimes even their native parishes) were announced in the press.[39] The October 1843 meeting in Charlottetown produced more than two hundred names of Irishmen and their places of origin. The 15 July 1844 repeal subscribers in Charlottetown numbered more than a hundred. The individual rural assemblies normally enlisted fewer people, but there can be no doubt about the widespread commitment of the Island's Irish – and many non-Irish as well – in support of the Repeal Movement. For instance, Daniel O'Connell's release from prison in 1844 ignited a giant celebration around a bonfire in Charlottetown. The *Palladium* on 8 October 1844 reported the demonstration in these words:

Scarcely had the English Mail arrived here on Friday morning, when the pleasing news of the reversal of the judgement against the Liberator and his co-patriots spread like magic throughout the community. During the day, no unusual display of patriotic feeling was made on the part of the sons of Erin, while the "green Flag" glittering joyously in the breeze at the summit of the tower of the new Catholic Chapel furnished convincing testimony to the intelligence. In fact, it might be said that the reception of this national intelligence, afforded general gratification to the Liberal portion of the community, without regard to creed or clime. And why should it be otherwise when the grand object of triumph is the liberation of the advocaters of universal freedom.

At the close of the evening, a public demonstration, befitting the occasion, bore evidence to the general exultation felt in the community. A large bonfire was lighted at the North suburbs of the town, dissipating by its "long broad flame" the heavy darkness which but a moment before, enveloped every surrounding object; while the corruscations of innumerable lights shot forth from the windows of those who could lay claim to one throb of Irish patriotism, or one feeling of respect and admiration of the great Advocate of Irish Liberty. The illuminations, though hastily, and by many, unexpectedly got up, were creditable to the National and Catholic feeling of Charlottetown, and will long be a source of pride and gratification to all who participated in that feeling. We rejoiced to observe our Protestant Brethren and natives of different soils from our own, felt disposed on that occasion, to bury their national and religious prejudices, and join in the noble revelry of celebrating the liberation of O'Connell.

The Repeal Movement, as manifested in Prince Edward Island, focused Irish attention on a major political issue and helped to bolster the immigrants' sense of identity and solidarity. Furthermore, as a just cause pursued by legitimate political means, the Repeal Movement also won support from freedom-loving people of various national backgrounds. At New London, for instance, Scots Presbyterians joined in support of the Irish repealers.[40]

Ultimately, the Repeal Movement in Ireland failed, but not for lack of popular support or able leadership. For one thing, the Great Famine of 1845–48 devastated the land and drew humanitarian attention to that immediate overriding crisis and away from the long-standing political issue. For another, in the post-famine era, continual agitation for home rule or dominion status – now exacerbated by Irish outrage over both the famine and the cruel evictions that followed in many places – met with evasions, delays, broken promises, and virtual rejection by the parliament in London. Thus, many Irishmen argued that it was British procrastination, insensitivity, and stubbornness that spawned the future violent uprisings and internecine warfare. In this crucible the Irish Free State was eventually born. By then, many Irish people had become so disenchanted with the British misunderstanding, mistreatment, and mismanagement of their country that they were determined to establish a completely autonomous Irish republic. All these developments in the old homeland were observed by the Island's Irish people with unflagging but nonviolent interest.

OCCUPATIONS AND PROFESSIONS

A belief persists that Irish immigrants generally were unskilled, uncouth, and unemployable except as labourers. The census of 1848 goes far toward controverting this belief. It is true that more immigrants to Charlottetown were general labourers than tradesmen or craftsmen, but the Irish were well represented in a wide spectrum of occupations. In 1848 both the Catholic priest Malachy Reynolds and the Episcopalian minister David Fitzgerald were Irish-born. So were physician Dr J.H. Conroy, publisher Edward Whelan, lawyer Edward Neil, and teachers James Foley, P.F. Doyle, and E.L. McCormack. Irish merchants in Charlottetown included Dennis Reddin, Daniel Brenan, Pierce Gaul, Edward Kickham, Cornelius Little, John Costin, Thomas Broydrick, and others.

There were butchers (John Blake, Thomas Gleeson), bakers (William Murphy and John O'Neil), and a cabinet maker (James Garland). The building trades included carpenters William Duffy, James Cahill, James Welsh, Michael Delaney, and James Carroll; masons John McGrath and William Broydrick; and plasterer John Egan. Timothy Condon and Thomas Logan were gardeners. Captain Doyle, Thomas Lynch, and John Toole were shipwrights. Four of the many truckmen were Peter Darcy, Michael Hickey, James Hughes, and Thomas McKenna. Among the Irish immigrants there were shoemakers galore: Morris Kelly, James Mahoney, James Tracey, Martin Brennan, Thomas Hennessy, and several others. Also a large number of tailors: Patrick Goodman, Patrick Quirk, Patrick Gaffney, John McIvor, and Richard Walsh, to name a handful. Joseph Weeks was an innkeeper, and Joseph Pippy and James Riely ran boarding houses. James Quinn, Francis Cahill, and Denis Fennessy were among the town's blacksmiths, while James McKenna, John Kennedy, and James Kelly were coopers. John Bowers was a saddler, Moses Hayes a bellman, and John Cain a tanner. While dozens of Irish labourers are listed in the 1848 census, there was only a small number of pensioners and firemen, and one engineer. The only worm cutter listed was Patrick Flinn.

Some Irish Women

The nineteenth-century nominal censuses tell very little about the women of that time. Invariably the named householders were men, and therefore the women were usually counted only as unnamed numbers. Children, guests, roomers, and boarders were similarly counted but were not identified by name or occupation.

Of the Charlottetown Irish women whose names do appear in the censuses, only a few are given full names: in 1828, Catherine Kanwell (Cantwell?), Mary Conoly, Bridget Cahill, and E.L. McCormack; and in 1861, Mary Dunn ("widow, huxten"), Ann McGronan ("laborer"), and Mary Kenady ("spinster"). Most women listed in these enumerations were called widows or given no designation. Some occupations, however, are indicated, such as "boarding-house keeper" (Mrs Ryan, Mrs McKenna, Mrs Whelan), "teacher" (Mrs McCormack), grocer

(Mrs Hardy), all in 1848; and, in 1861, publicans (Mrs Salinger and Mrs McCarron), "laborer" (Mrs Walsh and Mrs Neal), "washer-woman" (Mrs Gleason), "weaver" (Mrs Power), "vestmaker" (Mrs Gorman), "needler" (Mrs Goodwin), a "deys maker" (Miss Hanpin) and a "mantese" (Mrs McDaid), a few "hucksters" (Mrs McCourt, Mrs Nation, Mrs Clarkin), and one "lady" (Mrs Keoghan). Other occupations open to women in the mid-nineteenth century are not indicated in these lists.

Journalists

Remarkable in this review of immigrants' occupations is the fact that the Charlottetown Irish were notably active in the profession of journalism. Patrick Reilly, whose style, according to a fellow journalist,[41] was "modeled after that of the Irish agitators of 1848," was a regular contributor of diatribes and editorials to the *Patriot*. Edward Whelan, a native of Ballina, County Mayo, exemplified the combative, crusading journalism of the mid-nineteenth century. When he came to the Island as a protegé of Joseph Howe in 1843, he founded the *Palladium* (1843–45) and then the *Examiner* (1847), in which he fearlessly advocated responsible government, free schools, and free land, and more than incidentally he kept his fellow Irish well informed about events in Ireland. P.R. Bowers succeeded Whelan as editor of the *Examiner* and later established his own paper, the *New Era*.

Edward Reilly, printer and politician, edited the *Herald*, founded in 1864 as a successor to the *Vindicator*. After Reilly died, John Caven became the owner. When Caven became a professor at Prince of Wales College he suspended publication of the *Herald* until a new owner resumed operations in 1882.[42] Joseph F. Brennan became editor of the *Islander* after A.E. MacDougall acquired it from Judge W.H. Pope. Peter McCourt had published the *Advertiser* in Georgetown from 1876 to 1882 before taking up his career in Charlottetown and founding the *Watchman* in 1890.[43] From 1843 to 1847 E.A. Moody was editor and proprietor of the *Morning News and Semi-Weekly Advertiser*, but when he died his son-in-law John J. Pippy changed the name to the *Advertiser* (in 1854), and later he sold the business to J.J. Rice. Pippy went to Boston, where he prospered, and Rice later became a Methodist minister in Ontario.[44] The Irish, who boast the oldest vernacular literature in Europe and whose modern writers are often honoured as masters of the English language, were well represented here by articulate members of the press. (Chapter 10 contains further information on the occupations of the Irish immigrants.)

EDUCATION

The respect for learning that is often found among Irish people was also in evidence in early Charlottetown. In the 1840s, except for the Central Academy, a boys' high school, there were no public schools. Boys usually attended private schools for six or seven years, and girls did so for a few years longer; but many youngsters could not afford to pay tuition charges and therefore received little or no formal education. Patrick B. Doyle for many years conducted a licensed school on Water Street. According to the 1848 census, P.F. Doyle and James Foley also taught in the city. About 1844 the National School was founded on Kent Street (later it was called the Normal School or the Model School). Mrs E.L. MacCormack taught English and music there.

Early in the 1840s Father Malachy Reynolds's nephew, John Kenny, BA, taught at the Central Academy (later called Prince of Wales College). E.L. MacDonald recalled that Kenny's Irish dialect was a source of some amusement: He would address a dull student as "You stult you" (pronounced "stoolt"), and when a student made a wild guess in answer to a question, Kenny would say, "You are not within a bray of an ass of it!"[45] After teaching in Charlottetown for two years, he returned to Ireland.

Another Irish-born man of learning was Edward Roche, father of James Jeffrey Roche who became editor of the *Boston Pilot* later in the century. He taught at a school attended by the poorer children.[46] An able mathematician, Roche was an examiner at St Dunstan's College and at Queen's Square School. The latter, originally called St Patrick's, was founded in 1868 and was staffed by the Christian Brothers from 1870 to 1877. It provided education for the Catholic boys of the town, just as Notre Dame Academy and St Joseph's School (both conducted by the Sisters of the Congregation of Notre Dame) provided academic studies for the Catholic girls. When the new School Act governing public schools prohibited the teaching of religious doctrine, the Christian Brothers left; but until 1962 the school on Queen's Square remained *de facto* a bastion for the boys of St Dunstan's parish.

From the 1850s other Catholic institutions also served the growing Irish population of the city. From the start, daughters of Irish families attended Notre Dame Academy, and dozens of these young women later joined the sisterhood so that they might extend Christian education to younger generations. St Joseph's Convent and its school were established for the training of children on the western side of the town. In that building St Andrew's Hall was a popular place of assembly.

When St Dunstan's College was opened in 1855, two of the original seven registrants were from Charlottetown: William and Michael

Leahy. Thomas and Henry O'Mara enrolled in 1857; Myles Gahan in 1858; and James Roche, James Broderick, and Patrick Begley in 1859. Of the twenty students registered in the first five years of St Dunstan's College, eight were from Charlottetown, and eighteen had Irish surnames.

Scholars generally recognize that Irish interest in learning had become legendary during the Dark Ages in Europe, when Ireland's monastic "universities" did much to preserve and revitalize Western civilization. To this tradition American civilization appended the practical value of education as a means of social progress. Knowledge, always admired by the Irish as a virtue and a reward in itself, had now become a power. It was statesman Charles Gavan Duffy's rooted opinion that education was the agency without which the Irish people could accomplish nothing. Sentiments and sympathies would not suffice; conviction was necessary.[47] Duffy was proved right. By means of education the children of poor immigrants were enabled to gain positions of honour and responsibility. In nineteenth-century Charlottetown, the Irish Catholic people supported the schools sponsored by their church, and even after this school system was secularized they held to their traditional interest in education both for its own sake and for the practical benefits it promised.

SOCIO-ECONOMIC AND ETHNIC MIX

In 1848 – a pivotal year, marking the end of large-scale Irish immigration to the Island – the population of Charlottetown was 4,062. English-born residents numbered 555, Scots-born 180, and Irish-born 874. In addition, 325 had come from other British colonies (and therefore would have included some people of Irish descent); only 12 were from foreign countries. Whether these official figures account for all the newly arrived Irish who took up residence in Charlottetown in 1848 is doubtful. By then half the people residing in Charlottetown (2,105) were Prince Edward Island natives. Perhaps between 700 and 900 of them were of Irish descent. Thus, at mid-century, the Irish constituted more than 40 percent of the population and were the largest ethnic group in Charlottetown.[48]

Another piece of information contained in the 1848 census comes from the following notation by the census officer, C.D. Rankin:

In procuring the materials for the preceding statistics Nuisances came under my nose that were of an extremely repulsive character and must inevitably engender and propagate Disease. I have seen many families in extreme destitution of the means of subsistence, living in places resembling Pig Styes more than the dwellings of human beings; the squalid misery of many living in the back streets, lanes, and alleys, and the inferiority of the air they inhale, must prove very injurious to the health of the community in general. These are the most prominent particulars to which I consider it my duty to direct public attention.[49]

At this distance it is not possible to gauge to what extent the Irish augmented the poor rolls in Charlottetown. Predictably, Irish names appear in reports from the public asylum (which evidently housed indigents and disabled persons as well as the mentally ill), and no doubt other incapable individuals were beneficiaries of private charities. It would be wrong, however, to assume that the Irish generally were a burden on Island society. First of all, though many were materially poor when they arrived, not many – other than some *Lady Constable* survivors – were destitute refugees from the infamous Great Famine. In fact, the great majority had paid their own passage to Canada. Secondly, as has been shown, many of the immigrants were young able-bodied people familiar with various trades, capable of acquiring skills, and willing to work.[50] For such immigrants and for their children the Island and its capital city offered prospects for security and comfort unavailable to them in Ireland.

Thirdly, quite commonly Irish families came to the Island clothed in ordinary homespun and carrying basic household possessions, perhaps some tools or implements, and even a little money. From their members came sturdy rural tradesmen and farmers, as well as the shopkeepers and craftsmen of the town. The plain fact is that the Irish immigrants were found at every point in the economic spectrum, from pauper to patrician, from indigent outcasts in the asylum, through respectable workers on the land or in the town shops and trades, to honourable incumbents of the governor's mansion.[51] In this respect the Irish were no different from, and certainly not inferior to, the other immigrant groups who populated the colony.

The census of 1848 clearly supports the observation of a touring journalist who remarked that the Irish "compose a large proportion of the population of Charlottetown."[52] In 1848 Roman Catholics in Charlottetown numbered 1,492. There were 1,137 Anglicans, 765 Methodists, 573 Presbyterians, 72 Baptists, and 9 Bible Christians. Two reasonable assumptions are that at least three-fourths of Charlottetown's Irish people were Roman Catholics and that the Irish were also represented in Anglican and Methodist communions, and in smaller numbers in Presbyterian congregations.

The same census reveals another noteworthy feature of life in mid-nineteenth-century Charlottetown: the intermixture of people from

England, Scotland, and Ireland within the same household or boarding house, and the resultant variety of sectarian loyalties found under the same roof. Mrs Donald's place, for instance, housed two Irish, two British colonists, and three who were Islander-born; of these seven, four worshipped at St Dunstan's, two at the Kirk, and one at St Paul's. Druggist W.R. Watson headed a household consisting of an Irishman, an Englishman, a Scotsman, three British colonists, and four Island-born, a diversity reflected in their religious affiliations: four Roman Catholics, four Kirk members, and two Methodists. W. Harvey, a tailor, had a household of fourteen Island-born, seven Irishmen, one Englishman, and three Scots; thirteen of these people attended the Church of England, five the Kirk of Scotland, and seven the Church of Rome. Chief Justice Jarvis's residence consisted of six Anglicans, three Roman Catholics, and one Methodist. Druggist Thomas DesBrisay's household included ten Anglicans, three Baptists, three Free Church members, one Methodist, and one Roman Catholic. In the residence of the queen's printer, J.D. Haszard, there were twenty-one people, including four Irish; on Sundays, they were counted as twelve Anglicans, six Roman Catholics, two members of the Kirk, and one Baptist.

Within the compact boundaries of mid-nineteenth-century Charlottetown, therefore, three of the main ethnic groups and several church congregations lived in close proximity and engaged in peaceful interaction. Generally, the townspeople maintained their original national loyalties and respected one another's sectarian differences. While familiarity did not immediately lead to an indiscriminate mixture or assimilation, it did engender a cultural coexistence that perpetuated their diverse national traditions. In other words, the Island capital could not be called a melting pot that summarily subsumed its ethnic components. Although differences were perhaps respectfully attenuated to avoid unpleasant confrontations, they were neither blotted out nor denied. This state of cultural interaction was precarious, for the possibility of friction, even open conflict, was ever-present. So, too, was the possibility of a levelling assimilation. A third possibility was mutual respect and enrichment.

How, then, does one account for the longevity of Irishness in Charlottetown?

AN IRISH TOWN?

A few additional generalizations about the Irish community may be permitted here. As the family was the principal transmitter of values, and as "mixed" marriages were then very rare, the traditions of the homeland were effectively handed down and cultural identity was normally preserved. Furthermore, the traditional value system was staunchly reinforced by both the church and the school. To this day, even across a continuum of six or seven generations, many Charlottetonians perceive and proclaim themselves to be Irish. In fact, they are Irish in descent, in surname, in physical features, and in personal and communal outlook. Furthermore, they warmly acknowledge spiritual ties, however remote, with Ireland. Their ancestors came in sufficient numbers to constitute the capital's largest ethnic group, and their ethos retained sufficient vitality to imprint its character upon the capital's history. Thus, Charlottetown was once known to many as an Irish town.

Nor was the town cut off from the country. Regardless of milieu, outward signs of Irishness were seldom lacking. One such sign was evident when scores of Island homes displayed portraits of Ireland's emancipator, Daniel O'Connell, and thousands of people turned out on 6 August 1875 to celebrate the O'Connell centennial in Charlottetown. The *Examiner* reported that special trains from Tignish, Alberton, Summerside, Mount Stewart, Georgetown, and Souris converged on the capital, and that on each train one or two passenger cars were literally packed with people, and eight to ten freight cars were jammed with passengers. Celebrants who lived nearby came on foot or by carriage.

The festivities began with the celebration of a High Mass and an eloquent sermon by the vicar general. Then the procession set out from Rochford Square and marched through the town to the Kensington grounds. The parade was led by the city marshal and policemen and by Galbraith's band, followed by the parade marshal Charles Quirk and his aides. The marchers carryied a full-length portrait of Daniel O'Connell painted by the renowned artist Robert Harris. The Benevolent Irish Society turned out in full regalia. The St Charles Temperance Society (of Summerside) and the St Patrick's Total Abstinence Society were also in the parade, preceding the carriages bearing Senator George Howlan, the Hon. James Warburton, and parade organizer Daniel Brenan. At the end of the line the Rustico band played martial music for a "motley multitude of Irishmen from city and country."[53]

An oration was delivered by Senator Howlan. On the grandstand were the lieutenant-governor, the bishop, the chief justice, and other public figures. Sports events were directed by Judge Rowan Fitzgerald, B. Warburton, and William Welsh; Mrs Fitzgerald awarded the prizes to Hugh Trainor, Hugh McGonnell, and others. That evening there was a brilliant display of fireworks, along with entertainment in Market Hall, "the most remarkable feature of which was the recital by John LePage, Esq., of his poem on O'Connell's Centenary."[54]

The observance of the O'Connell centennial was organized by James Reddin, W.W. Sullivan, William Welsh, Thomas Handrahan, Owen Connolly, John Quirk, R.R. Fitzgerald, Thomas Foley, and P.R. Bowers.[55] The public display of Irish sentiment on this occasion was indicative of the strong Irish presence, numerically and culturally, both on the Island generally and in Charlottetown.

MEMORIALS FOR THE IRISH IMMIGRANTS

While Hibernia's public heroes and saints have been duly honoured, Charlottetown has publicly memorialized very few of the thousands of heroic homemakers and honest labourers who passed through the city in the nineteenth century.[56]

Streets and Tablets

Only a handful of street names evoke memories of the immigrant generation. DesBrisay Crescent is specific enough (and Upper Hillsborough Street was formerly called DesBrisay Street). Longworth Avenue commemorates another well-known early family, and Esher Street is a corruption of the Irish word *eiscir* (esker: glacial deposit), referring here to the name of the Longworth family estate in County Westmeath. Riley's Lane is named for a person now forgotten, but Connolly Street is called after a merchant and banker who emigrated from Donagh, County Monaghan, as a poor lad and rose to business eminence. Today his sandstone bust on the parapet of an office building on Queen Street – the only memorial sculpture atop any building in the province – suggests that Owen Connolly still presides over the city where he amassed a personal fortune and endowed many charitable causes. Edward Whelan is memorialized on a tablet in front of Province House, as a "Father of Confederation," and a room in the Coles Building is also named in his honour. The memory of Robert Kelly, a tradesman of old Charlottetown, is recalled by his name-plate being affixed to a building in the new Harbourside development; the name plate of James Reilly on an apartment dwelling at 27 Water Street also reminds passers-by of the building's original owner.[57]

Gravestones

Most immigrants were privately memorialized (if at all) on tombstones in several graveyards around the city. The Elm Avenue (University

Avenue) Protestant Cemetery dates from 1789, though the ground was
not consecrated until 1826. Here one discovers a stone for James
Bardin Palmer, an Irish barrister and politician who died in 1833 and
whose remains rest near those of his daughter Anna Louisa. Nearby
rests Mary, the fourteen-year-old child of Thomas and Anne Scott of
Belfast, who died in 1838. There is also a marker for Willie, the young
son of the Reverend David Fitzgerald. Fade Goff is buried here too; he
was a prothonotary and clerk, and first president of the Benevolent
Irish Society. A memorial to James McComb of Flurry Bridge, County
Louth, and another to Elizabeth Wood of Coote Hill, County Cavan,
stand not far from the gravestones of the Longworth family from
County Westmeath. Pastor Theophilus DesBrisay rests here among his
flock.

In the Roman Catholic Cemetery on Longworth Avenue, officially
dedicated in 1843, stand other granite or sandstone reminders of Irish
immigration. Dennis Reddin, for instance, is buried here, and so are
two generations of Corcorans: Michael and Ann, and James and Emily.
Alice Fennessy, wife of Thomas Fennessy of the parish of Golden, Tipperary, also is buried here, beside her four-year-old son, John. Michael
Lantry, of County Offaly, and his eleven-year-old son who died in 1860
share a gravesite, as do seventy-five-year-old James Hearn and his five-
year-old granddaughter. Some County Monaghan natives are interred
here: Michael Trainor's wife Mary, who died in 1869, Owen Trainor
(1871), and Ellen Trainor (1879); also Catherine McKenna's husband
Charles (1866) and her brother Owen McCarvill (1854). The families
of William and Helen Malone, and John and Mary Handrahan are
named on another stone. In a small cluster of memorials, the Hon.
Edward Whelan is commemorated, along with his son and daughter.
Other monuments, unfortunately, have been effaced by long exposure
to severe weather or, having been broken, were removed and dumped
along the breastwork at Victoria Park.[58]

Many tombstone inscriptions in St Peter's Cemetery in Sherwood
also serve as footnotes in the annals of Irish Charlottetown. They attest
that John Doyle and William Howlen were born in County Wexford;
Bassal Haiden in Kilkenny; James Cahill in Tipperary; and John
Leonard in County Laois. Among the Ulster natives buried here are
John McArty (a baker) and Peter Curran (a merchant), both of County
Down.

Here, too, one learns about Ellen Kickham, age sixty-four, and her
son-in-law Richard Ryan, age forty, who died in 1845. (Mr Ryan may
have been the shoemaker from Cashel, Tipperary.) There is also a
marker erected by Edward Kickham for his wife Mary, who died on 31
October 1845 age thirty-three, and for their two infant children. (Kick-

ham and his brothers Thomas and John were cousins of Charles J. Kickham, the distinguished novelist and patriot from Mullinahone, County Tipperary.)

James Reilly of Mount Meath, a merchant, was only thirty-one when he died on 7 April 1824. Two days later his year-old son also died, leaving a disconsolate widow and mother to inscribe these words:

> Do thou preserve the silent tomb
> Till wife and mother shall ask room
> Time was like thee possessed
> And time shall be where thou abideth.

It is possible that James Reilly had arrived in Charlottetown on 22 May 1822, for a passenger of that name was registered on the *Relief* (Simon Dodd, master) from Liverpool.

In 1828 Thomas Kelly erected a stone in memory of his father, Cornelius Kelly, who died on 15 December 1827, at age sixty. In 1834 James Cahill, a blacksmith, recorded the death of his twenty-nine–year-old wife Eliza and their two infant children. (He may have been the native of New Inn, Tipperary, who arrived in 1828 and resided in Charlottetown until his death in 1871.)[59] A merchant named John Doyle, a native of Oulart, County Wexford, was in his fiftieth year when he died in 1833, leaving a widow and two children. The Hon. Edward Kelly erected a stone for Moses Keough, his wife Catherine, and their son Daniel, natives of County Wexford.

In the same graveyard are buried Moses Roach and his brother-in-law Thomas Doyle. Other stones commemorate Sergeant Thomas Bennett (died 1863) and his family; Patrick McKenna, who died in 1870, thirteen years after his wife; Helena Brenan, wife of Daniel Brenan, who died in 1862; Patrick Walker, who died in 1877; and Dennis Lyons, his wife Margaret, and their son James, all of whom passed away in the 1870s.

By the 1870s the more extensive burial grounds on St Peter's Road – the Roman Catholic Cemetery and the People's Cemetery – had been consecrated. In the Roman Catholic Cemetery particularly, numerous Celtic crosses signal the Irish origins of many of the deceased. Scores of Irish family names confirm the sculptural evidence, and dozens of inscriptions reinforce the first impressions by alluding to the native Irish county or village of the deceased.

By the 1870s, of course, the stones were recording the passing of the later, northern Irish immigrants as well as the many descendants of both the colonial pioneers and the southeast immigrants. In the several graveyards in the Charlottetown area, as in dozens more through the peaceful countryside, the records of family names, places of origin, and dates of birth and death, carved in stone, proclaimed belief in a glorious resurrection and a world without end.

Each of the ethnic groups that helped transform Prince Edward Island from a tiny colony in the British Empire to a distinctive province in Canada has had its own claim upon the capital city. No immigrant group has ever possessed it exclusively, it is true, but no settlers ever felt more at home in Charlottetown than the Irish.

CHAPTER NINE

Storm over Belfast:
An Irish Retrospective

> I have lived in important places, times
> When great events were decided, who owned
> That half a rood of rock, a no-man's land
> Surrounded by our pitchfork-armed claims.
> I heard the Duffys shouting "Damn your soul"
> And old McCabe stripped to the waist, seen
> Step the plot defying blue cast-steel –
> "Here is the march along these iron stones."
> That was the year of the Munich bother. Which
> Was more important? I inclined
> To lose my faith in Ballyrush and Gortin
> Till Homer's ghost came whispering to my mind.
> He said: I made the Iliad from such
> A local row. Gods make their own importance.
>
> Patrick Kavanagh, "Epic"

For the Irish settlers of Prince Edward Island, the transition from Old Country ways to new colony ways was not free from anxiety, particularly with respect to political conduct and social issues. Indeed, the most discordant event in the Island's political history occurred during an 1847 by-election. Known as the Belfast Riot, it is the least understood political event of nineteenth-century Prince Edward Island, especially as the myths that have arisen from it are much better known than the facts.

Although the Irish people have been generally tight-lipped about the Belfast Riot, it is incumbent upon anyone attempting to tell the story of Irish immigration and settlement to clarify the traditional Irish understanding of what happened on that notorious occasion. However, the following account does not exonerate those who precipitated or participated in the violence. Its aim is simply to review

the issues, personalities, events, and attitudes, and to throw brighter
light on the Irish perception of what occurred and why. Examining
the Belfast incident in this way should illuminate several facets of the
Irish settlers' adaptation to the culture of Prince Edward Island.

The Belfast Riot of 1847 was a composite of two violent clashes and
three elections – the first election invalidated, the second aborted, and
the third uncontested:

1 In the Island's general election of 1846, polling was conducted
  between 10 and 14 August. In the third district of Queens County,
  known as the Belfast District, Reform candidates John Little and
  John MacDougall were apparently elected. However, the election in
  that double riding was invalidated when the legislative assembly
  upheld the charge of the Conservative candidates William Douse
  and Alexander MacLean that extremely rough behaviour at the
  Cherry Valley–Vernon River Poll had prevented some voters from
  freely exercising their franchise.
2 In the subsequent by-election on 1 March 1847, which was contested by the same four candidates, a much more serious riot broke
  out at the Pinette poll. Perhaps four hundred persons were involved.
  The voting had to be called off, but only after three men had been
  killed and many more injured.
3 In the rescheduled by-election on 19 March 1847, which was conducted under the watchful eyes of a company of infantry, a company
  of cavalry, and 120 special constables, the Conservative candidates
  were unopposed and therefore were declared elected after about one
  hundred votes were taken and only one hour had elapsed.

  The by-election violence at the Pinette poll was the central crisis in
the drama, the most outrageous of the series of events that constituted the Belfast Riot. Ever since then, the dark shadow of that civilian atrocity has troubled the collective conscience of numerous
Islanders.

WHAT HAPPENED AT PINETTE

The events of the 1 March 1847 by-election in the third district of
Queens County are recorded in three contemporary documents: a news
report in the *Royal Gazette*; Sheriff William Cundall's eye-witness
report to the colonial secretary;[1] and Lieutenant-Governor Henry Vere
Huntley's offical letter of 23 March 1847 to Earl Grey at the Colonial
Office in London.[2]

First, on 2 March 1847 the *Royal Gazette* informed the public that an election riot had broken out near the Pinette hustings shortly after noon the previous day and caused the death of two men, Malcolm MacRae early in the fighting and James Cain later. This was the most critical episode in the Belfast Riot story.

Next, Sheriff Cundall reported that most of the noonday aggressors were stick-carrying Irishmen, chiefly from County Monaghan, who were supporters of John Little and John MacDougall (Reform Party candidates). In the melee, Malcolm MacRae was killed and many other men were injured, he stated. When order was restored the balloting resumed. At about two-thirty a second outbreak occurred when more than two hundred stick-wielding voters, mainly Scots from Pinette and Flat River, supporters of William Douse and Alexander MacLean (Conservative candidates), clashed with the Irishmen who were guarding the hustings. During the encounter two young Irishmen, James Cain and Michael Mulcahy, were slain and many combatants were injured. The returning officer called off the balloting.

Lieutenant-Governor Huntley then rescheduled the cancelled election for 19 March 1847. In his report to the Colonial Office, he attributed the 1 March outrage to sectarian factions seeking to gain political control by electing members of their respective churches (Roman Catholic and Presbyterian). He later modified this hasty judgment.

Soon after these tragic events many Islanders sensed that the violence that had reached its climax at the Pinette poll held deeper social and political meaning than any common election-day "dust-up" or ordinary "local row." In their search for the underlying cause, some thought the disorderly conduct was incited by the customary election-day drinking; others blamed inflamed political partisanship; not a few attributed the disgraceful melee to ancient nationalistic rivalries; and still others faulted unresolved sectarian animosities.

Generally, Irish partisans were reluctant to memorialize or mythicize the Belfast Riot. Their composite view of it was matter of fact, and their consistent explanation of the root cause was down to earth, literally. To judge the Belfast Riot through Irish eyes requires that one see the situation as informed Irish contemporaries probably saw it leading up to the fateful encounter.

THE GEOGRAPHIC SETTING

In Ireland, Belfast is the second-largest city, a place long noted for its busy port, for shipbuilding, and for general manufacturing. To this day, Belfast's slums, sectarian strife, and political struggles stand in contrast to its classical public buildings, fine churches, and renowned university.

In Prince Edward Island, Belfast popularly refers to a rural district a few miles long fronting on Orwell and Hillsborough bays and the Northumberland Strait in Lots 57 and 58 in Queens County (see map 10). That whole district embraces Newtown Cross, Eldon, Pinette, Roseberry, Flat River, Surrey, Valley, and Iona. Enclosed in it is the specific locality of Belfast, a small rural area – not a village or town – between Lower Newtown and Mount Buchanan. The folk notion persists, supported by Warburton's *History*, that its name is an anglicized or corrupt form of the early French settlers' name for part of that area, *La belle face*. On the other hand, Rayburn's study of Island place names credibly insists that the district was named around 1770 by its first proprietor (Captain James Smith, RN, commander of HMS *Mermaid*) for the city in northern Ireland. The original Irish form of the toponym is *Béal Feirste*, meaning the ford or crossing of the sandbank.

Regardless of the source of the place name, from 1803 when Lord Selkirk (1771–1820) established his extensive colony, Presbyterian Scots from the Isles and Highlands have been the predominant residents of the Belfast area. Only a few Catholic Scots held land there. A small number of Catholic Scots who were thought to be part of Selkirk's expedition probably settled beyond the pale in Kings County; but several families of Catholic Irishmen from Waterford, Wexford, and Kilkkenny (some via Newfoundland) had leased some of the poorer acreage in Iona and Valley and in Upper and Lower Newtown by the 1820s. Land seekers from County Monaghan infiltrated the same localities in the early 1840s. However, even by mid-century, when Irish immigration to the surrounding townships had peaked, the small Irish minority within the Selkirk townships could be described fairly as living alongside rather than among the Scots, and neighbourly relations were guardedly tolerant rather than warmly harmonious.

According to the 1841 census, in the four Selkirk townships there were 197 native-born Irishmen and 1,221 native-born Scotsmen. In addition, there were 1,894 Island-born persons (almost all of Scots parentage, but a few being of Irish parentage), and 101 persons from other British colonies. Clearly, then, the Island place name Belfast never denoted an actual Irish settlement, and no substantial connection ever existed between the Island district and the Irish city.

Most graphically, at the centre of the Belfast district, on a knoll sheltered by birch and maple trees and overlooking a stream that winds down to the Pinette River, stands the elegant St John's Presbyterian Church. Erected by the Scots in 1823, the wooden building with its three-tiered Christopher Wren steeple remains a handsome and revered symbol of the predominant ethnic and religious realities of the area.

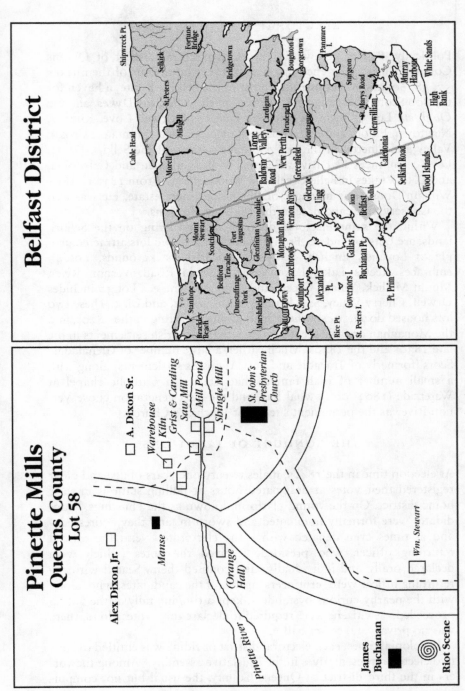

Map 10. The Belfast District was the scene of the Island's most notorious riot.

ELECTORAL BOUNDARIES

Politically, Belfast lies within the third electoral district of Queens County. This district encompasses six townships. Four of them (Lots 57, 58, 60, and 62) constituted most of the Selkirk Estate, a haven for the 800 Scots who emigrated in 1803 on the *Polly*, the *Dykes*, and the *Oughten*. Lot 57 includes the communities of Orwell Cove, Kinross, Newtown, Eldon, and Belfast. Lot 58 includes Iona (Montague Cross), Valley and Pinette. In the less populous portion of the Selkirk Estate, Lot 60 embraces Flat River, Beatons Mills, Culloden and Caledonia, and Lot 62 takes in Belle Creek and Wood Islands. From 1833 to 1861 William Douse was manager of this 80,000–acre estate. He was also the Conservative candidate in the 1846–47 elections.[3]

Within the same electoral district, and bordering on the Selkirk lands, are Lots 49 and 50. From the outset these two lots attracted people of Loyalist, English, Scottish, and Irish backgrounds. Lot 49 embraces Keefes Lake, Lake Verde, Pisquid Road, Vernon River, Mount Mellick, Village Green, and Millview, whereas Lot 50 includes Orwell, Cherry Valley, Seal River, Vernon Bridge, and Uigg. These two lots housed dozens of southern Irish families starting in the 1820s, and the Monaghan arrivals greatly augmented those Irish settlements in the late 1830s and the 1840s. Much earlier, a large number of Glenaladale Scots (formerly of Tracadie and Fort Augustus settlements) along with a small number of Irish families had erected a Catholic chapel at Waterside (1804) on Pownal Bay, and the next generation chose Vernon River as the permanent site for St Joachim's Church.[4]

THE CONDUCT OF ELECTIONS

At election time in the 1840s, males twenty-one years of age and older registered their votes at designated hours at polling stations in their home district. On the voting platform, known as the "hustings," candidates were formally nominated and sworn in, and they addressed – and at times even debated with – the electorate. Next, the official returning officer, who presided, received the votes (which were declared orally and individually) and counted them. Seated with the returning officer were scrutineers, agents of the candidates, who, along with the nearby curious bystanders, kept a running tally as the voting proceeded. As citizens were required to declare their votes aloud, there was no privacy, no secret ballot.

In colonial times, each electoral district or riding was entitled to have two elected representatives in the legislative assembly.[5] Among the voters in the third district of Queens County, the usual but not compulsory practice was to "vote the ticket," that is, to vote for the candidates supporting one's basic ideology, or the "party" of one's choice. Political parties as such were still in an early evolutionary stage, and party policies on many issues were not as clearly defined or as binding on individual elected members as they later became. By the 1840s, however, there were two camps, and the main issue (but not the only one) that distinguished them was the Land Question. The Conservatives generally defended the interests of the proprietors and large landowners, while the Reformers were expected to represent the aspirations of the tenantry.

More than anything else, the individual candidate's stance on major issues determined voter support, though his personality, local reputation, and influence also were important factors. Certainly, local issues could and sometimes did take precedence over matters of more intrinsic or more general importance. Often the polling process in any electoral district lasted more than one day, with the returning officer moving the poll from one station to another as required. The retinue of curious or avid party members were free to follow him from poll to poll.

Even before the Belfast incident, weaknesses in the electoral system had been obvious, and certain undesirable and, indeed, dangerous customs had emerged to exploit the weaknesses. Candidates who realized that they were doing poorly in the early voting, for instance, would intensify their campaigning among the local voters, making promises, offering inducements, or applying threats or other pressure. The closer the election contest, the greater was the pressure applied to the harried voters. At times, electors were assaulted near the hustings either before or after voting. In such hazardous circumstances, some eligible persons chose not to vote at all.

The electioneering practices of the time gave rise to another form of harassment. Commonly, supporters of a certain party or candidate paraded to the hustings in groups, sometimes to the accompaniment of music, singing, and shouting, waving symbolic banners or wearing the coloured ribbons or sashes of their favourites. The intent was twofold: to demonstrate party strength or candidate support and to coerce or harass followers or candidates of the opposing party. Such boisterous pageantry generated interest and enthusiasm, of course, but sometimes these practices degenerated into brawls – especially if, along the way, the rival marchers encountered one another. Sometimes, to make matters more hazardous, marchers tasted their "election rum" on the way to the polls (normally, they would expect to have their "treat" after voting). Some imbibers became jubilant, others pugnacious. At times voting was conducted amidst cheers and jeers, threats and fights, harsh words, and blunt weapons. All these forces had some bearing on what happened at Belfast in 1846 and especially in 1847, for in the latter instance both factions wielded staves and cudgels, and the outcome was disastrous.

A VIOLENT SOCIETY

Myth has made the Belfast Riot of 1847 memorable. However, placed in the context of nineteenth-century Prince Edward Island's tendency to election violence, the incident itself should not seem exceptional. Violence had already been in vogue prior to 1830; when Roman Catholics were first permitted to cast votes in elections, Bishop A.B. MacEachern had "warned his people to refrain from violence, and practice a spirit of forgiveness and toleration in all things."[6] It now appears evident that if there had not been so many casualties at the Pinette poll in 1847, that riot would probably have received no more notoriety than numerous other election clashes.

It is also apparent that the official custom of open voting and mobile polling sometimes precipitated conflicts among those who were inclined to fight. As well, the unofficial custom of providing voters with "election rum" sometimes fuelled political passions. Similar practices (followed by similar disorder) were no less common in the neighbouring colonies. In such circumstances, to speak of the Belfast tragedy (as Edward Whelan did) as a customary election battle that got out of hand was, in effect, to acknowledge two disgraceful facts: that election protocols were primitive and inadequate, and that election violence was common. In the subsequent debates in the assembly, these conditions were cited to explain the circumstances but not to justify the events of the riot.

AN AGE OF DISORDER

Those who deplored the disgrace at Belfast could reflect on many other instances of unruly behaviour in the Island colony. As early as the general election of 1787, the victory of Alexander Fletcher's followers had been disallowed because of interference and violence at the Charlottetown poll. The 1831 by-election that seated William Cooper, leader of the Escheat Party, had produced a riot at St Peters. And the 1846 general election in Kings County's third district, as well as Queens', was disputed on the grounds of riot and intimidation. In 1850 another "disgraceful row" occurred when a supporter of William Douse splintered a cane on the head of a political opponent at a rally near the Lot 48 ferry. Tempers flared and fists flew at Kinkora and Searletown in the 1857 election when, it was alleged, Dennis O'Meara Reddin, Edward Whelan, and some Charlottetown tavern owners incited Irish voters. In 1859, though no actual violence was reported, it was alleged that Monaghan settlers in the Hope River area were determined to keep possession of the poll and to shillelagh all who opposed them.

More to the point, in the 1834 election the factions headed by Douse, a Tory, and Douly Rankin, who favoured the Escheat Party, had clashed violently at Pinette.[7] Afterwards, Douse's property in the Belfast district was twice vandalized, and he had fears for his personal safety. These disturbances, it should be noted, occurred in the intensely Scottish community a few years before any Monaghan immigrants arrived in the vicinity.

In the same time frame, the festering Land Question had provoked many instances of violence. Milton Acorn, "the people's poet," writing nearly 150 years later, memorialized a "revolt" in 1837 in East Point and several other populist risings.[8] Hay River was then a well-known hotbed for escheators. A disturbance there on 20 December 1836 involved the well-known escheators Cooper, LeLacheur, and MacIntosh.[9] The Cunard estate at East Point was the scene of a house burning in 1843 after two hundred tenants of Lot 45 – in retribution for the eviction of a neighbour – had chased the sheriff and besieged an employee of the land agent. That flare-up required about forty special constables from the Charlottetown garrison to restore order. Nearby that same year, a sensational verbal clash disturbed the peace of St Margaret's Church when John MacIntosh, an ardent Reformer, defied the landlord-priest, the Reverend John MacDonald. Several years later the widely disliked Donald MacDonald (also of the Glenaladale family) was wounded in what was termed "an awkward blunder," and his brother resorted to arming himself with two guns. In this connection, John C. MacMillan tells the readers of his history: "The tenants with whom Father John [and his brothers] had to deal were, in many instances, a stiff-necked and refractory class of people. They were mostly emigrants from Ireland and Scotland, or immediate descendants of such, and were full of the notion that landlordism was a deadly exotic utterly unsuited to the free soil of Prince Edward Island."[10]

Besides the earlier tenant unease on the Cunard and MacDonald lands, a tenant outbreak in 1863 occurred on the Melville estate. In another incident, in March 1865 the tenants of Fort Augustus caused a disturbance when the sheriff attempted to serve writs upon members of the Tenant League: in all directions the farmers blew their tin trumpets (normally used to call in workers from the fields at mealtimes) as a signal to their neighbours to assemble in order to intimidate the sheriff and chase him from the area. Many times members of the league defied authorities in this manner. They ignored the lieutenant-governor's order to disband, and when the land agents and sheriffs demanded their rents, the farmers resisted with force. Finally, the colonial administrator brought in from Halifax a British contingent of eight officers and a hundred and thirty soldiers, who put an end to the resistance in Kings County. This action, along with the military crackdown on the 1866 parade in Charlottetown, suppressed the Tenant League.

Non-political issues also provided occasions for riotous behaviour. In 1830 residents of Dundas violently objected to restrictions on their importation of rum.[11] In the 1870s the townspeople of Souris became embroiled with American fishermen. In 1877 Charlottetonians witnessed a pitched battle near the Orange Hall on "the glorious Twelfth of July." Tense situations such as these always contained the potential for mob violence. The surprising fact is that despite all the clashes there were relatively few serious casualties.

Nineteenth-century Prince Edward Island, then, had its full share of group violence. In this respect the Island resembled many other colonies in the British Empire and, indeed, factions within Britain itself. Therefore, what happened at Belfast in 1847, though it clearly had some unique aspects, was far from unprecedented. It certainly was lamentable, though, the more so because of the loss of life and the numerous serious injuries that occurred in a small rural community.

FATALITIES AND INJURIES AT BELFAST

Although violence and intimidation were judged to have interfered with normal election proceedings at the polls in August 1846, as Douse and MacLean had charged in their successful petition to the assembly (in which the Tories then held a slim voting majority), those skirmishes produced no fatalities or serious injuries. Voiding the August 1846 election results, however, enabled both sides to prepare not only to cast ballots in the by-election but also to get ready for a battle. And that is exactly what happened. As noted above, in the subsequent by-election on 1 March 1847, they clashed at the Pinette poll in Belfast, where three men were killed at the scene and others may have died later from injuries received that day. Scores of combatants carried physical and psychological scars of that battle throughout their lives.

Of the three known fatalities – Malcolm MacRae (also spelled McRae), age forty-four, of Flat River in Lot 60; James Cain (also spelled Kane, Kean, Keane), age eighteen, of the Town Road in Lot 66; and Michael Mulcahy (also spelled Mulcahie), age about eighteen, of Sparrows Road, in Lot 66 – only Mr MacRae was eligible to vote.[12] The two Irish youths seem to have been mere apprentices in the hurly-burly exercise of Island election politics.

Inquests into the three deaths concluded that the homicides were committed by persons unknown, and no criminal charges were laid.

Several accounts of MacRae's death exist (though they are inconsistent in details and sometimes confusing), but no similar records were kept for the two Irish youths. It is doubtful that whoever killed MacRae knew that he was a native of Applecross, Ross-Shire, Scotland, or that whoever killed young Cain and Mulcahy knew they were sons of Irish immigrants from County Waterford. It is most unlikely that their assailants had deliberately set out to kill any one of them.[13]

Finally, it is reasonable to assume that young Cain and Mulcahy were not the only "outsiders" at the Pinette hustings. The by-election had attracted widespread interest, for voting control of the assembly depended on the outcome: the winning party would hold the balance of power. At stake, therefore, were matters that affected the whole Island, not only the Belfast polling area. Furthermore, the fact that the regular election had been nullified once on controversial grounds gave the return contest added notoriety and interest. All these circumstances considered, it is entirely believable that some non-voters (besides Cain and Mulcahy) were present and that some of the "outsiders" actively demonstrated their support for one or other of the contending parties.

THE CANDIDATES

In the elections in the Belfast district in 1846–47, the dominant personage was unquestionably the Conservative candidate William Douse. And if Douse represents the giant, the Reform candidate, John Little, could be cast as the potential giant killer. Their respective running mates, Alexander MacLean and John MacDougall, had only secondary or supporting roles.

The Secondary Players

Alexander MacLean (Conservative) and John MacDougall (Reform) were both of Scottish descent. Except for different political leanings, they had much in common. Both lived and farmed in the electoral district they wished to represent in the assembly, MacLean in Portage near Eldon, and MacDougall in Orwell Corner. Both men had some experience in public service, and each enjoyed a reputation in his district as a gentleman of good character – a neighbour who was reliable, sensible, and low key. MacLean was called *Gasda* in Gaelic, meaning "goodfellow," a term equally applicable to MacDougall. Similarly, MacDougall's exhortation to the electors for the 1 March 1847 by-election could just as well have been attributed to Alexander MacLean. MacDougall hoped that the voters' conduct would earn for them "the character of independent men," without compromising their rights and privileges by any disregard of the law, or their claims to the freedom of election, by submitting to any undue influence that might be exercised against them.[14]

William Douse (1800–1864)

Formidable is a word that fairly describes William Douse.[15] Born in Devizes, Wiltshire, England, he had emigrated to Prince Edward Island when he was twenty-one years of age. He married Esther Young and they had twelve children. He and his family lived in Charlottetown and attended the Anglican church.

Douse was a big man; he weighed over 300 pounds. He had courage; he had rescued a drowning man at sea. And he was enterprising; at various times he had been a shipbuilder, auctioneer, brewer, farmer, and a dealer in potatoes. Most important, he was well known as Lord Selkirk's estate agent, with power of attorney, responsible for tracts of land exceeding 100,000 acres in Queens County: Lots 57, 58, 60, and 62 in the third electoral district and Lot 31 (about thirty miles to the west) in the second electoral district. In this capacity he issued the leases and collected rents from hundreds of families – duties that were widely perceived as having some bearing on his conduct and success as a politician.

Douse strengthened his own financial position when he personally acquired 14,000 acres of the New Wiltshire estate (Lot 31) in 1855, five years before the government purchased the remainder of Lord Selkirk's holdings on the Island. In several ways Douse personified the worldly virtues of the enterprising man of business, the powerful resident land agent. He lived by the generally accepted code of that office and the common practices of an acquisitive society. Moreover, most of the time between 1834 and 1862 he represented the third Queens riding in the assembly.

Although rank-and-file Irishmen were reputed to recoil almost instinctively at the very sight or mention of a landlord's agent, some Irishmen may have voted for Douse in some of his elections, and some may even have taken up staves to ensure his victory in 1834. By 1846, however, his reputation among the Irish was markedly tarnished and he was being compared to James Yeo, the powerful "ledger giant" of Lot 9.[16] Like Yeo, Douse allegedly intimidated settlers on the estate he administered by insidiously calling attention to records of rents, debts, payments, and arrears. To any tenant who was in debt or in arrears, such a mean-spirited act implied the threat of foreclosure or eviction.

A staunch Conservative, Douse always supported the proprietors in land-control issues, and he was unsympathetic to populist causes. At the same time, he obtained road improvements for his constituency and generally treated his long-term Scottish leaseholders and freeholders with sufficient respect to garner their support. In addition, he won enough votes from small landholders and complacent or compliant tenants to control the riding – except in 1838, when he chose not to run, and in 1840 when he actually lost. Whether Douse's political success can be attributed to his power or his popularity remains an open question. Realists, recognizing the tenants' dilemma, have assumed that very few insecure tenants would be so courageous or foolhardy as to court the disfavour of their land agent by publicly voting against him. For secure leaseholders who were not subject to the land agent's threats, the Irish believed that Douse found other ways of "sweetening the pot."

John Little (1820–1864)

To electors in 1846 and 1847 John Little, first son of Cornelius Little and Brigid Costin, was known as a promising twenty-six-year-old lawyer who had served his five-year clerkship under Edward Palmer, had become an attorney in 1840 and a barrister in 1842, and had opened a law office in Charlottetown and in Georgetown.[17] Following in his father's path, Little was politically committed to the liberal Reform ideology. An active Catholic, he co-founded the Charlottetown Auxiliary of the Catholic Institute of Great Britain and was a member of the St Dunstan's Total Abstinence Society. Proud of his Irish heritage, he joined the Benevolent Irish Society and publicly supported the Repeal Association. In the person of John Little, the Irish community saw a rising star.

Who was John Little? To the Irish that question meant, Who were his forebears and where did they come from? In Island society as in old Irish society, such questions established a person's basic credentials. On his mother's side, John Little could be identified as a descendant of the Costins of Clashmore, County Waterford. Several members of that family had distinguished themselves in religious vocations of the Catholic Church. Others, living close to the port of Youghal in County Cork, had become involved in the Newfoundland trade and left Ireland after 1745.[18]

About 1787 John Costin (1760–1843), an immigrant son of that well-known Waterford family, had established his branch of the family on Prince Edward Island and purchased more than four hundred acres at Crown Point on Squaw Bay (Alexandra, Lot 49) as well as business interests five miles away in Charlottetown. In the colonial town he was recognized as a leader among the Irish Catholics, for he was a devout man, had some formal education, and was "endowed with rare intelligence, sound judgment, and high moral principles, all of which were supported by a fearless courage." John Costin's daughter Brigid married

Cornelius Little, and they established their home in Charlottetown. When their first son was born, in 1820, they christened him John.

John Little's father, Cornelius (1791–1864), was the son of Philip Little and Margaret Leonard of Dunshaughlin, in County Meath, Ireland.[19] Philip's descendants relate that he had been severely wounded at Vinegar Hill in the Rebellion of 1798. Another family tradition holds that young Cornelius, disappointed with the outcome of Robert Emmett's 1803 revolt, later left the family home at Rathbeggin. Equipped only with his father's blessing and a modest legacy, it is said, he wandered through Scotland, France, Maryland, and Nova Scotia, finally reaching Prince Edward Island after 1810. Once established in Charlottetown, Cornelius opened a grocery business, accepted appointments from time to time (wharfinger, fence viewer, fish inspector), supported Reform candidates at political rallies, and became an active member of St Dunstan's parish and the Benevolent Irish Society. He and his wife Brigid lived on Water Street, where they brought up their nine children "in the best Irish Catholic tradition."

Three of their sons eventually became lawyers. When John, the eldest, was nominated for a seat in the assembly in 1846, the Irish voters undoubtedly knew (or soon learned) his background and character. Reform constituents particularly noted that Little had earned a measure of professional distinction in an 1844 lawsuit against John MacDonald, the landlord-priest. MacDonald had taken legal action against one of his parishioners, John MacIntosh, an advocate of escheat in the assembly, who had confronted him in St Margaret's Church. In the bitter court case, Little had assisted Counsel Charles Binns in the successful defence of MacIntosh.

In Irish eyes John Little – scion of a highly respected family, a promising lawyer, a devout Catholic, an ardent Irishman, an articulate temperance advocate, and a convinced Reformer – was well qualified to challenge a Goliath such as William Douse. Most Irish voters, presumably, would be inclined to support him. And they would not be alone.

MEN OF THE CLOTH

It has been said that the Belfast debacle contributed to friction between the large Presbyterian population and the small Catholic minority in the district. Because, as we have seen, bigotry was pervasive (even when latent or subdued) and because sectarianism was a volatile factor (especially when mixed with politics), religious divisions were alternately respected, feared, suspected, appealed to, and denied. The potential for sectarian conflict existed in many places on the Island, but actual clashes were usually avoided. Often the role of the clergyman proved critical. For this reason, it may be instructive to scan the careers of Belfast's two leading clergymen at that time.

The Reverend John MacLennan

To Irish Catholics, Belfast's Scots Presbyterian minister, John MacLennan, was known mainly by his excellent reputation and good works.[20] His church and manse were only a few hundred yards from the hustings where the 1847 violence erupted. At that time his house became a temporary shelter for injured and dying men, and the minister himself testified at the inquest for Malcolm MacRae.

MacLennan, the first pastor of St John's Presbyterian Church, had arrived from Scotland in 1823 and served that congregation for twenty-six years. He also assisted in the founding or functioning of several other Presbyterian churches on the Island. He was a fluent speaker of both Gaelic and English. Never has a derogatory word or any hint of prejudice been recorded concerning him. During the fray, he was not threatened, nor was his church or manse ever in danger. Despite the cherished local legend that his son had prepared many of the staves and clubs used by the Scottish combatants at Belfast, the minister's reputation as a man of peace was never sullied. In 1849 MacLennan returned to Scotland, where he died three years later. He was buried there, at Kilchrennan. A stone monument memorializing him still stands in the peaceful churchyard at Belfast, Prince Edward Island.

The Reverend James Brady

As pastor of St Joachim's Church in Vernon River, James Brady resided on the periphery of events in Belfast.[21] From Vernon River he served the mission chapels in Fort Augustus, Tracadie, and Covehead, and later the missions in Baldwins Road and Iona. Many of the participants in the fray at Pinette poll were from his flock.

Shortly after emigrating from County Cavan in the province of Ulster, Brady had completed his studies in theology at St Andrew's College in Prince Edward Island and was ordained in 1838. Immediately he was appointed rector of the college and pastor to missions extending from Tracadie to Vernon River. Soon he incurred the disfavour of the autocratic MacDonalds of Tracadie, resident proprietors of Lots 35 and 36, who accused him of being a leveller and an escheator who preached anti-landlord propaganda.

Although Brady's personal sentiments probably favoured the tenants rather than the proprietors, there is no solid evidence that he had a hand in the debacle in the third Queens district. It is believable that both Brady and MacLennan may have agreed to counsel their respective congregations against the use of force during the election, but the rumour that Brady betrayed his word and countenanced violence is without factual foundation. His parishioners no doubt knew where he stood on social issues, including the Land Question. He was never a proprietor's man; nor was he known to be an advocate of violence.

In 1861 Brady dutifully accepted a transfer from Vernon River to Kinkora and Seven Mile Bay, but his loyal parishioners were so dismayed at his leaving that they protested to the bishop. As it turned out, he served only several months in his new parish when he became ill and was forced to retire to his brother's home in Webster's Corner near Fort Augustus. When he died a year later, more than three hundred carriages formed the funeral procession. His people erected a marble monument near St Joachim's Church to commemorate the Reverend James Brady and "the many virtues which adorned his character."

NATIONAL PRIDE? SECTARIAN PREJUDICE?

Without necessarily placing blame on any group involved in the Belfast Riot, it is incumbent upon historians to clarify the political and social issues that influenced the aggressive Irish supporters of the Reform Party, in particular, during the 1846–47 elections in the third district of Queens County. Otherwise, unreliable myth will continue to prevail over undeniable reality.

Historian Ian Ross Robertson presents a challenging keynote for discussing what happened at Belfast when he writes: "While it is true that those on one side were Scottish Protestants and those on the other were Irish Roman Catholics, it is far from certain that the causes of the riot can be reduced to religion, or 'religion and nationality.'"[22] Robertson's reasoning adds weight to the traditional Irish opinion, for at no time did the Irish participants think of the election in the Belfast area as essentially a nationalistic or "racial" struggle between themselves and their Scottish neighbours. On the Island generally, the numerous Scots and the minority Irish got along reasonably well; that is to say, they normally kept their distance and exercised caution and forbearance. This relationship existed even within the Selkirk townships.

Certainly, the national histories of the two Celtic groups had differed in some significant ways, but as settlers in a faraway colony, they realized that they held much in common. They could be, and were, rivals without being enemies. In the compelling concerns of politics, for instance, neither national group consistently voted *en bloc* along party lines. Not all Irish voted for the Reformers, and not all Scots voted for the Tories. Indeed, in the contest in question, many of the supporters of the Reform Party must have been Scots; otherwise, the 1846 election results could not have been so close. At the same time, although a few of the Irish voters may have favoured the Conservatives, there can be no doubt that in the third district of Queens in 1846 and 1847, the Irish voters overwhelmingly supported the Reform ticket. On the opposite side, judging by the official tallies within the four Selkirk townships, the strong majority of the Scots who voted obviously favoured the Tory candidates.

As if to ensure ethnic balance, in this election, each of the political parties had nominated a Scotsman to be the running mate of a non-Scotsman (English-born Douse and Irish-descendant Little) in the dual riding. Incidentally, the two Scots were permanent residents of the district, whereas the two non-Scots could be termed "outsiders" whose permanent homes were in Charlottetown. Regardless of the ethnic mix and balance on the ballots, some people later came to believe that the Pinette election encounter had somehow been a heroic re-enactment of supposed ancient Celtic grudges or mythical racial hostilities. The Irish participants, painfully familiar as they were with faction fights and brawls among Celtic kinsmen, did not place such an august interpretation on the donnybrook at the Pinette hustings. Even if ethnic rivalries or clannish differences had been minor motivations for a few of the rioters, in most Irish minds they had not been the principal cause of the riot.

The earliest Irish settlers in the area had in fact maintained a reasonably respectful coexistence with the Scots majority. After all, the Irish electorate (practically all of whom were Catholics) remembered with abiding gratitude that the noblest citizen of the Selkirk estate, Dr Angus McAulay of Belfast, spiritual leader, physician, and legislator, had been "an uncompromising friend of the Catholic Cause" during the struggle for political emancipation.[23] In the view of the Irish participants, who were always aware of Scottish and Irish differences, the colonial Belfast Riot most certainly was not precipitated by nationalistic Irish-Scots hostility, ancient or contemporary.

Equally dubious is the opinion that the Irish electors were chafing from the so-called Bible Question of 1845 – a petition to require Bible reading in the Central Academy in Charlottetown. Although some Selkirk settlers may have regarded the brash, rambunctious Irish newcomers as an irritant on the fringes of their peaceable Presbyterian precincts, this was an entirely separate matter, unrelated to the public school Bible-reading issue. Argument over the proposed use of the Bible in the public schools had already been put to rest in the Protestant-majority assembly, and it was not revisited in earnest (and even then in a much more general context) until 1857–58, ten full years after the Belfast incident.

Busy, hard-working immigrants had other compelling concerns on their minds. Actually, until the mid-1850s, as Professor Robertson has noted, "the surprising circumstance was the dearth of religious hostility."[24] In any event, if the matter had been raised, informed Catholics would probably have been untroubled by William Douse's personal stand on the Bible Question, while militant Protestants would probably have strongly disagreed with him and found ample cause to abstain from voting for him. Although Douse favoured religious instruction for youth, he thought it imprudent, in view of the sectarian differences, to introduce the Bible into the public school curriculum.[25]

It was only after the 1 March 1847 election that the speaker of the assembly, W.H. Pope, rang the biblical alarm bell when he speculated that "combinations are in the course of formation, not merely of a political, but of a religious character," and that "a very bad feeling is getting up, that religious differences are appealed to, for political purposes."[26] Lieutenant-Governor Huntley was no less simplistic in his initial impression that "the outrage in the first instance originated in a determination of the voters of different religious persuasions residing in the district named to return members of their respective churches to the Assembly."

At least as tenable was the unpublished opinion that this contest – which pitted a Presbyterian and an Anglican against a Presbyterian and a Roman Catholic – must have created a prickly predicament for Selkirk electors, who may have been inclined to vote on exclusively-sectarian lines. Perhaps it was for this reason that the lieutenant-governor, on reflection, evasively disconnected the riot from any feeling "beyond that of the respective parties engaged in it, desiring to obtain the ascendancy."[27] Even though sectarian awareness was implicitly present in this election, as it was in virtually every other riding and perhaps every other Island election, the Irish never argued or agreed that the Bible Question as such caused the Belfast Riot. In the context of the 1846–47 election, this particular issue may never seriously have crossed their minds.

The Central Issue

Even so, while some gentlemen in high public office assigned specious, spurious, or superficial reasons for the Belfast encounter instead of acknowledging the root cause of the conflict, several members of the assembly did perceive and did declare that certain proximate matters – non-nationalistic, non-ethnic, non-biblical, and non-sectarian – were foremost in the minds of the discontented Irish voters. Furthermore, these assemblymen fully realized that any people who could be persuaded to fight for their national myths or traditions or for their sectarian beliefs would also – when adequately provoked or motivated – fight for worthy social principles or political objectives, for their civil rights, or even for the normal opportunity to earn a decent family living. In short, contemporary Irish spokesmen and others did not believe that the root cause of the conflict at Belfast was drunkenness, ethnicity, or narrow sectarianism, though they certainly were familiar with all of these factors. Instead, the Irish contended that the compelling concern of the irate Irish electorate was the Land Question, not only in socio-political theory but as it directly affected them in their practical quest as would-be settlers on the Island. Historian Edward MacDonald states the matter most cogently: "The central issue was a passionate one, the Land Question."[28]

THE CONTENTED SCOTS?

Consider, first, the situation of Scottish leaseholders in the Belfast area. Between the far-sighted vision of the founding Lord Selkirk and the actual administration of the Belfast-area settlement there were several deep discrepancies. As a colonizer or developer, Selkirk evidently believed in promoting freeholding rather than tenancy, and in this respect his views were certainly more liberal than most Island proprietors. In Selkirk's PEI colony, we are told, "leases were relatively generous and terms of purchase were reasonable."[29] In fact, by 1807 Selkirk "had sold or granted for services 16,222 acres of his holdings to over 150 individuals ... over half that total on Lots 57 and 58."[30] Those who did not own their farms outright usually held very long leases. For this reason, the original Scottish settlers (who then constituted perhaps 90 percent of the people on the Selkirk estate) should have been generally pleased with their situation. Indeed, at first the Skye settlers called their new home an Isle of Contentment. Hardly a generation passed, however, before some of those same Scottish settlers and their heirs expressed discontent with the terms of their leases and protested by withholding their rents.

These weeds of discord began to sprout in Selkirk's peaceable plantation soon after William Douse became the administrator in 1833. It would be unjust to think of Douse as the sole cause of the troubles; he was merely a forceful and faithful agent of the controversial proprietory system. Within five years he "was complaining to Selkirk that tenants who had shown no previous sympathy for escheat [confiscation] were now refusing to pay their rents."[31] His attempts to evict the protestors met with violent resistence and some damage to his own property in the Belfast district. "Discontent was rampant. It was

expressly directed against the land agent," states historian Kenneth A.
MacKinnon, referring to action taken by tenants in 1836. On that
occasion a Scottish leader, Coun Douly Rankin, presided at a meeting
in Belfast that supported both a court of escheat (to settle claims to disputed lands) and a statutory exclusion of land agents from the assembly. "Douse responded," says the historian, "by advertising the sale of
Rankin's lease and rent arrearages."[32]

Despite Douse's frequent political victories, the notion that he regularly treated all his Scots tenants with kindness and deference is indeed
questionable. It is clear, though, that as a shrewd land agent he preferred to deal with the more or less contented Scots than with the more
or less contentious Irish. By 1847 he had evidently persuaded Scots residents to set aside the admonitions of their remarkable pioneer, Dr
Angus MacAulay. In his 1820 appeal to the electors of Queens County,
MacAulay (who was known to have challenged even the Earl of Selkirk
himself in matters of justice for the tenants) had revealed his contempt
for the agents of absentee proprietors when he declared: "Resident
gentlemen engaged in Agriculture or Commerce are linked with your
interest in the Province. Strangers however well inclined are not to be
confided in, more than plausible Agents of absent Proprietors, who
have often gulled the industrious community here, and men of rank at
home. I shall only add, ... 'There are but two reasons for not trusting
an Attorney with your money: one is, when you do not know him very
well, and the other is when you do.'"[33]

THE DISCONTENTED IRISH

Aside from the real rumblings among the Scottish tenantry, the Irish
had a very substantial grievance of their own: Douse refused to grant
them long-term leases. Acting within his legal rights, he offered them
leases of only twenty-one years, and he charged them a higher rental
than usual. Some Irish immigrants were infuriated by this particular
form of discrimination. When they left Ireland they thought that they
had escaped from landlord despotism and land-agent arrogance. They
had expected to enjoy in the colony the same rights, privileges, and
opportunities in law and society as all other British subjects. They were
astounded to meet with such blatant bigotry in New Ireland.

Like their fellow settlers from Scotland, Irish immigrants who chose the
rural way of life were earnestly desirous of rising above the status of mere
peasants and assuming the dignity and duties of independent farmers.
Therefore, they considered it insulting and exploitive when they were
offered only fifteen-year leases or even twenty-one-year leases and were
charged higher than normal rates. After all, several years of invested

labour without income were normally required just to clear and prepare the wilderness land for crops. Following this period of toilsome servitude, as historian McNutt points out, "Most infuriating of all was the possibility of eviction or the raising of rental rates."[34] It was public knowledge that Douse had tried to evict rent withholders on the Selkirk estate in March 1838, only to meet stout resistance from Scots tenants armed with clubs and pitchforks.[35] Like their Scottish kinsmen before them, the new Irish immigrants sought reasonable security through longer leases at reasonable rates. But they were refused. So like their Scottish kinsmen before them, some of them felt obliged to resort to force.

Some neighbours who observed the Irish reaction to Douse's land policy must have realized that among the darkest, most dreadful images of sorrowing Ireland were indelible recollections of poor hungry peasants being evicted from their humble cottages under the supervision of the land agent and constables. It was common knowledge, too, that similar evictions had sometimes been enforced in several places on the Island, though bravely resisted. In such circumstances it is understandable that Douse, as a reputed representative of the potentially cruel system and as a land agent who had actually requested the use of armed force against some poor tenants, would not enjoy the favour of the Irish newcomers to the region. Still, audacious as it may seem, Douse was the person who sought to consolidate his power and extend his influence over the tenantry by being chosen to represent them in the legislative assembly.

Thus, of emphatic importance is the Irish contention that, about 1840, William Douse had arbitrarily altered leasing policies within his business jurisdiction (that is, in the four Selkirk townships of the third electoral district of Queens) in such a way as to shut off the inflow of new Irish immigrants while simultaneously protecting the clannish interests of long-settled Scottish tenants. To the Irish, the message was clear: they were not wanted. They surmised that there were two major reasons for their being ostracized: first, Douse certainly did not want any more anti-landlord rabble rousers in his constituency; second, those Selkirk residents who may have felt threatened by the rapid growth of Irish immigration and settlement probably approved of the curtailment of the Irish Catholic influx into their relatively comfortable Scots Presbyterian precinct.

In this connection, some Scottish tenants may well have wished to revive Lord Selkirk's early idealistic concept of establishing an exclusive colony in which Scottish settlers would strive to preserve their Gaelic language and perpetuate their Highland culture.[36] Unfortunately perhaps, neither Selkirk nor his settlers had diligently pursued these early objectives, and in time their appeal diminished. To what

extent Selkirk's uncodified vision still motivated some Scottish combatants at Belfast cannot be determined. For their part, the Irish
immigrants never expressly faulted the desires of any Selkirk settlers
to preserve the cultural integrity of their community. What the Irish
strongly resented was the ploy used by the land agent to impede normal access on customary terms to unoccupied lands on which they, as
citizens, hoped to settle their families. From the Irish point of view,
the Douse-modified land policy in the Belfast district was deliberately
discriminatory.

Precisely what Douse did, it seems, has been alluded to in a marginal
notation presumably made by the 1841 census enumerator, who wrote:
"Some of the settlers in the back woods rec'd their land at 6d sterling
per acre per annum, others at 8d, but the general rent over all the four
Townships was a shilling sterling per acre for 999 years, until last year
when the price of land was unaccountably raised by the agent to 1/4
cur'y per annum and the term of the lease curtailed to 21 years."[37]

The property rights of the established Scottish leaseholders and other
residents in the Selkirk settlement remained secure and untouched by
the new rules and the increased rates. Perhaps it was for this reason
that the unaffected residents never openly expressed opposition to the
new regulations, nor did they indicate to what extent (if any) these regulations influenced their strong support for Douse at the polls. On the
other hand, on this particular local land issue, no one, not even col-
leages within Douse's camp, rose publicly to his defence.

In contrast to the general neutral silence or tacit approval, the Irish
response was explicit and unmistakable. For his discriminatory leasing
practices, candidate Douse incurred the wrath of the disadvantaged
newcomers from County Monaghan. The Irish criticism of Douse was
substantive: his short-lease rules so patently directed against the new
immigrants, along with his flaunting of the rent ledgers at election
time, were two palpable charges against him. These charges reminded
the Irish of bitter experiences in their long-distressed and currently
famine-devastated homeland – experiences which predisposed many of
them to strongly oppose the landlord-tenant system in their adopted
land which agents such as William Douse so offensively espoused.

Irish historian R.B. McDowell once observed that "in Ulster, competition for land led to rural rioting between catholics and protestants,
rioting culminating in the 'battle of the Diamond' and leading to the
formation of the Orange Society [in September 1795]."[38] Paralleling
that Ulster experience, the founding of the Orange Order in Prince
Edward Island has sometimes been traced or attributed to the colony's
Belfast Riot.[39] Furthermore – as if to reinforce the parallels – in New
Ireland, as in Old Ireland, there were nineteenth-century land wars and

land leagues and land reforms. In each place the commoners generally stood together and eventually prevailed.

Quite apart from such historical coincidences, it is little wonder that historian Robertson, writing about Prince Edward Island, should have stated: "From what is known of the voting patterns of the Irish, and from literary evidence which survives concerning their activities at public meetings and political affrays and other occasions, there can be no doubt that they were, as a body, strongly committed to the reform cause, and opposed to leasehold tenure."[40] In fact, so active were the Irish in their opposition to the excesses in the land system that the *Examiner* once editorialized: "It used to be slanderously said that no class of people in the Island resisted the payment of rent but Irish Catholics."[41] As the Irish settlers themselves saw it, in the third Queens district, "the man from Devizes," an autocratic land agent and hard-nosed politician, had dared to say "Boo," to the Monaghans. That was asking for trouble.

ACTION AND REACTION

In their opposition to William Douse in 1846 and 1847 the Irish chose to be aggressive. They believed that he exercised unfair control over many tenants within the four Selkirk townships but had little power and less appeal in Lots 49 and 50. Their resort to muscular persuasion at the polls, therefore, was intended to serve an obvious dual purpose: to discourage voters in the four Selkirk townships from voting Conservative (or from voting at all), and to encourage voters in Lots 49 and 50 to vote Reform. This meant confronting head-on those who supported Douse. Hence they employed the same strong-arm tactics often practised in the United Kingdom, elsewhere in Canada, and elsewhere in Prince Edward Island, as well as in their own district. They marched boldly to the hustings in force, carrying shillelaghs or other sticks, and shouting their slogans in support of John Little and John MacDougall. Such action not only proclaimed their own political preference but signified a threat to those who held contrary views. In this instance, though, the plan failed. Douse's well-armed supporters were not easily intimidated. In fact, they reacted with such typical Celtic vigour that their counterattack matched their opponents' challenge. They met violence with violence.

As a result the noisy, pugnacious demonstration degenerated into a free-for-all which ultimately led to three deaths and scores of injuries. Earnest as the combatants were, it cannot be said that either side really anticipated such a tragic outcome; after the heat of battle, both factions grieved over the casualties they had caused and the losses they had suffered. Some defenders later took some satisfaction from their part in the dubious battle, and the aggressors never denied their part of the responsibility for the fray. Nor did either side lessen its commitment to the social and political objectives at stake in that election. Although the overt battle was over, the underlying cause of the conflict had yet to be addressed.

THE REAL CAUSE

A review of the political events leading up to the fatal encounter at Pinette helps account for the real cause of the 1847 riot. In the Legislative Assembly debate on the Douse-MacLean petition to nullify the August 1846 election in the third district of Queens County, the temporary incumbent John Little rebutted minor and secondary charges before he took up the main issue. These reported words are at the heart of his statement:

With regard to the real causes which induced the people of the third District to take part against Mr. Douse – many of them were lease holders, holding their property on short leases at a heavy rent charge. They asked for long leases – they were reviled, spurned and treated with contempt. They therefore declared that they would not support him, and, when this fact was made evident to him, he abused them in the foulest epithets – called them scoundrels and other opprobrious names, and even leaped off the hustings and challenged them to fight ... When, however, Mr. Douse saw that the men whom he had reviled – these Monaghans with short leases – were determined to assert their rights, then he became enraged, told them they would be glad to eat "humble pudding" with him yet – quitted the hustings and returned to Charlottetown.[42]

No attempt was made to refute Little's charges.

In the Assembly debate concerning the 1 March 1847 by-election, Reform member Alexander Rae (second Prince district) echoed Little's judgment in these words: "I believe there is another feeling prevalent in the District of Belfast, and that is one of strong prejudice against a person who has once, twice and thrice stood on the hustings there, and that this feeling is created and fostered by the tenure on which that individual has placed the tenants. The unfortunate fact of the twenty-one years leases has caused a strong feeling against him."[43] No attempt was made to deny Rae's allegation.

Between the August 1846 general election and the 1 March 1847 by-election, the accusations against Douse remained unrefuted. In fact, even three years later, in a letter Douse wrote to the *Islander* (5 July 1850), he was still adamant in his land policies. Gloating over his fifth personal election victory in the Belfast riding, he ridiculed the "scheming pennyless agitators" who would give the tenants false hopes of "free land tenures" and other reforms.

Reform members of the Assembly always recognized the power that Douse wielded in his own constituency, and even in the debates before the 1847 riot they had attacked both his policies and his practices. Speaking with the strong convictions characteristic of his Monaghan countrymen, Assemblyman Robert Mooney (second Queens district) had this to say about the 1846 allegations of violence at the poll made by Douse and MacLean:

They speak of intimidation ... as if there was not a greater intimidation daily practised on the tenantry than all that had occurred at this election. Did they never hear of the intimidation of the Rent Roll? ... These Monaghans of whom we have heard so much came to this country to seek that justice which was denied to them at home. The "forty-shilling freeholders," who were shut out from voting in Ireland, came here to place themselves among freemen and to acquire – if not for themselves, at least for their children – the rights and privileges of electors ... Place, Sir, the tenantry of this Island on a fair footing – and do not tell them that they must vote this way or the other way, but leave them to vote according to their consciences. They were too much threatened as it was. They hardly dared to attend a meeting, for the rod was held out to them; and what right has any one to threaten them: they, as well as myself, have sworn allegiance to the British Queen. Give them justice, and that's the way to bind the Monaghans to you.[44]

George Coles, leader of the Reform Party, who was strangely ambivalent about the events of the 1846 election and who willingly conceded "the misconduct of Mr. Little's friends," took this stand: "If the House are determined to protect the rights of the subject, and put down the club and such means of intimidation, let them also put down the influence of the Rent Roll and Ledger."[45] Reform member John W. LeLacheur (third Kings district) expressed much stronger views. Citing historical instances of politics and violence as a context for the 1846 debacle, he declared: "The oppression of the tenantry was the cause of all these outrages. In the election now before the Committee, the same spirit has been shown, the same desire to revile and oppress the tenantry. With regard to the rioting at Belfast, it appears to have been private quarrels that led to it."[46]

Throughout the Assembly's committee debates, members cited numerous instances of electioneering violence and intimidation. In the same session of the Assembly, a formal protest was lodged against the validity of the August 1846 election results in the third district of Kings

County. But although this petition also alleged riot and intimidation, the two elected Reform members, LeLacheur and Thornton, retained their seats.

Dr J.H. Conroy (third Prince district), singled out the unpopular land-lord of Green Park, James Yeo, as an example of a politician who used the rent ledger for "gross and unblushing" intimidation of voters, and in the same breath he spoke with disdain of William Douse who, he said, "seems from the evidence we have heard to have lorded it over the Ten-antry of the District with all the magnificence of a petty tyrant over his vassals ... He, poor man! puffed up in all the pride and pomp of 'a little brief authority,' descended from the hustings and threatened the voters with the awful thunder of the artillery of his delegated Rent Roll."[47]

Both Mooney and Conroy spoke fervently about the Irish immi-grants' historical sensitivity about the Land Question. Both Rae and John MacIntosh (first Kings district) spoke firmly in favour of reform-ing the electoral system as a means of averting violence.[48] Rae point-edly linked the two issues by remarking, "I trust that when means are to be devised to prevent intimidation at elections, the rent rolls and prosecution for debt will not be forgotten." MacIntosh was also criti-cal of the tactic of the rent roll. He blamed "the system of land hold-ing which enables some persons to intimidate quite as effectively, and more so, than with the stick or bludgeon." He expressed the belief that no election in the previous fifteen years had had less violence than that at Belfast and Lot 49 in 1846.

Edward Whelan's Views

Finally, Edward Whelan – then a new member of the Assembly, who philosophically insisted upon using only just means to achieve social reforms – seemed almost complacent about the relatively slight vio-lence in the third district of Queens in 1846. He said, "As great a dis-turbance may frequently be seen at a fair or market as that which took place at this election," and he went so far as to maintain that "it is utterly impossible to conduct a contested election without a certain amount of excitement and some degree of intimidation."[49] In attempt-ing to establish a realistic perspective on the incidents in question, however, he was careful not to express approval of violence.

Nor did Whelan condone the evils of landlordism. As Professor Robertson points out in his essay on the Land Question, "For a gener-ation Whelan stressed the centrality of the land question and came back repeatedly to his early argument that the Scots and the Irish of Prince Edward Island were facing a common and historic foe: land-lordism."[50] In fact, only nine days after the calamitous 1847 by-election, and on behalf of residents of the Belfast constituency, Whelan presented to the assembly a petition that touched the very heart of the matter: "A petition of the divers inhabitants of the Third Electoral District of Queen's County, praying that measures may be adopted with a view to effect a purchase of the right of the proprietors of the soil of this Island in order to enable the Petitioners and others to become freeholders of the improved and wilderness lands, at a reasonable rate."[51]

While legislators continued for years to wrestle with the Land Question, frustrated tenants formed themselves into tenant leagues. Eschewing party loyalties, national origins, and sectarian differences, these leagues strengthened the members' resolve to defy the law, resist the payment of rents, and conduct disturbing protests. Until the tenant leagues were finally suppressed in 1866, they were the most effective means that tenants had for expressing grievances.

Although Whelan strongly disapproved of the tenant leagues' defiance of the law – a stand that is said to have deeply displeased his constituents – he was just as vocal as any other Reform member in arguing that the real issue behind the Belfast Riot was "a contest between landlord and tenant." In Whelan's mind, the Land Question was the leading public issue on the Island, and "all other items in the political agenda were to be considered in its light."[52]

John Little's Farewell

The *Royal Gazette*'s reporting of the Assembly debate of 31 January 1847 reflected the responsible sentiments that John Little had expressed while pleading his own case: "Mr Little was as anxious as any honorable member could be, that all feeling should be laid aside, and that every matter connected with the Third District Queens County should be fairly investigated and brought forward. If his return was jeopardized by this, he was aware he had to abide by the decision of the House, and that decision would be given – not upon forms and prejudices, but upon the merits of the evidence adduced. But both as an individual and as a member of the House, he wished the provisions of the Law to be duly complied with."[53]

Little was in all respects an honourable man. Nor did it go unnoticed among his constituents that before he was required to relinquish his seat in the Assembly, he had introduced an issue of justice related to the Land Question, namely "A Petition ... securing to Tenants ejected from their lands, compensation for their improvements."[54]

REVISITING THE DARKLING PLAIN

Four months after the Belfast Riot, Irish and Scottish residents of Vernon River and vicinity (St John's civil parish) addressed several resolutions to Lieutenant-Governor Huntley.[55] One resolution stated that the "lamented proceedings" at the Belfast election had "been erroneously attributed to Irishmen in particular." The resolution charged that in fact a candidate had "infuriated with religious prejudice the feelings of a certain party of the Electors" and had not observed "the principles of sobriety and good order," and that this candidate had maltreated and assaulted "certain other Electors who had constitutionally opposed him." The meeting declared its determination "to aid the public authorities in bringing the guilty parties to speedy and condign punishment."

Huntley prudently replied that he thought "any attempt to attach the sole guilt of the outrages to either party would be repugnant to the facts of the case." As he was "confident in the repentant feelings of the parties implicated," he was not inclined to pursue the matter further. Instead, he hoped "that a veil would for ever have been thrown over those excesses which at the time plunged the District in mourning, and that a dreadful lesson having been received, all would seek to atone for their errors, by encouraging and practising in all future differences charity and christian forebearance."

Huntley's response to the petition was admirably conciliatory. Despite the demands of the Vernon River citizens' petition and a *Royal Gazette* editorial, no formal inquiry was ever conducted. As a result, the veil of official silence thrown over the shameful event unintentionally but effectively transformed plain facts into popular myths. For decades, residents in the area brooded over what had happened at Belfast, and a century and a half later students of Island history continued to probe the basic questions.[56] Throughout, low-key Irish voices have maintained that a demagogue's verbal insults and subtle intimidation can be just as infuriating as physical assaults; that the labelled aggressors at Belfast were not the only culpable participants in the riot; that the leasing regulations instituted on the Selkirk estate in the 1840s intentionally discriminated against the Irish immigrants; and that the ultimate cause of the bloody conflict was tangible and deep rooted – in the land itself.[57]

On a small scale, in a localized setting, and in a disorderly manner, tenant potency had challenged proprietor power. To the extent that possessing the land was the central issue behind the effort to control the Pinette poll, the "local row" fought in James Buchanan's ten-acre field exemplified the "epic" quest of virtually all immigrants to Prince Edward Island.

CHAPTER TEN

An Island of Destiny

Having traced the century-long odyssey of the Irish immigrants and settlers in Prince Edward Island, we may now view the same Irish exiles and their families as citizens putting down permanent roots in Canada's smallest province. Between 1769 and 1880, Prince Edward Island progressed from a fledgling British colony to a full-status province in Canadian Confederation. By the latter date, Irish immigration to the Island had long ceased, and nearly all the fertile land was occupied. Many among the second and third generations were beginning to claim their inheritance. For others, outmigration had begun, but not yet on a large scale.

In 1864 the historic conference in Charlottetown initiated the political process of binding the several provinces into one nation. Nine years later, Prince Edward Island formally joined the Confederation. On that occasion the Irish settlers transferred their formal allegiance to their newly constituted homeland, and without having to divest themselves of their cultural possessions or hereditary loyalties, they embraced citizenship in Canada – a nation they and their compatriots had helped to create.

"Ultimately the Irishman abroad retains an interest in his native country," states Ruth Dudley Edwards, "but commitment to his new country eventually comes with acceptance by the indigenous community."[1] That process of adaptation clearly applies to the nineteenth-century Irish immigrants, who did not shake off their "exile" or "alien" mentality until they were recognized as normal citizens, equal both in law and in social practice. Just as the colony itself cautiously approached its destiny as a province of Canada, so the Irish settlers gradually adapted to the Island way of life.

During the several decades of immigration and settlement up to 1850, the Irish had come from all thirty-two counties of Ireland and established themselves in every township on the Island (see map 11). In religion they were not so diverse; nine out of ten were Roman Catholics. These immigrants in their totality and diversity truly represented "the Irish abroad." In the three decades of acceptance and adaptation after mid-century, however, their children and grandchildren came to typify "the Islanders at home." By then they had acquired property, conducted businesses, participated in politics, and assumed leadership roles in church and secular society. Remarkably, in this progress the Irish people held fast to their filial affection for the Old Country even while they cultivated and demonstrated their allegiance to Prince Edward Island and Canada.

THE STATUS OF THE ISLAND'S IRISH

For Irish residents no less than for other Islanders 1864 was a pivotal year. At that time people of Irish birth and descent made up slightly less than one-quarter of Prince Edward Island's population and about 40 percent of Charlottetown's population. For well over ten thousand Irish immigrants, Charlottetown had been the principal port of entry into the New World. For most of them, Prince Edward Island had become the new Emerald Isle, rich in resources and opportunities, a true *Inisfail*, their Island of Destiny. At its outset the year 1864 held no exceptional promise, only a routine rehearsal of familiar occupations, challenges, hardships, diversions.

John Murphy, for example, continued to operate the North American Hotel, the city's largest hostelry, as a place of comfort and good cheer on Kent Street, and Edward Whelan pursued his vigorous style of partisan journalism in the *Examiner*, a newspaper advocating social reform on the Island and supporting majority-Irish interests abroad. The publishing firm of Reilly and Doyle took a more explicit sectarian stance in the pro-Catholic *Vindicator*. Around town, the Irish stood out at every turn. Patrick Reilly was a tailor, Maurice Kelly a shoemaker, and Peter Halloran a blacksmith and carriage maker. Both James Reddin and John Higgins ran combined groceries and dry goods businesses, and the McKenna family had a grocery at Pownal and Richmond streets. John Conoly was a brewer and James Walsh a grocer and liquor dealer. Andrew and Thomas Doyle from Wexford were sail makers and builders. A young law clerk from Hope River had just come to public attention as secretary of the Catholic Young Men's Literary Institute; he was the future premier, William W. Sullivan. And a poor immigrant from County Monaghan, Owen Connolly, on his way

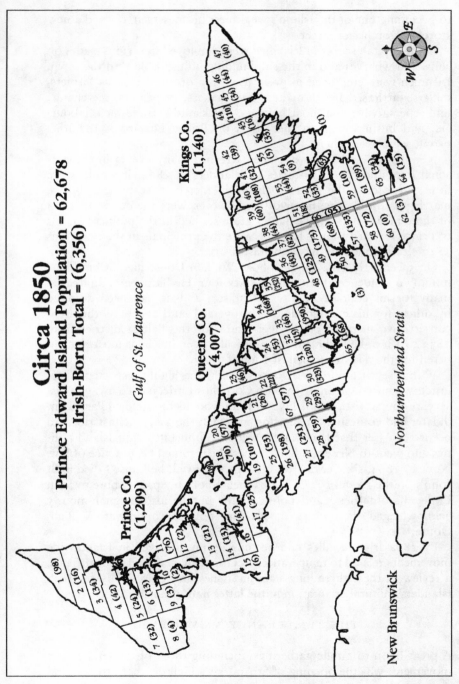

Circa 1850

Prince Edward Island Population = 62,678

Irish-Born Total = (6,356)

Gulf of St. Lawrence

Prince Co.
(1,209)

Queens Co.
(4,007)

Kings Co.
(1,140)

Northumberland Strait

New Brunswick

1 (98)
2 (16)
3 (34)
4 (42)
5 (24)
6 (13)
7 (32)
8 (4)
9 (3)
10 (2)
11 (76)
12 (2)
13 (21)
14 (13)
15 (6)
16 (41)
17 (25)
18 (70)
19 (107)
20 (57)
21 (26)
22 (22)
23 (46)
24 (53)
25 (53)
26 (198)
27 (251)
28 (59)
29 (293)
30 (323)
31 (120)
32 (15)
33 (46)
34 (168)
35 (352)
36 (452)
37 (82)
38 (44)
39 (60)
40 (108)
41 (32)
42 (39)
43 (16)
44 (110)
45 (34)
46 (46)
47 (40)
48 (125)
49 (173)
50 (68)
51 (182)
52 (33)
53 (44)
54 (9)
55 (5)
56 (63)
57 (133)
58 (72)
59 (10)
60 (0)
61 (89)
62 (3)
63 (34)
64 (15)
65 (68)
66 (95)
67 (57)
(1)
(3)

Map 11. By the mid-nineteenth century, Irish families had settled in virtually every township on the Island.

to becoming one of the Island's wealthiest businessmen, opened a new store on Dorchester Street.

In the capital, scores of Irishmen were employed in various trades on ships and wharves and in the shipbuilding industry. Beyond the town, Irishmen were employed in every township on the Island as farmers, millers, farriers, harness makers, sail makers, carpenters, merchants, innkeepers, fishermen, boat builders, blacksmiths, tradesmen, labourers, and businessmen. In the 1860s on Prince Edward Island Irish people were everywhere.

Newspapers and other documents record many events in the personal lives and family histories of Islanders in 1864. It would serve little purpose in the present chronicle merely to catalogue births, marriages, and deaths; noteworthy, however, were the deaths in 1864 of three men – two whose names are inscribed in the political annals of Prince Edward Island, for they were the principals in the notorious 1847 election incident in the Belfast district.

On 5 February 1864 English-born William Douse died at his Charlottetown residence at the age of sixty-four. He had been admired by many for his courage in a rescue at sea, and he had been despised by others for his conduct as a controversial land agent. As the arch-conservative member of the legislature for the Belfast district from 1832 to 1860, he had a stormy political career, but he is most remembered for the disastrous Belfast Riot of 1847.

Within seven months of Douse's death, the highly respected Charlottetown businessman, Irish-born Cornelius Little, passed away in his-seventy-fourth year. It was his son John who, as the Reform Party candidate, had contested the election at which the 1847 Belfast riot had occurred. After that lamentable incident, John Little quit Island politics and went to Newfoundland, where he resumed his practice of law. Now, in 1864, six weeks after his father's burial, he himself died in St John's. In the *Examiner*, Edward Whelan not only paid tribute to John Little, his old friend and political ally, but he also magnanimously acknowledged the virtues of his late political opponent, William Douse.[2]

By 1864 Irish families had become deeply involved in Island-wide movements related to temperance, sectarianism, and land reform. Thus, a review of these three long-standing issues may help clarify the Irish Islanders' cultural adaptation in the latter half of nineteenth century.

THE TEMPERANCE MOVEMENT

A great boon to public gatherings, including those of the temperance movement, was the opening of St Andrew's Hall in Charlottetown on

13 July 1864. Early in March the building, which had been the old St Andrew's Church near Mount Stewart, was transported fifteen miles along the frozen surface of the Hillsborough River to its new site on Pownal Street. This herculean project had enlisted the services of 500 men and 120 horses. Among the Scots, who were mainly responsible for the undertaking, it was a deservedly memorable event.[3] Soon the lower section of the building was converted into classrooms for St Joseph's School, conducted by the Sisters of the Congregation of Notre Dame, and the newly constructed upper floor became a meeting room called St Andrew's Hall. The school enrolled over one hundred pupils that September. Meanwhile, the hall had been put to use on 17 July when Bishop Peter MacIntyre called a meeting to organize a temperance society. Over the years, St Andrew's Hall accommodated many cultural and business activities, and St Patrick's Temperance Society and the Benevolent Irish Society came to be designated "benefactors of the house" at St Joseph's Convent.[4]

When Dennis O'Meara Reddin, president of the St Dunstan's parish temperance group, spoke on the evils of intemperance on 7 November 1864, he was carrying on a tradition that had originated locally in 1841, when Father Malachy Reynolds had been the driving force behind the founding of the St Dunstan's Total Abstinence Society.[5] Reynolds and laymen such as Cornelius Little, P.B. Doyle, and Richard Welsh were distressed by what they considered the excessive use of spirituous liquor in the small colony. "Demon rum," particularly, was cheap and plentiful. Bishop Bernard D. MacDonald's strong support of the temperance movement encouraged the Charlottetown organizers, who modelled their society on the crusade that Father Theobald Mathew had inaugurated in 1838 in County Cork. Among Irish immigrants the "chief vice was drunkenness," states historian William Forbes Adams, but taking "Father Mathew's pledge was as good as the best letter of recommendation"[6] for these same people. At the time, insobriety was a national scandal in Ireland, and in America it was the most disadvantageous characteristic associated with Irish immigrants. To combat this situation, Father Mathew called on the Irish people to pledge themselves to total abstinence from alcoholic beverages. Not without controversy and personal hardships, during the last eighteen years of his life he saw his movement spread to every nation to which Irish people emigrated. As a result, millions of people around the world took the pledge of lifelong sobriety. Paradoxically, in the homeland itself, even though alcoholism was still considered the nation's second most grievous social problem (after poverty), Ireland had the highest proportion of teetotallers in all of Europe.

As Father Mathew had relatives in PEI, he was particularly disappointed that he was unable to visit the Island during any of his North
American tours. However, some immigrants had taken the pledge of
total abstinence from the famed Irish apostle of temperance and wore
religious medals blessed by him.[7] But it was the crusade of the Catholic
clergy, led by Bishop MacDonald and his successor Bishop MacIntyre,
that ensured several thousand Catholic enrolments in the society here.
In July 1874, MacIntyre established the St Patrick's Temperance Society to suppress the sale of spirituous liquors on Sunday and to abolish,
as far as practicable, the traffic generally. By 1877, every Catholic
parish on the Island had a total abstinence chapter, and the bishop saw
fit to issue a pastoral letter on the subject and to form a diocesan council. Several of the temperance societies eventually formed their own
bands and conducted parades and concerts on St Patrick's Day and
other occasions. As well, they frequently held teas and picnics and
other social and educational gatherings, as they did in 1864 in Rustico,
Kinkora, Charlottetown, and elsewhere.[8]

The temperance movement was already very strong among Protestant groups at this time, and occasionally the Protestant and Catholic
churches joined forces in the cause of temperance. As early as 1845,
the Independent Total Abstinence Society had united with the St Dunstan's group in sending Father Mathew a letter of homage and financial assistance.[9] And in 1864 an interdenominational temperance rally
in Kinkora attracted two thousand people. Such cooperative efforts
promoted good will, as indicated in an open letter by "a Protestant" in
praise of the late Patrick Stephens of Orwell: "Belonging to the order
of 'Sons of Temperance' was to him a qualification of the highest order.
He was no bigot."[10]

Beneficial as the temperance movement was, and numerous as its
adherents were, two offsetting factors were constantly present: first,
not all total abstinence pledgers persevered in their resolution (those
who slipped were known as "backsliders"); second, teetotalism was far
from being universally accepted. On the Island, as in Ireland, temperance movements have waxed and waned over the decades. This is one
of the cultural similarities among Irish people on both sides of the
Atlantic.

SECTARIANISM

Meanwhile, a more grievous issue that had been simmering for a long
time began to boil. Strident sectarianism polluted public life in the
1860s. In Prince Edward Island religion and politics were virtually
inseparable. A plethora of speeches, articles, letters, editorials, and

reprints inflamed the passions and choked charitable impulses. Combative journalism and hyperbolic oratory, the customary media of the day, were often vehicles of invective. These public exercises in mutual antagonism contained little matter for the mind. The avowedly Protestant papers (the *Protestant and Evangelical Witness* and the *Monitor*) contended against the professedly Catholic ones (the *Vindicator* and the *Examiner*). The other papers also usually took sectarian and political sides. Sometimes the sectarian eruptions that later generations would regard as foolish or tedious deeply affected the lives of nineteenth-century Islanders.

Considerable consternation emerged, for instance, when the peculiarly Irish product called the Loyal Orange Institution (LOI), also known as the Orange Order) was imported into Canada and successfully marketed on the Island. For some people, no doubt, Orangeism satisfied an appetite; for others it was bitter fruit. In either case, Orangeism was a glaring symptom, not the root cause, of the scandal of sectarianism. What made that politico-religious fraternal organization the centre of controversy was the propagation of its adamant ultra-Protestant and ultra-Loyalist principles in a society that often held different beliefs. Catholics in particular took umbrage at the Orange view that "the tenets and structures of Catholicism were threats, seen as the epitome of disloyalty and moral laxity."[11] There can be no doubt that for the large number of Irish Catholics in Prince Edward Island, Orangeism was an unwelcome intrusion.

The Orange Order

Founded in Loughgall, County Armagh, in 1795, the Orange Order was transplanted to British territories overseas by immigrants who believed strongly in the defence of Protestantism and in loyalty to the British monarchy. King William III, the Prince of Orange, who had defeated James II, the deposed king of England, on Irish soil near the Boyne River, is the principal symbol of the Orange Order. "The Glorious Twelfth" (12 July 1690, the date of the decisive battle), is still observed in parts of Ireland and also abroad as a day for Orange celebrations. Traditionally, Green nationalists (the Catholic majority) have viewed the Orange institution as a peculiarly Irish legacy of British imperialist policies and as an auxiliary agency of sectarian apartheid and political partition. At the beginning of the twenty-first century, Orangeism still stands for militant Protestantism and implacable Unionism, especially in sectors of the six counties of northeastern Ireland.

Since their establishment in eastern Canada, the Orange lodges have lost their original Irish stamp and have enrolled people of diverse national origins. Meanwhile, their common bond has remained dedicated Protestantism and occasional concerted political action. In the latter half of the nineteenth century the potential for open conflict was always present, but in later decades Orange activities generally appeared to be fraternal and sociable rather than militantly sectarian or strongly political.

From its inception, the Orange Order in Prince Edward Island was supported mainly by Scotsmen and Englishmen. The Island's Irish Protestant population was probably less than 10 percent, and only about half of them were of the militant Ulster variety. The Anglo-Irish establishment families who had helped found the nondenominational Benevolent Irish Society were generally indisposed to join or ardently support this militant sectarian fraternity. Nevertheless, the traditional linkage between Irish Low Churchmen (the more militantly Protestant members of the Church of Ireland) and the Orange movement was maintained on the Island by such Irish clergymen as David Fitzgerald (deputy grand chaplain, LOI) and Robert T. Roach (grand lodge chaplain, LOI), who were Anglican Church rectors in Charlottetown and Georgetown, respectively.[12] It is difficult to ascertain how many Irish laymen were active members of the Orange Order here, but there do not appear to have been many.

Another view of the beginnings of Orangeism on the Island holds that "the Murderous riot, some years ago, at Belfast, led to the formation of Orange Lodges in the Island."[13] While the Belfast myth may have been an initial factor (four Lodges were indeed formed in the Selkirk townships), probably more significant were the 1850s debates in the legislature and the press over the use of the Bible in the Island's public schools. On the strength of the Bible controversy, the Orange movement helped elect the all-Protestant Conservative government of 1859. After that, Orange lodges became more numerous and more assertive. The Boyne Lodge had been instituted in Charlottetown in 1849. By the 1860s, there were thirty-three Lodges on the Island (two of them in Charlottetown), and the Grand Lodge of Prince Edward Island was established with George P. Tanton as deputy grand master in 1862. Of the fifteen primary lodges at that time, four were in the order's Belfast district, under District Master Daniel Fraser: Thistle (Belfast), Sword (Woodville), Prince Edward (Lot 49), and Lyon (Orwell).[14] On 17 March – always a sacred date in the Irish calendar – PEI's provincial secretary, W.H. Pope, chose to introduce his 1863 bill to incorporate Orange lodges in the colony.[15] The legislation was duly passed by the assembly and readily approved by Lieutenant-Governor

George Dundas; but it did not receive royal assent, because the Duke of Newcastle, secretary of state for the colonies, decisively disallowed the Act as being detrimental to the public interests (just as Lieutenant-Governor Alexander Bannerman had done in 1852). Incorporation, therefore, was postponed, but the political initiative of Pope and the acquiescence of Dundas showed the increasing political strength of the Orange movement on the Island.

It has been argued that this Orange show of strength may have been a reaction to the steady progress and increasing assertiveness of Catholics. Almost from the founding of this British colony, Catholic Scots and Catholic Irish, outnumbering the Catholic Acadians who were already here, began to infiltrate what was initially supposed to be a Protestant stronghold. By 1830 most legal limitations on the civil rights of Catholics had been rescinded. By mid-century heavy Irish immigration had made Catholicism, at nearly 44 percent, the largest single denomination. Then came the drawn-out bitterness over educational issues and the use of the Bible in public schools. As well, there were the aggressive practices of the Tenant League, some of which were notable in Catholic districts. Each step represented a perceived threat to, or erosion of, political control by the original establishment. Just as the Orange Order in Ireland had come into being to protect the entrenched interests of the Protestant community, so too the Orange lodges on the Island were determined to check encroachments on what many Protestants considered to be their hereditary domain.

Both as an outspoken editor and as a Liberal politician, Edward Whelan, a Green Irishman, saw red on the Orange issue. He had wide support in assailing the Orange cause. As the Duke of Newcastle understood, the majority of the Irish people on the Island were profoundly offended by the importation of practices that had caused so much hostility and suffering in their homeland. A pro-Orange newspaper, the *Monitor*, summarized the 1864 partisan contentions of Whelan and his supporters "that Orange Lodges are a bane to society wherever they exist; that their object in this Island is not to protect Protestantism against the encroachments of Popery, but to keep the present government in power; that the Roman Catholics were disposed to live in peace with their fellow-subjects; that the Orange Lodges tended to engender strife and ill-feeling in the community."[16] Connected with Orangeism, in the minds of Liberal leader George Coles and others, was Governor Dundas' establishment of the Volunteer companies to augment the military force. The Volunteers armed a thousand men – very few of whom were Catholics. Suspicions grew not only that the Volunteers were systematically Orange-dominated but also that they would be used, if necessary, to suppress the agitated tenantry. Such policies and practices, many Islanders realized, resembled those that intensified distress in Ireland under British occupation.

Although the Orange organizations renounced overt violence, some of their tactics and public demonstrations had the effect of provoking hostile reactions among their Irish Catholic neighbours. In this way the covert violence of sectarian animosity ignited sporadic clashes in the country, and an Orange-versus-Green wrangle in Charlottetown in 1877 almost exploded into a donnybrook.

No Surrender

One of the fears of Lieutenant-Governor Bannerman in the 1850s became a reality twenty-five years later. In 1852, when Bannerman learned that an Orange association had been formed in Charlottetown, he expressed concern about "the evil tendency of all class Societies inasmuch as they cannot fail to disturb the public peace by creating animosities and feuds." His intention was to discourage the formation of all such organizations, and to urge islanders not to join the Orange, Ribbon, or any other society that imposed on its members "oaths, obligations or tests which were not authorized or required by Law."[17] But Bannerman succeeded only in postponing the trouble. The predictable, if not the inevitable, occurred on "the Glorious Twelfth" of July 1877.

A group of people who had attended the Orange Lodge picnic at West River returned to Charlottetown in the evening and were met at the wharf by a large crowd of Protestants, who marched with them up Queen Street to their headquarters.[18] There the procession disbanded, some members going home and others going upstairs to the lodge's rooms. Suddenly, from across the street, someone fired a gun. No one was injured. Then, according to the *Patriot*, Orangemen and attackers engaged in jostling and fighting.[19] A volley of pistol shots fired from within the building and apparently aimed above the heads of the people in the street slightly wounded a boy in the arm. The rioters meanwhile continued to pelt the lodge's door and windows with stones.

Senator Haviland and Dr Jenkins pleaded with the rioters to desist, and the stipendiary magistrate R.R. Fitzgerald (son of the ardent Anglican minister) was very active in his endeavours to prevail upon the rioters to disperse, but his efforts were for a time unavailing. Eventually Fitzgerald "made terms with them," and the rioters agreed to disperse if he would persuade the Orangemen to haul down their flag. However, when the flag did come down, "the rioters set up a tremendous shout of triumph," and this so offended the Orangemen that they raised their flag again, whereupon the stone throwing was resumed. (As the street was being paved, there was no shortage of ammunition.) At Fitzgerald's repeated request, the Orange side again lowered their flag, and the Green men sent up another triumphant cry. The crowd then marched away, singing and cheering. Their numbers were variously estimated at between twenty and three hundred men and lads.

Next morning "there was a rush to the hardware shops for revolvers. The Protestants of the city were determined that the disgrace of yesterday should be wiped out." A citizens' meeting at the Orange Hall condemned the actions of Fitzgerald and the police. Once again the Orange flag was raised and, in anticipation of trouble, one hundred special constables were sworn in. By afternoon, surprise arrests were being made among the Green rioters, who were then on parade, and the captives were escorted to the county jail. A company of volunteers commanded by Major Morris remained on duty overnight.

Arrested were Alex McCabe, John Thornton, Richard Power, Patrick Malone, James Carroll, Patrick McKenna, Nicholas Collins, Martin Carroll, Patrick McGuigan, Frank McGuigan, Frank Dalton, Patrick Brennan, Michael Dooley, Gerald Sweeney, Thomas McCluskey, John Potter, Mr Callaghan, Mr McKinnon, Frank McAdam, Frank McCarthy, John Mahoney, Bernard McCarey, William McDonald, and Angus McDonald. In addition, warrants were issued for John Power, Thomas Smith, Owen McCloskey, John Walsh, Henry Halfpenny, Patrick McKenna, Daniel McNeill, Thomas Butler, Angus McDonald, John Corrigan, and Francis Keenan.

A rumour circulated that Owen Connolly had paid the collective fines, amounting to $2,500. What is known with certainty is that Connolly submitted to a meeting of the Catholic congregation of Charlottetown the following resolution, seconded by Thomas Handrahan and Patrick Blake: "Whereas certain disturbances took place on the 12th of July, instant, on account of which aspersions have been cast upon the Catholics of this City, Therefore Resolved, that the Catholic citizens discountenance and repudiate all connection and sympathy with the disturbances on Thursday night last. Further Resolved, that we deeply regret there should be, in this mixed community, processions calculated to excite angry feelings and ill-will."[20]

This 1877 disturbance is now viewed in the context of the easily aroused sectarianism of the late nineteenth century, when parades and demonstrations were sometimes intended to be provocative. The wonder is that riots were not more frequent, for some politicians were not above "playing the Orange card" of bigotry, nor were public men such as Edward Whelan slow to counterattack and ridicule Orange activities. The foot soldiers, both Orange and Green, exemplified the saying, "You can't hold an Irishman back when there's a fair or a fight."[21]

The Orange Order, though historically rooted in the sectarian strife of northern Ireland, has been perceived in Canada as an institution of militant Protestantism and not – and this emphatically applies in Prince Edward Island – an institution of distinct Irish character or even, in many places, of significant Irish membership. In Charlottetown, Protestant Irish leaders, secure in their religious affiliations and respectful of the consciences of others, were rarely associated publicly with the Orange movement. In contentious times Catholic Irish leaders usually advocated restraint and generally pacified their more temperamental brethren.

A later generation of Irish descendants, mindful of the riot of 1877 and other confrontations, noted the prudent admonition of Lieutenant-Governor George DeBlois to the Orange Lodge Convention that was held in the city sixty years later. DeBlois expressed the hope that the Orange assembly would cause no disturbance to any religious group in the province. He need not have worried. Some years earlier, the Orange Lodge had graciously thanked the Catholic sisters at the Charlottetown hospital for the loan of dishes and bingo cards needed for a Twelfth of July party. Civility, at last, was beginning to dislodge "the troubles."

LAND REFORM

In the gradual process of mutual acceptance and adaptation, another long-standing problem, one of an altogether different order, challenged the Island's Irish settlers (and others) in the form of landlordism. Haunted by the memory of marauders, usurpers, planters, absentee landlords, rackrenters, and evictors in the Old Country, the Irish immigrants sought, above all, security in the land. The children of poverty-stricken peasants and small farmers were determined to become strong farmers in the New World. In Prince Edward Island, the Irish pursued their passion for land vigorously. Not the Irish alone, to be sure, but other immigrants as well who wished to become permanent settlers and independent farmers resisted the neo-feudal proprietory system of land tenure on the Island. It took more than a century to wipe out that system, and to this prolonged revolution the Irish settlers certainly contributed their fair share.

The Tenant League

In the 1860s the Land Question was still the Island's foremost social and political problem. In 1864 the Tenant League was formed, with the

explicit resolve that its members would refuse to pay rent to proprietors who would not agree to sell land to them. This radical collective
action was brought on in part by Britain's 1862 rejection of further
land reform in the Island colony. To cite the words of Island historian
F.W.P. Bolger, "The tenants were determined to achieve by illegal
means what they were unable to secure by legislation."[22] Generally,
Irish immigrants, well acquainted as they were with the ways of civil
disobedience in dealing with long-standing grievances, were prepared
to embrace Tenant League tactics.

The 1853 Land Purchase Act had enabled the Island's government to
purchase estates of over 1,000 acres if the owners were willing to sell.
The government then subdivided these estates and sold the individual
farms to the incumbent tenants on reasonable terms. Perhaps one-
quarter of the Island, including the vast Worrell and Selkirk estates,
passed into the hands of small farmers under this legislation. But this
was not enough. "Public meetings, noisy demonstrations, and the use
of force," writes historian Bolger, "were the order of the day in the
mid-1860's." In the spring of 1864 tenants held rallies in at least fifteen
localities from Rollo Bay to New London. At Covehead, Crapaud,
Donagh, Tenmile House, Monaghan Road, and Baldwins Road, in
Lots 37, 48, 49, 50, and 51, the Irish were numerous and frequently
dominant; and there is no denying that they were deeply committed to
the struggle for land reform. This is not to say that all Irish people were
in full sympathy with all the practices of the Tenant League. For
instance, Edward Whelan, deputy leader of the Reform Party and an
ardent advocate of justice for the tenants, insisted on using only constitutionally acceptable legislative means to achieve tenants' rights, and
he firmly rejected recourse to violence and law-breaking. Those who
chose to stand with Whelan in this instance seemed to be following the
Irish tradition exemplified by Daniel O'Connell. On the other hand,
this tradition was modified by County Monaghan's statesman hero,
Charles Gavan Duffy, whose experience had taught him that sometimes the use of civil disobedience and even force was justified. Many
chose to travel that road.

A Visitor's Impressions

Since the Land Question was such a matter of concern, it is not surprising that twenty years after the Belfast Riot, John Francis Maguire,
a distinguished Irish publisher and parliamentarian visiting the Island,
observed: "Leaving the shores of Ireland, where the land question is
the one which most stirs the heart of its people, I cross the Atlantic,
and reach a small Island of which not very many in the old country

have ever heard; and to my amazement, I find this irrepressible land question the question of the colony."[23]

Maguire was from Cork City, and he drew his impressions of the Island from conversations with Irish immigrants and from newspaper accounts of the short-lived but influential Tenant League. Whereas Ireland's tenant league, the Land League, was concerned mainly with fixity of tenure, he noted that the organization on the Island was much more radical, seeking freedom for "the actual cultivators from the obligation of rent-paying, by converting the occupying tenant into a fee-simple proprietor." The Irish immigrant farmers, Maguire stated, "were soon drawn into the League, as they sympathized with its object, which was not so much to abolish the payment of rent, as to compel the proprietors to sell their estates on fair terms."[24] Maguire's perception was correct; and even though the league itself was suppressed, its objective was ultimately achieved. In retrospect, it may be reasonably argued that the numerical and political strength of the Irish immigrants from 1840 onwards contributed importantly to this outcome. Arguably, their forceful action in the third Queens district by-election of 1847 created a significant though distressing episode in the long struggle for possession of the land.

The Island's tenant revolt was indeed a call to action. Sam Fletcher led the Tenant League in parade on St Patrick's Day in 1865. Demonstrations and the danger of violence increased, and eventually the Island's government brought in British troops from Halifax to quell what some regarded as an incipient uprising. This police action put an end to the tenants' threatened violence, but the problem remained. The solution came in 1873, when Prince Edward Island joined Canadian Confederation, partly in return for a satisfactory land-purchase agreement.

SOCIAL PURSUITS

Even the weighty issues of the day could not suppress the traditional gregariousness of the Irish. They turned out for almost every meeting, rally, and social gathering on the Island. During the 1850s and the 1860s, lectures were a leading form of public entertainment. For this purpose, Kilkenny-born Thomas Phelan, rector of the cathedral, had founded the Catholic Young Men's Literary Institute in 1856. Over the years, the institute sponsored hundreds of lectures. Among the invited speakers in 1864 were the schoolmaster Edward Roche, the St Dunstan's College rector, the Reverend Angus MacDonald, and the journalist and politician Edward Whelan. One talk in early March, highly praised for the speaker's research, knowledge, and delivery, was given by Patrick Bowers on "The influence of O'Connell and his contemporaries in promoting civil and religious liberty in the British Empire." Bowers's presentation evidently did not persuade the editor of the *Protestant*,[25] who later that year reprinted an article which claimed that the name of Daniel O'Connell was "almost unknown" and ridiculed a proposal to erect a monument to his memory in Dublin. Evidently the local editor did not know that far from being "almost unknown" to the Island's Irish Catholics, Daniel O'Connell was virtually a household god.

Among the popular diversions in the 1860s, musicales and sacred concerts held a cherished place. St Dunstan's Cathedral had its own St Cecilia Choral Society, consisting of 150 voices under the direction of the Reverend Azade Trudelle. In December 1864 a sacred concert to help defray the cost of the cathedral's new organ was attended by "many of the *elite* of the City, Protestant as well as Catholic."[26] The soloists included Miss M.A. Conlan and Mr John Gahan. Accompaniments were by Miss McCormack and Mr H. Gaffney. "Some Irish and Scotch popular airs were played on the organ," the *Examiner* reported, "and the performance of them afforded the fullest and most gratifying testimony of its powers."

Early in April, David Fitzgerald, rector of St Paul's (Anglican) Church, Charlottetown, gave a public lecture at the YMCA on "The Lakes of Killarney." The lecture was illustrated with "beautiful dissolving views on a large scale" by H.J. Cundall, assisted by young Robert Harris.[27] Fitzgerald, a graduate of Trinity College in Dublin, was very active in his ministry from 1848 to 1885. In 1864 he was chaplain to the legislative council.

Nostalgia for the Old Country, so evident in songs and stories, opened the way for commercial exploitation of sentimental Irishness. The *Examiner* of 27 June 1864, for instance, carried an advertisement for "MacEvoy's Hibernicon, or a Tour in Ireland." This pictorial and musical exhibition was staged at the Temperance Hall on Prince Street. The show purported to be a "series of splendid paintings covering 10,000 [square] feet of canvas," painted by two French artists and depicting "the principal cities, public buildings, magnificent lakes, mountains and even river scenery of Ireland." These illustrations were accompanied by vocal and instrumental renditions of "immortal Irish melodies." The show was directed by Professor J. MacEvoy who, the notice assured, "is favourably known in Boston." The 11 July *Examiner* reported that the exhibition was a popular success, "delightful and amusing."

Another diversion that summer was the Benevolent Irish Society picnic at Warren Farm on 4 July. The outing was organized by John

Dorsey, Charles McKenna, Francis McKenna, James McQuaid, Peter Mullins, Edward Reilly, and Peter Trainor. Tickets were sold at stores owned by Martin Hogan, Francis McCarron, J.A. McKenna, John Murphy, James Reddin, P. Walker, and W.R. Watson. The steamer *Heather Belle* was hired for the day to ferry families from Pownal Street wharf to the Rocky Point site. Violinists and the St Dunstan's College band were also engaged. On the picnic grounds, a notice admonished, "No one but the person authorized will be allowed to sell liquors and refreshments." After several hours at Warren Farm, the happy picnickers boarded the steamer for a trip around Hillsborough Bay before returning to the city.

Earlier in the year the Benevolent Irish Society had elected S.W. Mitchell as president, Owen Connolly as vice-president, J. Reddin as assistant vice-president, J.A. McKenna as treasurer, and H.A. Bennet as secretary. The Committee of Charity consisted of John Dorsey, William O'Brien, Francis McCarron, Peter Mullins, Edward Ryan, William Walsh, and Michael Traynor.[28]

Observance of St Patrick's Day in 1864 included the traditional parade to the cathedral for religious services at ten o'clock. Marching in the procession were members of the BIS and the Irish Volunteer Corps. In the evening the St Cecilia Choral Society presented selections from the works of Rossini, Lambillotte, and Thomas Moore's *Irish Melodies*. Unlike some other years, in 1864 there were no untoward incidents at all.

THE CHARLOTTETOWN CONFERENCE

The fortunate event that superseded all activities, Irish and otherwise, and made 1864 memorable was the Charlottetown Conference. This political conference was convened on 1 September for the purpose of discussing the union of the three Maritime colonies. Because interest in the proposal was only lukewarm, the official conferees agreed to permit visitors from the Province of Canada to attend, first as observers and then as advocates for their own proposal for the union of all British North American colonies. By agreement, the conference took place behind closed doors, and there was no direct press coverage of the several working sessions.

The significance of the conclave, though not the verbatim proceedings, eventually became public knowledge. In retrospect, it is clear that the Charlottetown Conference set aside the notion of Maritime union, accepted the concept of national union as worthy of careful study and formulation, and established friendly relationships among the leading statesmen and architects of the future Confederation. In short, the

Charlottetown Conference clearly prepared the way for the Quebec and Westminster conferences, which adopted the grand design for Canadian nationhood.

At the time, few people in Charlottetown grasped the full import of the meetings taking place during the first seven days of September. So blasé were Island officials, in fact, that they had made no special preparations for welcoming, accommodating, or entertaining their guests. Charlottetown residents assumed that something unusual was going on when a large steamer, the *Queen Victoria*, anchored in the channel for several days and more than normal traffic circulated around the Provincial Building and Government House. Before long, the distinguished visitors who were attending the conference and various social gatherings about the city were identified as, among others, John A. Macdonald, George-Étienne Cartier, George Brown, Alexander T. Galt, Hector L. Langevin, Samuel L. Tilley, Charles Tupper, Jonathan McCulley, and Thomas D'Arcy McGee.

Details of the Charlottetown Conference have been expertly elucidated by Dr Francis W.P. Bolger in his book *Prince Edward Island and Confederation*. For our purposes, however, the following notations may be in order. Charles Stanley, Viscount Monck of County Wicklow, who had been appointed governor general of British North America in 1861, formally facilitated the meeting; but once the participants convened, they themselves generated the momentum for the historic discussions. The chairman of the conference was John Hamilton Gray, premier of Prince Edward Island. Other Island delegates were W.H. Pope, George Coles, A.A. Macdonald, and Edward Palmer. Although several of the participants may have had distant Irish connections, Thomas D'Arcy McGee, the Province of Canada's minister of agriculture, was the only native Irishman among the visitors. However, one of the Island's delegates, former premier Edward Palmer, was son of the Dublin-born lawyer James Bardin Palmer. Edward Whelan, who as a youth had immigrated to Canada from Ballina, County Mayo, did not attend the Charlottetown Conference, but three weeks later he was appointed to the Island delegation for the Quebec Conference.[29] The Irish may therefore claim a small but astute representation among the Fathers of Confederation.

The Circus Came to Town

At first some of the visitors were unable to find lodgings, because so many Islanders had descended on the capital's ten small hotels in order to attend Slaymaker and Nichol's Olympic Circus, which had set up tents on the corner of Queen and Fitzroy streets. Gaudy advertisements had invited islanders to see "the most beautiful *Equestriennes*, the most accomplished Riders, the most daring Acrobats, the finest Stud of Horses, the most learned Dogs and the most Comical Monkeys." Individual performers included Mlle Caroline, an "accomplished *Maitresse de Cheval*" from New York; Mlle Elizabeth, "premier *Equestrienne*, whose Classic *Scenes de Cirque* fully entitled her *nom D'artiste of La Riena D'Arena*"; Miss Frank Nixon, "the Exquisite *Danseuse*, in her Graceful and Elegant Poises and Charming Acts"; and the Snow Brothers, "the Hyper Excellent Acrobats, with their worldwide celebrated Troupe of Acting Dogs and Monkeys." Is it any wonder, then, that Islanders were at least temporarily distracted from the affairs of state being enacted at Charlottetown's Provincial Building three blocks distant?

Hospitality on a Grand Scale

After the circus departed, interested townspeople turned to the social events attendant upon the assembly of visiting statesmen. Although the local government was at first criticized for its aloofness and lack of hospitality, the entertainments, once launched, were indeed impressive. They began with a dinner at Government House on the opening evening. On 2 September, the provincial secretary W.H. Pope invited the conference members to Ardgowan, his home on Mount Edward Road, for "a grand *déjeuner a la fourchette*, oysters, lobster and champagne and other Island luxuries." The next day the delegates held a luncheon aboard the *Queen Victoria*, and Premier John Hamilton Gray responded with an elegant dinner at his Inkerman residence. On 5 September George Coles entertained at his farm near the city, and on the sixth the attorney general Edward Palmer served luncheon at his home before the guests attended a formal ball at Government House. The following day the visitors held a reception aboard their steamer for Lieutenant-Governor and Mrs Dundas and a large group of ladies. On the final day of their visit, the Canadians toured the north-shore beaches, and that night they attended a triumphal banquet and ball in the building where they had met for their historic conference.

When the government announced the ball and supper on 5 September, Edward Whelan, writing in the *Examiner,* expressed delight that graceful hospitality would be displayed "on a grand scale" and that "no expense would be spared to make it creditable to the colony."[30] In proposing one of the toasts at the banquet, Whelan was eloquent. The editor of *The Protestant and Evangelical Witness,*[31] on the other hand, had professed "aversion to balls and champagne suppers ... customs which are a delusion and a snare," but when he was invited to preview a table "literally groaning under the choicest viands," he conceded that the sociable evening had some genuine merit after all.

Lieutenant-Governor and Mrs Dundas received the guests in the Council Chamber and at ten o'clock led them to the tastefully decorated Assembly Room for dancing. The Legislative Library was turned into the refreshment room, where champagne and other wines were plentiful and where D'Arcy McGee entertained many people with the "admirable dexterity of his wit." After midnight, supper was served in the Supreme Court room. The *Examiner* reported:

Everything that could minister to the taste of the epicure, from substantial rounds of beef and splendid hams, to the more delicate trifles of the *cuisine*, were in great abundance – salmon, lobster salad, oysters prepared in every shape and style, all the different kinds of fowl which the season and the market could afford – all vegetable delicacies peculiar to the season – pastry in all forms – fruits in almost every variety – wines of the choicest vintage – were in greatest profusion, leaving scarcely an inch of vacant space on the wide table. There was never such a "spread" prepared in Charlottetown, and the caterer, Mr. John Murphy, of the North American Hotel, well deserved all the praise which he received for it.[32]

Indeed, the genial John Murphy, caterer extraordinary, earned his footnote in history. This banquet, the climax of a week of hearty dining and imbibing, was no perfunctory state gathering. It was the most scintillating social function in Island legend. "The most brilliant Fête that has ever occurred in Charlottetown," the *Examiner* effused, "the Provincial Building teemed with more festive life than it ever did before." The first guests arrived about eight-thirty Thursday evening; the last revellers departed after four o'clock Friday morning. This party was, in the words of the once-skeptical but now-captivated editor, "as magnificent an entertainment as was ever given in Charlottetown."

Incidentally, partaking of the culinary largesse that evening was a young bandsman of Welsh parentage. "One of the gentlemen told him to fill his pockets," his mother wrote in a letter, "so the following morning he had a store of good things to distribute around the house." Another benefit came to him twenty years later when, as an accomplished portrait painter, he was commissioned to paint Canada's most historic and perhaps best-known picture, *The Fathers of Confederation*. The artist was Robert Harris (1849–1914).[33]

A local spin-off from the conference was a public lecture on 6 September by the eloquent D'Arcy McGee. An accomplished poet himself, he spoke on the lyrical works of Robert Burns and Thomas Moore. (Earlier in the year a literary soirée had included readings from the same two poets by local journalists Patrick Bowers and Edward

Reilly.)[34] The well-attended McGee lecture, sponsored by the Catholic Young Men's Literary Institute, was given in St Andrew's Hall on Pownal Street. The Charlottetown audience, which included some of the conference delegates on the platform, felt especially privileged to have heard one of the 1,300 public addresses that D'Arcy McGee delivered in his career. Four years later this Father of Confederation was assassinated in Ottawa by a purported Fenian sympathizer.[35]

THE CULMINATION

The promising political events of 1864 proved to be a valuable prologue to what took place nine years later. In July 1873, after considerable debate and political soul-searching, Prince Edward Island somewhat reluctantly but formally joined Canadian Confederation. Anticipating joyous ceremonies in Charlottetown that year, the enterprising tailor Pat Reilly announced the arrival of bolts of a fancy tweed called Dufferin Checks: "Very handsome, and ought to be fashionable just now, seeing that the Governor General is about to visit us. Gentlemen, give us a call, if you are in want of Pants and Vests in Dufferin Checks."[36]

The Island's entry into Confederation was ceremonially marked by the state visit of the governor general of Canada and his wife. Atop the welcoming arch erected at the Provincial Building gate were the Gaelic words of greeting, *Céad Míle Fáilte,* and from the central flagstaff hung a green banner inscribed with the name Dufferin in gilt letters.[37] The Right Honorable Frederick Temple Blackwood, Earl of Dufferin, Baron Clondeboye of Ballyleidy and Killeleagh in County Down, Knight of St Patrick and Knight Companion of Bath, was formally welcomed to Charlottetown on 18 July and began a nine-day round of state and social events. These included a levée and reception, two public balls, excursions through the country, Sabbath services at both St Paul's and St Peter's Anglican churches, and a regatta in Charlottetown harbour for which Lord Dufferin offered several hundred dollars in prizes.

Ireland-born and Oxford-educated, Lord Dufferin was gentlemanly, prudent, and very well informed about the land tenure system and related emigration issues in Ireland. That he was an enlightened statesman with a liberal outlook is evident from the fact that although he was an influential landowner in Ireland's most Protestant county, he publicly favoured both disestablishment of the episcopal church and extensive land reform in Ireland. His credentials suited well the policies of the British prime minister William Gladstone.[38]

In Charlottetown, Dufferin and his wife, Lady Hariot Georgina Hamilton, favourably impressed all who met them. For the delegates of the two presbyteries who presented addresses, the governor general's friendly reply was a reminder that Presbyterianism had a very large following in his native county. For those citizens who may have been wary of Confederation, his speeches tended to engender confidence in the new dominion and to strengthen the ties of loyalty to the British crown.

Among the delegations to greet the Dufferins was the Benevolent Irish Society, headed by President James Reddin. He was accompanied by Vice-President J. McCarron, Martin Hogan, Henry Hughes, John A. McKenna, Patrick Foley, Maurice Blake, Peter Doyle, and John Walsh. "We know that in welcoming Your Excellency we do honor to a distinguished son of the Emerald Isle," the BIS address gushed, "that dear old land around the memories and associations of which the Irish heart so lovingly and fondly entwines itself."[39] Dufferin's reply was not so sentimental. He spoke of his efforts to mitigate long-standing differences between Britain and Ireland and of his pleasure at finding in Canada no group "more loyal, more devoted to the institutions of the Dominion, and more jealous of the glory and unity of the Empire" than the Irish immigrants. He also noted that the process of Confederation had taken place under three successive Irish-born governors general and that Prince Edward Island's joining the new nation could be credited in part to the wise administration of his fellow Irishman, Lieutenant-Governor William Robinson.

On the evening of 26 July a torchlight parade to the wharf, where the vice-regal steamer *Druid* was moored, sent "the beau ideal of an Irish nobleman"[40] and his lady on their triumphant way. They left with the happy knowledge that Prince Edward Island's entry into Confederation had fulfilled a small but indispensable portion of Thomas D'Arcy McGee's grand vision for Canada.

THE IRISH DESCENDANTS

Soon after the formalities and fireworks were over, the Islanders realized that joining Confederation involved much more than producing a good show. It signalled essential changes in political outlook, economic prospects, and the way Islanders lived. No longer merely a tiny colony in a vast empire, Prince Edward Island had become an integral part of a new nation, a province in the Dominion of Canada. This commitment helped unify Island society, define its character, and chart its destiny.

In return for joining Confederation, the Island delegation had astutely persuaded the federal government to make three important concessions: to assume the heavy debt incurred in building the Island railway; to end the Land Question by funding the purchase of the remaining proprietorial estates; and to ensure continual communication between the Island and the mainland.[41] With the securing of these liberating agreements, the long century of colonization and settlement ended.

The Legacy

Perhaps the most beneficial legacy the settlers conferred on later generations was the institution known as the family-owned farm. It became the mainstay of the Island's economy and the symbol and surety of a rewarding way of life. It was a concept that appealed to the Irish settlers. At the time of joining Confederation, the Island was 90 percent rural; more than 20,000 people were farmers or agricultural workers (over 72 percent of the workforce), and there were numerous blacksmiths, millers, coopers, and other tradesmen as well. There were no large industrial or processing plants. When this socio-economic structure could no longer accommodate the employment needs or satisfy the natural ambitions of the increasing population, many young people chose to emigrate. Among them were some who would have preferred to remain in farming, but arable land was rarely available; and in the home the traditional rule of primogeniture was normally invoked, whereby the eldest son inherited the farm and his siblings had to leave. That practice became known as "one for the farm, the others for the road." In such circumstances, emigration was a necessary option in many families.

Providentially, the Island's status at the end of the colonial settlement era was comprehensively documented by two publications: the national census of 1881, which listed members of each household by name, approximate age, and marital status; and the 1880 Meacham's cadastral *Atlas*, which graphically identified every Island property by location and the name of the owner or lessee. Together these publications personalized the inventory of human resources and formed a permanent record of Island society at a pivotal time in its history. The 1881 census officially confirmed, among other things, significant migration among the Irish people; there was a trend to leave the Island in order to settle elsewhere in North America.

On the Move

One hundred years after the Island had been tentatively named New Ireland, the residents of Irish origin and the much larger number of Irish descendants totalled 25,400 – approximately 23 percent of the 108,900 persons enumerated in the census. As the Irish had constituted one-quarter of the population in 1850, the census presaged a significant downturn. Two social factors influenced the impending decline: immigration from Ireland had ceased, hence there was no replenishment after 1850; and despite a high birth rate, Irish outmigration was substantial and continuing. A.H. Clark attributes Irish emigration partly to the fact that the Irish were relative latecomers to the Island and often had to settle on poorer land in the western and inland areas.[42] Between 1881 and 1901 the number of people claiming Irish origin declined by 13 percent. Looking ahead, the Irish would represent less than one-fifth of the Island population by 1951.

During the same period (1881–1951) the Scots also lost considerable ground, dropping to 32 percent from 45 percent of the population. Meanwhile, the English and the Acadian descendants generally remained on the Island, thereby increasing numerically and proportionally. In the seventy years after the 1881 census, the English increased from 20 percent of the population to 30 percent, and the Acadians increased from 10 to 16 percent.

The high birth rate assured a natural increase in the Island population, but limited economic opportunities, normal restlessness and personal ambitions assured continuing emigration. Even the Island's excellent resources in agriculture and fishing could not bolster the sluggish economy of the late 1860s. The economic collapse actually encompassed all three Maritime provinces. As Alan R. Brookes explains, after the American Civil War the demand for lumber, fish, foodstuffs, and coal declined drastically. The age of wooden sailing ships came to an end, along with its attendant trades and commercial activity. The great timber market also slumped. In fact, a major transition occurred as a result of Confederation: considerable trade and commerce from Great Britain was transferred to central Canada. As Brookes states, "The persistent depression and economic dislocation which characterized these years (1860–1900) in much of the Maritimes provided the overriding motives for out-migration."[43]

Discontentment with the economic disruptions in the Maritime region did not diminish the Islanders' emotional attachment to their home, but it did force thousands of people to leave. They scattered to California, Colorado, Iowa, and several other states, but they found the Boston area the most compatible and welcoming location in the United States. This relationship had developed from decades of north-south trade, and the familiar sea lanes of "the age of sail" provided easy access for Islanders who chose to move to the Boston area. "It was the Highlanders and the Irish who, in turn, led the great outward migration from the Island after 1880."[44] Since then, in Prince Edward Island (as in Ireland), leaving home to find vocational fulfilment has become almost a normal expectation – though not necessarily the primary aspiration of Island youth. However, whether they remained at home or emigrated to a distant land, many descendants of the settlers continued to take pride both in their Island and Canadian birthright and in their Irish heritage.

The Irish Settlers Memorial, Charlottetown, Prince Edward Island

Epilogue

At the beginning of the twenty-first century the most visible sign of the Irish presence in Prince Edward Island is an eloquent statement in stone honouring the Irish settlers.[1] Located on a peaceful point of land fronting Charlottetown's spacious harbour, the Irish Settlers Memorial not only pays homage to the Irish pioneers but also celebrates the heritage belonging to their Island descendants. It was dedicated on Canada Day 2001.[2]

The memorial blends spirituality and secularity in icons representing religious faith and social history.[3] First in view stands a tall, elegant Celtic cross atop a hawthorn-planted hillock. (A Celtic cross differs in structure from the standard Latin cross in that it has a circle superimposed at the intersection of the upright post and the transverse piece.) In religious terms, the cross may signify the humanity and divinity of Jesus Christ. It is also a traditional symbol of Ireland. The Celtic cross in Charlottetown is an unadorned version of the famed Cross of Moone in County Kildare. It was sculptured from fine Quebec granite.

The second major component of the memorial is a large circle of thirty-two flagstones, one from each county in Ireland. This concept enables each descendant of an Irish settler to cherish in a tangible way the particular flagstone of his or her ancestral home. The stones are equal in size and shape but individually distinctive in geological composition and natural coloration. At the centre of the circle of county stones rests a sturdy bronze plaque. Embossed on it are heraldic images of the two homelands, along with the inscription, "In honour of the Irish Settlers of Prince Edward Island."

At the base of the Celtic cross, a semi-circular granite bench provides an ideal vantage point for viewing the harbour. A mile or so away, directly across the open water from the memorial, the narrows between the Keppoch headland and Rocky Point can be seen. Through this passage, scores of immigrant ships, having endured the strenuous month-long Atlantic crossing, sailed into the safe harbour. After they passed through the gently swirling eddy known as Three Tides – where the Hillsborough, North and West rivers meet – the ships slowly sailed by the point where the future memorial would stand. When finally their ships moored at Charlottetown's dockside, the sea-weary passengers disembarked and began their new life in Prince Edward Island.

The Irish Settlers Memorial is the only monument celebrating Irishness in the province, but some other public edifices, mainly carry-overs from the nineteenth and twentieth centuries, are also reminders of Irish immigration. Several churches, for instance, are named after Irish saints: two for St Patrick (Grand River and Fort Augustus), two for St Columba (the Presbyterian church in Marshfield and the Roman Catholic church in Fairfield), and one each for St Malachy (in Kinkora), and St Brigid (in Foxley River). The Old Country continues to be remembered in a score of early Island place names that were transferred or derived from the original home places of the settlers: Avondale, Donagh, Emyvale, Fodhla, Kinkora, Monaghan, Tyrone, Waterford, and others.

Irish-consciousness is clearly found in various organizations and traditional programs that have thrived for generations. Pre-eminently, the charitable, cultural and social activities of the Benevolent Irish Society – highlighted by the annual church parade and banquet on St Patrick's Day – have maintained Irish traditions uninterrupted since 1825. The Celtic Heritage Association, which in 1990 presented to the province a facsimile edition of the Book of Kells, later erected the Irish Settlers Memorial. Meanwhile, for nearly twenty years, the New Ireland Society's musical and genealogical programs have stimulated Irish awareness in Prince County. The largely Monaghan-settled communities of Fort Augustus, Emyvale, Kinkora, and Emerald continue to flourish as centres for Irish social and cultural events and as liaison points between the Island and Ireland.

Augmenting these activities, the Prince Edward Island Museum and Heritage Foundation and the Prince Edward Island Genealogical Society have sponsored public history and genealogical seminars, lectures, and workshops about Irish immigration and related matters. On the academic level, the University of Prince Edward Island offers courses in Irish history and literature, and occasionally courses in the Irish language (in cooperation with Saint Mary's University in Halifax). The university has sponsored public lectures, symposia, and exhibitions, as well as the 1997 convention of the Canadian Association for Irish Studies. It has also supported research for the present volume on the Irish settlers.

In Exile. Painting by John Burden

These and other outward signs confirm that neither time and distance nor countercultural forces have broken the bonds of kinship
between the Island and the Old Country. Many thousands of fifth-,
sixth-, and seventh-generation islanders still identify with Ireland and
speak of themselves as Irish. Mary Robinson, the former president of
Ireland, aptly characterized such persons as "men and women whose
pride and affection for Ireland has neither deserted them nor deterred

them from dedicating their loyalty and energies to other countries and cultures."4

Irishness, it seems, is not territorial; it is hereditary and portable. Known as the Irish mystique, it extends to all points of the compass, and it embraces over seventy million people beyond the shores of Ireland. In this number, of course, are counted the descendants of the Irish settlers of Prince Edward Island5 – men and women who have shown, in their own distinctive ways, that they have not forgotten who they are and where they came from.

Notes

CHAPTER ONE

1 Harry Baglole, "Patterson, Walter," in *Dictionary of Canadian Biography* (*DCB*) (Toronto: University of Toronto Press, 1966–   ), 4, 605–11. See also Nicholas Flood Davin, *The Irishman in Canada* (Toronto: McClear, 1877), 167–8. For a racy account of Patterson's administration, see Walter Stewart, *True Blue, The Loyalist Legend* (Toronto: Collins, 1985), 135–9.

2 Concerning Lord Egmont's life and public career, consult especially J.M. Bumsted, "British Colonial Policy and the Island of St. John, 1763–1767," *Acadiensis*, Autumn 1979, 3–18. See also W.S.MacNutt, *The Atlantic Provinces: The Emergence of Colonial Society, 1712–1757* (Toronto: McClelland and Stewart, 1965), 64–5; Robert G. MacPherson, ed., *The Journal of the Earl of Egmont: Abstract of the Trustees' Proceedings for Establishing the Colony of Georgia 1732–1738* (Athens: University of Georgia, 1962); Andrew MacPhail, "The History of Prince Edward Island," in *Canada and Its Provinces,* vol. 13, ed. Adam Shortt and Arthur G. Doughty (Toronto: Glasgow, Brook and Co., 1914); Duncan Campbell, *History of Prince Edward Island* (Charlottetown: Bremner, 1875; reprint, Belleville: Mika, 1972), 10–17. D.A. MacKinnon and A.B. Warburton summarize Egmont's proposals in "A Historical Sketch," in *Past and Present of Prince Edward Island* (Charlottetown: Bowen, 1906), 21–3.

3 J.M. Bumsted clarifies the importance of Lord Egmont's plan in the *Acadiensis* article cited in n 2, above. Duncan Campbell's *History* opines, "Nothing more fantastic has been conceived outside of Utopia" (339). Other writers call Egmont's plan "utopian," "quixotic," and "feudal fantasy." Incidentally, Egmont's notion to import Dominican slaves was never carried out, though some black slaves were held in the early

colony; in fact, in March 1781 the assembly passed an act declaring that the baptism of slaves would not exempt them from bondage. A number of black families came to the Island at the time of the American Civil War. Their story is told by Jim Hornby, *Black Islanders: Prince Edward Island's Historical Black Community* (Charlottetown: Institute of Island Studies, 1991), Island Studies 3.

4 R. Douglas, *Place-Names of Prince Edward Island with Meanings* (Ottawa: King's Printer, 1925), 23–4 and *passim*. Also Alan Rayburn, *Geographical Names of Prince Edward Island* (Ottawa: Department of Energy, Mines and Resources, 1973), 47 and *passim*.

5 Lots 40 and 59 were bestowed on fishing companies that had established operations on them before Holland's survey; and Lot 66, consisting of only 6,000 acres, was reserved for the crown. Lot 67 contains 27,000 acres. For maps, see *Illustrated Historical Atlas of Prince Edward Island* (Philadelphia: J.H. Meacham, 1880; reprint, Belleville, Ont.: Mika Publishing, 1977).

6 Edward Walsh, "An Account of Prince Edward Island, 1803," *The Island Magazine,* Spring/Summer 1984, 9–13, introduction by H.T. Holman. In this connection see *British Parliamentary Papers: Papers Relating to Canada 1842–46, Colonial Canada 16* (Shannon, Ireland: Irish University Press, 1970), 12–15.

7 Public Record Office (PRO), CO 226, 494, Executive Council Minute, 25 October 1865, cited in Francis W.P. Bolger, *Canada's Smallest Province: A History of Prince Edward Island* (Charlottetown: Prince Edward Island Centennial Commission, 1973), 180.

8 Quoted by Maire and Conor Cruise O'Brien, *The Story of Ireland* (Toronto: Thomas Nelson Canada, 1972), 78. On St Patrick's Day 1847 the PEI Assembly passed an act to repeal the Act of Abduration which had been imposable upon Roman Catholics. See *Royal Gazette,* 2 June 1847. Political privileges were not granted to women until the twentieth century.

9 Campbell, *History,* 207–24. Davin, *Irishman in Canada,* 167. A.H. Clark, *Three Centuries and the Island* (Toronto: University of Toronto, 1959), 61, 88. Clark's map (fig. 27) shows the French, Scottish, and other settlers of 1798 and notes that the "other" group included chiefly English names (with some Irish, Welsh, or German) and that around Charlottetown, where they chiefly concentrated, these must have been largely people who had come directly from England. The present chapter is concerned primarily with the important minority that Clark refers to as "some Irish." Some of the Irish-born colonial pioneers were buried in the old Elm Avenue cemetery in Charlottetown and in the graveyard commemorating the Hyde and Crosby families in Meadowbank; also in several other sites.

10 Walsh, "Account of PEI."

11 Orlo Jones and Doris Haslam, *An Island Refuge: Loyalists and Disbanded Troops on the Island of Saint John* (Charlottetown: Abegweit Branch, United Empire Loyalists' Association of Canada, 1984). This is a comprehensive study. *The PEI Genealogical Society Newsletter*, February 1984, is dedicated to the United Empire Loyalists, 1784–1984.

   For information on the English settlers, see Bruce S. Elliott, "English Immigration to Prince Edward Island, Part One," *Island Magazine*, Fall/Winter 1996, 3–11, and "Part Two," Spring/Summer 1997, 3–9. Bruce S. Elliott, *Irish Migrants in the Canadas: A New Approach* (Montreal: McGill-Queens, 1988) is also interesting.

12 Edward MacDonald, *New Ireland: The Irish on Prince Edward Island* (Charlottetown: PEI Museum and Heritage Foundation, 1990).

13 An English nobleman, Viscount George Townshend, Lord Lieutenant of Ireland, was granted Lot 56 in the 1767 lottery. This unsuccessful Irish toehold is described in chapter 5. An Irish army officer, General Hunt Walsh, received Lot 11, where the Irish settlement described in chapter 2 developed.

14 Baglole, *DCB* 4: 606. For a good sketch of his life, see ibid., 605–11.

15 R.J. Dickson, *Ulster Immigration to Colonial America, 1718–1775* (London: Routledge and Kegan Paul, 1966), 154.

16 Clark, *Three Centuries*, 66. The place referred to is probably New Ireland, off the north coast of New Guinea, named in 1767.

17 Clark's opinion is shared by Campell, (*History*, 55–6, 65). See also comments by Davin, *Irishman in Canada*, 167–8.

18 Dickson, *Ulster Immigration*, 158.

19 Ibid., 152, 154. For a concise biography of Thomas DesBrisay, see F.L. Pigot, "Desbrisay, Thomas," in *DCB*, 5: 249–50.

20 A.B. Warburton, *History of Prince Edward Island* (Saint John: Barnes, 1923), 167–8. Dickson devotes a chapter to DesBrisay's activities as a recruiter (*Ulster Immigration*), 152–80. Stephen A. Royle and Catriona Ní Laoire, in "DesBrisay's Settlers" (*Island Magazine*, Spring/Summer 2002), trace DesBrisay's advertising campaign in Ireland.

21 W.A. Carrothers, *Emigration from the British Isles* (New York: Kelley, 1971), 2. Dickson (*Ulster Immigration*), 163.

22 Public Archives of Prince Edward Island (PAPEI). Selkirk Papers, vol. 59. See also MacDonald, *New Ireland*, and Royle and Laoire, "Desbrisay's Settlers," 19–23.

23 Pigot, *DCB*, 5: 249. See also J.M. Bumsted, *Land, Settlement, and Politics on Eighteenth-Century Prince Edward Island* (Kingston and Montreal: McGill-Queen's University Press, 1987), 61.

24 Bolger, *Canada's Smallest Province*, 46.

25 Robert Allan Rankin, "An Island Refuge," in *An Island Refuge*, ed. Jones and Haslam. See also Pigot, *DCB*, 5:250.

26 For a succinct account of the minister, see Robert Critchlow Tuck, "Des-Brisay, Theophilus," *DCB*, 6: 197–8.

27 Percy Pope, "The Church of England in Prince Edward Island," in *Past and Present of Prince Edward Island,* ed. D.A. MacKinnon and A.B. Warburton (Charlottetown: Bowen, 1906), 241–4 and 248n. Rev. R. Grant had been appointed chaplain to the governor, but he did not serve. In 1773–74, during short visits from his appointed place at Fort Cumberland, Rev. John Eagleson voluntarily performed divine services in six places on the Island.

28 Pope, *Church of England*, 247. For other accounts of Thomas Des-Brisay's activities, see Tuck, *DCB*, 6: 197–8; Dickson, *Ulster Immigration,* 127, 152–64; and MacKinnon and Warburton, *Past and Present*, 29–30.

29 Elinor Vass, "The Ready Touch: John Ready and Prince Edward Island, 1824–1831," *Island Magazine*, Fall/Winter 1990, 30–7. Vass reveals that despite Ready's Irish name, he was born in England. He served under the 4th Duke of Richmond, Lord Lieutenant of Ireland, and thereby acquired extensive knowledge of that country.

30 Phillips Callbeck (c. 1744–90) may have been born in Bath, England (Jones and Haslam, *Island refuge*, 51). However, "family tradition suggests that he was born and educated in Ireland" and emigrated in 1770 from England (H.T. Holman, "Callbeck, Phillips," *DCB*, 4: 128–9).

31 The Colcloughs, whose extensive landholdings in Wexford included Tintern Abbey, were highly regarded by their tenants. Notably patriotic, some family members took part in the rising of 1798 on the rebels' side. Caesar Colclough became chief justice in Newfoundland after his tenure in PEI and then returned to his estate in Wexford. His career deserves further study, for an opinion in Wexford holds that Colclough may have been sent to the colonies in order to cool his ardour for the Irish cause of 1798 rather than to reward his opposition to it (interview with Sean M. Cloney, Dungulph, Wexford, 3 July 1985). See also J.M. Bumsted, "Colclough, Caesar," *DCB*, 6: 160–4; Campbell, *History of Prince Edward Island*.

32 Warburton, *History*, 241. Davin, *Irishman in Canada*, 168. Lt. Gov. Fanning was a graduate of Yale University and had served as a royalist officer during the American Revolution. After 1804 he lived in retirement on the Island.

33 While the Island's nineteenth-century Irish immigrants were very rarely thought to be violent rebels, they strongly supported Daniel O'Connell's two peaceful movements: for Catholic Emancipation and for Repeal of the Union. The loyalist stance of some Anglo-Irish families, however, may have been shaken by these two causes, as well as by the Great Famine, the rising of 1848, and other stirrings for Irish independence from Britain.

34 John McKenna, "Early Irish Settlers in Prince Edward Island," *Guardian* (Charlottetown), 10 February 1928 (report of an address). Mayor McKenna may have relied on Warburton's *History* (95). Correspondence between two students of military history, Douglas Morton and Gordon McCarville, attempts to clarify an issue that McKenna's talk raises. Morton's research reveals: "During the siege (and subsequent fall) of Louisbourg in 1758, a number of British regular units participated. In the summer of 1758, a fleet of ships was sent from County Cork with reinforcement troops (no confirmation that these were in fact Irish troops, or just British troops stationed in Ireland at that time). There were no Irish regiments in North America at this time, as they were in combat in what now is part of Germany. Irish troops came to America during the American Revolution." Morton notes specifically: "The convoy from County Cork landed first in Halifax and then went to Louisbourg. The ships were then sent to Ile St Jean under orders of General Amherst and commanded by Lord Rollo. The ships were used to take off the former French inhabitants. Accompanying Lord Rollo were 500 troops, but these were not the same men that had crossed the Atlantic with the convoy from County Cork. The 500 were the 35th Regiment of Foot (the Royal Essex Regiment), and two companies of the 60th Regiment of Foot (Kings Royal Rifle Corps). Both of these regiments are listed as being in North America in 1757, a year before the convoy from County Cork arrived" (personal correspondence, 23 March 1987).

35 Peter McCourt, "The Benevolent Irish Society," in *Past and Present of Prince Edward Island*, ed. D.A. MacKinnon and A.B. Warburton (Charlottetown: Bowen, 1906), 241.

36 Tuck, *DCB* 6: 197–8.

37 Pope, "Church of England," 250.

38 Roman Catholics, too, sometimes used public taverns for religious services. In 1812 Bishop J.O. Plessis of Quebec celebrated mass in McPhee's Tavern on Dorchester Street in Charlottetown. See Francis W. Bolger, *Memories of the Old Home Place: Prince Edward Island* (Toronto: Oxford University Press, 1984). For a light account of the first parliament, see Lorne C. Callbeck, *My Island, My People* (Charlottetown: Prince Edward Island Heritage Foundation, 1979), 21–3.

39 MacPhail, "History," 308, 311.

40 Telephone interview with Waldron Leard, Souris, June 1997.

41 Jones and Haslam (*Island Refuge*, 366–86) reprint the 1841 Claimants List as taken from the *Journals of the Council*. See also Donna Collings, "Journal of the Legislative Assembly of PEI – 1841 – Loyalists and Disbanded Soldiers" in PEI *Genealogical Society Newsletter*, September 1998, 23–5; also in *Journals of the House of Assembly of Prince Edward Island*, 1841, appendix J, 32–4. Concerning the Loyalists, who made up

one-fifth of the Island's population in 1783, see J.M. Bumstead, *Land, Settlement and Politics on Eighteenth-Century Prince Edward Island* (Montreal and Kingston: McGill-Queen's University Press, 1987), and "The Loyalist Question on Prince Edward Island, 1783–1861," *Island Magazine*, Spring/Summer 1989, 20–8.

The 1841 Claimants List includes the following selection of Irish names: John Breen, Charles Carroll, John Casey, Patrick Connolly, Peter Connolly, Peter Cosgrove, John Dowling, Michael Doyle, Thomas Doyle, Jeremiah Dayley, Martin Dwyer, Patrick Dwyer, Thomas Dwyer, Thomas Geary, John Griffin, C. Kilcash, Thomas Landrican, Stephen McConnell, Barnaby McCrossan, Michael Malone, Michael Maloney, John Murphy, Michael O'Brien, John Purcell, John Quigley, Francis Reilly, William Reilly, Thomas Reynolds, John Sullivan, David Walsh, and Walter Walsh.

42 The first Scottish Catholic priest on the Island was the Rev. James Mac-Donald. He came with the settlers of Tracadie and served from 1772 until he died in 1785.

43 Francis W.P. Bolger, "The First Bishop," in *The Catholic Church in Prince Edward Island*, ed. Michael F. Hennessey (Charlottetown: Roman Catholic Episcopal Corporation, 1979), 28. See also Emmet J. Mullally, "A Sketch of the Life and Times of Right Reverend Angus Bernard MacEachern, the First Bishop of the Diocese of Charlottetown," *Canadian Catholic Historical Association Reports* 13 (1945–46): 71–105. See also John C. MacMillan, *The Early History of the Catholic Church in Prince Edward Island* (Quebec: Evenement, 1905), 64ff. The great Scottish bishop, an authentic Island hero, had no real connection with Ireland even though it is reported that Hugh MacIntyre of Savage Harbour was "born in Ireland in 1789 and emigrated to this Island with his parents and his uncle, Bishop MacEachern" (*Charlottetown Herald*, 3 May 1871). Family tradition explains that "Irish Hugh" MacIntyre was actually born off the coast of Ireland in a Scottish vessel that was bringing his parents and his uncle (the future bishop) from Scotland to St John's Island (telephone interview with Mrs Joanna MacIntyre Peters, Charlottetown, 30 March 1987).

44 Clark, *Three Centuries*, 61.

45 Cited in MacMillan, *Catholic Church*, 110–11. Concerning the abbé DeCalonne, see especially Wilfrid Pineau, *Le clergé français dans l'Ile du Prince-Edouard 1721–1821* (Quebec: Ferland, 1967), 63–87; also Bolger, "The First Bishop," 30–1; and Pope, "Church of England," 257n.

46 Cited in MacMillan, *Catholic Church*, 111–12.

47 Ibid. It seems that both MacMillan's and DeCalonne's observations have some justification. Whatever the circumstances in 1800, in April 1840 the PEI assembly saw fit to enact a law to prevent any further immigration of Newfoundlanders who had been convicted of felonies or misdemeanors

(*Acts of the General Assembly of Prince Edward Island*, 1840, 3 Vict, cap. 16, 553–4). The moral problems had important social dimensions: Newfoundland was the leading source of the visible poor among the colonial Irish of PEI, and in the early nineteenth century the Island became a small dumping ground for so-called riff-raff and other unproductive citizens cast out from Newfoundland. These unfortunate people then became a charge on the meagre public resources of PEI.

48 Pope, "Church of England," 236. English immigrants were sometimes subjected to similar charges. Governor Patterson, critical of Robert Clark's New London settlers of 1773 called them "wild youths" and "all the vagabonds of the Island" (Benjamin Chappell, "Day Book," 1775, in PAPEI).

49 MacMillan, *Catholic Church,* 128. Incidentally, Arthur P. Monaghan incorrectly identifies "the first Irish cleric ministering on Prince Edward Island" as Michael Fitzgerald, "who came in 1823 from Newfoundland." See Patrick J. Corish, ed. *A History of Irish Catholicism* (Dublin: Gill and Macmillan, 1968), 17.

50 MacMillan, *Catholic Church,* 164–5.

51 J.A. Ready, "Lot Twenty: From Forest to Farm, II," *Prince Edward Island Magazine,* July 1899, 192–4. The Park Corner Pioneer Graveyard was a burial site for Irish pioneers, both Protestant and Catholic.

52 J.A. Ready, "Lot Twenty: From Forest to Farm," *Prince Edward Island Magazine,* June 1899, 151.

53 Francis W.P. Bolger, *Prince Edward Island and Confederation, 1863–1873* (Charlottetown: St Dunstan's University Press, 1964), 5.

54 Francis W.P. Bolger, "The Beginnings of Independence, 1767–1787" in *Canada's Smallest Province,* 54.

55 Ian Ross Robertson, "Highlanders, Irishmen, and the Land Question in Nineteenth-Century Prince Edward Island," in *Comparative Aspects of Scottish and Irish Economic and Social History, 1600–1900,* ed. L.M. Cullen and T.C. Smout (Edinburgh: John Donald, 1976), 227. A speaker at the Catholic Young Men's Literary Institute designated the Island as "the Ireland of America" (*Islander,* 25 May 1860). Albert County, New Brunswick, also has a claim to the same title. An informative collection of historical essays on the Irish in New Brunswick, edited by P.M. Toner, is entitled *New Ireland Remembered* (Fredericton: New Ireland Press, 1988).

CHAPTER TWO

1 Specifically, the name refers to descendants of Haylen Brenach, son of "Philip the Welshman." Other Walshes are descended from Philip's brother David. For more general usage, the name takes in many of the

Welsh who crossed over to Ireland with the Normans in 1172. See
Edward MacLysaght, *Irish Families* (Dublin: Hodges and Figgis, 1957),
281.

2 Concerning Colonel Hunt Walsh's career and the Battle of Quebec, see
John Knox, *The Siege of Quebec and the Campaigns in North America
1757–1760*, ed. Brian Connell (Mississauga: Pendragon House, 1980).
See also Captain John Knox, *An Historical Journal of the Campaigns in
North America for the Years 1757, 1759, and 1760*, ed. Arthur G.
Doughty. 3 vols. (Toronto: Champlain Society, 1914; reprint, New York:
Greenwood Press, 1968). One of the original subscribers was Col. Hunt
Walsh, 56th Regiment of Infantry.

3 *Burke's Peerage* (949), 2067–8. Concerning the home estate itself, Rev.
John Canon O'Hanlon notes: "Ballykilcavan House and Demesne, the
seat of Sir Hunt Walsh, Bart., have been greatly admired for the tasteful
appearance they present to the eye of the traveller along the high road
from Stradbally to Athy, the grandly wooded heights around lending a
great charm to the landscape" (*History of the Queen's County*, 1: 335–6;
see also 2: 629.)

4 In 1764, for example, Rev. Raphael Walsh signed the lease of Drumneen
farm to Thomas Large of Derryclony. John Large, possibly a descendant
of Thomas Large, became the Walsh family's land agent in Prince Edward
Island in 1817.

5 J. Clinton Morrison, Jr, *Along the North Shore: A Social History of
Township 11, P.E.I., 1765–1982* (St Eleanor's, PEI: J. Clinton Morrison, Jr,
1983), 58. Foxley River was named by surveyor Samuel Holland in 1765
to honour Henry Fox (1705–74), 1st Baron Holland of Foxley. See R.
Douglas, *Place-Names of Prince Edward Island with Meanings* (Ottawa:
Acland, 1925), 25.

6 For a succinct sketch of James Bardin Palmer's business career, consult
Morrision, *Along the North Shore*. See also Basil Greenhill and Ann Gifford, *Westcountrymen in Prince Edward Island* (Toronto: University of
Toronto Press, 1967); and H.T. Holman, "Palmer, James Bardin," DCB, 6:
565–9.

7 Greenhill and Gifford, *Westcountrymen*, 57.

8 Ballykilcavan Papers, letter from J.B. Palmer to Benjamin Johnson Esq.,
24 December 1803. (Evidently Johnson was handling some of the Walsh
business affairs at that time.) The Ballykilcavan papers are in the Walsh-
Kemmis family archives at Ballykilcavan, County Laois. The papers cited
here were made available courtesy of Peter Walsh-Kemmis (Ballykilcavan), assisted by Dr J.W. Carter (Ballyfin).

9 Ballykilcavan Papers, letter from J.B. Palmer to (Walsh), 23 May 1807.

10 See, for instance, J.M. Bumsted, "The Loyal Electors of Prince Edward
Island," *Island Magazine* 8 (1980): 8–14; Holman," DCB, 6: 565–9; and

Stanley C. Johnson, *A History of Emigration from the United Kingdom, 1815–1830* (Oxford: Clarendon, 1972).

11 Public Archives of prince Edward Island (PAPEI), *The Drumneen Lease* (6 July 1764). This document is listed in the National Library of Ireland Reports on Private Collections, no. 34: Walsh Papers. It is in the Walsh-Kemmis family archives at Ballykilcavan, County Loais.

12 Orlo Jones, "Legal Documents Puzzle Genealogist," *Guardian* (Charlottetown), 12 October 1983.

13 PEI Museum and Heritage Foundation, genealogical file; Morrison, *Along the North Shore*. It is possible that more than one John Large lived in Prince Edward Island and that family historians and others at times confuse the Large families.

14 An estimated 10,000 Huguenots may have emigrated to Ireland between 1685 and 1750. For background on the Irish Huguenots, see C.E.J. Coldicott, ed., *The Huguenots and Ireland* (Dublin: Glendale Press, 1987).

15 PAPEI, 25/105. Sir John Allen Johnson Walsh was General Hunt Walsh's nephew and heir. In this document the family name is spelled Walshe.

16 PAPEI, 42/306. Power of attorney to James Warburton was granted by Sir Edward Walsh of Brockley Park, Queens County, Ireland, 4 December 1834.

17 Morrison, *Along the North Shore*, 376. The Warburton pedigree identifies Richard Warburton of Garryhinch (1637–1717) as clerk of the council to Henry Cromwell, Lord Deputy of Ireland in 1654; afterwards clerk assistant to the House of Commons in Ireland in 1662; and member of parliament for Ballyshannon, 1695–1711. See Burke's *History of the Colonial Gentry* (London: Heraldry Today, 1970), 804–5. James Warburton was a member of the sixth generation in Ireland.

O'Hanlon's *History of the Queen's County* (2, 629) has this footnote: "Garryhinch, the fine seat of Colonel Warburton, is situated on the borders of this [Queen's] and the King's County; 'tis disputed in which county the house stands, as the course of the river Barrow (which is the boundary) has been changed, and consequently the house is not now on the same side as it formerly was." Today all that remains of Garryhinch House, razed by fire in 1914, is a forlorn shell of the stately mansion, overgrown with weeds and wild creepers and trapped by trees so tall and thick that they hardly permit light or warmth to touch the damp ruins.

18 The Warburtons and Walshes were already known to one another. James Warburton's father, John Warburton, had served at Quebec as aide-de-camp to the victorious General James Wolfe; see I.R. Robertson, *The Prince Edward Island Land Commission of 1860* (Fredericton: Acadiensis, 1988), 65. In 1779 the same John Warburton won the parliamentary seat for Queens County in a contest with General Hunt Walsh, 264 votes

to 262. (Dublin: National Library of Ireland Report on Private Collections, no. 34. Walsh Papers, dated 1779.)

19 Information on the Warburton residences in Ireland courtesy of Dr J.H. Carter, Ballyfin, County Laois. See also, Morrison, *Along the North Shore*, 55.

20 Ibid., 377.

21 At this time Warburton himself acquired (for 10 shillings and "for divers other good considerations") 500 acres to augment his original 100 acres in Woodbrook. In 1840, to pay the land tax, Walsh had sold 5,535 acres.

22 PAPEI, 72/382, Land Conveyance Records. The indenture of 2 June 1856 was co-signed by Hunt J. Walsh and John Allen Johnson-Walsh, and registered 1 July 1856. The successive proprietors of Lot 11 had been Lieutenant-General Hunt J. Walsh, 1767–95; Rev. Dean Raphael Walsh (brother of Lt. Gen. Walsh), 1795–1808; Sir John Allen Johnson-Walsh (son of Lt. Gen. Walsh's sister Olivia and her husband, Allen Johnson) 1808–31; Sir Edward John Johnson-Walsh (first son of Sir John Allen Johnson-Walsh), 1831–48; and Rev. Sir Hunt Henry Johnson-Walsh (second son of Sir John Allen Johnson-Walsh), 1848–56. See also William M. Glen and Elizabeth A. Glen, "Lot 11: Report of Inspectors Craswell and Anderson circa 1856," in *P.E.I. Genealogical Society Newsletter*, November 1998, 25–30.

23 John Stocks Powell, *Portarlington: A Planted Town* (Birmingham: Frenchchurch Press, 1990), 73. Powell states: "In the nineteenth century the Warburtons were still at Garryhinch holding down many government offices, a target for Ribbonmen and Land Leaguers. It was people like the Warburtons who gave their support to the Penal Laws of the 1700s, who approved of the militia in 1798, fought emancipation, sat on Grand Juries, served ejectment notices and generally did the work of the Protestant Acendancy" (29).

24 "The Purchase of Lot 11," *Islander*, 9 November 1855, 2.

25 In testifying before the PEI Land Commission in 1860, Warburton conceded that he would favour escheat (governmental confiscation) of proprietorial lands under certain circumstances. (See Robertson, *Land Commission*, 60–9.) Ironically, had escheat been invoked for the owner's failure to meet all the terms of the original grants, Lot 11 itself might have been forfeited. As it was, it remained underpopulated and relatively underproductive, and therefore yielded little revenue to the proprietor. Practical economics more than altruism, it may be argued, influenced the decision to sell Lot 11.

26 Morrison, *Along the North Shore*, 478. Warburton's 1846 running mate in the first district of Prince County was Wexford-born Nicholas Conroy of Tignish. Greenhill and Giffard refer to James Yeo as "The Ledger Giant of Port Hill" (*Westcountrymen*, 44).

27 See Morrison, *Along the North Shore*, 377, and Robertson, *Land Commission*, 60–73. Two other Warburton sons had distinguished careers. One became a renowned surgeon, the other mayor of Charlottetown and a member of the legislative assembly.

28 Morrison provides concise genealogical notes on the families of Lot 11 in his *Along the North Shore*, 259–479. This book, the most comprehensive source available on the area, is an excellent community history.

29 Mountmellick (the Irish *Mointeach Miliuc* means "bogland of the marsh") was then popularly known as the "capital of Quakerism" outside Dublin, and Rosenallis became the site of a Quaker graveyard.

30 Robert S.P. Jardine and L. Ann Coles, *Some Immigrants from Offaly and Laois* (Kensington, PEI: Offaly and Laois Family History Society, 1992). See also *Examiner*, 20 February 1865, for obituaries for Thomas Smallman and John Kilbride, Sr.

31 Morrison, *Along the North Shore*, 10.

32 Ibid., 188–92; and Alfred E. Burke, "First Catholic Settlers of the Mission of St Bridget, Township Eleven," in "Histories of the Parishes of Prince Edward Island" (typescript in PAPEI 2352/252); also available at University of Prince Edward Island (UPEI) collection. St Brigid's Church construction began in 1868 and lasted five years. The building was designed by architect John McLellan. It is 30 by 60 feet and had twenty-seven pews and a choir gallery. Jeremiah Dalton was responsible for the exterior construction and McLellan for the interior finish, including the altar (letter from Hon. Joseph Murphy to Amy Pope, 12 July 1886, courtesy of L.B. Murphy of Summerside, PEI). The first trustees were Joseph Murphy and James Kilbride.

33 Morrison, *Along the North Shore*, 199–211. "Goin' to School" gives a comprehensive account of schooling in Township Eleven.

34 For a graphic description, see David Weale, "The Gloomy Forest" *Island Magazine*, Spring/Summer 1983, 8–13.

35 Morrison (*Along the North Shore*, 92–3) lists twenty-three vessels launched in Lot 11 between 1840 and 1886, the largest being a 430–ton barque, 125 feet long.

36 Walter O'Brien, "Bristol Notes," *Guardian* (Charlottetown), 4 October 1983, 12. See also Cornelius Howatt, "The Farm Family," *Canadian Antiques Collector* 8, no. 1 (1973): 61–5; David E. Weale, "The Mud Diggers" in *Island Magazine*, Fall/Winter, 1978, 22–30; and Sir Andrew Macphail, *The Master's Wife* (Montreal: Macphail and Lindsay, 1939).

37 Elinor Vass, "Early Agriculture in Prince Edward Island and the Role of the Agricultural Societies, 1827–1845" (unpublished essay written in December 1975 for Professor David Weale's course, Special Studies in History, at the University of Prince Edward Island).

38 In composing this section I drew upon the following sources: Edward

MacLysaght, *The Surnames of Ireland* (Dublin: Irish Academic Press, 1999), 6th edn; *Irish Families* (Dublin: Hodges and Figgis, 1957). P.W. Joyce, *Irish Local Names Explained* (Dublin: Fred Hanna, 1979); James O'Connell, *The Meaning of Irish Place Names* (Belfast: Blackstaff, 1979); Donal F. Begley, *Handbook on Irish Genealogy* (Dublin: Heraldic Artists, 1984); lectures by and conversations with Donal F. Begley (chief herald, Dublin) and Padraig Ó Siadhail (chair of Irish Studies, Saint Mary's University), and correspondence with Joseph Fitzgerald (East Hartford, Connecticut).

39 Concerning the presence of English names in Ireland, the chief herald offers this explanation: "The main causes of the widespread introduction of British names were the plantation of Ulster in the first decade of the seventeenth century and the Cromwellian Settlement of the 1650s. The Plantation of Ulster had a very considerable and permanent effect on that province, until then the most completely Irish part of Ireland. It is of interest, however, to note that in only two of the nine Ulster counties do English or Scottish names now predominate (Antrim and Down) and these were not among those 'planted': this condition is due rather to modern commercial infiltration. The Cromwellian Settlement was different because the immigrants it introduced were widely scattered over the country. In this case they were for the most part eventually assimilated and became an integral part of the Irish nation. Generations of intermarriage with native Catholic Irish have made them, apart from a few landlord families, otherwise indistinguishable from their neighbours who bear Gaelic or Hiberno-Norman names" (MacLysaght, *The Surnames of Ireland*, xiv–xv).

40 Cecil J. Houston and William J. Smith write: "Geography mattered, and it is necessary to pose questions: 'Who were the Canadian Irish?' 'Where did they come from?'" ("Irish Emigrants to Canada: Whence They Came" in *The Untold Story: The Irish in Canada*, ed. Robert O'Driscoll and Lorna Reynolds (Toronto: Celtic Arts of Canada, 1988), 30).

41 To our knowledge, the Irish language was not widely used in Township Eleven or elsewhere on Prince Edward Island, but it did linger in family usage for a generation or more, and some Irish expressions infiltrated the Island English dialects. Examples of Irish influence on English usage in Prince Edward Island may be found in T.K. Pratt, ed., *Dictionary of Prince Edward Island English* (Toronto: University of Toronto Press, 1988).

CHAPTER THREE

1 T.F. O'Sullivan, *Goodly Barrow: A Voyage on an Irish River* (Dublin: Ward River Press, 1983), is an informative and entertaining account of

Ireland's second-longest river. Kevin Whelan, ed., *Wexford: History and Society* (Dublin: Geography Publications, 1987), contains informative essays on County Wexford.

2 A thousand years ago Reginald the Dane built a round tower at Waterford, a landmark still in use as a museum. Strongbow the Norman recognized the importance of the harbour, and his son-in-law, William Marshal, founded the town of New Ross, 25 miles upstream on the Barrow. In 1650 Cromwell's son-in-law, General Henry Ireton, occupied Waterford. The Irish name for the city is *Port Lairge*.

3 Edmund Spenser, "The Faerie Queen" (book IV, canto xlii), in *The Works of Edmund Spenser: A Variorum Edition*, vol. 4, ed. Edwin Greenlaw et al. (Baltimore: Johns Hopkins Press, 1966), 147.

4 By 1800 a road system and some canals had been constructed, but the Bianconi car (Ireland's first public transport) was not developed in Clonmel until 1815, and the railroad did not come until 1835.

5 Essential to the understanding of the Ireland-Newfoundland migration is John J. Mannion's *Irish Settlements in Eastern Canada: A Study of Cultural Transfer and Adaptation* (Toronto: University of Toronto Press, 1974). See also John J. Mannion, *The Peopling of Newfoundland* (St John's, 1977).

6 Helpful background studies on the Newfoundland–Prince Edward Island connection include William Forbes Adams, *Ireland and Irish Emigration to the New World from 1815 to the Famine* (New Haven: Yale University Press, 1932); W.A. Carrothers, *Emigration from the British Isles* (New York: Augustus M. Kelley, 1971); Helen I. Cowan, *British Emigration to British North America: The First Hundred Years* (Toronto, 1961); C. Grant Head, *Eighteenth Century Newfoundland: A Geographer's Perspective* (Toronto: McClelland and Stewart, 1976); Thomas P. Power, ed., *The Irish in Atlantic Canada 1780–1900* (Fredericton: New Ireland Press, 1991); J.D. Rogers, *A Historical Geography of the British Colonies*, vol. 5, part 4: *Newfoundland*, revised by C.A. Harris (Oxford: Clarendon, 1931); and Robert O'Driscoll and Lorna Reynolds, eds., "The Irish in Atlantic Canada," in *The Untold Story: The Irish in Canada* (Toronto: Celtic Arts of Canada, 1988), 169–250.

7 See Nicholas J. de Jong and Marven E. Moore, *Shipbuilding on Prince Edward Island: Enterprise in a Maritime Setting 1787–1920.* (Hull: Canadian Museum of Civilization, 1994).

8 On this and other matters pertaining to Newfoundland, my frequent conversations with Dr Cyril Byrne (Saint Mary's University, Halifax) proved a very helpful supplement to the readings cited. Byrne writes about the Irish thalassocracy in "The First Irish Foothold in North America," in O'Driscoll and Reynolds, *The Untold Story*, 1: 171–4. See also Kildare Dobbs, "Newfoundland and the Maritimes: An Overview," in Ibid.,

175–94. Of more specialized interest is the collection of papers in the Ninth Annual Seminar of the Canadian Association for Irish Studies, edited by Alison Feder and Bernice Schrank, entitled *Literature and Folk Culture: Ireland and Newfoundland* (1977), in which R.B. Walsh's paper, "Aspects of Irishness," 7–31, is particularly valuable.

9 Paul O'Neill, *The Oldest City: The Story of St John's, Newfoundland* (Erin, Ontario: Press Porcepic, 1975), 54.

10 In Prince Edward Island the Acadians, English, Scots, and Irish had, each in turn, felt the pangs of serious poverty. The painful events most meaningful to the Irish settlers were the 1811 colonization attempt by Lord Townshend (chapter 5 of this study), the 1848 arrival of the famine ship *Lady Constable* (chapter 8), and the post-1815 surge of refugees from depression-stricken Newfoundland (discussed in this chapter).

11 Cecil J. Houston and William J. Smythe, "Irish Immigration to Canada: Whence They Came," in O'Driscoll and Reynolds, *The Untold Story*, 27–35. Andrew Hill Clark, who holds a contrary view, states: "The great majority of Highland Scots and Southern Irish had come as poverty-stricken immigrants and had advanced their circumstances very slowly over the years; they were yet in the 1850's (and many of them late in the eighties) as close to the level of European peasantry as one would be likely to find in the New World"; see his *Three Centuries and the Island: A Historical Geography of Settlement and Agriculture in Prince Edward Island, Canada* (Toronto: University of Toronto Press, 1959), 91.

12 Oscar Handlin, *Boston's Immigrants* (New York: Atheneum, 1976), 38. Professor Handlin (Harvard University) states: "Subjection began to affect the life of the common Irishman only with the changes in land tenure during the Cromwellian invasions. With Cromwell came a host of land-hungry retainers who had to be satisfied at the expense of the native Irish. The great confiscation created a landlord class of foreign birth and religion while the policy of surrender and regrant destroyed the communal basis of land ownership and concentrated what land was left to the Irish in the hands of a few, reducing the remainder to the position of rent-paying tenants. Ruinous wars decimated the population from 1,300,000 in 1650 to less than a million in 1660, and confiscations and anti-Catholic penal laws aimed at depriving 'the majority of the Irish people of all wealth and ambition' – frankly 'to make them poor and keep them poor.' Finally, changes in the land laws destroyed security of tenure, the only safeguard against rapacious absentee landlords."

Professor R.B. Walsh (University College Dublin) also blames the Cromwellian conquest, along with subsequent confiscations and the exploitation of Ireland's resources, for the cultural and economic poverty that beset the country; see Walsh, "Aspects of Irishness," in Feder and Schrank, *Literature and Folk Culture*, 8–9.

13 Public Record Office (PRO), CO 194/64, F/123, Fort Townshend. Governor Hamilton to Lord Bathurst, 4 December 1821.

14 *Acts of the General Assembly of Prince Edward Island*, 1840, 3 Vict. cap 16. The burden of caring for the aged and infirm and for the mentally and physically disabled refugees was carried by the struggling colonies. The depressed economy of Newfoundland after 1815 – and that neglected colony's consequent decision to deport many of its chronically poor people – accounts for numbers of Irish persons in Charlottetown's asylum and workhouse. In the spring of 1839, another time of great distress in Newfoundland, the *Colonial Herald* published the names of unfortunate individuals and families who received public assistance in Charlottetown; in 1844 a House Committee on Paupers and Lunatics was appointed and thereafter, from 1844 through 1860, the *Journals of the House of Assembly* listed, among others, dozens of Irish paupers. Throughout this period – but especially with the arrival of 400 refugees from Ireland's disastrous potato famine in 1847 – the Benevolent Irish Society and other charitable agencies administered assistance to the poor.

15 *Limerick Evening Post*, 16 April and 29 June 1818.

16 Stanley C. Johnson, "Shovelling Out Paupers," in *A History of Emigration from the United Kingdom to North America, 1815–1830* (Oxford: Clarendon, 1972).

17 Cited by Helen I. Cowan, *British Immigration before Confederation*, Canadian Historical Association Booklets, no. 22 (Ottawa: Leclerc, 1968), 66. See also Cowan, *British Emigration to British North America*, 68.

18 Peter Gallant, *From Ireland to Prince Edward Island: An Index of Irish Immigrants Based on Obituaries and Death Notices in Prince Edward Island Newspapers 1835–1910* (Charlottetown: PEI Genealogical Society, 1990.) County Kilkenny's 79 persons from Mooncoin, Gowran, Graignamanagh, Thomastown, etc., settled in 35 Island locations; Wexford's 49 persons (from Bannow, Adamstown, New Ross, Gorey, Rathdowney, Newbawn, etc.) scattered to Tignish, Rustico, Charlottetown, Farmington, and 25 other Island places; over 40 natives of Carrick, Clonmel, Fethard, Mullinahone, Thurles, etc., in Tipperary, settled in two dozen Island places; 6 County Carlow people lived in 5 separate communities; and 25 County Waterford immigrants settled in 15 different places. These settlers mingled with one another and with settlers from other nations.

19 P.M. Toner, ed., *New Ireland Remembered* (Fredericton: New Ireland Press, 1988.)

20 George Freeman Sanborn, Jr, "The Story of the 'Elizabeth,'" unpublished article, Tilton, New Hampshire, 30 September 1979. See also D.C. Harvey, "Voyage of Thomas Curtis," in *Journeys to the Island of St. John or Prince Edward Island, 1775–1832* (Toronto: Macmillan, 1955).

21 Sean Spellissy, *Limerick, the Rich Land* (Ennis: O'Brien, 1989), 51–2.
22 Tim Severin's *The Brendan Voyage* (London: Hutchinson, 1978) is tangentially relevant here in that Severin replicated St Brendan's reputed sixth-century journey, thereby demonstrating the possibility that the saint's legendary voyage to America had taken place – as Kerry people generally believe it did. The key historic document is the *Navigatio Sancti Brendani Abbatis*. A fine translation from the Latin is by John J. O'Meara, *The Voyage of Saint Brendan* (Dublin: Dolmen, 1978). One of the many interpretations is that by Dr George A. Little, *Brendan the Navigator* (Dublin: Gill, 1946). Other books featuring the Brendan tradition include Geoffrey Ashe, *Land to the West* (London, 1962), Paul H. Chapman, *The Man Who Led Columbus to America* (Atlanta, 1973), and S.E. Morison, *The European Discovery of America* (New York, 1971).
23 Eibhlín Ní Mhurchú (Eileen Murphy), "An tIascach a Bhí" (The Fishing That Was), *Céad bliain 1871–1971* in eagar ag Mícheál O Ciosáin (Muintir Phiarais, Baile an Fheirteáraigh, 1973), 194–5 (translation by Joseph Fitzgerald, East Hartford, Connecticut).
24 Liam Kelly, Geraldine Lucid, and Maria O'Sullivan, *Blennerville: Gateway to Tralee's Past* (Tralee: Blennerville Windmill Co., 1989).
25 "Canada Emigration," *Limerick Evening Post and Clare Sentinel*, 21 and 25 March 1828 (National Library of Ireland microfilm). A.C. Buchanan was an emigration agent based in Derry.
26 Cited by Edward MacDonald, *New Ireland: The Irish on Prince Edward Island* (Charlottetown: PEI Museum and Heritage Foundation, 1990), 6.
27 Orlo Jones and Douglas Fraser, "Those Elusive Immigrants," *Island Magazine* (Charlottetown), pt. 1, Fall/Winter 1984, 36–41, and pt. 2, Summer 1985, 33.
28 Point Prim Light was built in 1846 by Richard Walsh, assisted by blacksmith Thomas Robinson, both from Charlottetown. Architect Isaac Smith designed the 60-foot circular stone tower with its polygonal lantern. Late in the nineteenth century the tower was sheathed and shingled.

CHAPTER FOUR

1 R. Douglas, *Place-Names of Prince Edward Island* (Ottawa: King's Printer, 1925), 40–1. Alan Rayburn, *Geographical Names of Prince Edward Island* (Ottawa: Queen's Printer, 1973), 95. S.B. O'Leary states: "The town was named for a Michael O'Leary who was ship-wrecked at West Cape in about 1837. He had to make a road through the woods to the other side of the island for supplies. His path became known as O'Leary's Road, and finally as O'Leary's town" (*Irish America*, November 1990, 7).

2 Arthur O'Leary, an officer in the Hungarian Hussars, was killed by High Sheriff Abraham Morris's bodyguard in Carriganimma, County Cork, in 1722. His wife was Eibhlin Dubh Ni Chonaill ("Eibhlin Dubh") of Derrynane, aunt of Daniel O'Connell. She composed the classic "Lament for Art O'Leary."

3 Dr O'Leary's wife was the daughter of Patrick Scully and Mary Dunn, natives of County Tipperary. Scully was a farmer and woodranger in Souris West (information courtesy of Judge George Mullally, Souris, March 1992). See also Alice Green et al., *Footprints on the Sands of Time: A History of Alberton* (Summerside: Williams and Crue, 1980), 244–5; and *Daily Colonist* (St John's, Nfld), 30 July 1888.

4 Rayburn, *Geographical Names*, 66.

5 Green et al., *Footprints*, 140–2.

6 Rayburn, *Geographical Names*, 65.

7 Ibid., 33.

8 Ibid., 94.

9 Ibid., 37.

10 Ibid., 72. Rev. Richard Ellsworth, who taught school there in 1915–16, informed me that the place name commemorated teacher Lauretta O'Brien, daughter of Edward O'Brien (interview, July 1982).

11 Rayburn, *Geographical Names*, 126. A family history of Wilson Shea of Tignish indicates that ancestor William Shea, whose family came by boat to Horse Head from Antigonish, Nova Scotia, in 1845, proposed the name of his native county, Waterford.

12 See John Cousins, "James Heron Fitzgerald: Pioneer Schoolmaster," PEITF *Newsletter*, October 1980, 30; and John Cousins, "James H. Fitzgerald and 'Prince Edward Island, Adieu,'" *Island Magazine*, 1980, 27–31. See also Public Archives of Prince Edward Island (PAPEI) 3704 and 3261/1, Diaries of J.H. Fitzgerald.

13 J.H. Fitzgerald, "Letter from Mount Hemlock," *Summerside Progress*, 31 December 1866, 2. Fitzgerald moved to Richmond, also called Fitzgerald Station, where he lived most of his life. On the occasion of the change of name from Quagmire to Wellington in 1862, Fitzgerald (secretary of the community meeting) recorded the decision in these exuberant words: "After a few names being suggested to the meeting the name of the celebrated Irish hero of a Hundred Battles was finally adopted, viz. 'Wellington'; so after giving three cheers to perpetuate the name of the great and victorious General and eminent statesman, and, I may say, in great measure, the preserver of the Crown for the present illustrious Royal Family and the perpetuation of one of the greatest dynasties that the sun ever shone upon, the meeting separated, but not until they took a good libation of Mr. Allen's strong beverage, generously given by his worthy hostess." For a history of the community, see *By the Old Mill Stream: His-*

tory of Wellington 1833–1983 (Wellington: Senior Citizens History Committee, 1983).

14 O'Halloran told of the guns being fired in the port of Cork to announce the coronation of the king in 1820 (John Cousins, public lecture, 1985). The *Martin* made several voyages between Ireland and Prince Edward Island.

15 Vance Griffin, interview, 20 August 1983. Marriages arranged by parents were not uncommon.

16 Inez Butler Howard, ed., *The History of St Mark's–St Bernadette's Parish 1879–1979* (Burton, PEI: St Mark's Parish, 1979), 36. This booklet contains useful information on pioneers in the parish and district. See also A.E. Burke, "The Mission of St Mark," in "Histories of the Parishes of Prince Edward Island" (typescript in PAPEI; also at UPEI).

17 *Palladium*, 2 May 1844.

18 This information is drawn from public lectures by, and occasional personal conversations with, John Cousins of Campbellton. See John Cousins, "Tom Dunn and the Irish Folk Tale in Prince Edward Island," in *Celtic Languages and Celtic Peoples: Proceedings of the Second North American Congress of Celtic Studies*, 1989, ed. Cyril J. Byrne, Margaret Harry, and Padraig Ó Siadhail (Halifax: Saint Mary's University, 1992).

19 Edward D. Ives, *Larry Gorman: The Man Who Made the Songs* (Bloomington: Indiana University Press, 1964), and *Drive Dull Care Away: Folksongs from Prince Edward Island* (Charlottetown: Institute of Island Studies, 1999).

20 Ives, *The Man Who*, 25–6.

21 Robert A. Rankin, "Larry Gorman and 'Monaghan's Raffle'," *Island Magazine*, 32–3.

22 Ives, *The Man Who*, 28.

23 Ibid., 42–4. In public lectures John Cousins has identified Mick O'Brien of Centre Line Road as a man who vexed Gorman. When Mick asked Larry to write a song about his brother (who was an inoffensive person), Gorman pilloried Mick the wife hunter instead.

24 Ives, *The Man Who*, 30–32.

25 Ibid., 35. John Cousins, folklorist and teacher from Campbellton, notes that the Gull Decoy himself had married a Scottish Presbyterian, Peggy Stewart of West Point. When his brother's daughter died and was interred in consecrated ground, the Gull Decoy exhumed the body and placed it outside his brother's door. The song was composed in the late 1860s or early 1870s (conversation with John Cousins). See also Ives, *Drive Dull Care Away*, 84–6.

26 "The Baptists," in Ives, *The Man Who*, 38–9.

27 Surnames of pioneer families along that coast include O'Connor, Howard, Doyle, Griffin, Sheen, Locke, Frizzell, Morrissey, Donahue,

Kelly, Coyle, Coughlin, Trainor, Sullivan, Dalton, Luttrell, Colfer, Butler, Kaughan, O'Halloran, Stone, Callaghan, Aylward. See *History of St Mark's–St Bernadette's Parish,* 25–36.

28 Meacham's 1880 map shows at least the following recognizably Irish surnames: Bulger, Carroll, Dignam, Dougherty, Dunn, Foran, Gamble, Keefe, Kelly, McMullin, Nelligan, and Smallman; see *Illustrated Historical Atlas of Prince Edward Island* (Philadelphia: J.H. Meacham; reprint, Belleville, Ont.: Mika, 1977). Proprietor William Hill's 1826 list of inhabitants included John and Mary Keefe, Peter and Eliza Carroll, Richard and Mary Roe, Thomas and Sarah Fitzgerald, Lawrence and Judith Kinch, John and Jane MacAlduff, and widows Mara and Hogan, in Lot 5; and John and Mary Kilbride, Martin and Mary Lynch, and widow Quin, in Lot 6; see H.T. Holman, "Counting Heads, William Hill's Mysterious Lists," *Island Magazine,* Fall/Winter 1990, 38–41.

29 For more information on Tignish and vicinity, see Reginald Porter, "The First Irish Settlers in Tignish," *Abegweit Review,* Spring 1983, 27–33, and *The Souvenir Program of the Centennial Celebration of the Church of St Simon and St Jude* (Tignish, 1961).

30 Porter, "Settlers in Tignish," 27–8.

31 P.M. Toner, ed., *New Ireland Remembered: Historical Essays on the Irish in New Brunswick* (Fredericton: New Ireland Press, 1988).

32 Rev. A.E. Burke in *L'impartial,* centennial edition (Tignish, 1899), and Georges Arsenault, *The Island Acadians, 1720–1980,* trans. Sally Ross (Charlottetown: Ragweed, 1989), 183–4.

33 In fact, within three generations another type of problem arose: "The majority of entries of marriages note that the parties had to be dispensed from the impediment of consanguinity, usually in the third or fourth degree and sometimes double"; see Emily Elizabeth Cran, "A Brief History of the Parish of St Simon at St Jude, Tignish, Prince Edward Island," (photocopy, Tignish, 1971), 23.

34 The PEI Museum and Heritage Foundation display at the Confederation Centre of the Arts (1990) noted that "though English was an adopted tongue, the Irish had their own way with it. In syntax, inflection, and figure of speech, the heritage of Ireland persisted in PEI."

35 Georges Arsenault states the matter succinctly: "On the one hand the French Canadians maintained that language was the guardian of the faith; anyone who became anglicized risked losing the Catholic faith. On the other hand, the anglophone clergy, particularly of Irish descent, was convinced that English would sooner or later become the dominant language of the Country: consequently it should be favoured to ensure the expansion and the unity of the Catholic Church" (*Island Acadians,* 184). In any event, French was one of the two official languages in Canada.

36 Reprinted in *Souvenir Program of Centennial of St Simon and St Jude.*

English translation: "Let us never forget to observe faithfully the precepts that they have taught us: love of country, preservation of our beautiful French language, obedience to the law, and an inviolable fidelity to our religion."

37 Rev. A.E. Burke, in the centennial edition of *L'impartial* (1899). Social historian Georges Arsenault is more acutely aware of conflicts centred in language preservation and in hierarchical appointments; see Arsenault, *Island Acadians*, 183–4. A bishop of Acadian descent was first appointed in New Brunswick in 1912, and one in Prince Edward Island in 1992. It is not known what portion of the Island's Acadians are descendants of the Bretons and therefore may be considered Celts. Art O'Shea's *A.E. Burke* (Charlottetown: Clark, 1993) is a concise biography of the pastor of Alberton.

38 In this chapter the information pertaining to families has been gleaned from community histories, family histories, tombstones, and conversations with descendants.

39 A person named Flo McCarthy from Killarney died in Kildare Capes in 1884.

40 Patrick Fitzgerald, *Fitzgerald 1858–1993* (Summerside: Williams and Crue, 1993), a family history.

41 A Witness, "Dreadful Shipwreck at Tignish," *Examiner* (Charlottetown), 5 November 1866.

42 F.H. MacArthur, *Legends of P.E.I.* (Charlottetown: Irwin, n.d.) 70–2. The author is specific about the year 1786.

43 Francis W.P. Bolger, *Prince Edward Island and Confederation, 1863–1873* (Charlottetown: St Dunstan's University Press, 1964), 3.

44 Douglas, *Place-Names*, 33; and Rayburn, *Geographical Names*, 71.

45 The Earl of Kildare married Emilia Mary, daughter of Charles, second Duke of Richmond and Lennox (whose name Samuel Holland also is assigned to places in PEI). About 1753, perhaps to placate him, for he sometimes displayed revolutionary tendencies, Kildare was dubbed the first Duke of Leinster. His magnificent Dublin residence later became the seat of the Irish parliament. Lord Edward Fitzgerald became the most popular hero of the Fitzgerald dynasty when he died for Ireland in the insurrection of 1798.

46 J.B. Cahill, Halifax, N.S., correspondence with author, 8 August 1986; *Summerside Progress*, 31 December 1866. Patrick Cahill's tombstone is in Tignish cemetery.

47 Clohossey family history. See n 51 below.

48 PAPEI, O'Connor-Foley diaries. The quotations about Kildare, PEI, are taken from these diaries.

49 Green et al., *Footprints*. The information that follows concerning Alberton businessmen is drawn largely from the same source. Rayburn (*Geo-

graphical Names, 33) notes that *Cascumpeque* is the older spelling for *Cascumpec*.

50 The Inheritors et al., *History of St Anthony Parish 1803–1980* (Bloomfield, PEI: Bloomfield Historical Society, 1980).

51 Edward Clohossey's account of the Clohossey family, including this letter, appeared in the *Abegweit Review*, Spring 1988, 129–47.

CHAPTER FIVE

1 Lawrence Doyle, "Prince Edward Isle Adieu," in *Lawrence Doyle: The Farmer-Poet of Prince Edward Island. A Study in Local Songmaking* by Edward D. Ives (Orono: University of Maine Press, 1977), 67. John Cousins argues a strong case concerning authorship of this song, in "James H. Fitzgerald and 'Prince Edward Isle, Adieu,'" *Island Magazine* 8 (1980): 27–31. He credits Fitzgerald with this song.

2 *Illustrated Historical Atlas of Prince Edward Island* (Philadelphia: J.H. Meacham, 1880; reprint, Belleville, Ont.: Mika Publishing, 1977), 11. This atlas rates the soil as good in the vicinity of St Peters, Souris, Rollo Bay, and East Point, but swampy and second class in many other sectors.

3 Mary MacDonald and Irma Stewart, *Historical Sketch of Eastern Kings* (private publication, 1972), 43. This is an informative local history.

4 Alan Rayburn, *Geographical Names of Prince Edward Island* (Ottawa: Department of Energy, Mines and Resources, 1973), 46.

5 See comments on Lot 43 in Kenneth MacKinnon, "Captain John MacDonald and the Glenaladale Settlers," *Celtic Languages and Celtic Peoples: Proceedings of the Second North American Congress of Celtic Studies, 1989* (Halifax: Saint Mary's University, 1992), 678–9.

6 The village name and similar geographic designations in that area derive from the early French fishing base named in honour of the Compte de St Pierre (Rayburn, *Geographical Names*, 190).

7 Rayburn, *Geographical Names*, 61.

8 Public Archives of Prince Edward Island (PAPEI), 1848 census.

9 See also *Palladium*, 22 February and 4 March 1844, for similarly detailed reports from Repeal meetings at St Peters, East Point, and Georgetown.

10 Annabelle Powell, *P.E.I. Genealogical Society Newsletter*, November 1982.

11 Ibid.

12 Frederick Marryat, *Frank Mildmay, or The Naval Officer* (Boston & New York: Dana Estes, 1896), 154–5. Research may yet reveal to what extent Marryat's novel depicted the actual settlement at Spry Point.

13 Powell, *Newsletter*. Before England had established a standing navy, such impressment of able-bodied merchant seamen was a common practice. See C. Grant Head, *Eighteenth-Century Newfoundland*, Carleton Library no. 99 (Toronto: McClelland and Stewart, 1976), 93.

14 Powell, *Newsletter*.
15 Ibid.
16 PAPEI, Governor J.F.W. DesBarres and Council, Minutes, 18 July 1811.
17 Marryat, *Frank Mildmay*, 156–7.
18 PAPEI, 1848 census.
19 J.C. Underhay, "Bay Fortune," in *Past and Present of Prince Edward Island*, ed. D.A. MacKinnon and A.B. Warburton (Charlottetown: Bowen, n.d.), 391a-2a; see also 602.
20 Adele Townshend, "Drama at Abells Cape," *Island Magazine*, Spring/Summer 1979, 34. See also C.P. Flocton, "The Murder of Abel," *Prince Edward Island Magazine*, December 1901, 346–52; and *Prince Edward Island Gazette*, 3 September 1819, 3.
21 Marryat, cited in Townshend, "Drama," 34.
22 Underhay, cited in Townshend, "Drama," 34.
23 Townshend, "Drama," 34.
24 Underhay, "Bay Fortune," 392a; Townshend, "Drama," 35.
25 *Prince Edward Island Gazette*, 3 September 1819, 3. This article states the facts as understood at the time of the tragic incident. Later articles by Adele Townsend and J.C. Underhay (cited above) are more detailed and more interpretive than the original report.
26 *Prince Edward Island Register*, 3 September 1819.
27 *Prince Edward Island Gazette,* 2 February 1820.
28 Townshend, "Drama," 35–6; George Cheverie, "Growing Up in East Point," *Abegweit Review*, Fall 1990, 14–16.
29 George A. Leard, *Historic Highlights* (Charlottetown: Historical Society of Prince Edward Island, 1955), 46.
30 See, for instance, Adele Townshend, "Wreck of the 'Sovinto,'" *Eastern Graphic*, 13 and 20 September, 1978.
31 *Royal Gazette* 22 June 1822.
32 George Keefe, "A Visit to East Point," *Abegweit Review*, Winter 1985, 123.
33 Edward MacDonald gives the year 1822; see his *New Ireland: The Irish on Prince Edward Island* (Charlottetown: Prince Edward Island Museum and Heritage Foundation, 1990), 36.
34 Adele Townsend, *Ten Farms Become a Town: A History of Souris 1700–1920*, compiled from the Leard Papers by Adele Townsend (Souris, 1986), 14–15. The information cited here is attributed to Tommy Harris, great-great-grandson of Mrs Moses Harris, the last survivor of the ship-wreck, who died in 1886 at age 104.
35 Doyle, "The Picnic at Groshaut," in Ives, *Laurence Doyle*, 21–2.
36 Judge George Mullally of Souris, told me this story. The late Dr Augustine MacDonald and Jack Lawlor were Souris residents. Concerning Dr

MacDonald, see Sasha Mullally, "Dr. Roddie, Dr. Gus and the Golden Age of Medicine," *Island Magazine*, Fall/Winter, 1977, 3–9.

37 MacDonald, *New Ireland*, 36–8, and others reinforce this point.

38 Edward D. Ives, "The Farmer Poet," in *Maine Studies* 92 (1971): 2.

39 Rayburn, *geographical Names*, 115–16. Townsend, in *Ten Farms*, 153, suggests that Souris means "Harbour of Smiles."

40 Alfred E. Burke, "Catholic Settlers of the Mission of St Mary" in (PAPEI, *Histories of the Parishes*).

41 *Souris, P.E.I.* (booklet, n.d.), 3.

42 Ibid.

43 Adele Townshend, Charlottetown public lecture, 10 November 1981.

44 Burke, "Catholic Settlers." Judge George Mullally of Souris informed me that of twenty Irish surnames in the 1841 census in Lot 44, only one (Mullally) was still found in that area in 1997. Descendants of other Irish colonials are still there but under different surnames acquired by inter-marriages through several generations.

45 Newspaper clipping, dated 17 March 1890 in Souris, in author's personal files.

46 Peter McGuigan, "The Lot 61 Irish: Settlement and Stabilization," *Abegweit Review*, Spring 1988, 33.

47 Letter from John McNally, East Point, PEI, North America, to Ulick Nallen, Longford, Parish of Crossmolina, County Mayo, Ireland, 11 January 1832 (courtesy Mrs Maura Nallen, Cullies, Cavan, County Cavan, Ireland).

48 In the latter sentence, McNally is evidently referring to leasing 100 acres of woodland for five pounds a year – a common rate at that time. He cautions his brother, however, that it would take at least five years to cut the trees, remove the stumps, and prepare the land for crops.

CHAPTER SIX

1 The Rev. Richard Ellsworth was prominent among Island residents who related anecdotes such as those cited here.

2 Chapter 9 in this study offers a detailed account of the Belfast Riot.

3 The contribution by the descendants of the Monaghan settlers to the Catholic Church in Canada is the more remarkable, perhaps, considering that no clergy from their home diocese of Clogher accompanied them on the transatlantic voyage.

4 For a commentary on Ireland's 1826 election, see Rev. Martin Cahill, "The 1826 General Election in County Monaghan," *Clogher Record* 5, no. 2 (1964): 161–83; also Sir Charles Gavan Duffy, *My Life in Two Hemispheres*, introduction by John H. Whyte (London: T. Fisher Unwin,

1898; reprint, Shannon: Irish University Press, 1969), 1: 5. Other citations from Duffy come from the same source.

5 For a comprehensive background of electoral violence, riots and other shameful practices in nineteenth-century Ireland, see K. Theodore Koppen, *Elections, Politics, and Society in Ireland 1832–1885* (Oxford: Clarendon Press, 1984).

6 William Carleton, "The Tithe Proctor," in *The Works of William Carleton* (New York: Collier, 1881), 2: 372. Although the story is based on events that had occurred in Limerick and Kilkenny, it was indeed relevant to County Monaghan readers. They, too, had experienced the obnoxious tax, the repressive system, and the secret societies, and they knew real-life counterparts for the overbearing bailiff, the treacherous informer, and the suffering peasants. Even though Carleton's viewpoint sometimes infuriated his readers, his portrayals serve as a graphic complement to historical records. The Tyrone-Monaghan region is clearly depicted in Carleton's *Traits and Stories of the Irish Peasantry* (1842), ed. D.J. O'Donoghue (London: Dent, 1896).

7 Dennis Carolan Rushe, *Historical Sketches of Monaghan, from Earliest Times to the Fenian Movement* (Dublin: Duffy, 1895), 75–81.

8 Ibid., 76.

9 Ibid., 76–7.

10 Ibid., 77–8.

11 Ibid., 78.

12 Ibid., 92.

13 Quoted in Carleton, *Works*, 2:414.

14 In Prince Edward Island in 1843–44, hundreds of Irish immigrants signed Repeal Association petitions urging the British government to rescind the Act of Union, and they sent money to Daniel O'Connell's headquarters to support the Repeal campaign. Long afterwards, islanders debated whether Britain's refusal to accede to Ireland's desire for Home Rule under the crown (a status somewhat similar to Canada's) led to further uprisings and, eventually, to the political separation of most of Ireland from the United Kingdom.

15 Carleton, *Works*, 2: 362.

16 Ibid.

17 Quoted in Peadar Livingstone, *The Monaghan Story: A Documented History of the County Monaghan from the Earliest Times to 1976* (Enniskillen: Clogher Historical Society, 1980), 208.

18 Quoted in ibid., 263.

19 Denis Carolan Rushe, *Monaghan in the Eighteenth Century* (Dundalk: Wm Tempest, 1916; and The Desert, Armagh: Celtic Reprints, n.d.), 10.

20 Rushe, *Monaghan*, 111.

21 Rushe, *Historical Sketches*, 97.

22 William Carleton, *The Life of William Carleton* (London: Downey, 1896), 1: 29.

23 J.E. McKenna, *Diocese of Clogher: Parochial Records, Monaghan* (Enniskillen: Fermanagh Herald, 1920), 1: 218–19.

24 Quoted in Benedict Kiely, *Poor Scholar: A Study of the Works and Days of William Carleton (1794–1869)* (New York: Sheed and Ward, 1948), 47.

25 Ibid.

26 Quoted in Thomas Brendan O'Grady, "William Carleton's 'The Fair of Emyvale,'" *Abegweit Review*, Winter 1985, 36. "The Fair of Emyvale" first appeared in *The London Illustrated Magazine*, 1853.

27 Livingstone, *Monaghan Story*, 211. Canon Livingstone offers an interesting account of the blight's inception in Ireland (216–17). See also Brian Ó Mordha, "The Great Famine in Monaghan: A Coroner's Account," *Clogher Record* 4, no. 1–2 (1960–61): 29–43; and no. 3 (1962): 175–86.

28 For information in this paragraph, I am indebted to Theo McMahon, editor of the *Clogher Record* (personal interview, June 1989.) The statistics here are derived from Livingstone, *Monaghan Story*.

29 J.B.D. Cotter, *A Short History of Donagh Parish* (Enniskillen: Fermanagh Times, n.d.), 3.

30 Livingstone, *Monaghan Story*, 217–18. This book provides much information on the famine years in County Monaghan.

31 For further information on these parishes and on the whole area under discussion, consult Patrick J. Duffy's excellent atlas: *Landscapes of South Ulster: A Parish Atlas of the Diocese of Clogher* (Belfast: Institute of Irish Studies, Queen's University, 1993).

32 Livingstone, *Monaghan Story*, 560–74 and *passim*.

33 Rushe, *Monaghan, passim*.

34 Ibid., 7.

35 Ibid., 90.

36 Ibid., 21.

37 McKenna, *Diocese of Clogher*, 218.

38 Archbishop John Hughes's birthplace was near Augher, County Tyrone, just north of the Monaghan county line. (It is believed that relatives of the archbishop may have emigrated to Prince Edward Island.)

39 McKenna, *Diocese of Clogher*, 274.

40 Rushe, *Monaghan*, 88.

41 McKenna, *Diocese of Clogher*, 272.

42 Owen Connolly and many other Monaghan settlers of Prince Edward Island were among the contributors to the building of the cathedral in Monaghan town.

CHAPTER SEVEN

1 What is now called the Fort Augustus area (a place name derived from Scotland) was then designated on the MacDonald estate map as Moydart in Lot 36 and St Martin's in Lot 35, totalling 18,750 acres.

2 See, for example, Peter Anson, *Underground Catholicism in Scotland* (Montrose, 1970), 172–3; Alphons Bellesheim, *History of the Catholic Church in Scotland, 1760–1800*, 4: 218–20. Apparently Father Wynne was assistant to the aging and infirm Rev. Alexander Forrester. See also Rev. Allan F. MacDonald, "Captain John MacDonald, 'Glenaladale,'" in *The Canadian Catholic Historical Association Report*, 1964, 21–37. Marie E. Daly of the New England Genealogical Society, Waltham, Massachusetts, has also researched Rev. John MacDonald and the Glasgow Irish.

3 Lorne C. Callbeck, "The Glenaladale Pioneers," in *My Island, My People* (Charlottetown: Prince Edward Island Heritage Foundation, 1979), 12. Of greater importance, J.M. Bumsted points out that most of the Glenaladale settlers were neither driven from their homes nor victimized by oppression; rather, they chose to leave Scotland and paid their own way to do so in the hope of improving their circumstances. Among the people from South Uist who were indeed being intimidated by sectarian pressures, only eleven families were so poor that they had to have their passage paid by the Scottish Catholic Church. See Bumsted's articles in the *Island Magazine* 8 (1980): 8–14; and "Highland Emigration to the Island of St John," *Dalhousie Review* 58 (1978): 511–27. Professor Bumsted's many publications contribute very significantly to our understanding of the Island's Scottish settlements. *The Arrival of the First Scottish Catholic Emigrants in Prince Edward Island and After* (Summerside: Journal Publishing, 1922) is a commemorative booklet.

4 Rev. John MacDonald was educated at Ampleforth (1819–20), St Sulpice, Paris (1820–22), Scots College, Rome (1822–23), then Paris on Scots funds (1824–25). See Christine Johnson, "Secular Clergy of the Lowland District 1732–1829," *Innes Review* (Glasgow), Autumn 1983, 75. It is believed that Father MacDonald agreed to serve the early years of his priesthood in Glasgow in return for the financial assistance he received during his studies in Europe. He worked under the jurisdiction of the Rev. Andrew Scott, builder and pastor of St Andrew's Church, Glasgow, who became bishop in 1825 and served until 1836. He died in 1846. Scott's relations with the Irish people were not always cordial, partly because he did not support the work of Daniel O'Connell in Ireland. See James Edmund Handley, *The Irish in Scotland, 1798–1845* (Cork: Cork University Press, 1945), 285. Handley attempts to give a balanced view of both the Scottish resentment and the Scottish acceptance of the Irish.

5 *Souvenir of the One Hundred and Fiftieth Anniversary of St Andrew's Cathedral* (Glasgow: John S. Burns, 1966), 4.

6 Ibid., 10–11. In 1830 St Andrew's Church served about 50,000 parishioners, most of whom were Irish or of Irish descent.

7 According to a Scottish tradition, St Patrick in his youth was taken captive by Irish raiders near his supposed birthplace, Dumbarton. "From the Gorbals to Gweedore" in *Odyssey: Voices from Scotland's Recent Past* (Edinburgh: Polygon Books, 1980), 1, ed. Billy Kay, succinctly states the kinship between the two peoples: "Gaelic Scots [*Scoti*] of Ulster crossed to Argyll in the fifth and sixth centuries and gave Scotland her name, her initial experience of Christianity, and her ancient tongue."

8 Cited in Handley, *Irish in Scotland*, 160.

9 Ibid., 294.

10 Ibid., 239. Anson, *Underground*, 233, pointedly observes that these Irish migrants did not bring even one priest with them: "They were often left as sheep without shepherds, except for the ministrations of the far from sufficient Scots priests; hence the wholesale lapses from their religion, especially in Galloway ... The Irish bishops gave no sign that they were interested in the spiritual welfare of the ever increasing number of Irish families who abandoned their homes to seek their fortunes in a foreign country, where there was little or no provision for the practice of their religion."

11 Handley, *Irish in Scotland*, 240.

12 Ibid., 242.

13 Ibid., 261–2.

14 *Souvenir*, 9.

15 *Glasgow Chronicle*, 2 April 1830.

16 *Prince Edward Island Register*, 25 May 1830.

17 See Peter Gallant, *From Ireland to Prince Edward Island: An Index of Irish Immigrants Based on Obituaries and Death Notices in Prince Edward Island Newspapers 1835–1910* (Charlottetown: P.E.I. Genealogical Society, 1990).

18 Rev. Alfred E. Burke, "Mission of St Patrick, Fort Augustus," in "Histories of the Parishes of Prince Edward Island" (undated typescript in PAPEI; also in the University of Prince Edward Island collection).

19 G. Edward MacDonald, *New Ireland: The Irish on P.E.I.* (Charlottetown: Prince Edward Island Museum and Heritage Foundation, 1990), 35.

20 Callbeck, "The Early Dawsons," in his *My Island, My People*, 74–83. Dawson's activities as a lay preacher are also noted in George A. Leard, *Historic Bedeque: The Loyalists at Work and Worship in Prince Edward Island* (Bedeque: Bedeque United Church, 1948), 16.

21 *Royal Gazette*, 27 October 1840.

22 John McKenna, "Early Irish Settlers in Prince Edward Island," a lecture reported in the Charlottetown *Guardian*, 10 February 1928.

23 Ibid.
24 *Colonial Herald*, 4 June 1842, and *Royal Gazette*, 31 May 1842.
25 *Royal Gazette*, 20 September 1842.
26 *Colonial Herald*, 6 and 20 May 1843, and *Islander*, 19 May 1843.
27 McKenna, "Early Irish."
28 Ibid.
29 McKenna believed that a monument had been erected to commemorate the *Miracle* victims. After reasonable searching I have found no monument and no record of one ever having been erected in Pictou, Nova Scotia, or in the Magdalene Islands. The *Royal Gazette*, 8 June 1847, reported: "The ship *Miracle*, Elliot Master, from Liverpool, G.B., bound to Quebec, (31 days out) with 408 passengers, was cast away at Magdalen Islands on the 9th inst. Sixty-four were drowned, and thirty others had died of fever."
30 McKenna, "Early Irish." See also Lorne C. Callbeck, *The Cradle of Confederation* (Fredericton: Brunswick Press, 1964), 137–8, and Edward MacDonald, "The Ill and the Dying," *Island Magazine*, Fall/Winter 1994, 35–9.
31 *Acts of the General Assembly of Prince Edward Island*, 1846, cap. 4; 1847, cap. 1; 1848, cap. 1.
32 Ibid., 1846, cap. 1. This act covered the provision and distribution of seed and food, and the mode of repayment.
33 D.J. Lake, *Topographical Map of Prince Edward Island* (Saint John: W.F. and H.H. Baker, 1863).
34 Other names included E. Lafferty, Mrs McGuirk, J. Herring [?], G. Beard, P. Brogan, T. Brady, M. McBride, Doyle, P. McNally, W. Hickey, O. Callaghan, J. McManus, J. Burnett, J. MacDonald, Sr, and A. McDonald. Near and beyond Glenfinnan Lake were John Cumusky, W. McGuirk, J. Garland, H. Cumusky, P. Lafferty, P. Doyle, M. Cumusky, P. McMahon, J. Mallaly, J. King, E. McAvene [?], P. Holland, J. Murnaghan, J. Frisk, B. Crehan, McCully, T. Crehan, Mrs Koen, and J. White.
35 Other names included P. Goodfellow, J. O'Brien, J. McMahon, J. Morgan, P. McKenna, W. Lynn, W. Smith, P. McQuilland, J. Queen, F. Loughran, F. Queen, Mrs Queen, J. Trainor, J. McAree, John Trainer, H. Fitzsimmons, F. Dennis [?], P. McMahon, J. Fitzgerald, J. Burns, J. Kelly, Mrs Murray, Miss Kelly, J. Burns, J. Callaghan, T. Murray, T. Cumusky, M. Trainer, F. Conly, Jas. Kelly, John Kelly, P. McKoen, J. Wisener, M. Hughes, P. Trainor, J. Fitzsimmons, J. McAdam, J. McCleary, J. Smith, J. Burns, J. Finnegan, J. Corley, P. Clerkin, W. Fields, P. Wood, P. McCullough, F. Kelly, and J. Kelly.
36 For a survey of names (1970) and other information on the families of Monaghan, see Peadar Livingstone, *The Monaghan Story* (Enniskillen: Clogher Historical Society, 1980), chap. 32.

37 Brendan O'Grady, "The Monaghan Settlers," *Abegweit Review*, Spring 1983, appendix 2, 76–9.
38 See, for instance, *The Dictionary of Canadian Biography*; and D.A. MacKinnon and A.B. Warburton, *Past and Present of Prince Edward Island* (Charlottetown: Bowen, 1906).
39 A short history of the Parish of Donagh by Canon Cotter merely refers to people emigrating from the Leslie estate in 1843 and founding St Joseph's Mission at DeSable, Prince Edward Island; and Canon Livingstone's comprehensive work *The Monaghan Story* merely states: "The Emyvale area suffered badly during the Famine and the village entered a period of decline. Many emigrated, including some with the surname McCluskey, and established a colony of Prince Edward Island, Canada" (569).
40 The Belfast Riot of 1 March 1847 was the most notorious clash involving the Scots and Irish. It was not simply a nationalistic fracas; religious and political rivalries were thought to have been factors as well. At root was the land issue. There were numerous injuries and three deaths. There are many accounts of this incident, including L.C.C., "Election Days of Old," in *Pioneers on the Island,* vol. 2, ed. Mary C. Brehaut (Charlottetown: Historical Society of Prince Edward Island, 1959), 30–2. This subject is treated at length in chapter 9 of the present study.
41 The first Island community to commemorate St Patrick was Grand River, where in 1780 a band of Scottish highlanders from the islands of Barra dedicated their log chapel to Ireland's patron saint. This was possibly the first mission in all Canada to be named for St Patrick.
42 Some of their names are found, for instance, among persons who attended the 1844 Repeal Association meeting in the Covehead district: Patrick Berrigan, David Bride, William Carroll, James Devon, Darby Flinn, Patrick Grinley, Michael Howlett, Patrick Kavanaugh, Thomas Kelly, John Lannergan, Richard Mahar, John Mullin, Edmond Mullin, Daniel Mullins, Nicholas Mullins, Patrick Murphy, Simon Power, Martin Read, Matthew Riordan, and Michael Riordan (*Palladium*, 22 February 1844). Mary Sullivan gave me information on the Berney (or Bearney) family of County Carlow.
43 Sources consulted for this section include Desi Nantes et al., "A History of Kelly's Cross Parish," 1974, and Alfred E. Burke, "Mission of St Joseph, DeSable" and "Mission of St Anne, Township Sixty-Five." All three are in "Histories of Parishes of Prince Edward Island" (PAPEI; also available at UPEI). Other sources are acknowledged in specific footnotes.
44 MacKinnon and Warburton, *Past and Present of Prince Edward Island*, 604–5. Information about Mr and Mrs John Creamer is incomplete and conflicting. Thomas Bradley, Sylvia McGaughey, Rosemary Trainor, and Mercedes Donahue assisted me concerning some details.
45 Jean Layton MacKay, "Lord, William Warren," DCB, 9: 532.

46 Callbeck, *My Island, My People*, 96.

47 Brehaut, ed., *Pioneers on the Island*, 2: 94.

48 Nantes et al., "A History of Kelly's Cross Parish."

49 O'Grady, "The Monaghan Settlers," appendix 1, 75.

50 Conversations with Brendon Campbell, 1996. Mr Campbell provided me with information on the settlers from County Tyrone, and the families in Kellys Cross and other Island settlements. Concerning another group of Tyrone immigrants, see Edward T. McCarron, "Altered States: Tyrone Migration to Providence, Rhode Island During the Nineteenth Century," *Clogher Record* (Monaghan, Ireland), 1997, 145–61.

51 *Daily Examiner* (Charlottetown), 20 September 1900.

52 Burke, "Mission of St Anne, Township Sixty-Five."

53 Ibid. For a short account of the edifying life of Rev. Patrick Moynagh, see J.E. McKenna, *Diocese of Clogher Parochial Records* (Enniskillen, Monaghan, 1920), 273–5.

54 Noted in *Journals of the House of Assembly of Prince Edward Island*, 1850.

55 Sources consulted for this section include Alfred E. Burke, "Mission of St Malachy, Kinkora," in "Histories of Parishes of Prince Edward Island"; MacKinnon and Warburton, *Past and Present of Prince Edward Island*; Kevin Farmer, "History of Kinkora" (unpublished essay, St Dunstan's University, 1960), and *Around Kinkora Area: A Socio-Cultural History of Five Communities in Prince Edward Island* (Kinkora: Maple Leaf Senior Citizens Club, 1991); and David McKenna, "Kinkora, an Ideal Village" (unpublished essay, 1972). Other sources are acknowledged in specific footnotes.

56 "Really, the Island potato industry got started when the Irish immigrants trying to escape the starvation of the 1845 Potato Famine settled and began to farm here." So states the "P.E.I. Potato Country" map, issued by the provincial Department of Tourism in 1982. That statement is not accurate.

57 Burke, "St Malachy's Mission, Kinkora," in "Histories of the Parishes of Prince Edward Island" (PAPEI; also in UPEI).

58 Mary McKenna, in "Newton Community" (unpublished paper), discusses education in Newton.

59 *Guardian* (Charlottetown), 31 May 1985.

60 In 1830, however, he was active in business and even served as official agent for his brother Roderick (*Royal Gazette*, 28 September 1830).

61 A.B. MacEachern to Archbishop Joseph Signay, 21 March 1835, (IPE, 1: 132), cited in F.W.P. Bolger, "The First Bishop," in *The Catholic Church in Prince Edward Island, 1720–1929*, ed. Michael F. Hennessey (Charlottetown: Roman Catholic Episcopal Corporation, 1979), 51.

62 MacMillan, *The History of Catholic Church in Prince Edward Island*, discusses MacDonald's career (*passim*).

63 It is noteworthy that the assistant legal counsel for MacIntosh was John Little, Reform candidate at the ill-fated Belfast election of 1846–47 (MacMillan, *History*, 47.) The Belfast incident is treated at length in chapter 9 of the present study.

64 The author consulted this book in the Diocesan Archives, Charlottetown, in the 1980s. The book has since disappeared.

CHAPTER EIGHT

1 Orlo Jones and Doris Haslam, eds., *An Island Refuge: Loyalists and Disbanded Troops on the Island of Saint John* (Charlottetown: Abegweit Branch of the United Empire Loyalist Association of Canada, 1983).

2 The census of 1798 accounted for 78 heads of families in Charlottetown Royalty. Of these, close to 20 percent appear to have been Irish: Rob. Callehan, John Carroll, John Condon, James Connoly, Peter Connolly, Nichs Counahan, Colo Desbrisay, Martin Dwyer, Thomas Geary, Robert Kiley, Francis Longworth, Patrick O'Neal, and possibly Wm. Burk, Thomas Murray, Peter Stafford, and a few others. In total, perhaps 57 of the 424 persons enumerated (over 13 percent) were Irish. See Duncan Campbell, *History of Prince Edward Island* (Belleville, Ont.: Mika, 1962), 207–24. See also the census of 1841 and 1848.

3 John C. MacMillan, *The Early History of the Catholic Church in Prince Edward Island* (Quebec: Evenement, 1905), 110–11. See also chapter 1 in the present study.

4 See, for example, chapter 1, notes 23 and 24 above.

5 *Prince Edward Island Register*, 6 May 1825.

6 Peter McCourt, "The Benevolent Irish Society," in *Past and Present of Prince Edward Island*, ed. D.A. MacKinnon and A.B. Warburton (Charlottetown: Bowen, 1906), 241–2.

7 Ibid.

8 *Prince Edward Island Register*, 21 March 1826.

9 Ibid.

10 Edward MacDonald, "The Ill and the Dying ..." in *Island Magazine*, Fall/Winter 1994, 35–9. John C. MacMillan, *The History of the Catholic Church in Prince Edward Island from 1835 till 1891* (Quebec: Evenement, 1913), 71; Sister Carmel MacDonald, "An Era of Consolidation," in *The Catholic Church in Prince Edward Island 1720–1979*, ed. Michael F. Hennessey (Charlottetown: Roman Catholic Episcopal Corporation, 1979), 65–6. The latter two works both refer to the 400 immigrants but not to numerous deaths. See also John McKenna, "Early Irish

Settlers in Prince Edward Island," *Guardian* (Charlottetown), 10 February 1928. Governor Huntley's notation to Lord Grey is also relevant: "Four hundred sick and half-starved Irish immigrants landed at Charlottetown, after taking a ship in Ireland for Charlestown, near Baltimore" (Public Record Office CO 226/71, Huntley to Grey, 28 June 1847).

11 *Royal Gazette*, 25 May and 1–25 June 1847. At the 24-acre Partridge Island quarantine station in Saint John's harbour a Celtic cross was erected in 1927. In 1847 alone 14,892 Famine refugees arrived at Partridge Island, of whom 601 died there of typhus and another 595 died in Saint John. Nearby, in 1848, at Hospital Island in Passamaquoddy Bay, off St Andrew's, 48 quarantined Irish emigrants died of fever. A memorial stone in St Michael's Cemetery in Chatham, New Brunswick, tells of tragedy at Middle Island on the Miramichi River: the *Looshtauk* of Dublin, sailing from Liverpool in April 1847, lost 175 souls to fever during the seven-week voyage and 96 more at the quarantine station. Of the 220 survivors, 167 remained in the Miramichi area, and the others went on to Quebec. See Caroline Daley and Anna Springer, *Middle Island Before and After the Tragedy* (Miramichi, NB: Middle Island Irish Historical Park, 2002), and T.P. Power, "The Emigrant Ship: The Transportation, Regulation, and Reception of Irish Immigrants in New Brunswick, 1815–1855," in *Celtic Languages and Celtic Peoples*, ed. Cyril Byrne et al. (Halifax: Saint Mary's University, 1989), 694.

12 *Acts of the General Assembly of Prince Edward Island*, 1842, cap. 5; 1846, cap. 9; 1848, cap. 3. Consult *Royal Gazette*, 25 May and 1, 4, 8, 11, 15, 18, 22, and 25 June 1847; *The Islander*, 4, 11, and 18 June 1847; and Edward MacDonald, "The Ill and the Dying: Family Records from the *Lady Constable* Affair," *Island Magazine*, Fall/Winter 1994, 35–8.

13 E.L.M. [Elizabeth L. MacDonald], "Charlottetown Fifty Years Ago," *Prince Edward Island Magazine*, July 1901, 139.

14 Ibid., 138–9. The following are among those who are known or believed to have come on the *Lady Constable* in 1847. From County Fermanagh were Aeneas McCabe and his son James, Dennis Rooney, Owen McCarville, and Patrick McCloskey; others who may have been from the same county include Bernard McTeague, John Goodman, Edward Kelly, John Finegan, and Patrick Dunn. From County Monaghan came Daniel Hughes, Terence Slavin, and John H. Ranahan. Robert McAllister and Margaret McAllister were from County Antrim, and Owen O'Neill was from County Armagh. Also from northern Ireland were Mr and Mrs Matthew Kelly, Felix Mulligan, Patrick Young, and John McCarvill; Patrick Gormley (Lot 61), James Farmer (Kinkora), and James McMahon were probably from Ulster too. It is also possible that the Tipperary men Daniel Mullen and Edward Feehan, as well as Michael and Mary Christopher of Waterford, arrived on the *Lady Constable*.

15 *Islander*, 23 March 1866.

16 *Examiner*, 5 March 1865.

17 *Examiner*, 30 July 1866.

18 See various issues of the *Herald*, the *Islander*, and the *Examiner* between January 1865 and April 1869.

19 Irene Rogers, *Charlottetown: The Life in Its Buildings* (Charlottetown: Prince Edward Island Museum and Heritage Foundation, 1983), 27. One of the original powder magazines still stands at the Brighton compound.

20 For general background on Fenianism, see Hereward Senior, *The Fenians and Canada* (Toronto: Macmillan, 1978).

21 It is of interest to note that one hundred and fifty years after the Great Famine, British Prime Minister Tony Blair, issued an apologetic statement to the Irish people, stating: "Those who governed in London at the time failed their people by standing by while a crop failure turned into a massive human tragedy ... That one million people died in what was then part of the richest and most powerful nation in the world is something that still causes pain as we reflect on it today." The prime minister's statement was reported in the *New York Times* and the *Washington Post* on 3 June 1997 and in other publications around the world.

22 J.B. Pollard, "The Visit of King Edward VII to Prince Edward Island," *Prince Edward Island Magazine* (forthcoming), 371.

23 Concerning the social life of the period, see J.E.W., "Charlottetown Past and Present," *Prince Edward Island Magazine*, March 1902, 17–21.

24 Rogers, *Charlottetown*, 66–7.

25 *Prince Edward Island Gazette*, 16 August 1820.

26 Rogers, *Charlottetown*, 278.

27 James P. Gaffey, *Francis Clement Kelley and the American Catholic Dream*, 2 vols (Bensenville, Ill.: Heritage Foundation, 1980).

28 Rogers, *Charlottetown*, 119.

29 Ibid., 119–20.

30 *Charlottetown City Reports*, 1877–84, 59–60, 75–7.

31 *Examiner*, 2 February 1857.

32 Frank MacKinnon, *The Government of Prince Edward Island* (Toronto: University of Toronto Press, 1951).

33 Besides the reverend gentlemen mentioned in the text, Methodist clergy included William Ryan, Robert Cooney, James Buckley, and William McCarty; Baptist preachers with probable Irish connections were Joseph Cahill, M.C. Higgins, and David Rice; and Anglicans with Irish ties included Cornelius Griffin, Robert T. Roach, and Trinity graduate Joseph William Forsythe. Five Roman Catholic priests born in Ireland are named in this chapter; seven others are Edward Walsh, William Dollard, Thomas Quinn, James Duffy, Stephen T. Phelan, James Phelan, and William Phelan.

34 Elinor Shipley Duckett, *Saint Dunstan of Canterbury* (New York: Norton, 1955), 29–30.

35 Father MacDonnell's remains are interred in the crypt of St Dunstan's Basilica in Charlottetown.

36 Terrence M. Punch, "Larry Doyle and Nova Scotia," in *Talamh An Eisc: Canadian and Irish Essays*, ed. C.J. Byrne and Margaret Harry (Halifax: St Mary's University, 1986), 175.

37 *Colonial Herald*, 15 July 1843.

38 *Palladium*, 15 January 1844.

39 *The Palladium* reported on Repeal meetings on the Island in various issues of 1843–44 and gave lists of subscribers in the issue of 28 December 1843 and the issues dated 7 March, 2 May, and 15 August 1844. For lists reported in the *Register* (Halifax), see Terrence M. Punch, "A Prince Edward Island Repeal List of 1843," *Island Magazine*, Fall/Winter 1986, 29–31, and "A Prince Edward Island Repeal List of 1843, Part II," *Island Magazine*, Spring/Summer 1987, 33–6. These lists contain useful information for genealogists and family historians.

40 *Colonial Herald*, 26 August 1843.

41 J.H. Fletcher, "Newspaper Life and Newspaper Men," *Prince Edward Island Magazine*, June 1900, 107–13.

42 W.L. Cotton, "The Press in Prince Edward Island," in *Past and Present of Prince Edward Island*, ed., MacKinnon and Warburton, 115–18.

43 Ibid., 119–20

44 Ibid., 115.

45 E.L. MacDonald, *Charlottetown Fifty Years Ago*, 337.

46 Ibid., 332.

47 Charles Gavan Duffy, *My Life in Two Hemispheres* (London: T. Fisher Unwin, 1898), 61.

48 At the same time Charlottetown Royalty, a belt of several thousand acres bounding the north side of the town, had a population of 655, made up as follows: 127 English immigrants, 59 Scots, 74 Irish, 35 from British colonies, 4 foreign, and 356 born in Prince Edward Island.

49 PAPEI, 1848 census, 29 November 1848.

50 MacMillan, *History of the Catholic Church in P.E.I.*. See also John Francis Maguire, *The Irish in America* (London: Longmans Green, 1868), 30–1.

51 Three of the Island's governors were born in Ireland: Walter Patterson (1769–87), Sir Dominick Daly (1850–59), and William Robinson (1870–74). Edmund Fanning (1787–1804) was of Irish descent, and Col. John Ready (1824–31), though born in England, may have had Irish family connections. Concerning Col. Ready, see Elinor Vass, "The Ready Touch: John Ready and Prince Edward Island, 1824–31," *Island Magazine*, Fall/Winter, 1990, 30–7.

52 Cited in MacMillan, *The History of the Catholic Church in P.E.I.*, 55.

53 *Examiner*, 9 August 1875.

54 Ibid.

55 Ibid., 21 June 1875.

56 In 2001 the Celtic Heritage Society for Prince Edward Island (founded in 1990) erected at the Charlottetown waterfront a memorial to the Island's Irish settlers (see Epilogue).

57 Rogers, *Charlottetown*, 302.

58 The PEI Heritage Foundation has since retrieved some of the headstones that had been desecrated.

59 *Islander*, 21 April 1871.

CHAPTER NINE

1 *Journals of the House of Assembly of Prince Edward Island* (JHA) Cundall to Haviland, 2 March 1847; *Islander*, 5 March 1847.

2 Public Record Office (PRO) CO 226, vol. 71, Huntley to Grey, 23 March 1847.

3 Lord Selkirk also owned Lot 31, which was separated by some thirty miles from the Belfast district and therefore is not relevant to the present account. Selkirk also purchased Lot 53 in Kings County. For background on the proprietor, see J.M. Bumsted, "Lord Selkirk of Prince Edward Island," *Island Magazine*, Fall/Winter 1978, 3–8.

4 By 1852, sixty Irish families formed the Roman Catholic mission in Iona, and they erected St Michael's Church on the Lot 58 side of the line road. This parish encompassed all of Lots 57, 58, 60, and 62 but drew its adherents from Upper Newtown, both East and West Montague Road, Montague Cross, and Valley. About 1902, Rev. James Phelan (a native of Mooncoin, County Kilkenny) conferred the name Iona on the district and the name Fodhla on the railroad station. See Arthur O'Shea, "The Iona Parish," *Abegweit Review*, Spring 1988, 89–106.

5 The Island's dual-riding system prevailed until the provincial election of 1996, when the number of seats was reduced from sixteen dual ridings to twenty-seven single constituencies.

6 John C. MacMillan, *The Early History of the Catholic Church in Prince Edward Island* (Quebec: L'Evenement, 1905), 278. As early as the general election of 1787 there were charges of disorder and violence. See F.W.P. Bolger, "Prince Edward Island Rejects Confederation," *Canada's Smallest Province: A History of Prince Edward Island* (Charlottetown: PEI 1973 Centennial Commission, 1973), 67; and J.M. Bumsted, "Parliamentary Privilege and Electoral Disputes in Colonial Prince Edward Island," *Island Magazine*, Fall/Winter 1989, 22–6. The Tenant League agitation that required the intervention of troops is explained in Bolger, 180.

7 Kenneth A. MacKinnon, "Rankin, Coun Douly" DCB, 8: 740–2; *Royal Gazette*, 13 September 1836.

8 Milton Acorn, *The Island Means Minagoo: Poems for Prince Edward Island* (Toronto: NC Press, 1975).

9 *JHA*, 3 February 1837, 32–5, 143. Reg Phelan, "Prince Edward Island Land Struggle," *Cooper Review* (Charlottetown), 1988, 21–33, gives some views of a social activist.

10 MacMillan, *Early History*, 289.

11 Greg Marquis, "Rum Riots of Dundas," *Island Magazine*, Spring/Summer 1998, 8–12.

12 A century after Malcolm MacRae was killed in the Belfast Riot, he was regarded as a martyr to the cause of liberty. An illustrated tribute printed 29 December 1947 reads:

  "The Year was 1847 ...

  "Malcolm McRae was beaten into unconsciousness, left in a ditch to die. He was a voter in the Third District, Prince Edward Island, who had, the previous year, voted against certain members who were later unseated on charges of intimidation and violence.

  "Now a new election was called – but Malcom McRae was warned not to vote. In those days he was not protected by the secret ballot – yet Malcolm McRae determined to set out for the polls, risking his life for the right to vote.

  "Today, because of the courage of men like Malcolm McRae, you run no risk at all in your free, unhampered exercise of the franchise." The exact circumstances of Malcolm McRae's death remain somewhat obscure. One account indicates that he was assaulted right at the hustings, before the riot began. Another implies that he was waylaid by a gang on his way home from the polling place. A third story states that he was wounded in the melee in the field and managed to betake himself to the minister's manse, where he died. A notation in the George Leard files (PAPEI) states: "Big Rory [MacLeod] was in the line up to vote – a McRae man ahead of him was first at the poll he was killed by an Irishman who in turn was killed by Big Rory."

13 The bereaved father of James Cain, one of the two young Irishmen slain in the Belfast Riot, expressed forgiveness to the unidentified killer of his son.

14 *Royal Gazette*, 15 February 1847.

15 See H.T. Holman, "Douse, William" in DCB, 9: 222–3, and Nicholas deJong, "Charlottetown's Good Samaritan of the Deep," *Island Magazine*, Spring/Summer 1987, 24–6. See also *Royal Gazette*, 11 January 1848.

16 For a deft sketch of James Yeo, see Boyde Beck, "The Ledger Giant," *Prince Edward Island: An Unauthorized History* (Charlottetown: Acorn Press, 1996), 73–6.

17 Information on John Little's career may be found in PAPEI, "Roll of Attorneys," *Colonial Herald*, 10 October 1840, 16 January 1841, and 20 January 1844; *Royal Gazette*, 1 February and 19 July 1842, and 14 March 1843.

18 Arlene Hood, secretary of the Prince Edward Island Genealogical Society, Charlottetown (PAPEI), provided me with genealogical information on John Costin and his family.

19 Information on the Little and Costin families is drawn largely from interviews in Dublin in 1985 with Sean P. Little and Brendan Little, descendants of the Hon. Philip Francis Little, and through correspondence with Sean P. Little. Although the descendants of Cornelius Little and Brigid Costin (who were married in Charlottetown on 19 February 1816) made important contributions to society, the focus in this study is limited to son John Little's place in the political histoty of the Island. John Little's brother Joseph I. Little became chief justice of Newfoundland, and his brother Philip Francis Little became the first prime minister of Newfoundland under responsible government.

20 See Jean M. MacLennan, *From Shore to Shore: The Life and Times of Rev. John MacLennan of Belfast, P.E.I.* (Edinburgh: Knox Press, 1977), and "MacLennan, John" in DCB, 8: 569–70; and Ada MacLeod Putnam, *The Selkirk Settlers and the Church They Built at Belfast* (Toronto: Presbyterian Publications, 1939).

21 Aspects of Rev. James Brady's career are treated briefly in John C. MacMillan, *The History of the Catholic Church in Prince Edward Island, 1835 till 1891* (Quebec: L'Evenement, 1913); and Edward MacDonald, *The History of St. Dunstan's University, 1855–1956* (Charlottetown: Board of Governors of St Dunstan's University and Prince Edward Island Museum and Heritage Foundation, 1989).

22 I.R. Robertson, "Highlanders, Irishmen, and the Land Question in Nineteenth-century Prince Edward Island," in *Comparative Aspects of Scottish and Irish Economic and Social History 1600–1900*, ed. L.M. Cullen and T.C. Smout (Edinburgh: John Donald, 1976), 234. Dr Robertson also deals perceptively with the Belfast Riot and the Bible Question in "Religion, Politics and Education in Prince Edward Island," chap. 2 (MA Thesis, McGill University, 1968).

23 MacMillan, *Early History*, 235. In the Legislative Assembly on 12 February 1847, Alexander Rae introduced a "Bill for dispensing with the Oath of Abduration at present required to be administered to persons of the Roman Catholic persuasion, on their acceptance of office." The bill received second reading on 15 February 1847 and was passed 20 February. See JHA 15 and 20 February 1847, and *Royal Gazette*, 2 June 1847. Catholic Emancipation had been granted in 1830.

24 I.R. Robertson states: "Even between Protestant and Roman Catholic

there does not seem to have been much outright hostility until the late
1850s, when it became profitable for one political party to exploit religious loyalties for its own purposes" ("Highlanders," 235).

25 The *Islander*, 12 April 1845, reported Douse as having stated in the
assembly that "he wished not to cause unhappiness in any part of the
community [and he] had no desire to offer distraint on the free liberty of
conscience in others, or of their free exercise of religious opinions."
Douse concluded that the proposal for use of the Bible for instruction
would have his full support "were it not carrying out a sectarian principle in a public school ... but as matters stood, he felt it his duty to oppose
the amendment."

When the sectarian controversy reached its peak in 1856, Charlottetown's Roman Catholic bishop, Bernard D. MacDonald, took a similar
stand, for which he was criticized by the Protestant press. He believed
that to work well, the mixed schools should adopt the system found in
the Irish National Schools. He stated in part: "Prayers and all religious
exercises, as well as the reading of Scripture from any version not
approved by all, must be discontinued. Nothing favorable or unfavorable
to any religious denomination must be inculcated. If the friends of education wish our mixed schools to prosper, their wish can only be realized
by allowing those schools to be godless, under the present circumstances
of the country" (quoted in MacMillan, *History of the Catholic Church*,
125).

26 In the second volume of his *History* (271), MacMillan states that "the
Catholic people, as a rule, distrusted Mr Pope"; and Robertson (in
"Whelan, Edward" DCB, 9: 832) refers to W.H. Pope as "the *bete noire*
of Island Catholicism." Perhaps the Irish sensed that Pope was a political
opportunist. On the other hand, in his later career Joseph Pope (father of
W.H. Pope) was regarded as a staunch friend of the Irish Catholics of
Kinkora. (See *Islander*, 12 March 1847, report of Assembly debates; and
the 19 March issue for more on the question of bigotry).

It is worth noting that Joseph Pope and his sons, James C. Pope and
W.H. Pope, were all successful nineteenth-century politicians. Against this
background, the following news item concerning the late-twentieth-cen-
tury Assemblyman Peter Pope is relevant: "The Summerside Member of
the Legislature began his address by introducing to gallery guests his
great-great-grandfather, whose picture is displayed to the far right of Mr
Pope's seat in the Legislature. He noted his father, a shipbuilder, built the
first wharf in (Green's Shore) Summerside and donated the land to the
people of Kinkora for a church. 'And that is why to this day the Catholic
people always support the Pope' he said to raucous laughter." (*Guardian*,
14 April 1984).

27 PRO, CO 226, vol. 71, Huntley to Grey, 23 March 1847.

28 Edward MacDonald, *New Ireland: The Irish on Prince Edward Island* (Charlottetown: PEI Museum and Heritage Foundation, 1990), 17.

29 W.S. MacNutt, "Political Advance and Social Reform 1842–1861," in *Canada's Smallest Province*, ed. Francis W.P. Bolger (Charlottetown: PEI Centennial Commission, 1973), 129. See also Alan Buchanan, "Introduction," *Belfast People: An Oral History of Belfast, Prince Edward Island*, ed. Susan Hornby (Charlottetown: Tea Hill Press, 1992), 2; and Holman, *DCB*, 9: 222–3.

30 Bumsted, "Lord Selkirk of Prince Edward Island," 5.

31 Holman, *DCB*, 9: 223. MacKinnon, *DCB*, 8: 742.

32 MacKinnon, *DCB*, 8: 742. See also *Royal Gazette*, 13 September 1836.

33 *Prince Edward Island Gazette*, 22 May 1820.

34 MacNutt, "Political Advance," 129.

35 MacKinnon, *DCB*, 8: 742.

36 Bumsted, "Lord Selkirk of Prince Edward Island."

37 PAPEI, 1841 census.

38 R.B. McDowell, "The Protestant Nation (1775–1800)" in *The Course of Irish History*, ed. T.W. Moody and F.X. Martin (Cork: Mercier, 1967), 241.

39 Interesting to note on the Island scene, the *Examiner*, 9 May 1864, cites Duncan's assertion in the legislature that "the murderous riot, some years ago, at Belfast, led to the formation of Orange Lodges in the Island." (Duncan was critical of the Duke of Newcastle's refusal to grant the Orange Order's application for legal recognition.) Whether by cause or coincidence, in 1863 (as MacMillan's *History*, 236, observed) there were four Orange lodges in the Belfast constituency.

40 Robertson, "Highlanders," 233.

41 *Examiner*, 14 December 1836.

42 *Islander*, 6 March 1847; *Royal Gazette*, 8 February 1847. Official statements about the Belfast elections and riot are in the *Journal of the House of Assembly*, March 1847, and appendix I.

43 *Islander*, 13 March 1847.

44 *Royal Gazette*, 2 March 1847.

45 Ibid.

46 Ibid.

47 *Islander*, 5 March 1847; *Royal Gazette*, 2 March 1847.

48 *JHA* and *Royal Gazette*, 2 March 1847.

49 *Royal Gazette*, 2 March 1847.

50 Robertson, "Highlanders," 233.

51 *JHA*, 10 March 1847.

52 I.R. Robertson, "Party Politics and Religious Controversialism in Prince Edward Island from 1860 to 1863," *Acadiensis*, Spring 1978, 54–5.

53 *Royal Gazette*, 31 January 1847.

54 *JHA*, 4 February 1847. Before the end of July 1847, Reform candidate John Little closed his law office in Charlottetown. He joined his brother Philip Francis (1824–97), who in the meantime had opened his own law office in St John's, Newfoundland, and as partners they developed a lucrative practice there. Later, the youngest brother, Joseph Ignatius (1835–1903), also joined them. According to descendants of Philip Francis Little, John was "the person who laid the fortune of this particular generation of the family and most of them owe their success in life to John's hard work and generosity" (personal correspondence with Sean P. Little, 1985).

   John Little died in Newfoundland in 1864. He had lived long enough to see his brother Philip Francis become a member of the Newfoundland House of Assembly, lead the Liberal Party in its crusade for responsible government, and become the first prime minister of Newfoundland (1855–58) and a justice of the Supreme Court (1858–66). John Little's youngest brother, Sir Joseph Ignatius Little, later became chief justice of Newfoundland's Supreme Court. A tombstone in Belvedere Cemetery, St John's, Newfoundland bears this inscription: "John Little, Barrister at Law, died October 1865 in his 47th year, an honest, charitable, and religious man."

55 Patrick O'Donnell of Vernon River presented the resolutions to the lieutenant-governor on 12 July 1847.

56 The general election of 1850 further indicated that it would take more than disorderly resistance and formal petitions to wrest from William Douse the seat of power in the Belfast area riding. A worthy challenger, Archibald McNeill, a schoolteacher from Mount Vernon (Lot 50), received over 80 percent of the vote in Lots 49 and 50 where, he said, "the people are not frightened of Rent Rolls and act independently." However, in the Selkirk settlement where, said McNeill, tenants were warned that "ejection and ruin would result if they dared to vote against the agent," Douse won out by a large margin. See "The Belfast Election [1850]," *Examiner*, 3 July 1850.

57 The continuing importance of land in Prince Edward Island is comprehensively treated by Douglas B. Boylan et al. in *"Everything Before Us": Report of the Royal Commission on the Land*, 2 vols (Charlottetown: Queen's Printer, 1990).

CHAPTER TEN

1 Ruth Dudley Edwards, *An Atlas of Irish History* (London: Mathuen, 1973), 132.
2 *Examiner*, 8 February and 14 November 1864.
3 For descriptions of this herculean feat, see John C. MacMillan, *The*

Catholic Church in Prince Edward Island from 1835 till 1891 (Quebec: L'Evenement, 1913), 256–9; and Amy Pope Berlinquet, "A Leaf from the Annals of St Joseph's Convent," in *Prince Edward Island Magazine*, June 1904, 201–6.

4 Berlinquet, "A Leaf," 206.

5 *Examiner*, 14 November 1864. Another lecture, by Rev. Angus MacDonald, was reported in the *Examiner*, 28 November 1864.

6 William Forbes Adams, *Ireland and Irish Emigration to the New World from 1815 to the Famine* (New Haven: Yale University Press, 1932; reprint, Baltimore: Genealogical Publishing, 1980), 202, 215. See also MacMillan, *Catholic Church*, 79–92. Fuller information on Father Mathew's crusade is found in Colm Kerrigan, *Father Mathew and the Irish Temperance Movement, 1838–1849* (Cork: Cork University Press, 1992); and Elizabeth Malcolm, *Ireland Sober, Ireland Free: Drink and Temperance in Nineteenth-Century Ireland* (Dublin: Gill and Macmillan, 1986).

7 MacMillan, *Catholic Church*, 86. Mary Mathew, Father Mathew's niece, was married to Patrick Stephens of Orwell, PEI. See also Arthur O'Shea, "The Iona Parish," *Abegweit Review*, Spring 1988, 89–106.

8 MacMillan, *Catholic Church*, *passim*.

9 Ibid., 90.

10 *Examiner*, 25 July 1864.

11 Cecil J. Houston and William J. Smyth, *The Sash Canada Wore: A Historical Geography of the Orange Order in Canada* (Toronto: University of Toronto Press, 1980). This is a comprehensive study of Orangeism in Canada. A recent study of Orangeism in Ireland is *A Short History of Orangeism* by Kevin Haddick-Flynn (Dublin: Mercier, 2002). For an extended, partisan view of the Bible controversy and other sectarian issues in Prince Edward Island, see MacMillan, *Catholic Church*.

12 *Vindicator*, 30 December 1863 and 20 January 1864.

13 James Duncan, cited in *Examiner*, 9 May 1894.

14 R.H. Spencer, "Loyal Orange Association," in *Past and Present of Prince Edward Island*, eds. D.A. MacKinnon and A.B. Warburton (Charlottetown: Bowen, l923), 230–8. In his essay, Spencer emphasizes the religious character of Orangeism. Haddick-Flynn also calls attention to this matter in his *Short History of Orangeism*.

15 MacMillan, *Catholic Church*, 238.

16 *Monitor*, 14 April 1864. Although Whelan was a severe critic of Orangeism, he was not anti-Protestant.

17 PAPEI, Minutes of the Lieutenant-Governor in Council, 6 May 1852.

18 A second lodge was located a few blocks away, on Richmond Street.

19 *Patriot*, 19 July 1877. The account given here is based mainly on the *Patriot* report. See also MacMillan, *Catholic Church*, 315–18.

20 *Patriot*, 19 July 1877. See also MacMillan, *Catholic Church*, 317.

21 Professor J.J. Coyle fondly told about his grandfather (the janitor of the Market Place) and old Jimmy Johnston who would ostentatiously "sign" or "cross" themselves when the banner portraying "King Billy" passed. "A wonder you weren't arrested!" exclaimed a bystander.

22 Francis W.P. Bolger, *Prince Edward Island and Confederation 1863-1873* (Charlottetown: St Dunstan's University Press, 1964), 9.

23 John Francis Maguire, *The Irish in America* (London: Longmans Green, 1868), 30-1. Maguire is commemorated by a fine public statue in Cork City.

24 Maguire, *Irish in America*, 31.

25 *Protestant and Evangelical Witness* (Charlottetown), 10 September 1864.

26 *Examiner*, 12 December 1864.

27 Robert C. Tuck, ed., *The Family Harris: Letters of an Immigrant Family in British North America, 1856-1866* (Charlottetown: Ragweed, 1983), 132.

28 *Examiner*, 28 March 1864.

29 See Ian Ross Robertson, "Whelan, Edward," DCB, 9: 1976, 828-35; MacMillan, *Catholic Church*, 267-75; and G. Edward MacDonald, "Dear Clark, Edward Whelan and the Election of 1867," *Island Magazine*, Fall/Winter 2002, 19-28.

30 *Examiner*, 5 September 1864.

31 *Protestant*, 10 September 1864.

32 For accounts of these festivities, see *Examiner*, 12 September 1864; *Protestant*, 10 September 1864; and *Monitor*, 15 September 1864.

33 Tuck, *The Family Harris*, 139. Harris's large mural, painted in 1884, was destroyed in a fire that extensively damaged the Parliament Buildings in Ottawa in 1916. Copies of that painting are based on Harris's preliminary cartoons.

34 *Examiner*, 21 March 1864. There was no report of the text of D'Arcy McGee's address on this occasion.

35 Thomas D'Arcy McGee was a controversial politician in Ireland; he transferred his allegiance to Canada. Fuller information on him is found, for instance, in Josephine Phelan, *The Ardent Exile* (Toronto, 1951). See also section 7, "Thomas D'Arcy McGee and the Making of the Canadian Nation," in *The Untold Story: The Irish in Canada*, vol. 1, ed. Robert O'Driscoll and Lorna Reynolds (Toronto: Celtic Arts of Canada, 1988), 451-554. The Chair of Irish Studies at Saint Mary's University in Halifax, Nova Scotia, is named in his honour.

36 *Patriot*, 17 July 1873.

37 *Patriot*, 24 July 1873.

38 William Leggo, *The History of the Administration of the Right Hon-*

ourable Frederick Temple Blackwood, Earl of Dufferin, K.P., G.C.M.G.,
K.C.B., F.R.S., *Late Governor of Canada* (Montreal: Levell, 1878).

39 *Patriot*, 24 July 1873.
40 Leggo, *Dufferin*, 25.
41 Bolger, *Prince Edward Island and Confederation.*
42 Clark, *Three Centuries and the Island* (Toronto: University of Toronto Press, 1959), 125.
43 Alan A. Brookes, "Out-Migration from the Maritime Provinces 1860–1900: Some Preliminary Considerations," *Acadiensis*, Spring 1976, 28.
44 Clark, *Three Centuries and the Island*, 208.

EPILOGUE

1 The Irish Settlers Memorial project was undertaken by the Celtic Heritage Association for Prince Edward Island. This group was formed in 1990, the Island's "Year of the Irish." At the time of the memorial's completion, the CHA executive consisted of George Mullally (chairman), Michael Hennessey (secretary), Charles Duffy (treasurer), and committee members Anna Duffy, Brendan O'Grady, Colman O'Hare, and Hon. Marion Reid. The past Chairman was George O'Connor.
2 The Hon. Marion Reid, OC, former lieutenant-governor of Prince Edward Island, presided at the ceremonial unveiling of the bronze plaque. The Reverend Eric Dunn delivered the invocation.
3 *The Book of Three Tides*, a special publication reserved in the public libraries of Prince Edward Island, records the dedication ceremonies and lists all the contributors to the Irish Settlers Memorial project. The architect and designer of the memorial was Trevor Gillingwater of Montreal.
4 The Hon. Mary Robinson, "Cherishing the Irish Diaspora," address to the Houses of the Oireachtas, 2 February 1995.
5 In the 2001 census of Canada, 27.87 percent of Prince Edward Island's population identified their ethnicity as Irish. That is more than 37,000 people.

Index

Abell, Edward, 104–5
Abell, Susannah, 104
Abells Cape, 104–6
Acadians, 13, 30, 80; and Irish, 71, 80–2; at Souris, 112
Act of Abjuration, 260n8
Act of Union, 123, 131; retribution for Rebellion of 1798, 128
Aeolus incident (1811), 100–4, 108
Agitator (1839), 154
agricultural conditions: County Monaghan, 134, 136–7
Alberton, 80, 90–1; Irish in, 90
alcohol abuse: in Charlottetown (1791), 20, 23; and cheapness of rum, 186; DeCollone's view, 176; DesBrisay's view, 20
Alexander (1771), 13, 143; (1819), 64; (1820), 67
American Revolution, 142, 174; and Irish Loyalists, 21; and privateers, 18, 19
Ancient Order of Hibernians, 182
Anglican Church, 13, 18,

116, 128; in Charlottetown, 186–7; clergy, 186, 200, 245; colonial pioneers, 4; in County Laois, 37; in Lot 11 (1881), 34; and Orange Order, 238; use of tavern for service, 21
Ankatel, 74
Anna (1834), 63
Annandale, 95
Antelope (1844), 65
Ascendancy, Anglo-Irish, 7, 12–13, 129, 130; in early Benevolent Irish Society, 179; rejection of Orange Order, 238; rejection of Poyning's Law, 129; township acquisition in PEI, 14
Assembly. *See* Legislative Assembly
Atlanta, 100–2
Avalon Peninsula: Irish from, 54, 55
Avondale, 161, 256

Baldwin Road, 115, 158, 161, 162, 217
Baltic, 97
Bannerman, Gov. Alexander, 239, 240
Barony of Truagh, 118
Bear River, 109

Beatons Mills, 208
Bedeque, 63, 74
Belfast, Ireland, 60, 61, 152, 166; Des Brisay's immigrants, 16; immigrants to PEI, 153; ships for PEI, 59, 61, 151–6, 166, 170
Belfast Riot (PEI), 204–30; ethnicity of participants, 205–8; the four candidates, 213–16; the Irish and William Douse, 222–6; land tenure, the real cause, 226–9; the Scots and Douse, 221–2; the three deaths, 212–13; voting before the secret ballot, 208–12
Belle Creek (Lot 62), 208
Benevolent Irish Society, 170, 177–9, 246; in Emerald, 170; in Souris, 113–15; women admitted, 179
Benjamin Shaw (1823, 1829), 60
Bernard, Joseph, 81
Bible Question, 238
Bishop Estate, Armagh, 169
Black Kesh, 131
Bloomfield, 91
Bloomfield Corner, 91

Printed in the USA
CPSIA information can be obtained
at www.ICGtesting.com
LVHW042146100524
779540LV00001B/3